Network Marke... For Dummies...

D0472445

Questions You Should Ask Before Joining a Network Marketing Company

- Would the integrity of the company's leadership inspire you to follow them?
- Is the company mission-driven or get-rich-quick motivated?
- Does the company's corporate philosophy fit your personal philosophy?
- Does the company's product sell at retail?
- Does the company have a proven and effective training program?
- Does the company's product line include a reasonable number of consumables?
- Does the company depend on glitz, glitter, and hype to sell its opportunity, or will the company and opportunity survive a factual examination of the claims made at company-sponsored opportunity meetings?
- Would the company's income and product claims pass muster with regulatory bodies, or do they sound too good to be true?
- Would the opportunity give you a real chance to make a positive difference in the lives of those you sponsor into the business?
- Does the company want to load you up with products that you must sell before you can recoup your investment?
- Does the company tell you in understandable terms what volume of activity you must maintain in order to receive the residual income from the organization you have built?
- Does the local Better Business Bureau have a file of unresolved claims against the company?
- Do you expect the company or your upline to bring people into your business or do your work for you?
- Are you totally convinced of the righteousness of your cause and of its value to those you will work with?
- Do you understand why it's important to become a product of the product?
- If you succeed with this company, would you have more of the things money will buy and all the things money won't buy?

For more information about these questions, read Chapters 4 through 6.

How to Succeed in Network Marketing

Set goals! A study at UCLA found that people who had a balanced goals program earned an average of $7,411 per month. People without a goals program earned an average of $3,397 per month. Those with goals programs were also happier and healthier and got along better with the folks at home. A goals program helps the network marketer focus on the really important things in life.

Learn how to build relationships. Network marketing is not about sales. Even if you've never sold a thing, you can still succeed in this profession. The people who earn the most money in network marketing are the people who know how to form relationships with other people.

Chapter 10 zeroes in on the skills you need to succeed in network marketing.

For Dummies: Bestselling Book Series for Beginners

Network Marketing For Dummies®

Cheat Sheet

Zig's Golden Rule Philosophy

You can have everything in life you want if you will just help enough other people get what they want.

The Hallmarks of a Top Network Marketing Company

Many of the networkers represented in this book helped us compile this list of hallmarks of a top network marketing company:

- ✔ Integrity and honesty
- ✔ Full disclosure about the company's ownership, financial strength, product development, and distributor relationships
- ✔ A mission statement along with ethics standards and values
- ✔ A simple, duplicatable marketing system that people from all orientations can follow with a reasonable expectation of success
- ✔ Products that have been tested for reliability and marketability
- ✔ A fair compensation plan that's easy to understand and rewards both full-time and part-time distributors
- ✔ Support for the associates in the form of outstanding marketing materials, conference calls, and national meetings
- ✔ An experienced management team
- ✔ Training that teaches people what to do and how to do it so that they can become successful within a reasonable period of time
- ✔ Technology that makes it easy for distributors to recruit, train, sell products, and manage their organizations, and for retail customers to buy products

Chapter 5 discusses these hallmarks in more detail.

The Ten Commandments for Network Marketers

1. Thou shalt build your business on a character foundation and practice the Golden Rule as you build.

2. Thou shalt not make unto anyone false perceptions of the income opportunity or the "miracles" your products will work on their health.

3. Thou shalt not take the name of your company for granted or use it in vain, thereby becoming a product of the product.

4. Thou shalt remember your workdays to keep them productive and the Sabbath to keep it holy.

5. Thou shalt not kill the dreaming spirit of any new distributor and remember that you are responsible *to* those you sponsor, but not *for* them.

6. Thou shalt not commit any impurity within your organization or company worldwide.

7. Thou shalt not bear false witness concerning any part of the company's growth, mission, or products.

8. Thou shalt not covet thy crossline's sales organization, nor steal the downline of another company.

9. Thou shalt remember to keep God first, family second, and your company third in priority.

10. Thou shalt honor thy upline and downline that thy days within the company may be long and enable you to build a substantial residual income.

See Chapter 22 for more information about the qualities and characteristics of top network marketers.

For Dummies: Bestselling Book Series for Beginners

You,_____ , hold in your hands
the roadmap to success in network marketing
and the keys to a balanced life.

Praise for Zig Ziglar

"Arguably the most sought-after motivational speaker in the world, Zig Ziglar is a household name and a true success legend. He is a world-renowned author, lecturer, sales trainer, and destined to be a network marketing icon."

— *Network Marketing Lifestyles Magazine*

"If Zig Ziglar didn't already exist, Network Marketing would have to *invent him.* The theme Zig has been promoting for the past half century — 'You can have everything in life you want if you will just help enough other people get what they want' — is at the heart of network marketing. Which is exactly where Zig Ziglar is, too."

— Clifton H. Jolley, Ph.D., President, Advent Communications

"I first heard Zig Ziglar speak in 1977. The impact of that experience helped shape my philosophies regarding family, relationships, and business. My consulting firm now helps hundreds of network marketing executives incorporate Zig's timeless 'service to mankind' principles into their business plan blueprint for distributor success. His 'no hype' values-based message has reached millions, making Zig Ziglar the world's master networker."

— Michael L. Sheffield, President of Sheffield Resource Network and Chairman of the Multi Level Marketing International Association

"Zig Ziglar's unique mastery of the skill of instilling hope enlightens the hearts and minds of millions, freeing them to become all they can be."

— Peter Lowe, President and CEO, Peter Lowe International

"I met Zig when I was 18 years old, 23 years ago. He told me to always reach farther than I thought I could, and if I did that consistently I would see many successes in life. He has had a tremendous impact on my life. His books and tapes are on my A list."

— Dan Gaub, Director, MARKET AMERICA

Praise for Zig's Books, Tapes, and Training Seminars

"Zig has been a primary source of faith and confidence that I could make it through the struggles and disappointments and succeed, as long as I kept the right attitude and never quit. Twenty-five years ago, his book *See You at the Top* empowered me to get to the top of my company, with over 350,000 distributors. Thank you, Zig!"

> — Ray Gebauer, Platinum Presidential, Mannatech Inc.

"Simply . . . I have everything that Zig has ever written or recorded as part of my library . . . . The impact that he has had on my life has been extraordinary . . . and my success is due to a HUGE part in the teaching and wisdom he has so unselfishly shared . . . . A brilliant mind and beautiful heart . . . that's Zig."

> — Doug Firebaugh, Chairman/CEO, PassionFire International

"When I committed to following the goals program in Zig's book *Over the Top*, I went from wishing and hoping to a focused activity that started making my dreams come true. The steps are simple and they give you laser focus. Thanks, Zig."

> — Priscilla Harrison, Diamond Super Star, Starlight International

"I was tired of being an 'average' salesperson. Zig's *How to Stay Motivated* tape series made me realize that the critical element of goal setting was missing from my daily life. I began to apply his techniques, and over the next 12 months, I consistently outsold not only my peers, but more importantly, the competition! I've taken his breadth of knowledge on selling and personal empowerment into the network marketing industry, where I now earn a residual six-figure income."

> — Todd Falcone, Network Marketing Consultant, ProSTEP, Inc.

"When Zig Ziglar spoke at our company's annual conference he had a profound impact on my professional *and* personal development. The following year, applying Zig's time-tested wisdom, I achieved our company's highest manager level, becoming the fastest 5-star Manager in Canada (to date!). Zig's bottom-line message is the importance of 'old-fashioned' values and integrity . . . the same 'state-of-the-art' technology necessary for us to achieve principled success in both our business and private lives in the new millennium!"

> — Jon Miller, 5-Star Manager, BodyWise International

"Using Zig's books and tapes: *See You at the Top* and *Secrets of Closing the Sale,* and using network marketing as our vehicle, we moved quickly from the 'outhouse' to the penthouse!"

— James and Louanne Davis, Horizons Marketing

"When I first heard of Zig Ziglar, I was in my 30s, and having received two graduate degrees I thought I had pretty much read or at least heard of most of what was available in the area of personal development. After being inspired by the messages and delivery contained in *Take Charge of Your Life,* I began a new stage of my life, which led me straight into network marketing. Because of Zig's teachings I was able to be successful — earning six figures in one month early in my career — and more importantly, teaching others to do the same."

— Ken Rudd, President and CEO, Premier Systems, Inc.

"Zig's 'How to Stay Motivated' audio series really came at the right time in my life. It's helping me pinpoint what I really want and need, and the best way in getting there. Playing his tapes makes me constantly rediscover the truths that I need to make not only my life fruitful, but my family and friends also. Thank you, Zig."

— Vic Carrara, Affiliate, Business Success Strategies, United Kingdom

"I vividly recall the first time I heard Zig say: 'You can have everything you want in life if you will just help enough other people get what they want.' These words capture the very heart and soul of the network marketing way of life. I can attest from personal experience that *it works!* There is not a net-worker alive who can take a detour around this motto and expect to make it to the top."

— Atticus Killough, FreeLeads.Com

"One of the first things I tell new prospects is to renew their mind. The only way to do that is to read more. If you want to make it to the top, read Zig's book *See You At The Top,* which includes the quote, 'You need a check up from the neck up.' Because it's all about attitude."

— Lee Lemons, Excel Communications

Network Marketing FOR DUMMIES®

by Zig Ziglar with John P. Hayes, Ph.D.

WILEY

Wiley Publishing, Inc.

Network Marketing For Dummies®

Published by
Wiley Publishing, Inc.
111 River Street
Hoboken, NJ 07030
www.wiley.com

WILEY

About the Authors

Zig Ziglar (Dallas, Texas), speaker, author, and authority on high-level performance, is chairman of the Zig Ziglar Corporation, which is committed to helping people more fully utilize their physical, mental, and spiritual resources. Hundreds of companies use his books, tapes, and videos to train their employees. Zig has traveled more than 5 million miles, addressing over 300,000 people every year at the Peter Lowe Success Seminars and at businesses, sales organizations, schools, and church groups. He also reaches countless numbers through television and radio appearances. Zig is the author of 17 books, including 10 best-sellers like *Secrets of Closing the Sale, Raising Positive Kids in a Negative World,* and *See You at the Top,* which has sold over 1.7 million copies, and his two most recent books, *Success For Dummies* and *Something Else to Smile About.* He also develops and markets training audio- and videocassettes for worldwide distribution. His works have been translated into more than 38 different languages and dialects.

John P. Hayes, Ph.D. (Dallas, Texas), enjoys a multi-faceted career as author, speaker, trainer, and businessman. *Network Marketing For Dummies* is his 17th book in an impressive list of titles that includes business books and biographies. A "Signature Series Speaker" for Ziglar Training Systems, John speaks to small businesses, entrepreneurs, distributorships, and franchise companies on marketing and strategic planning. He also coaches individuals and companies to help them build more satisfying and profitable businesses. John is a member of the Board of Directors and a marketing advisor for The Dwyer Group, one of the world's largest franchise companies. He is senior counsel to Bizcom Associates, a Dallas-based public relations firm. You can request a copy of John's free Special Report: *The Network Marketing Checklist,* by sending him an e-mail at: info@hayesworldwide.com. Type "NM Checklist" on the subject line. Or visit his Web site at www.drjohnhayes.com.

Dedication

Dedicated to those courageous pioneers who brought network marketing to life years ago and created a multibillion-dollar industry that has produced numerous millionaires and opened the doors of opportunity for many thousands of "average," committed, hard-working men and women.

Authors' Acknowledgments

Writing *Network Marketing For Dummies* required the time, energy, and cooperation of a network of individuals, and we want to convey our personal thanks and gratitude to each of them. First and foremost, we want to acknowledge the network marketers who contributed their knowledge, expertise, and "heart" to the project. These people are:

Louise Adrian, Party Lite Gifts; Shapira Alexander and David Kohina, Dr. Nona International; Cathy Barber, Pampered Chef; Jimmy and Carol Bishop, Zig Ziglar Network; Jim Bruce, TVC Marketing; Mike Cheves, Zig Ziglar Network; David D'Arcangelo, author; James Davis, Horizons Marketing; Kamie M. Downen, Enviro-Tech International; Connie Dugan, Oxyfresh; Todd Falcone, ProSTEP; Dan Gaub, Market America; Ray Gebauer, Mannatech; John Greene, Pre-Paid Legal; Jennifer Harper, Henn Workshops; Priscilla Harrison, Starlight International; Dan Hollings, i360inc.com; Atticus Killough, AtticusKillough.com; Kim Klaver, MLM911.Com; Lee Lemons, Excel Communications; Melynda Lilly, Discovery Toys; Edward Ludbrook, Direct Sales World.Com; Jack Maitland, Nikken; Dayle Maloney, Nutrition for Life; Nuala McDonald, Kleeneze; Jon Miller, Body Wise International; Luis Mogas and Miguel Ganem, ORBIS; Rod Nichols, USANA; Russ Noland, Excel Communications; Tom Paredes, Nutrition for Life; "Tremendous" Bill Pike, Youngevity; Bill Porter, Zig Ziglar Network; Brett Rademacher, Recruitomatic.com; Fred Raley, Ameriplan USA; Jeff Roberti and Gordon Hester, National Safety Associates; Ken Rudd, Premier Systems, Inc.; Tim Sales, Nu Skin/Big Planet; Tom "Big Al" Schreiter, Nutrition for Life; Bob Schwenkler, Nikken; Gavin Scott, Kleeneze; Kathy Smith, Discovery Toys; Todd Smith, Rexall/Showcase; Arce Trujillo and June Sweetser, Rena Ware International; Vernon Walker, Zig Ziglar Network; Shawn Wheeland, New Image; Mark Yarnell, Legacy; and Colleen Zade, Epicure Selections. Each of these network marketers gave unselfishly of their time to be interviewed for the book. To all of you we extend our admiration for your success.

Two other network marketers endured lengthy interviews and then went out of their way to contribute to the book. Jan Ruhe, Discovery Toys, may know every network marketer of note *worldwide!* We know she has trained many of them, and those we interviewed showered praises upon her. Jan, consider us members of your fan club! We also are thankful for the devoted assistance of another trainer, Doug Firebaugh, Mlmleadership.com. Doug has produced some of the best products available to network marketers, and he is one of the most knowledgeable resources in all of network marketing. Doug, thanks for contributing so much to this profession.

Other professionals who contributed to the book include Jeffrey A. Babener, Babener & Associates; Travis Bond, vice president of sales and marketing, 2021 Interactive, LLC; Holly Cherico, Better Business Bureau; Bryan Flanagan, Director of Corporate Training, Ziglar Training Systems; Joe and Blake Gecinger, Century Small Business Solutions; N. Ridgely Goldsborough, *Network Marketing Lifestyles* magazine; Clifton Jolley, Advent Communications; Hilton and Linda Johnson, MLM University; Charles King, University of Illinois; Joseph Mariano, Direct Selling Association; and Kyle Wilson, Jim Rohn & Associates. Don Sherman straightened us out on several compliance issues; he's vice president of associate relations for the Zig Ziglar Network. Michael Sheffield, Sheffield Resource Network, is a consultant who never tired of our questions or requests; he contributed mightily to our work, even while traveling internationally to meet with his clients.

We greatly appreciate the thoroughness and the energy of our editorial triad at Wiley: Suzanne Snyder, Tina Sims, and Pamela Mourouzis, as well as Maureen Kelly and Ben Nussbaum. Please, ladies (and gent!), no more editorial queries! We could not have managed this project without the help of Zig's personal editor, Julie Ziglar Norman, and Laurie Magers, his executive assistant for more than 23 years. This dynamic duo flawlessly managed the writing and editing process and bolstered our confidence as we completed the book. Ron Wuerch, who provided his services as technical editor, contributed many good ideas and helped clarify the messages we wanted to get across.

Our gratitude also for Tom Ziglar, Zig's son and chief executive officer of the Zig Ziglar Network, and Richard Oates, Zig's son-in-law, and chief operating officer of Zig Ziglar Network, both of whom envisioned this book even before its authors; Bruce Barbour, Zig's super literary agent and friend to both authors; and Mark Butler, who as acquisitions editor had the confidence (and, might we add, the good judgment) to invest IDG's time and money in this book. Thank you, all.

Writing a book is an exhilarating experience and an awesome responsibility. Any errors or omissions are entirely ours and in no way reflect on the people who assisted us. When it's all said and done, we hope you, the reader, will have enjoyed the book as much as we enjoyed writing it for you. Thank you for reading.

Zig Ziglar

John P. Hayes, Ph.D.

Publisher's Acknowledgments

We're proud of this book; please send us your comments through our Online Registration Form located at www.dummies.com/register.

Some of the people who helped bring this book to market include the following:

Acquisitions, Editorial, and Media Development

Project Editor: Suzanne Snyder

Acquisitions Editor: Mark Butler

Copy Editors: Tina Sims, Ben Nussbaum, Maureen Kelly

Acquisitions Coordinator: Lauren Cundiff

Technical Editor: Ron Wuerch — Zig Ziglar Network Founding Associate, Presidential Founder/Silver Director

Editorial Manager: Pam Mourouzis

Editorial Assistant: Carol Strickland

Cover Photo: © FPG International / VCG

Composition

Project Coordinator: Dale White

Layout and Graphics: Amy Adrian, Beth Brooks, Maria Mitchell, Kristin McMullan, Brian Torwelle, Jeremey Unger

Proofreaders: Laura Albert, Andy Hollandbeck, Susan Moritz, Susan Sims

Indexer: Rebecca R. Plunkett

Publishing and Editorial for Consumer Dummies

Diane Graves Steele, Vice President and Publisher, Consumer Dummies

Joyce Pepple, Acquisitions Director, Consumer Dummies

Kristin A. Cocks, Product Development Director, Consumer Dummies

Michael Spring, Vice President and Publisher, Travel

Kelly Regan, Editorial Director, Travel

Publishing for Technology Dummies

Andy Cummings, Vice President and Publisher, Dummies Technology/General User

Composition Services

Gerry Fahey, Vice President of Production Services

Debbie Stailey, Director of Composition Services

Contents at a Glance

Cartoons at a Glance

By Rich Tennant

"It all started when Mr. Tolliver said he wanted to join Frank's downline."

page 9

"I think Dick Foster should head up that new network marketing initiative. He's got the vision, the drive, and let's face it—that big white hat doesn't hurt either."

page 133

"Mom and Dad are network marketing a new diet program. It's been proven quite effective when used on hamsters."

page 53

"I've been working on my network marketing business over 80 hours a week for the past two years and it hasn't bothered me OR my wife, whats-her-name."

page 181

It's the type of business that the whole family can participate in.

Dad—gramps has fallen asleep in the gorilla suit again.

page 309

Fax: 978-546-7747
E-mail: richtennant@the5thwave.com
World Wide Web: www.the5thwave.com

Table of Contents

Introduction

Almost every day, in just about every country of the world, people are sitting around their kitchen tables with family and friends saying something like this: "Sooner or later I'm going to figure out what I can do to make money on my own. I'm going to start my own business." Have you been a part of that conversation? Have you ever initiated it? Chances are, you have. Chances are, you're one of the many people who are looking for a financial opportunity.

If we could sit at your table during this conversation, we would ask you, "Why haven't you found an opportunity yet?" You probably would give us one or more of the following answers:

- "I don't have the money."
- "I don't have the experience."
- "I don't know how."
- "I don't know what to do."

We would then say, "Friend, if you'll give us a moment, we'll show you how you can overcome that challenge. We'll also show you how you can start changing your financial situation within a matter of a few weeks, and possibly as soon as several days." If you then gave us permission to continue, we'd pull *Network Marketing For Dummies* from our briefcase and begin to share it with you. And it wouldn't take much time at all for you to see that absolutely nothing is standing between you and a business of your own. Whether you said you wanted to work full-time or part-time, whether you dreamed about earning a few hundred dollars a month or multiple thousands of dollars a month, you would be able to get started sooner rather than later.

Why are we so confident about *your* financial future when we don't even know you? We're confident because we know people like you. We know they had doubts just like yours. We also know what they've accomplished financially and professionally, and we believe, as they would tell you they believe, that you can do it, too. *If you want to.* Oh yes, you really have to *want to,* because even though we can show you how to get started in your own financial enterprise, success won't come easy. You won't need a lot of money to get started, and neither experience nor education matters. But you *will* have to work hard. Hey, you're probably doing that already, aren't you? Except you're doing it for someone else's business when you could be doing it for your own.

Would you like to know more? Then let us show you the opportunities that exist in network marketing, or what you might know as *multi-level marketing*. It's all in this book. Even better, let us introduce you to more than 50 successful network marketers — we think of them as the masters of network marketing — and a dozen experts, who tell you through the content of this book what to do and how to do it so that you can build a successful and satisfying business of your own. Network marketing accounts for nearly $100 billion in sales worldwide. Network marketers sell thousands of products and services every day, and hundreds of companies are just waiting for you to join them. Put aside your fears, your objections, and any utterance that begins with "I don't" and begin to consider your future in network marketing.

What Network Marketing Isn't

If you read this book after someone recommends it to you (and we hope that's the case), that's network marketing. If you read this book and recommend it to someone else (we *really* hope that's the case), that's also network marketing. The fact is, we all participate in network marketing every time we share information about something we like or don't like. Now imagine getting paid for doing it. That's *professional* network marketing! And that's the subject of this book.

Would you like a technical definition? *Network marketing* is a system for distributing goods and services through networks of thousands of independent salespeople, or distributors. The distributors earn money by selling goods and services and also by recruiting and sponsoring other salespeople who become part of their *downline,* or sales organization. Distributors earn monthly commissions or bonuses on the sales revenues generated by their downline.

Wait a minute now. We can imagine some of you thinking, "Oh, network marketing. That's for salespeople. It's not for me." That's "stinkin' thinkin'," friend! It's jumping to a false conclusion. You don't have to be a super salesperson to build a network marketing business. Experience does *not* matter. If you're capable of communicating with people about products and services that you like, and hopefully use, then you're capable of building a successful network marketing business. This book covers plenty more about this topic. Give yourself the opportunity to consider the facts about this profession.

Here's what network marketing is and isn't:

- ✓ Network marketing, or multi-level marketing (MLM), isn't illegal, fraudulent, or unethical.
- ✓ Network marketing isn't an opportunity to get rich quick off the payments of others who join the organization. That's a pyramid scheme.

- ✔ Network marketing isn't a pyramid scheme, which *is* illegal and unethical.

- ✔ Network marketing isn't an opportunity to get rich quick. Period.

- ✔ Network marketing isn't built on simple mathematics where many losers pay a few winners. That's also a pyramid scheme.

- ✔ Network marketing isn't an opportunity to let someone else build a sales organization for you.

- ✔ Network marketing isn't just for salespeople.

- ✔ Network marketing isn't expensive. Unlike most other business opportunities, the start-up costs are low, almost always less than $500 and often under $100.

- ✔ Network marketing isn't a way for companies to sell huge amounts of inventory to distributors.

- ✔ Network marketing isn't a way for distributors to sell stuff that nobody wants or uses.

- ✔ Network marketing isn't a license to sell products and services at inflated prices.

- ✔ Network marketing isn't for people who aren't willing to work hard.

- ✔ Network marketing isn't for anyone who can't or won't follow a proven system that leads to business success.

As a profession, network marketing invites all people, regardless of gender, experience, education, or financial status, to jump on board and build a satisfying and potentially lucrative business. It's not a profession that everyone will master, however, but that's only because some people are unwilling to make the sacrifices and the commitment that's necessary to succeed. After reading this book, you'll know exactly what sacrifices and what level of commitment will be required of you. You'll also know the steps involved in mastering the profession. From there, your success in the profession is entirely up to you.

About This Book

You don't have to start reading this book at Chapter 1, and you don't have to read it from cover to cover. We wrote the book as a reference tool so that you can read sections and chapters if and when they appeal to you. For example, if you want to know how network marketers earn money and how much money they earn, turn to Chapter 8. Or if you're curious about the qualities that people need to succeed in the profession, first turn to Chapter 3 and then jump back to Chapter 22, which lists ten characteristics of top network marketers. When you're ready to join a network marketing company, read Chapters 4 through 8 to find out how to select a good company. If you're already a network marketer and you're counting on us to help you brush up on your prospecting and sales skills, check out Chapters 14, 18 and a couple others. You have the idea, don't you? It's your book, so read it *your* way. It doesn't matter where you start reading; just *start reading somewhere.* There's plenty here to help you achieve the results you want to get in network marketing.

Conventions Used in This Book

The one thing that's consistent about network marketers is that they're not! They're fiercely independent. Like any profession, this one has its own jargon — you know, words that make sense only to network marketers. In fact, the combination of the words *networking* and *marketing* is jargon. It's another way of saying *multi-level marketing,* which some people call *referral marketing,* and others call *relationship marketing,* and now the computer geeks have come up with *viral marketing!* You'll find that we use *network marketing* most of the time. We also use the word *distributor,* which is short for *independent sales representative,* which is a *consultant* to some, an *associate* to others. When writing about compensation, we prefer the term *compensation plan,* but we could have used *marketing plan* or even *pay plan.* But don't worry about the terms. We include a glossary to help you out — you know, a list of jargon words with their definitions.

Foolish Assumptions

Here are our assumptions about you:

You're tired of working for someone else. Or you're tired of meaningless work. Or, as network marketers like to say, you're sick and tired of being sick and tired! Then it's a good thing you're reading this book because network marketers work for themselves — they're mission driven, so they realize they're helping other people with the work they do — and they're about as enthusiastic as any group of professionals you'll ever meet.

You want to earn more money than you're earning now. Many network marketers want to earn a few hundred dollars a month; others want to earn tens of thousands every month. Either is possible in network marketing, and this book introduces you to people who are doing both.

You don't have a clue how network marketing works, but you want to find out. Or you already know about network marketing because you're in it. Maybe you're making a little extra money every month, too. But now you're ready to make a commitment and go full-time. This book shows you how.

What you *do* know about network marketing isn't positive. We wouldn't be surprised if you hide this book so that no one knows you're reading it — sort of the way people read the *National Enquirer.* Few will admit they read it, but it's the largest circulation weekly newspaper in the world, or one of them, at least. If you don't want people laughing at you, taunting you, or ridiculing your choice of reading material, we probably won't see you reading this book on an airplane or on the beach. But that's okay. We debunk the myths about network marketing. Of all the people we interviewed for the book, not one was afraid or ashamed to say, "I'm a network marketer," or "I'm in multi-level marketing." We think you'll feel that way, too, after you know the facts. And after you make some money as a networker, you'll no doubt place *Network Marketing For Dummies* on your coffee table at home.

You have dreams, and you're just not sure how to fulfill them while working at a J.O.B. — Just Over Broke — as the network marketers say. Wait until you read about the dreams that have been fulfilled by the networkers who tell their stories in this book. We're talking about people who bootstrapped their way to the top while clinging to their dreams. Some of these folks were broke, and some carried huge debts until they became masters of network marketing and then masters of their earthly destiny. You hold on to your dreams, and we'll show you a way to make them come true.

You're scared. Go ahead, admit it. We won't tell anyone, but it's important that you face the facts. Fear remains a crippling state of mind until you discover that it's merely False Evidence Appearing Real. You're scared because you don't know the facts about network marketing. You will, however, after you read this book.

How This Book Is Organized

This book includes five major parts; each part has been divided into chapters, and each chapter has been separated into bite-sized, modular sections. You can pick up the book and get a taste for what you want to know without necessarily reading the content that comes before. You can't read a novel that way, but by golly, you can read this book any way you want. Ain't it great to be a nonconformist? At least once in a while?

The following sections, bite-sized and modular, show you what's to be found where in the book.

Part I: Why Network Marketing Works

This is the non-how-to section of the book. While the other parts of the book include chapters that tell you how to do this and that, Part I is a little bit history, a little bit future, and a little bit "Will it work for me?" By "a little bit," we don't mean we've slighted these subjects. Not at all. But we don't beat 'em to death either because we know you're just "a little bit" interested in them. We begin with a fact-packed first chapter that explains how network marketing got started and how it has developed into a multi-billion-dollar business. We like what the experts are predicting about the future of network marketing, and you probably will, too. In good times and bad times, economically speaking, network marketing offers plenty of opportunity. And now with cyberspace, wherever that is, network marketing is marching into a new frontier. We wrap up this part with a chapter to help you decide whether network marketing will work for you. It'll work for just about anyone, but you'll want to make sure you have the right stuff.

Part II: Finding and Evaluating the Opportunities

Roll up your sleeves for Part II because this is where you can get your hands dirty. Before you plunk down your hard-earned cash to invest in a network marketing company, we think you ought to know as much as you possibly can up front. Yeah, it's true that we're talking about an investment of only a couple hundred to a few hundred dollars, give or take some, but we want to help you invest it wisely. Because there are so many network marketing opportunities to choose from and even more products and services to represent, you can easily get confused and discouraged. But not if you dig into each of these chapters. Our masters of network marketing and several of our experts provide laserlike insights so that you'll know which questions to ask, whom to ask, and why you want to ask them. Rarely does anyone get into this business with a working knowledge of their company's compensation plan, and we don't promise to turn you into a compensation plan guru. But you'll get the basics, at least, and then some. Besides, the majority of our masters said they didn't have a clue what the compensation plan was about when they got started!

Part III: Signing Up and Setting Up for Success

If you've owned a business before or you're currently in business, you may not have to spend much time in this part of the book. But that's not the case for most people who start a network marketing business. Imagine working hard for a couple years, making a good amount of money, and then getting a visit from the revenue collectors only to have them issue a demand note for extra taxes due! You can probably avoid such a disaster by consulting with professional advisers, including an attorney, an accountant, and a tax expert. Get their advice early in the life of your business and keep them fully informed of your progress. Network marketing isn't a hobby, so don't treat it like one!

Thinking of starting your business with a partner? Network marketing is like a magnet for partnerships, particularly between husbands and wives, parents and children, brothers, sisters, and so forth. Partnerships often thrive in this profession, but not always. We offer some good ideas to help you make the most of your partnership, should you decide to get into one.

After you sign up with a network marketing company, you have some planning to do. We get you going so that you get the best possible start in your new business.

Part IV: Sales and Marketing Skills to Help You Build Your Business

Now you're into the heart of the book. In this part, we take you through prospecting for customers, recruiting and sponsoring people in your downline, motivating your sales organization, building solid relationships with customers, sharpening your sales skills, and much, much more.

You discover in this part that network marketing isn't about selling. That's one of the hardest lessons for salespeople to learn when they transition out of traditional sales and into network marketing. This is a *relationship* business. The sooner you learn how to build and maintain relationships, the better. That's when the money starts flowing in your business, and it's when satisfaction skyrockets. Our masters of network marketing share lots of information about how to build your business.

Attracting and keeping customers are paramount to your success in network marketing, and we think you'll be delighted with our information about how to value customers and win their loyalty and friendship.

Part V: The Part of Tens

Zig calls the last part of the book the "quick-read" section. John calls it "the end of the book." You might call it the "beginning of the book" because it's a good place to begin! "Ten Plus Two Resources for Network Marketers." How about "Ten Business-Enhancing Ideas"? Or "Ten Ways to Get a Quick Start in Network Marketing." There's more! We tried giving you more than ten of everything — a baker's dozen we proposed to our editors — but they did their job by keeping us within the page allotment. Good thing, too, or we'd still be writing this section because it's so much fun.

Icons Used in This Book

Throughout the book, we placed icons in the margins to point out a particularly noteworthy piece of information, a memorable quote, an inspiring story, or a message directly from Zig to you. Here's what each of those icons means:

This icon directs your attention to ideas and information to help you build a more satisfying and profitable business.

We use this friendly icon to refresh your memory or let you know that we covered the same point earlier in the book.

This icon marks pearls of wisdom that come from our masters of network marketing, our experts, and sometimes from Zig.

We could have written a book of stories about our masters of network marketing. Instead, we condensed them and use this icon to point them out to you.

This icon keeps you from wandering off the network marketing path and possibly falling into deep water! If there is any possible way you can get into trouble, we let you know what it is and how you can avoid it.

When you see this icon, Zig is speaking directly to you.

Where to Go from Here

Where you go from here is purely a matter of what you want to know now. By reading the Table of Contents, you'll know what's where. Start reading wherever you like and return as often as you'd like. Have fun with the book and start to imagine what life would be like for you as a successful networker. Whatever you do, follow through on the ideas in the book. Because if you do, then we'll close by saying what Zig has been saying for many years: "We'll see you, and we do mean *you,* not just *at* the top, but *over* the top!"

Part I
Why Network Marketing Works

The 5th Wave   By Rich Tennant

"It all started when Mr. Tolliver said he wanted to join Frank's downline."

In this part . . .

*W*hen people talk about network marketing, also called multi-level marketing, they often don't know what they're talking about. Even when their comments are positive they're often wrong! And that's a shame because network marketing is a dynamic, exciting, and rapidly expanding profession worldwide. It's also a legitimate profession (though some will try to convince you otherwise) that generates wealth for millions of individuals and contributes positively to our global society. You're about to discover the truth about network marketing, and when you finish reading this part of the book you will be able to speak accurately and confidently about the subject matter. More importantly, you'll be able to make some critical decisions about your own possible involvement in the network marketing profession.

In good times and bad times, economically speaking, network marketing offers opportunities to people just like you. While network marketing may not be for everyone, we believe it's a profession worthy of your time and exploration because, when it's approached knowledgeably, it can deliver everything that you want to get out of life. The future promises great advancements for network marketing, and if you decide that the profession makes sense for you, the chapters that make up this part of the book will help prepare you to get the most out of network marketing.

Chapter 1

Don't Laugh — $100 Billion a Year Is Serious Business

You probably picked up this book to find out how to become a network marketer, but even if you don't know it, you already are one. You're very good at it, too. Whether at work talking to your boss, at the shopping mall bumping into a neighbor, or on the telephone catching up with a family member, you're likely to do some network marketing. It happens almost every time someone asks for your opinion. You're a spontaneous network marketer when you say things like

"I used it, and it didn't work. This one is much better."

"She's the best. I never go to anyone else."

"Ever since I started, I have more energy. Try it yourself."

"Just like that it went away. I bet it will work for you, too."

"You'll love it. Every kitchen needs at least one."

"I switched because I get more value. Go ahead and do it."

You say that's *not* network marketing? It's just sharing information, helping people make better decisions, and leading them to an improved quality of life, correct?

Precisely! Sharing information, helping people make better decisions, and leading them to an improved quality of life is network marketing. You probably do it every day because it's a natural behavior for all who are part of the human race. The only problem for you is that you're not getting paid for the stain remover you recommended, the lawyer you referred, the protein drink that enhanced your energy, the magnetized shoulder wrap that zapped your pain, the kitchen utensil you recommended, and the Internet service you use. You made all those recommendations but got paid for none of them!

You could have been paid. And in the future you will if you decide to join the ranks of professional network marketers who energize the fastest-growing channel of distribution in the world for products and services. We wrote this book to help you do just that. The network marketing profession welcomes everyone who wants to become a member, regardless of race, gender, education, or social or economic status. You have an equal opportunity to succeed and to create a lifestyle of financial freedom, luxury, and personal fulfillment, all of which may lead to happiness.

If you've dreamed about such a lifestyle and you're willing to apply yourself to network marketing, then your success is only a matter of time. Whether you choose to work part-time (as most network marketers do) to earn a few hundred dollars a month or to work full-time to earn thousands and sometimes tens of thousands of dollars a month, everything you need to know — from selecting a network marketing company, to finding a product or service that you want to promote, to attracting lifetime customers, and even to building your own self-perpetuating, income-generating sales organization — is included in this book. You won't succeed just because you read *Network Marketing For Dummies,* but you *can* succeed if you apply the principles and procedures we explain to you.

What makes us so confident that these principles will help you succeed? Quite frankly, it's because they work for top network marketers in the United States and several other countries. Every profession includes people who climb to the top and turn around to lend a helping hand to pull up those who want to join them. You're about to meet some of the people who are living extraordinary lives at the top of the network marketing profession. They told us their stories and gave us the benefit of their wisdom in hopes of helping you through the pages of this book. All you have to do now is decide whether you want to join them. If you do, continue reading!

"Like it or not," says Tom "Big Al" Schreiter, a network marketer for Nutrition for Life International and a professional trainer, "we're all practicing network marketing every day. It's nothing more than recommending and promoting the things we value. Whether you choose to get paid for doing it, or you do it for free, the world is a better place because of network marketing."

Getting the Facts about Network Marketing: You May Be Surprised!

Network marketing is not an industry. It's a method of distribution that's used by many industries, whose products and services include communications, health and fitness, vitamins and minerals, toys, business training, giftware, cookware, books and videos, skin care, jewelry, insurance, household goods, office supplies, dental supplies, and many more.

The Direct Selling Association (www.dsa.org), based in Washington, D.C., tracks data about network marketing companies and their independent representatives who are responsible for marketing and distributing products and services. Due in part to its stringent membership requirements and a hefty membership fee, the DSA counts only 140 or so network marketing companies among its members. Estimates place the total number of network marketing firms in the United States at approximately 1,000 (there are many more, actually — annual start-ups are discussed later in this section), and perhaps 3,000 worldwide. But even if more companies belonged to the DSA, statistics about network marketing would still be difficult to obtain. By its very nature, network marketing is entrepreneurial, and companies that adopt it are very independent. Out of fear of losing their distributors to one another, network marketing companies do not routinely share data with each other, or anyone else, for that matter. (Of course, publicly traded firms are required to report statistical and financial data.)

Through its annual Direct Selling Growth & Outlook Survey and other studies, the DSA publishes statistics that characterize network marketing. On a global level, the World Federation of Direct Selling Associations (www.wfdsa.org) conducts research and reports on network marketing in approximately 50 countries. Here's a summary of what these organizations report:

- ✔ Direct selling worldwide is more than an $80 billion industry and moving rapidly to the $100 billion mark. The U.S. market alone contributes approximately $30 billion, up from $14 billion in 1992, while Japan contributes approximately $30 billion. Germany and France contribute $3.5 billion each, while Brazil and Mexico each generate sales just shy of $3 billion. Several countries, including Italy, Taiwan, England, Argentina, and Malaysia, each produce more than $1 billion.

- ✔ The number of network marketing distributors worldwide (including those working part-time and full-time) is approaching 35 million. Of that number, 10 to 12 million are working in the United States, Taiwan is approaching 3 million network marketing practitioners, while there are more than 2 million each in Indonesia, Japan, Mexico, and Thailand.

✔ People of all races and ages and both men and women are engaged in network marketing. Women dominate the industry four to one. Senior citizens make up approximately 5 percent of the market, while the physically challenged account for more than 8 percent.

According to Michael Sheffield, consultant to hundreds of network marketing companies and president of Sheffield Resource Network in Tempe, Arizona (`www.sheffieldnet.com`), one of every ten American households includes someone who is involved in network marketing, or direct selling.

The numbers are impressive, but at least one insider thinks they're merely a third of the real numbers. Ridgely Goldsborough, publisher of *Network Marketing Lifestyles* magazine, a bimonthly sold on newsstands and by subscription, says, "If anyone asks me unofficially what I think the numbers are, I say they are three times whatever the DSA reports. The DSA's membership consists of only the largest companies, and there's a new network marketing company starting almost every day in this country."

Network marketing is expanding globally

According to the Direct Selling Association, more than 150,000 people worldwide join a network marketing company every week! Two percent of the U.S. population is engaged in network marketing, and the same holds true for Australia and South Africa. Meanwhile, network marketing has captured 1 percent of the populations of the United Kingdom and Mexico, 3 percent of Japan, and 4 percent of Canada. But in Taiwan, one of the most active networking countries of the world, 8 percent of the population is involved in network marketing!

The global expansion of network marketing is quite impressive. Within two years of its start-up in China, Tianshi, which sells Chinese herbs, attracted 3.5 million distributors. Within a year of expanding to Russia, the company added another 40,000 distributors! A boom market also awaits network marketing in India and Southeast Asia.

Leading network marketers across the world are optimistic about the growth of their profession.

For example, Arce Trujillo is a senior director for Rena Ware International in Lima, Peru. Rena Ware sells steel cooking utensils, water filters, and a variety of nutritional and household products. Arce has been a full-time networker for the last 28 years, and he's never been more enthusiastic about the future: "The next five years are going to be very positive because Peru is coming out of the recession, and we are going to be able to increase our reach to customers who at this time have no chance of [affording] our excellent products, but who are very interested in them," he says. "Currently, our [sales] organization includes about 500 active people, and we hope that in the next five years we will expand that number to 6,000!" Before becoming a network marketer, Arce worked as a messenger.

For detailed information about the global expansion of network marketing, visit these two Web sites: MLMSuccess.com at `www.mlmsuccess.com` and Direct Sales World at `www.directsalesworld.com`.

Who started network marketing anyway — and why?

The answer to the question "Who started network marketing?" may depend on whom you ask because professional historians have shown little interest in documenting the subject matter. In 1999, *Network Marketing Lifestyles* published a chronological history of Amway, arguably the best-known brand name in the direct selling industry. The chronology points to Carl Rehnborg as the father of network marketing. As early as 1915, while working in China as a manufacturer's sales agent, Rehnborg was studying the effects of diet and nutrition on health. Continuing his research when he returned to the United States, in 1934 Rehnborg launched California Vitamins (re-named Nutrilite Products in 1939), which sold multivitamin and multimineral food supplements. Rehnborg, his neighbor, Dr. Castleberry, and Lee Mytinger, a sales manager, added a multi-level compensation plan to the company in 1945, and thus was the beginning of network marketing.

In 1949, Rich DeVos and Jay Van Andel, who went to high school together in Grand Rapids, Michigan, signed up as Nutrilite distributors. They became a successful team, and in 1958, realizing that they could teach others how to build their own businesses as network marketers and fulfill their dreams, DeVos and Van Andel decided to broaden their product line and establish their own network marketing company, The American Way Association, the company that would become known as Amway. History has proved DeVos and Van Andel were right to think they could help others build their own businesses through network marketing. Before the end of the 20th century, more than 3 million people in 80 countries belonged to the Amway network.

DeVos and Van Andel weren't the only two entrepreneurs who latched onto network marketing and made a business of it. In California, Dr. Forrest C. Shaklee and his two sons founded Shaklee Products in 1956 to sell nutritional and household products. These two companies, Shaklee and Amway, blazed the trail for countless network marketing firms to follow. Besides their multi-level pay plans, these companies promoted financial independence and self-fulfillment through network marketing.

Michael Sheffield says that the number of company start-up attempts *annually* in the United States alone ranges from 1,000 to 1,500! "Maybe 500 of these companies actually get the money to get going," Michael explains. "The failure rate is usually 80 percent to 90 percent the first year, but this is not much different than small business statistics overall."

Michael says network marketing worldwide is growing at four times the rate of the industry in the United States. "The good news is that network marketing is expanding," he says. "Our clients are in South America, Mexico, South Africa, Russia, Vietnam, India, China, and many other countries." Michael estimates that another 500 companies are launched every year outside the United States. "Still," he points out, "most countries look to American companies to lead the way in network marketing."

Understanding How Network Marketing Works

The concept of network marketing is simple, and it consists of two primary principles. First, a company relies on independent representatives, or distributors, to sell its products and services directly to consumers. That's why it's called *direct selling*. The company is spared the expense typically associated with the middleman in business. In direct selling, you don't need retail space or massive and costly advertising campaigns. The independent representatives, using a variety of marketing vehicles, dynamically advance products and services to the point of purchase.

Second, the representatives are granted the opportunity to build their own independent sales organization and network of marketers — giving rise to the phrase *building a downline* (the term *downline* is discussed in the following paragraph). The representatives receive a percentage of the cash revenues generated monthly by the network. Some levels of the network pay a higher commission than others, as we explain in Chapter 8 when we discuss compensation plans.

Figure 1-1 illustrates a simple, clear example of a downline. John's downline consists of all the people under him in his sales organization. John is in Dave and Holly's *upline* (the line above them that continues even up above John). Dave and Holly are on John's first level. Liz, Paul, Keith, and Nina are on John's second level. There are two *legs* to John's organization. Dave's side comprises one leg of John's downline, and Holly's side comprises the other.

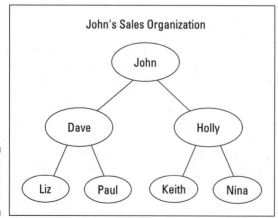

Figure 1-1:
A simple
downline.

On paper, the logic behind network marketing is simple, but the implementation is complex. The distributors depend on the network marketing company to provide desirable, quality products and services and to create the supporting systems — operations, marketing, sales, customer service, and personal development. The company depends on its distributors to learn and follow the systems and then to teach the systems to other distributors whom they sponsor in their downlines. The ultimate success or failure of a network marketing company depends greatly on the effectiveness of its systems and on the ability of its people to teach and follow them. For all of this to work, the parties must be committed, enthusiastic, and cooperative, not to mention fair and honest.

Network marketing companies build the "machine" that makes it possible for distributors to succeed. "For a very small investment, people can work from home and get all the tools and support they need directly from the company or the person who sponsored them," says Hilton Johnson, founder of MLM University (www.mlmuniversity.com), which provides sales training to network marketers. "So it works because people are given every chance to succeed without a lot of investment and without a lot of skills." Gavin Scott, a network marketer with Kleeneze in the United Kingdom, agrees wholeheartedly. (Kleeneze sells a variety of household products via catalogs.) "It's so simple to follow a proven system," he says.

Understanding Why Network Marketing Works

Veterans of the profession say that network marketing works for the following reasons:

- ✔ Even in a strong economy, many people need supplemental income. "Most people live paycheck to paycheck," explains Todd Smith, a Sarasota, Florida–based networker with Rexall Showcase International, which sells a variety of health and nutritional products. "Most people can't afford the nice things they want, or to send their kids off to college, and since there's seldom the opportunity to make more money in their full-time job, they start a part-time network marketing business. The risk is low, and the potential is great for a high financial return. As a result, there will always be the need for network marketing."

- ✔ People are looking for freedom from work and jobs they don't enjoy, and for money, and they can find both in network marketing. The combination is too tempting to pass up. "Where else can you find a concept that gives you more of what you want just for helping them distribute their products and services?" asks Kamie Downen of Honolulu, Hawaii. She and her husband, both in the military, are distributors of Enviro-Tech International, which is best known for its waterless car wash product.

✔ Time seems to be the one factor Americans value most, and network marketing can give them more of it by allowing them to work from home. They don't have to commute. They don't even have to get dressed! *Money* magazine conducted a nationwide poll in 1997 and discovered that 64 percent of Americans and 68 percent of women polled said that if they had a choice between more money or time off work, they would choose the time. Commenting on the survey results, *Network Marketing Lifestyles* magazine said the desire for more time may encourage more of America's dissatisfied workers to start their own network marketing businesses.

✔ The products and services are attractive, and they attract people to the profession. Network marketers are ground-breakers. They are often responsible for introducing new products and services. Phone cards are a good example. You know about phone cards — you can buy them in convenience stores for $5 and they're good for making long-distance phone calls. Networkers introduced those cards to the marketplace. "Many people have a positive experience with a network-marketed product, and then they're hooked," says Hilton Johnson. "They want to tell everyone about their experience, and in the process they build a business."

Choosing Network Marketing as a Career

Network marketing provides chances to succeed and get recognition in ways that more traditional forms of business have not. By the late 1960s, a combination of socioeconomic factors in America resulted in more women going to work, some because they wanted to, others because their families needed a second paycheck. In the 1970s and the following decades, many of these women gave up on corporate America when they were denied promotions to executive-level positions. As they considered their alternatives, many disgruntled employees discovered network marketing, and they couldn't resist the highly motivated, sky's-the-limit culture that some network marketing companies had created. Suddenly, upscale women and men found they could make the additional money they needed, or even replace and surpass their full-time incomes as network marketers. This is still very much the case today.

In the world of uncertainty, what network marketers call the world of the traditional J.O.B. (just over broke), you can get laid off because of a downswing in the economy or fired for any number of reasons: The boss doesn't like you, or she finds you intimidating, or he flat-out says you're not doing a good job. In network marketing, however, you can't get fired, regardless of your attitude or your productivity. Even earning more money than your sponsor (which often happens) isn't a problem, because the more business you do, the more you build your sponsor's business! It's really an amazing concept that attracts people for numerous reasons — money, yes, but there's so much more.

Reasons other than money

The desire to be recognized is one of the greatest motivators for people who join the network marketing profession. When work is a grind and people get no public recognition, they will look for something that's more exciting. Network marketing is often the answer because this profession makes a huge fuss over its people — all the time. And why not? People build businesses, and smart network marketing executives know it. That's why Mary Kay Ash wraps furs around the shoulders of her cosmetic-selling representatives and gives them pink cars to drive. It's why network marketing companies organize annual conventions: so they can praise their distributors and bring them on stage to publicly acknowledge their accomplishments. And the people love it, perhaps because most people are starved for this kind of attention.

People also join this profession because of the personalities of the people who make up the profession. Spend an evening with a bunch of network marketers, and you may be amazed by their positive attitudes, friendliness, and willingness to help each other. They don't keep secrets from their colleagues. If they find a solution to a problem, they want everyone to take advantage of it. Color, creed, gender, education, and seniority are issues that network marketers leave behind at their previous jobs.

Personal development is another motivator for people drawn to network marketing. Oftentimes, people are so beaten down by jobs, employers, coworkers, commuting, and the need to get ahead that they lose self-esteem. Then their attitude takes a nose dive, possibly followed by their health. Sooner or later, some of these folks look at themselves in a mirror and ask, "Why?" That's when the right network marketing company can rescue them. Most companies, through weekly telephone conference calls, regional and annual meetings, audio- and videocassettes, and workbooks, encourage their distributors to work on themselves harder than they work on their businesses. People with high self-esteem usually don't struggle as networkers. In fact, they're very good at it. And the more successful they become, the higher their self-esteem.

"People get involved in network marketing for many reasons other than money, and at first that amazed me," says Russ Noland, who gave up a lucrative real estate agency to become a full-time network marketer in Houston, Texas. "I thought everyone would be motivated by the money, but a lot of people are attracted by the recognition. Imagine someone who has gone to work every day for years, grinding it out and never getting any recognition, not even a pat on the back. As soon as they join a network marketing company and get a little success, they go to a meeting with hundreds or thousands of people, and they're asked to stand up so that everyone can cheer for them. That puts fuel in their boiler! They can't wait to get out there and do something so they can get recognized again."

Although people may think that they're getting into network marketing just for the money, David D'Arcangelo, author, television personality, and a former network marketer, disagrees. "Really they're attracted to the people. As a network marketer, you get a chance to teach other people and watch them succeed, and most people relish that opportunity. If things work out, you may even earn a tremendous amount of money." David was never a full-time network marketer: He dabbled in the profession just for the "fun of it, and because I liked the people," he explains. That fun led to a downline of 7,000 networkers, and even after David stopped actively working in the business, his commission checks continued to increase.

How could that happen? He didn't work, and he still got paid? And he got paid more? Yes! It's called residual income. It's one of the greatest benefits of network marketing, and we tell you all about it in Chapter 3.

"I was attracted to the opportunity for self-fulfillment," explains Arce Trujillo, a full-time network marketer in Lima, Peru, for Rena Ware International, a company that sells cooking utensils, water filters, and products for the home, as well as nutrition and skin care. "As a network marketer the past 28 years, I have achieved promotions, trips to almost everywhere in the world, financial stability, a happy family . . . and I continue working to achieve even more."

Another major bonus in network marketing is the ability to set your own hours and to work around your family's schedule. Throughout this book, you hear from women who chose network marketing simply because they didn't want to work away from home. They refused to send their children to day care, and they often sacrificed corporate positions and teaching careers. Men are also looking for ways to spend more time with their families, and it's not just American men, either. Tom Paredes tells a story about going to Puerto Rico to build his Nutrition for Life International business, and one of his first prospects was a veterinarian. Tom asked him, "If you could change one thing about your life, what would it be?" The response: "I'd like to get up in the morning and have breakfast with my children, take them to school, and then get home in time in the evening to have dinner with my family." Tom continues: "Here was an educated, professional man, and what did he want? More time with his family." Tom sponsored the veterinarian, who got what he wanted. "Today," says Tom, "he's still a vet, but he travels with me all over the world to train network marketers. He hangs a sign on his office door and says he'll be gone for a week or two. He has freedom of time, he has money, and he's home with his family when he wants to be."

Retirement isn't even a concept in this profession

Successful network marketers rarely retire, but it's not because they need the money. It's because they're having so much fun, and they would miss the personal and social rewards that network marketing provides. Dayle Maloney from Eau Claire, Wisconsin, is a case in point. He's the author of the book *I Could Have Quit $7,000,000 Ago,* which tells his story as a network marketer since 1983. Dayle has built a downline of 40,000 people in 16 countries, including Japan, Norway, Germany, and England. By the year 2000, he had earned more than $10 million, and that year he turned 65 — retirement age for most folks. But not Dayle. "I'm still working every day, and I'll spend 60 to 70 hours a week in my business, but it's not because I have to. It's because I want to. I don't even think about the money I'm earning. It's not important anymore. I'm touching lives, and those lives are touching more lives that touch even more lives. You don't give up something like that."

You could devote three to five years to network marketing and build an income that could survive even your own death. "I ask people if they would like a program that they could work for three years and then retire," says "Tremendous" Bill Pike, the most successful network marketer with Youngevity, a firm that sells antiaging products. Bill says there are no guarantees about how much money you will earn. Nonetheless, your residual income could continue for many years.

Measuring the interest in network marketing today

Perhaps the best indicator of the interest in network marketing today comes from Kim Klaver, Webmaster of www.mlm911.com. Kim built a lucrative business with National Safety Associates (NSA), which made its name selling water filtration systems. Several years ago, feeling the urge to "motivate and entertain" network marketers worldwide, Kim sold her business and launched her Web site.

"I had been a closet entertainer," says Kim, "and I wanted to help keep good people in the business. Plus, I saw the opportunity to attract a huge following." She says that the site floundered its first year, but due to strong word of mouth, she has yet to spend a cent on marketing. By 1999, the site was recording 10,000 to 40,000 hits daily, and by 2000: 100,000 hits a day! Kim explains, "The site has attracted leading distributors from as many as 150 network marketing companies, and they spread the word." In the last few years, Kim says, the site has built a subscriber base of 14,000 people. Kim sells a variety of products from the site and also promotes her speaking and training services. Visitors to www.mlm911.com can sign up for a free newsletter, as well as access the Discussion Board. Kim also posts information about free teleconferences that she conducts weekly.

Similarly, Russ Noland doesn't plan to retire. "Asking me when I'm going to retire is like asking me when I'm going to stop playing golf," he quips. "I can't imagine that I could stop talking to people about what network marketing has done for me. It's like a hobby now that makes me money. But I have an obligation to remain in the business. I've brought a lot of people with me, and I have much to offer others. Besides, it's fun! I'm around upbeat, positive people every day. How could you pass that up?"

You Get Out of It What You Put into It

You've heard it before, but it's true: You get out of it what you put into it. You can join one of the best network marketing companies. You can find a sponsor who's fabulously talented and willing to teach you. You can represent products and services that everyone wants to buy. But until you take action, nothing much is going to happen. You may be a natural-born network marketer, but you still have to work at it. When you join a company, you'll most likely receive a distributor's kit that contains audio- and videotapes, books, and a schedule of telephone conference calls and local opportunity meetings. There's your work. How often you listen to the tapes, watch the videos, read the books, join the conference calls, and attend the meetings determines how quickly and how well you advance as a network marketer.

The greatest indicator of success is your personal commitment to network marketing. "There's a day when you get into network marketing," says Jan Ruhe, a 20-year veteran of Discovery Toys and the most successful representative in that company. "But nothing happens until the day network marketing gets into you." There are no perfect network marketing companies, but that won't stand in your way to the top once you're committed.

Tom "Big Al" Schreiter recalls the failure that he experienced for nearly two years after he gave up a corporate job for network marketing in the 1970s. "Finally," he says, "I discovered my failure wasn't the company's fault, the sponsor's fault, the fault of the pricing, the weather, or the economy. It was *my* fault. Once I figured that out, it was easy to fix. But before then, I was only good at excuses. When network marketers think their lack of success is the fault of someone or something else, they're wrong. So many of them will change companies to address their failure, but if you're a lousy networker with one company, changing companies will just make you a lousy networker with another company. You've got to fix the basic problem, and the basic problem is *you.* Once I addressed the problem, I traded two bad years for what has now been 26 great years."

Research at Stanford University reveals that 95 percent of the people who buy an idea or concept are unable to follow through because they don't have the resources to do so — seminars, meetings, phone calls, training sessions, books, manuals, audiotapes, or CDs that are loaded with inspiring, informative material.

I have been training in the industry for over 30 years, and without exception, I can say to you that those people who take advantage of the things I just listed are the ones who succeed. Of those who never take advantage of any of these resources, I've never yet seen one who made it. The people who take advantage of most of them enjoy a degree of success commensurate with their effort, so take advantage of the books, tapes, and meetings your company has to offer you.

Of all the resources, I believe that the audiotapes you listen to in your car (Automobile University) are by far the most important factor in your success in network marketing and life. Over the years, I've received thousands of letters from people saying that my books and tapes changed and enriched their lives. The tapes pick them up when they are down, but interestingly enough, the biggest benefits come when they have listened so many times that they can finish the sentence, quote, story, or example. Here's why: At that point, the tapes turn into their self-talk, and those powerful affirmations change lives.

Regular attendance at the meetings is important, too. First, it helps you build relationships with others. Second, you get to participate in the excitement of the meeting itself. Third, you hear success story after success story. Fourth, you see people receiving praise and recognition. And perhaps for the first time, you will recognize and fully understand that you're part of something bigger than you — an opportunity to make a difference and have an influence in the lives of others and be rewarded handsomely in far more ways than just the dollar.

Network marketing advantage: It allows you to make a difference

People who really love what they do for a living will tell you that the money they earn is only half the equation. The other half is making a difference. They want to make a difference in the lives of other people. Making a difference is often more important than the money.

"Chills run up my spine when I see how we are helping mankind," says Tim Sales, a huge money earner in the Nu Skin network, and a popular network marketing trainer. "Our mission is driven by giving people the opportunity to live better lives. We contribute to charities, we provide funding for research, and we're behind many good causes. That's what drives us to remain long-term in network marketing."

Russ Noland, a top earner at Excel Communications, says he will never retire because he feels an obligation to remain in network marketing. He and his wife, Mary, used to work seven days a week in their own real estate sales agency selling more than $1-million worth of houses monthly. Once they discovered network marketing, however, they were able to give up the 14-hour-a-day grind, and that made a significant difference in their lives. First, it gave them their lives back. Second, it helped them earn more money than they ever thought possible. Third, it helped them make a difference in the lives of the other people they introduced to network marketing. "You don't retire from network marketing," Russ explains. "There's no need to. And who would want to? It's too much fun."

Chapter 2

Coming of Age: The Future Belongs to Network Marketing

● ●

In This Chapter

▶ Clarifying pyramids, Ponzi schemes, and network marketing

▶ Preparing for the challenges ahead

▶ Debating the pros and cons of industry regulation

▶ Looking forward to a new network marketing profession

● ●

*F*uture trends are lining up worldwide for network marketing to continue growing exponentially in the new millennium. Challenges lie ahead, including regulation and consolidation, but socially and economically, everything points to an invigorating spirit and newfound respect for network marketing. This chapter examines the issues that will impact network marketing in the early years of the 21st century. Predicting the future of any profession is always risky, but network marketing is changing fast, and the way we see it, it's going to get even more exciting!

Emerging from a Murky Past: Defining Legitimate Network Marketing

The debate over the legitimacy of network marketing ended more than 20 years ago, but try telling that to the critics who would have you believe that every network marketing opportunity is an illegal money-making machine, or a "pyramid scheme." There's a huge difference between the two, as the United States government pointed out in 1979. That year, after nearly a half decade of investigating the practices of the Amway Corporation, and during a time when pyramid schemes proliferated in the United States, the Federal Trade Commission (FTC) ruled that Amway's multi-level marketing program was a legal business opportunity. See Chapter 7 for additional information about the U.S. government's investigation of Amway.

In what has since been dubbed the Amway Safeguards Rule, the FTC established criteria for the operations of network marketing companies and drew the final curtain on the Dark Ages of this profession. In spite of what the critics claim (many of them former networkers with an ax to grind), separating the real opportunities from the "flop-portunities" suddenly became easier.

Understanding the difference between pyramids and network marketing

Think pyramids and network marketing plans are the same? Think again, advises the FTC.

The FTC explains that network marketing is a way to sell goods or services through distributors. Joining a network marketing company usually entitles the distributor to receive commissions on sales of products or services sold, as well as for recruiting other distributors. Pyramid schemes, on the other hand, have a similar structure but a completely different focus, says the FTC. Pyramid schemes reward members for recruiting new distributors, and generally overlook the marketing and selling of merchandise. Most states outlaw pyramiding. Why? Because they inevitably collapse. Sooner or later, the recruitment of new distributors comes to a halt. When that happens, the plan collapses and most of the people involved — except perhaps those at the very top of the pyramid — lose their money.

The FTC's Web site (www.ftc.gov) offers these tips to help you avoid an illegal pyramid scheme:

- ✔ Avoid any plan that offers commissions for recruiting additional distributors.

- ✔ Beware of plans that ask new distributors to spend money on high-priced inventory.

- ✔ Be cautious of plans that claim you'll make money through continued growth of your *downline* — the commissions on sales made by new distributors you recruit — rather than through sales you make yourself.

- ✔ Beware of plans that promise enormous earnings or claim to sell miracle products.

- ✔ Do your homework! Check with your local Better Business Bureau and state attorney general about any company you're considering, especially if the claims about your potential earnings or the product sound too good to be true.

For more information about how to tell the difference between a pyramid scheme and a legitimate network marketing business, visit the Direct Selling Association's Web site at www.dsa.org. You can also find articles on this subject in the Library of the Better Business Bureau's Web site at www.bbb.org.

Contradicting the pyramid theory

There's a difference between a legitimate network marketing company and a "pyramid scheme." Even though they are structured like network marketing opportunities, pyramids are illegal because they reward people for their recruiting efforts and generally overlook the marketing and selling of merchandise. Inevitably, pyramids collapse because sooner or later the members stop recruiting, and most of the people involved, except perhaps for the people at the very top of the pyramid, lose their money.

People may tell you that the network marketing company you're considering is a pyramid, and in their naivete they'll go on to explain that only the person at the top makes money. We find that argument humorous because it could just as easily be used to explain a traditional corporation, and perhaps even the company that employs this misinformed person. In a traditional company, the compensation packages of the chairman, the president, and the vice presidents are always more impressive than those of the people under them. True, they're not all doing the same type of work, but the money flows to the top in a corporation. Why should it be any different in network marketing?

That's where the similarities end, however. How often in a traditional corporation can an employee earn more than the boss? Or how often can the employee with the least tenure make the most money or move to the top of the payroll within a short period of time? In corporations, you don't often hear, if you hear at all, about such accomplishments. But in network marketing, these accomplishments occur frequently, as evidenced by many of the stories in this book. In network marketing, *every distributor,* regardless of education, gender, race, or creed, has an equal chance to make the big money or at least the amount of money he desires. The truth is that network marketers can control their financial destiny; people with jobs cannot. So which "pyramid" would you rather join?

Network marketing, when legitimately conceived and implemented, is *not* an illegal pyramid. Given the circumstances explained here, many people will choose network marketing over a job.

We're not talking about Ponzi schemes, either

A Ponzi scheme is closely related to a pyramid scheme because it revolves around continuous recruiting. In a Ponzi scheme, the promoter generally has no product to sell and pays no commission to investors who recruit new "members." Instead, the promoter collects payments from a stream of people, promising them all the same high rate of return on a short-term investment.

Ponzi schemes don't offer a real investment opportunity. The promoter uses the money from new recruits to pay obligations owed to longer-standing members of the program. The expression that best summarizes a Ponzi scheme is "robbing Peter to pay Paul."

Both Ponzi schemes and illegal pyramids are quite seductive, warns the FTC, because they may be able to deliver a high rate of return to a few early investors for a short period of time. Yet both pyramid and Ponzi schemes are illegal because they inevitably must fall apart. No program can recruit new members forever. Every pyramid or Ponzi scheme collapses because it cannot expand beyond the size of the Earth's population. When the scheme collapses, most investors find themselves at the bottom, unable to recoup their losses.

Going mainstream: Network marketing earns some respect

Even though network marketing was attracting thousands of people every week — in fact, more than 50,000 a week during the 1990s in the United States alone, according to the Direct Sales Association (DSA) — mainstream society, including the business media, avoided network marketing.

In the early 1990s, however, the editors at *Success* magazine courageously published a cover story about network marketing. Editors at other business publications would not have made such a decision for fear of appearing lowbrow. Network marketing was hardly considered a legitimate topic for a mainstream business publication. The coverage by *Success* created a fervor of interest, and one of the editors, Richard Poe, resigned and wrote *Wave 3: The New Era in Network Marketing* (Prima, 1994). The book became a best-seller, and Poe's credibility as a journalist contributed kindly to the profession.

So did the interests of a Harvard-educated marketing professor at the University of Illinois at Chicago who contributed editorially to *Success*. Dr. Charles King had investigated network marketing as an alternative career path for students during a major recession that started in 1990. By 1993, Dr. King had created an MBA-quality-level course for network marketing practitioners. He teamed up with several successful networkers to teach the course, and the university has offered it annually ever since, usually to a packed auditorium. Dr. King has since said, "More people are employed in direct selling and more money is transacted there than in any other single business-based career path. Direct selling doesn't attract the same level of prestige as becoming president of Chrysler, but it can be a very lucrative career path for Everyman."

During the 1990s, several major corporations — Sprint, MCI, Dupont, and Citigroup, to name a few — decided to use network marketing to promote *their* products and services. In fact, Sprint and MCI owe much of their success to network marketing: Networkers penetrated a market once dominated by AT&T. Network marketers delivered huge percentages of the market to the newcomers. During this same decade, Internet companies, Amazon.com being first among them, began offering a quasi-network-marketing opportunity online. They called it "affiliate" or "referral" marketing, but it included a modest pay plan. The Internet companies paid commissions to people who motivated their friends and associates to visit the sites and purchase products and services. It was another nod in network marketing's favor.

Many attorneys, consultants, speakers, networkers-turned-authors, and lobbyists who worked for the Direct Selling Association and other organizations contributed to the rising stature of the profession, and by the turn of the century, network marketing was no longer the "bad boy of business." It wasn't yet part of the mainstream, either, but it had made significant strides as a respectable business strategy.

Sizing Up the Challenges Ahead

Challenges in the earliest years of the 21st century will test network marketing's character, and the way the profession behaves will either jeopardize everything it has gained to date or move it several steps further up the ladder of respectability.

No one tracks network marketing more closely than Joseph Mariano, senior vice president and legal counsel of the DSA in Washington, D.C. He says that he's optimistic about his industry's future — after all, he's documented the figures that direct selling has produced "unprecedented growth, from 5 to 15 percent a year for the last 15 years." But he's the first to wonder whether this growth spurt can continue. "There's really some uncertainty about the future because network marketing is facing some new opportunities and challenges," says Mariano. "The outcome of the next two to three years will help us better assess network marketing's prospects for the next quarter century."

Calling on the profession to help itself

Ridgely Goldsborough, publisher of *Network Marketing Lifestyles* magazine, has an idea that would help the network marketing profession catapult itself into mainstream societies worldwide. "Talk to each other!" he urges, speaking directly to the leaders of network marketing companies. "We can't bring this industry together until it matures to the point that people will talk to each other." Why the silent treatment?

Two reasons: "First, the industry is fragmented," Ridgely explains. "Big companies have nothing in common with the little companies, so there's no cohesiveness. Most network marketing companies are small businesses, and their owners operate them independently. Second, one company doesn't want its distributors talking to those of another company, so it's a very insulatory industry. Even the big network marketing companies don't have an opportunity to speak to each other." Ridgely says that network marketing is being discovered every day by people from all walks of life, including many professionals such as doctors and lawyers. But who would know it? Without unity, network marketing misses the opportunity to make its voice heard.

Awaiting the impact of the Internet on network marketing

The greatest challenge to hit network marketing in the early years of the 21st century is being created by the Internet, which presents both opportunities and threats to this profession. This new technology, complete with e-mail, browsers, and Web sites, makes it possible for network marketing companies to attract, train, and educate distributors online, while also promoting sales of products and services to consumers. It will be interesting to watch how the profession responds to these new developments. Will the outcomes prove to be positive or negative? Only time will tell. (In Chapter 17, we tell you how you can take advantage of the technology to build your business.) Meanwhile, network marketers, or would-be network marketers, can use the World Wide Web to promote their business opportunities, legitimate or not. As a result, the Web has become a playground for scam artists, possibly proving disastrous for network marketing.

"The Internet is a safe haven for carnival barkers," says Mark Yarnell, one of network marketing's most celebrated practitioners, trainers, and authors. During a 13-year stint with Nu Skin International, starting with a mere $179, Mark earned $13 million! After retiring at age 46, he returned four years later as a distributor for Legacy USA, which markets a biotech health care product. "There's no way to police the Internet," says Mark, "and that frightens me because the people who want to take advantage of this industry are very convincing and manipulative. They know which buttons to push, and they always take good people down with them. A lot of people are going to get scammed by this technology."

Not if the FTC can help it! Internet scams were notorious by the mid-1990s when the FTC went to work to expose them and shut them down. *Law Enforcers Target Internet Pyramid Schemes* read the title of a 1999 FTC news release that went on to explain that the FTC and 26 state law enforcers targeted more than 600 Internet pyramid sites for law enforcement action. The news release included a statement from the director of the FTC's Bureau of Consumer Protection that promised to "sweep" the Internet in the future for pyramid scams.

The problem is, the FTC can't sweep often enough. "These 'Internet money games' pop up overnight, and they stay below the surface so that the regulators can't easily find them," says Michael Sheffield, who owns Sheffield Resource Network (www.sheffieldnet.com), which he says is the world's largest network marketing consultancy. If the Internet scams prevail in the next several years, network marketing will suffer another bout of criticism and skepticism. The critics will say, "We told you so. They're all pyramid schemes!"

Mark Yarnell says he expects an enterprising techie to come up with a way to use the Internet to expose scams before they have any chance of hurting consumers. "I think we'll see the day when we can go to a Web site and learn the truth about network marketing companies," says Mark, who lives in Vancouver, British Columbia. "Legitimate companies will disclose their earnings and the earnings of their average distributors, and before people join a company, they'll be advised to visit this site first. That should put the kibosh on the carnival barkers!"

Having Internet technology will not make you an instant millionaire

In addition to Internet scams, cyberspace technology poses a more subtle danger for network marketing. As consultant Michael Sheffield explains, "There are numerous offerings on the Internet that would have you believe you can spend the day in your pajamas and use the Internet to build an international business. If anyone tells you that, run as fast as you can. Network marketing always was and always will be a personal relationship business. The Internet can introduce you to someone who shows an interest in your business or your products, but you will have to get on the phone or get in front of that person and develop a relationship with them before they'll trust you enough to get into business with you. Yes, there will be exceptions, but very few."

Mark Yarnell agrees: "The Internet has been oversold as a tool for asking people to change careers. It's just nonsense to assume that the average person will pull up a Web site and give up a career in another profession just to pursue networking."

Oddly enough, if the Internet proved to be *that* effective for network marketing companies, it would nullify the need for networkers! "If all of a sudden we could recruit people and market products over the Internet," Mark explains, "there would be no need for distributors. If a network marketing company could just slap up a Web site and move products, the distributors are out of business." But that's not going to happen in a profession that relies on personal relationships.

Be cautious of any network marketing opportunity that you discover on the Internet. Investigate it just as thoroughly as you would any other investment opportunity. Chapter 5 explains how to investigate before you invest.

My son, Tom, has been following the progress of the Internet for several years, and even though I'm not personally online — I work through my executive assistant because of the volume of e-mails I receive — Tom's got me excited about the power of the World Wide Web. Nothing compares to the way that technology can bring people together for a common purpose. Tom calls the Internet a "hyper speed sifter" because it can generate leads and find prospects worldwide for just about any business. The Internet is an awesome tool, no doubt about it, but Tom points out that there's one thing the Internet can't do. It can't give you the personal support that you absolutely must have to succeed in network marketing.

Those who succeed in network marketing will tell you how much they depend on the personal support of people in their organization. Network marketers thrive on emotions. You can use the Internet to get information about opportunities and products, and I suggest you use it for that purpose. But you won't have much of a future in network marketing without support from at least one other networker who understands what you're going through and who is willing to mentor you, encourage you, and give you the hope that will keep you committed to the profession. What I've learned about the Internet is that it's high-tech. However, I've known for much longer that network marketing is high-touch. Make no mistake about that!

Using the Internet to solve three fatal flaws in network marketing

In spite of its potential for causing problems for this profession, the Internet is the perfect technology for solving three fatal flaws in network marketing, says Brett Rademacher, Webmaster of www.recruitomatic.com, a site that explores many of the opportunities that the Internet provides to network marketers.

The first flaw is lack of duplication. If you're the best recruiter for your company, you would like everyone in your downline to know how to recruit as well as you do. But it's a challenge to reach everyone in your downline and teach them your techniques so that they can duplicate your results. As Brett explains, "Eventually your organization is going to become so large, possibly with thousands of people, that you will have less influence on the people near the bottom of your downline. Who's going to teach those people how to do what you do? Probably no one. Or someone who's not as good as you. With Internet technology, however, that problem is solved. You can use a variety of media, including film and audio, to transfer your know-how and expertise to the Web, where it can be accessed by everyone in your downline, providing they know how to use a computer and Internet technology."

The second flaw is lack of timely communication within network marketing organizations. Traditionally, network marketing companies have used printed newsletters to communicate with their distributors. "But by the time you get the newsletter, the information is often out of date," says Brett. "Newsletters simply take too long." He also points out that there's often a communications gap between the company and certain distributors. "What happens if your upline (the person or people directly above you in the organization) drops out or becomes inactive? Who's communicating with you then?" The answer to this problem is e-mail. It's free and it's easy to use. You can send one e-mail or 100,000 with the same keystroke, and it's instantaneous. "Thanks to this technology," says Brett, "we now have 'sell-through' in network marketing. If your upline quits, you won't be left in the dark because the e-mail messages will sell through the entire organization. As long as you read your e-mail, you'll know what's going on with the company."

The third flaw: inadequate training programs. Network marketing depends on consistent, quality training. Traditionally, training occurs at meetings, but not everyone can get to meetings. Or the training may come on an audio- or videotape, but not everyone can learn that way. They need more interaction, and once again, the Internet provides the solution. You can hold a meeting in cyberspace with countless people simultaneously. They can be in the United States or several other countries. The Internet can step up the quality and quantity of training.

Don't turn up your nose when someone suggests that you learn how to use the Internet. Doing so may very well make the difference between a humdrum business and one that's flawlessly successful!

Regulating network marketing: the pros and cons

Network marketing executives and distributors are divided on the issue of government regulation. Some believe there's a need for a federal law that would mandate regulations across the board in network marketing. No such law currently exists, but some experts argue the law is necessary to protect the profession from those who want to use it for selfish and illegal reasons. Mark Yarnell, for one, favors such regulation: "If the carnival barkers in network marketing had behaved similarly in the stock market, they'd be in federal penitentiaries. Putting a stop to them is a matter for the U.S. government to step in and handle." Other experts, like Michael Sheffield, oppose federal regulation: "I'm violently opposed to government intervention," he says. "I'm in favor of self regulation. Where companies aren't in compliance, I want to see our industry associations help them make the right choices. If they don't, then that's when we ask the government to intervene and put the pressure to bring them into compliance."

Perhaps government intervention is the fastest way to put an end to bogus operators in network marketing. Federal and state regulations helped purify the franchise market in 1979 by approving a comprehensive Franchise Rule and could do so in network marketing, too. Companies could be required to issue disclosure documents revealing the inner workings and financial performances of their opportunities to prospective investors, for instance. Michael Sheffield grimaces at such an idea, however. A dozen times a year he's called to be an expert witness in network marketing legal battles, so he's familiar with the judicial scene. "The problem," he says, "is that many of the regulators just don't get it. They want to control this industry, but they really don't understand how it works. Do they have the knowledge to make appropriate laws for direct selling? Not without help from credible sources. Many regulators have difficulty in determining the difference between a legitimate company and one that's not, so there's a good chance they'll misinterpret important issues. That will hurt many good companies, many good distributors, and what is evolving as an important industry."

Based on these comments, legislators need to be educated about this dynamic profession. And that's where Joseph Mariano at the Direct Selling Association steps in.

Joe stays busy watching and responding to proposed legislation, which pops up frequently at the state and federal levels. He's not going to be out of work anytime soon, but he says he'd like to see the direct selling industry get its own house in order. "Are we [network marketing companies] realistic about what we're promising people?" he asks. "Are we making unrealistic earnings claims? Are we doing what we're supposed to do? We have nothing to be ashamed of, so let's not embarrass ourselves. The danger in overpromising and misrepresenting is that we'll invite the regulators to become more active in our industry, and we're seeing evidence of this. There's a large measure of misunderstanding about direct selling and network marketing, and we as an industry can do something about that by making sure we clean up our own act."

If the network marketing profession doesn't police itself, it's almost certain that additional state and federal laws will be enacted. Whether these laws are good or bad for the profession remains to be seen.

Predicting the effects of consolidation on network marketing

The Internet's role and government regulation are two of the three major challenges that will likely shape the future of network marketing. The third is consolidation, a phenomenon that's occurring in many industries today. Mergers and acquisitions are already underway. Most notably, Royal Numico, headquartered in the Netherlands, recently purchased Enrich and Rexall/Sundown, two of North America's largest network marketing companies that sell health-related products. A leading manufacturer and marketer of nutrition products, Royal Numico also owns another U.S.-based company: General Nutrition Centers, with more than 4,200 retail outlets worldwide. With sales hovering in the $2 billion range, Royal Numico controls a huge production and sales network in 40 countries. More acquisitions are likely for this giant among consolidators.

"We're going to see more consolidation," says Michael Sheffield, who consults with client companies worldwide, including China and Russia where network-marketing is booming. "The network marketing industry is maturing, and no one company is going to buy another just to eliminate competition and strengthen its distribution reach."

"As a result of consolidation," says Mark Yarnell, "I think in the next 20 years we'll have 100 solid companies rather than a thousand or more companies, with most of them scrambling for existence. As it happens now, every month we hear about distributors jumping ship, leaving one company and taking their downlines with them to another company where they think the grass is greener. But then they discover the grass is always greener until it's time to mow, and very few people get into the mowing in this industry. They just keep flipping from one company to another. Ultimately, that hurts network marketing, so the shakeout will do us some good."

Will fewer companies mean higher prices for products and services sold by network marketing companies? Michael Sheffield doesn't see it that way. "The days of high-priced products are coming to an end for this industry," he predicts. "Technology will play a big role in seeing to that. Now consumers can get on the Internet and comparison shop. They can look at the brand names along with the generic products. If a company wants to put a big price on a product, they'll have to do a good job of selling its value. Prices will be coming down."

But that means compensation plans — the plans by which distributors are paid — will have to be altered as a result. "Lower prices means there will be less margin for companies to share with their distributors," continues Michael. "Consequently, some companies will be forced to change their compensation plans, and that could create an uproar, particularly for companies that have been around for more than a few years. Distributor groups are beginning to realize that they don't work for the company. The company works for them. They can fire their company anytime they want when they just stop selling. The distributors with mature companies don't want the company to alter their comp plan since it usually affects their income. Keep the distributors happy, and the company may fail in the changing marketplace. Change the plan, and the distributor base begins to evaporate. It's going to be a real challenge for the larger companies."

The consolidation of network marketing companies, and the revision of compensation plans, could mean that it will become all the more difficult to create huge wealth in network marketing. "Don't get the idea that the maturation of the industry means that distributors will be earning less money," says Michael. "They will be earning a smaller commission per sale in many instances, but the technology of the Internet will give them a worldwide marketing reach that's broader than anything we've ever seen before for selling and sponsoring. Whatever distributors lose in commission, they'll make up in volume." However these developments turn out, they are not likely to affect the appeal of the profession. Most people join network marketing companies to earn a few hundred extra dollars a month — not to make a fortune.

Worrying about Saturation Is a Waste of Time

Skeptics of network marketing are easily agitated by the word *saturation*. In their passionate discourse to explain why network marketing can't work, they'll say geometric progression will cause the industry to collapse. "If your geometric progression produces what you claim it will," they'll argue heatedly, "you'll eventually recruit everyone on Earth until you're out of people!"

If that's true, Lee Lemons ought to be worried, and he doesn't seem to be. If he thought he was going to run out of people to recruit for his Excel Communications downline, he might change his marketing plan and focus on recruiting *everyone* just as quickly as possible. But he knows that wouldn't make good business sense because network marketing isn't for everyone (and he's not going to run out of people). "I'm out there every day prospecting," says Lee, "but I'm only interested in certain kinds of prospects. I'm looking for the people person. The man or woman who can build relationships and make friends. That's just not everybody. But that's the only kind of person who should get into this business."

Bob Schwenkler, an engineer-turned-networker in Boise, Idaho, doesn't seem worried, either. He and his wife, Trish, a former homemaker, became Nikken distributors in 1993. Seven years into the development of their business, they have 20,000 distributors working with them. Of that number, they personally recruited only 33; with Trish's guidance those 33 expanded into a network that includes distributors in 50 states and nine countries. Bob points out, "I can only see 15 levels deep, so I really don't know how big our downline is beyond that." Their efforts and sales generate a seven-figure income for the Schwenklers. "We're not worried about saturation," explains Bob. "Even if everyone in our city knew about Nikken, it wouldn't change things too much. We're not approaching all of them with a business opportunity. We're selling them a product. And there are always new products to sell."

If anyone knows when it's time to worry, it's Tim Sales. He spent nine years with an underwater bomb squad unit for the U.S. military. That was before he joined Nu Skin in 1990 and started building a financial empire. If Tim thought saturation could blow up his sales organization, thus ending his multi-million-dollar business, he'd be worried! But when people raise the saturation issue with Tim, he says he knows exactly what's happening. "If they're a prospect, or if they're already a network marketer, and they tell me the market is saturated, I tell them, 'There are as many excuses as there are people. You're searching for an excuse, and sooner or later you'll find something that gives you a good enough reason not to join, or to quit.'" Then Tim takes the kaboom right out of the saturation bomb when he asks, "Do you know anyone who doesn't have a refrigerator?" Of course the answer is "No." He then says, "It doesn't stop GE from selling more of them, does it?"

For those who are really concerned about saturation, let's approach it in a very logical way. Network marketing has been around approximately 50 years as we think of it today. In 1950, there were approximately 2.5 billion people on Earth. Today, in the year 2000, there are approximately 6.5 billion people on Earth and over 5 billion of them have not even heard of network marketing — or at least they've never listened to a presentation and are certainly not in the business. In other words, there are over 6.5 billion people to recruit. The explanation is very simple. There are far more people working on the population than are working at network marketing.

I encourage you to build your downline to your heart's content, because if you saturate your own area, all those other people all over the world are still potential prospects. Besides, if you could make certain the world was saturated, you'd have to recruit people to help you spend your money. You'd have lots of it!

Defining a New Profession

Network marketing, in one form or another, will survive the challenges we discuss in this chapter, just as it has survived major challenges in the past. However, network marketing as we know it today will soon cease to exist. A new profession is emerging, and no one knows what it will look like — or even what it will be called. It will likely be the result of the Internet crossing paths with traditional multi-level marketing concepts. This won't be just a North American phenomenon, either. The World Wide Web will see to that!

Michael Sheffield tells us, "The pure multi-level marketing model will have increasing difficulty competing in the evolving U.S. marketplace and eventually in the global marketplace. That's the model that says, 'Inviting your family, friends, and neighbors to an opportunity meeting is how you build a business.' This model won't disappear entirely, but it won't work as well in the future simply because people are putting a higher premium on their time. Meanwhile, the emerging model of MLM companies is offering distributors ways to leverage their time through technology, using new tools for communicating with prospects, training distributors, and educating their downlines. These technologies allow a distributor to reach out beyond family, friends, and neighbors, taking advantage of long-distance sponsoring opportunities." Michael says we'll always have the "high-touch" approach in MLM: Companies will continue to conduct opportunity meetings and build relationships one-on-one. "But how do you do that when there's an ocean between you and your customer?" he asks. "That's why it would be a mistake for MLM companies to ignore the 'high-tech,' which includes telemarketing, infomercials, direct mail, and, of course, browsing through cyberspace." These technologies lend themselves to the global marketplace, and that's why forward-thinking companies will use them. "Any MLM company that continues to limit its thinking to the traditional mold runs the risk of becoming a dinosaur," comments Michael.

In addition, there will be increasing pressure on companies to reinvent themselves to stay ahead of their competition. "It used to be that a company had to make revisions every three to five years," Michael explains. "But now, it's every 18 to 24 months. Why? Because as soon as a company begins promoting its new product or marketing system on a Web site, copycat competitors will figure a way to do it faster, cheaper, and sometimes even better. To get an edge, companies will have to move faster and be willing to reinvent themselves more frequently. This is where the newer companies have an advantage. When necessary, they can make changes easily and quickly, whereas the more established companies find change more difficult. Unfortunately, many will find themselves in the same situation as the department store chains that have disappeared in recent years unless they can change with the times."

"Turbulent and incredible" are the words Edward Ludbrook uses when he considers the emerging network marketing profession, which he prefers to call "direct sales." Ed is a London-based consultant who maintains the Direct Sales World.com Web site, which dispenses "independent, authoritative facts, statistics, and comment on the world of direct sales." He says of the next ten years: "We're going to see technology, and the opportunity for global expansion, shake up the bad business models and force direct sales companies to develop profitable business models that will focus on distributor retention and customer service and satisfaction. When this occurs, there will be fewer failures, more acceptance by governments, media, and the public, and a huge increase in sales volume, which will appeal to the stock markets."

Regardless of how this new profession develops, it promises to be exciting, fulfilling, and financially rewarding for network marketers.

"The real wealth hasn't been made yet in direct sales," says Edward Ludbrook. "It's still in the future. It will come in the next wave of development, when network marketing companies focus on building more profitable business models."

Chapter 3

Deciding Whether Network Marketing Will Work for You

In This Chapter

▶ Evaluating your desire to be a network marketer

▶ Judging whether you have the abilities to succeed

▶ Understanding how networkers earn their money

*T*his is where you find out whether or not network marketing will work for you and how to make it work for you. We'll tell you right off the bat that the degree to which network marketing *will* work for you boils down to one word: *desire*. Network marketing thrives on desire — the desire of people just like you who are hoping for a better life, a bigger reward, a more satisfying career, or perhaps the opportunity to live and work for a cause that would make a difference in their lives and the lives of other people. The more desire, the better network marketing will work for you.

Success Begins with Desire

With even a smidgen of desire, almost anything is possible, and that includes *your* building a career in network marketing. This chapter helps you answer the question: Will network marketing work for me?

We all want the same things out of life. We want to be happy, healthy, reasonably prosperous and secure, and to have friends, peace of mind, good family relationships, and hope. A career in network marketing can satisfy all these desires.

"I worked myself into a coma in the real estate industry," says James Davis, an associate of Horizons Interactive, an Internet marketing company. "I was working 18 hours a day, selling more than 100 pieces of real estate annually for seven years. I loved it, but it was killing me and I didn't know it." In 1994, at age 42, James had a stroke that ended his real estate career. "I was totally blind for a period of time," he recalls, "and I forgot everything. My wife would read to me at night, and that's how I started to regain my memory, and then eventually some of my sight returned, but I'm still legally blind. I couldn't drive anymore, so there was no way I could ever return to real estate. I had no disability insurance, but I had two mortgages, two car payments, real estate investment obligations, and a high standard of living, too. I had to do *something* to make a living."

For 18 months James couldn't work, and the doctors told his wife, Louanne, that he was dying and they couldn't help him. Ah, but they didn't consider James's desire. "I wanted to live," he says, "and even though I could barely walk, talk, or see and I had unbelievable pain on the left side of my body, I was determined to work again."

James's transition to success in network marketing was a heroic struggle. Shortly before his stroke, he had learned about Horizons Marketing, whose associates sold automotive products, pesonal care items, and nutritional products from their homes. "That looked like something I could do," he explains, "and so I started selling those products by mail order. I did okay, but the panic attacks were so bad for the first couple of years after the stroke that it was like electricity running through my veins every time the phone rang. How could I ever succeed in sales or network marketing?"

Once again, desire came to his rescue. "I needed to earn money — and fast," says James. I developed my 'single daily action plan' and I practiced walking by going to the mailbox every day to send a prospect a tape or a brochure. I practiced talking by calling prospects on the phone. It was hard, but I always heard that when desire meets opportunity, exciting things begin to happen."

Things really got exciting in 1997. That's when Horizons introduced an Internet program, making it an international marketing company. "Horizons showed me how a fellow like me could make a good living," James explains. "We went from 15 products to 800 million once we became an Internet mall, representing the products and services of 125 different companies." By 1998, when he was interviewed by *Upline* magazine, an industry publication, James says he was earning $8,000 a week!

"God gave me talents that I wasn't using," James says, paraphrasing a Scripture passage. "Once I read that, I had to take action. I can teach people how to make money using my products, and that's what I do now." And there's no doubt about it: Desire led him to do it.

One of the exciting things about this industry is the incredible growth people experience as a result of the fact that they can capitalize on their difficulties. The story that James Davis shares with us is one of many I've heard over a long period of time from people who have been bedridden or suffered a debilitating illness but still managed to maintain a decent standard of living because of the telephone, mail, and now the Internet. In the process of all this, many of them become better students, they read good, inspirational, informational books, they listen to recordings by inspiring people, and as a result are able to continue to be productive.

Becoming the Right Kind of Person for Network Marketing (Or Anything Else!)

ZIG SAYS

Regardless of your chosen profession or field of endeavor, I'm completely convinced that you've got to be the right kind of person and do the right thing in order to have all that life has to offer. Virtually anybody — including you, if you are of at least average intelligence, put your mind to the tasks you face, and make a serious effort at learning — can acquire procedures and techniques. However, the *kind* of person you are is ultimately going to determine your effectiveness and the level of success you achieve in whatever you do.

Over the years, network marketing has gained a reputation for attracting con artists and those who participate in exaggerated claims and overstatements of benefits and potential earnings. That's the reason I believe it's imperative that you concentrate on becoming the right kind of person and doing the right thing before you get really involved in network marketing procedures and techniques. Basically, you are what you do, and — as my mother said to me as a child — "People more attention pay to what you do than what you say." They follow the example that you set, and the example you set is determined by the kind of person you are. As Laurel Cutter, Vice Chairman of FCB Leber Katz Partners, says, "Values determine behavior, behavior determines reputation, reputation determines advantages."

What kind of experience do you need, and how do you become the kind of person that would become successful in network marketing? The good news is that changes can be made and substantial growth — even radical growth — can be made in minute steps.

1. Find out exactly where you are by taking the simple inventory in Table 3-1. This inventory is so important that I have included it in several of my books — *See You at the Top, Over the Top,* and *Success For Dummies,* to name a few. It contains a long list of qualities. I encourage you to make a dozen copies of this list and then carefully analyze it. Go down the list and check the qualities you feel you can honestly say you already have. Don't be too hard on yourself — if you have at least the seed of a quality, give yourself some credit for it. On the other side of the coin, you *do* need to be fair and honest. No one will see this but you.

2. Give one copy of the list (without any check marks) to at least one of your parents, your closest two friends, and an associate with whom you have worked for a period of time. Also, give a copy of the list to someone under whom you have served as a student, a church or synagogue member, a member of an athletic team, and so on. Ask these people to give you their honest evaluation of the qualities they think you have. Ask them to check the list and return it to you unsigned so you won't know whose evaluation you are reading. Ask them also to circle the qualities they feel you need or need to improve on in order to become all that you can be. This is important because whoever you are goes everywhere you go and does whatever you do. Consistency of action is one of the keys to success in network marketing.

3. Add to the list you made earlier the qualities that your family, friends, and associates have indicated they believe you have. You're going to be delighted to know you have so many positive qualities recognized not only by yourself but — equally important — by others. For 30 days, take the entire list of compiled qualities, get in front of a mirror every night before you go to bed and every morning before you start your day's activities, straighten your shoulders, look yourself in the eye, and with enthusiasm say, "I (insert your name) am an honest . . ." and go right down the list, claiming all of the qualities on the list. Understand that the eyes are the windows of the soul, and — in the 50 years I've been training people — this is the most effective, simple approach I've encountered to help people become more so they can do more and have more.

4. Every morning and every night for 30 days, claim these qualities. You will definitely see a change in yourself within the 30-day period. In most cases, your friends and coworkers will comment on the changes they notice in you. Then, starting on the 31st day, repeat the process, but every evening (in one-week increments) choose your strongest quality and the one you and your helpers have identified as needing help and say, for example, "I'm highly motivated and am becoming more consistent every day," or, "I'm very dependable and getting more cheerful every day." In other words, you will be claiming and reinforcing your strengths while confirming your improvement in the weak areas.

Literally thousands of people have assured us that they have experienced radical improvements in their lives through the use of this procedure. We have a free, trifold card — easy to carry in a pocket or purse — that contains this same information. If you would like one, send a stamped, self-addressed envelope to Ziglar Training Systems, Self Talk Card, 2009 Chenault Dr., Carrollton, TX 75006, and we will be happy to send you one.

Table 3-1	Self-Talk Affirmations	
Select the qualities that describe you, as well as those that you possess:		
Grateful	Teachable	Well-mannered
Dependable	Proud	Diligent
Thrifty	Resourceful	Extra-miler
Sober	Respectful	Affectionate
Supportive	Sincere	Attentive
Personable	Open-minded	Good-finder
Kind	Encourager	Visionary
Faithful	Humble	Hard worker
Authoritative	Self-controlling	Fair
Consistent	Creative	Humor
Good listener	Teacher	Common sense
Honest	Courageous	Competence
Intelligent	Enthusiastic	Experience
Goals oriented	Motivated	Training
Organized	Decisive	Knowledgeable
Responsible	Work smarter	Team player
Caring	Focused	Loyal
Conviction	Disciplined	Communicator
Commited	Persistent	Wise
Optimistic	Positive mental attitude	Energetic
Punctual	Momentum	Self-image
Self-starter	Confident	Integrity

Ways in Which Network Marketing Can Work for You

Experts say that network marketing can work for just about anyone, and although we think there's more than a little truth to that, such a statement could be misleading, depending on how it's interpreted. We believe that a number of factors can indicate an individual's compatibility with network marketing. For example, you have to have a lot of "want to." If you want to make network marketing work, there's a better chance that it will. Likewise, if you develop and maintain a good attitude about network marketing, even when it's not working the way you want it to, and you believe in yourself as well as your products and services, there's a good chance that you can build a successful career in network marketing. You also have to begin thinking like a business owner as opposed to an employee. There are other factors, too, and we lay them all out for you in the next few pages.

It works if you really want it to work for you

If you dream big, desire mightily, and are willing to do the necessary work, network marketing will work for you. Network marketing has no guarantees, and there are no secrets that a select few keep in reserve just for their friends, or for people who pay them large amounts of money. You can't buy success in network marketing. You simply need at least one reason to *want it* to work for you. Can you think of at least one?

Pick a date that represents exactly ten years in the future. Now write out what you imagine your life is like on that date. Write out where you live, how old you are, and the ages of your children. Now pretend that you are ten years in the future looking back at your life over the past ten years. Write out all the things that you would have accomplished, all the major experiences that you would have had. The trips that you will have taken. The advancements you will have made professionally. What kind of shape are you in? What is your day-to-day routine like? Will you be in good enough shape to really benefit from all the medical advances that were made in the past ten years? Looking back from the future, what will have been your greatest achievement? After your dream has "cooled off" for a week, go back to it and ask yourself how you will complete each step. Then write it all out.

It works if you have the right attitude

So much of what you do and who you become is controlled by your mental attitude. For example, you may think that you would be embarrassed to tell family and friends that you are involved in network marketing. Or you may be among those who say, "Only the people who get in at the beginning make any money in that industry."

Consider this: Since 1992, when Gavin Scott joined Kleeneze, a company that's well-known in the United Kingdom for its catalogs, which feature countless household and consumer products, he's heard all the excuses about why network marketing won't work or can't work. "I gave up a job in the shipyards to go with Kleeneze full-time," he explains, "and people still laugh at the idea that I'm in network marketing. But who cares if they laugh? I used to earn £8,000 (approximately $12,000), and last year I earned £260,000 (about $390,000). I joined Kleeneze 22 years after it started — far from being at the top — but now I have the company's biggest downline. It's all about attitude!"

For a comprehensive lesson in building and maintaining a positive attitude, see Zig Ziglar's book *Success For Dummies* (IDG Books Worldwide, Inc.).

I wish I could introduce you to all the talented people I've met through the years who are generally just one step ahead of the bill collector and often two steps ahead of the law. They're always looking for a deal and the fast buck. That's the wrong attitude. These people never build much or very high because they have no foundation to build on. Others with the right foundation end up living in the basement or building a shack on that foundation. They don't take all the steps to use the talent they have to get the richer life. Success and happiness are not matters of chance, but choice. You literally choose what you want in life. Then you develop a game plan to get it.

It works if you have a solid belief system

If you have a solid belief system — that is, you believe in yourself, your product or service, and your opportunity — network marketing can work for you. Unfortunately, many people who get into network marketing aren't believers. Todd Smith, a Sarasota, Florida–based distributor for Rexall Showcase International, which sells health and nutritional products, explains it this way: "The people who fail at network marketing are people who fail at most of the things they do in life. And that's because they have poor self-esteem, and they tend to blame everyone or everything without taking any responsibility themselves. You have to *believe* you can succeed in network marketing. And then you have to demonstrate to other people that you believe in your product and you believe in the opportunity. If you don't work the business, why would anyone believe you're convinced that it's of any value?"

The successful people in network marketing almost always say, "Once I saw the product (or the opportunity), I knew I could do it, too." They believed immediately. "As soon as I saw the spongeware pottery, the baskets, and the shaker boxes," says Jennifer Harper, a distributor of Henn Workshops, which sells the very products she mentions, "I loved them, and I knew right then I could talk honestly and enthusiastically about them night after night."

It works if you know your hot buttons

Knowing what you like and what you want out of life — the "hot buttons" that motivate you into action — goes a long way in helping you decide whether network marketing will work for you. "I wanted financial freedom," says Kamie Downen of Honolulu, Hawaii. While she and her husband are both in the military, they are also distributors of Enviro Tech International, a company that sells a waterless car wash product, as well as body care, nutritionals, and skin care products. "You don't make much money in the military," Kamie says, "and since I'm in military intelligence, I don't see many opportunities for me in the private sector. I don't want to work for the government when I leave the service, but I want financial freedom, and network marketing can deliver that." Kamie and her husband are Diamond distributors, one of the highest ranks in the Enviro Tech network.

Financial freedom is an oft-mentioned hot button by network marketers, but there are many "hot buttons," including the opportunity to work at home, the chance to be the boss, and the convenience of a flexible work schedule.

Kathy Smith, a Nashville, Tennessee-based distributor of Discovery Toys, which sells educational and unique toys for children, offers yet another hot button: the opportunity to travel! "I was an English teacher before I joined Discovery Toys, and on a teacher's salary, there weren't any big trips in sight, and there was no way to earn a trip. But trips motivate me, and since I've been in network marketing, I've earned many trips. I've spent a week in London, I've been to Hong Kong and China, where I walked on the Great Wall, I've been to Paris, to Hawaii a few times, and to Mexico several times. Without network marketing, I wasn't going to get any of these trips."

It works if you're looking for additional income

Although you can make big money in network marketing, not everyone gets into this profession to make big money. Trainers and experts in the industry say that most people are happy to earn enough money to pay for the products they buy, or to cover their car payments. In other words, they're looking for $300 to $500 a month. Almost anyone who's serious about network marketing and who's with a reputable company can earn that level of money within a few months — working just part-time. Many successful network marketers begin on a part-time schedule; once they start earning a few hundred dollars a month, they often decide to work full-time. Others, however, prefer a part-time business — they're taking care of young children, for example, and they have only a few hours a day to devote to network marketing. The schedule doesn't matter — if you have a need for additional income, network marketing can work for you.

Louise Adrian, an independent consultant with the Canadian division of Party Lite Gifts, which markets candles, wasn't thinking about earning extra money at the time she joined a network marketing company in the summer of 1990. (She left that company after nine years to join Party Lite Gifts.) Louise laughs when someone asks her how she got started in network marketing. "There wasn't much you could do if you wanted to stay home and raise your children, so I didn't know there were any opportunities for making additional income when my son was born 16 years ago. Not long after my second child was born, I went to a party at a friend's home and ended up getting into network marketing by accident. In fact, if I had known it was network marketing, I wouldn't have joined. I loved the products that were demonstrated at the party, and that's why I joined the company."

She later realized that she could earn a little extra money by selling the same products, so she bought a kit, and that was the beginning of what's become a very successful career. While working from home so that she could be with her children, Louise steadily moved up the company's ranks. Eventually, with both children in school and more time available to her, Louise became number one in *all* categories including recruiting, sponsoring, and earning trips. "With every promotion, I started making more money," she says.

The company hired Louise as its Canadian sales manager, but after 18 months, she wanted to return to being her own boss. That's when she found Party Lite Gifts. Within six weeks of joining the company, she had earned her first promotion. "Within the next year," she explains, "I expect to reach the level of regional vice president." At that level, she expects to be earning a six-figure income! "To this day I thank the person who got me involved in network marketing, even though she didn't tell me it was network marketing. I wouldn't be telling you this story now if it hadn't been for her."

It works if you're willing to learn from others

It's unusual to hear that someone succeeded in network marketing — even at the level of a few hundred dollars a month — without becoming a student of the profession and the business. No reputable network marketing company, or sponsor, would lead you to believe that you can make network marketing work all by yourself. In fact, they want to help you!

Too often, however, people appear not to want the help, or they won't make the effort to show up at training sessions or phone in to conference calls to get the help. If you want network marketing to work for you, humble yourself to learn from others.

Not so many years ago, little information in the form of books or tapes was available to network marketers. Neither were there many network marketing trainers, except those who worked within a specific company. People in the business had to depend on the people in their uplines (sponsors) or their corporate offices for education, and there's nothing wrong with that. That's the way network marketing is designed to work. Nowadays, however, with thousands of successful network marketers worldwide, individuals have many opportunities to learn from trainers and experts outside of a specific company. Many of these successful network marketers, through their books and tapes as well as seminars and telephone conferences, offer their personal stories and triumphs, and they share techniques and ideas that are not widely known in the business. All you have to do to get their help is ask for it and then be willing to follow their advice. You can find many of these trainers listed throughout the book. You may also wish to purchase *Network Marketing Lifestyles* magazine at a local newsstand.

It works if you're willing to invest in your network marketing career

For some odd reason, many people invest a few hundred dollars, or less, in a network marketing company, and they think they're entitled to a successful career or to at least make a little extra money. Network marketing doesn't work that way! Your initial investment covers the cost of your start-up kit, which usually includes a distributor's manual, some products, an audiotape that explains how to sell the products, some marketing materials consisting of brochures, and possibly some training materials.

A kit, no matter how big or pretty, doesn't turn you into a network marketer. The situation is similar to adding a new pet to your household. You can buy yourself the cutest puppy, but until that puppy is trained, you're going to have more than a few messes in your house! To train that puppy, you may have to read some books, listen to some tapes, watch a video or two, and possibly even join a training class with your pet. In other words, to be a successful pet owner, and to get the most enjoyment from your pet, you have to invest some money. That's what network marketing is like — to succeed in and enjoy your career, you must continuously make an investment of your time, effort, and/or resources. But hey, so do doctors and many other professionals. Would you want a doctor to operate on your heart if he hasn't had any advanced training since he graduated from medical school in 1960? You'd want a doctor who continued to invest in his career, and if you want to advance in your network marketing career, you need to invest both time and money on an ongoing basis.

You have to be before you can do, and you have to do before you can have!

It works if you have the right personality

What's the right personality? There's a good chance that it's *your* personality. People may tell you that it takes a *special personality* to succeed in network marketing. Well, that's right. And whether you recognize it or not, you *are* a special person. You were created that way!

Now, some personalities may be better suited to network marketing than others, but with the right attitude, network marketing has the potential to work for any personality.

"Anyone who is willing to learn and put their ego aside for a little while can succeed in network marketing," says Kamie Downen, whose story is featured earlier in this chapter. "Our company offers us a proven system that already works, but there are always people who want to reinvent the wheel. I was one of them! I thought I could do it better, and it took me some time to discover that I couldn't. That was a waste of my time. But I'm stubborn, and stubborn people are a good fit for network marketing. My husband is stubborn, too, and that's why we stick with this business and why we're making a success out of it."

"People with *burn* are most likely to succeed in network marketing," explains trainer Doug Firebaugh from Louisville, Kentucky. "Someone with burning in their heart to change their life because they're dissatisfied or they want more — *they* can succeed in this industry. People with burn are more likely to go get something done! The majority of people who get into network marketing don't succeed. The reason? Sometimes their uplines are weak, or their products aren't good, but usually it's because they don't have a strong burn in their hearts."

It works if you understand that network marketing is not a job

"When people make network marketing hard, or they say it's boring, that's because they're treating it like a job," says Carol Bishop, one of the most infectiously positive associates of the Zig Ziglar Network. Network marketing is anything but a job. No boss demands your accountability when you become a network marketer. Most days you don't have to be anyplace, such as behind your desk, at a certain time. Except for the initial training from the people in your upline, which may or may not happen (depending on your upline), it's not likely that you'll get a call from a superior who's going to tell you what to do, when to do it, and how to do it. No one schedules your work when you're a network marketer, and no one answers your phone — even the most successful network marketers usually answer their own phones. And no one, but no one, is going to bring you coffee!

When you become a network marketer, *you* are the boss. *You* set your own schedule, and *you* decide what you will do and how you'll do it. Do you want to make phone calls today? Or mail out audiocassettes? Do you want to do a little of both? Will you spend the morning writing a new classified ad for your buisness opportunity and placing it in newspapers, or will you spend the time studying your product information? Are you going to work at your desk or out on the patio? Do you want to get dressed or work in your pajamas? You didn't have these options as an employee, but as a network marketer you do. Want coffee this morning? Make it yourself! Or walk over to the donut shop, order some coffee and a blueberry scone, and read the newspaper. You can do that when you're a network marketer, and no one is going to say you can't!

The question is: *Can you handle that?* Because it isn't a job, and you'll fail if you treat it like a job, network marketing will work for you if you work it like a business. Not a hobby, either. A business! That means you must be self-directed and disciplined. Lots of work has to be done, and *you* have to do it without being told when and how.

Carol Bishop's husband, Jimmy, adds, "We make network marketing fun, and we keep it simple. That's everything a job *isn't,* and that's why we love networking. You have to work at it, that's true. But we have the systems already in place to show you what to do to duplicate our success. Just don't treat it like a job, because then you're going to take all of the excitement out of it."

If you need structure, including an office full of people, a boss to supervise your work, and a company to provide your benefits, you better keep your job.

Understanding the Money Issue

What we are about to tell you could change your future. We are going to tell you about linear and residual income, and once you understand the difference between the two, you might run out to sign up with the first network marketing company you can find. Consider yourself warned!

You're already familiar with linear income

Webster's New World Dictionary defines the word *linear* as "narrow and long." That gives you the perfect picture of linear income. *Linear income* is the financial reward, described in the following sentences, that you receive from a J.O.B.

"To me," says network marketer Kamie Downen, "it's the boss paying you what he thinks you're worth, and it's rarely as much as you think you're worth, but that's all you're going to get." In other words, the income is "narrow."

Kamie continues, "Most of us will work a long, long time, but with linear income, the pay doesn't always increase as much as we would want it to over that period of time. And then, once we stop working, the income stops, and sometimes we don't have a lot to show for the time we spent."

Thank you, Kamie. We couldn't have said it better ourselves!

Residual income is a whole 'nother story

Remember Elvis Presley? Who could forget him! He's been dead since 1977, but as long as there's music, the King of Rock and Roll will continue to be a part of it. Even though death short-circuited Elvis's career and prevented him from recording another song or performing in concert, he's still making money. In fact, Elvis will earn more money dead than he did alive! How so? *Residual income.*

While Elvis was alive, you can imagine that he was thrilled every time he heard one of his songs on the radio. The ole hound dog had to cherish the fact that the music industry loved him tenderly. But Elvis also knew that every time one of his songs aired on the radio, he earned a royalty, or what you might think of as a commission. Now he didn't get rich just because one radio station played his music; the money from one station didn't amount to much. But when thousands of radio stations played his records — sometimes two and three times a day, every day of the week, in many parts of the world — the result was a pile of money.

Now that Elvis has been dead all these years, radio stations still pay a royalty to air his music. Music retailers pay Elvis's estate a royalty on his CD sales, and T-shirt companies pay a royalty just so they can sell shirts with his like-ness on them. We don't know for sure, but Elvis's residual income for one year is probably larger than the gross national product of several small countries!

You can't sing, you say? That's quite all right, although some network mar-keters can belt out a tune and may even get paid well for doing so. But when it comes to earning residual income, network marketers will stick with net-work marketing. For many people, that's the way to make a pile of money!

If you sponsor two people to join you in business, and you earn just a little bit of money for everything *they* sell for as *long* as they sell it, and they each sponsor two people, who sponsor two people, who sponsor two people — after a period of time you have 70, 300, 1,500, maybe several thousand people in your downline, or sales organization. And you earn just a little bit of money for everything each person under you sells for as long as he or she continues selling it! That's residual income.

Perhaps the best attribute of residual income with many companies is that it keeps on paying you even after you stop working. And if you sell your business or turn it over to your children, that residual income keeps on paying even after you're dead. See there, you and Elvis may have a little more in common than you thought!

Is anyone working today who *wouldn't* want some residual income? If you do, you can imagine that millions of other people do, too. And some of them are likely to join you in business . . . that is, providing you've decided that network marketing will work for you.

Every legitimate network marketing company should offer at least two major possibilities and many smaller benefits:

- ✔ A real long-term opportunity to earn significant money, including residual income

- ✔ An opportunity to make a positive difference in the lives of others

Building residual income to secure your financial future

Even before his 41st birthday in 2000, Dan Gaub retired financially. But that's not the most amazing part of his story. He made his money and climbed to the top of his network marketing company, Market America, in less than five years. Market America sells many different products — from home care to personal care, as well as nutritional and educational products — through online malls.

Married and the father of two children, Dan was in a church ministry when a board member asked him to look at Market America. "My initial reaction was to tell him no, I wasn't interested," Dan recalls. "I had looked at network marketing in 1990, I investigated more than 60 companies, and I didn't join any of them because I didn't see any opportunities there. But

because this fellow was a friend and he was wealthy, I took a look at Market America. After I investigated it closely, I decided to join the company."

He's grateful now that he did. "I don't need [to work for] financial income ever again," Dan explains. "As I made money, I used it rather than spent it. I invested it and made some smart decisions. I still earn a tremendous income from Market America, and I'm a tremendous fan of the industry, but now I'm concentrating on designing a life for my family. I still work the business, I'm not sitting on the porch, but I don't work the business the way I used to. Now I select a few people at a time, I listen to what they want to achieve, and I help them get it."

Part II
Finding and Evaluating the Opportunities

The 5th Wave   By Rich Tennant

"Mom and Dad are network marketing a new diet program. It's been proven quite effective when used on hamsters."

In this part . . .

*1*f you know the right questions to ask and of whom to ask them, you can size up any situation, including whether or not you want to become a distributor of a specific network marketing company. In this part of the book, we tell you what those questions are, and we tell you whom to ask. And we do it all before you have to invest any of your hard-earned money in a network marketing opportunity that might not be right for you. Because network marketing is such an exciting profession, and because it includes a lot of excited distributors who want to recruit new distributors, people sometimes invest in a company that they know nothing about. *We don't want you doing that!*

No matter where you live in the world, and no matter what your goals are for joining a network marketing company, you can find one that satisfies your expectations and meets your standards. But you'll have to do some research. Come on now, research isn't all that horrible to do! Sure it takes time, and yes it requires you to analyze and think through situations, but remember — we're talking about your future! Whether you choose to work part-time or you decide to build a career in network marketing, we want you to be successful. So plan on doing some investigative work to find out about a company's management, products, compensation plan, and so forth.

Besides, we're going to lead you through the process. Just follow our suggestions: Ask the questions we pose and seek out the people who can honestly answer these questions. We're confident that you'll be better prepared to make some important decisions about network marketing and the companies and products that you would like to represent.

Chapter 4

Investigating Before You Invest

- -

In This Chapter

▶ Gathering information about industries that use network marketing

▶ Doing research on specific network marketing opportunities

▶ Knowing which questions to ask

- -

Selecting a network marketing company is a lot like selecting a dessert.

How's that?

In both situations you have many choices, and you can take all the time you want to look 'em over. What looks good? Pie? Cake? Ice cream? Fruit topped with whipped cream? The first choice is to narrow down the classifications; you can't have them all.

That's exactly what you have to do in selecting a network marketing industry. What do you like? Personal care? Home care? Wellness products? Family care? Inspirational products? Services? Educational products? All these industry classifications use network marketing for distribution. But you have to decide which industry you like best. Which one grabs your attention? Which one has "career" written all over it for you?

After you narrow down the dessert classifications, you still have one more decision to make. You've decided that the cakes look good. Great! But what kind? Chocolate? Marble? Two layers or one? The confusion intensifies as you make this final decision. The decision has to be one that will satisfy you, at least until another day.

Suppose that after much deliberation, you've decided that you like educational products. Wonderful. But any of the classifications would have been equally as wonderful, and they're all available through network marketing companies. Now the tough decision remains. What sort of educational products do you want to sell? Do you prefer books or videos? Maybe you can sell both, but do you prefer secular or Christian? Or would you rather sell educational toys? How about selling all of them? You can if you join a company that offers multiple product lines.

Even though the experts advise against it and many companies disallow it, some people choose to represent more than one network marketing company simultaneously. Doing so may not be an effective use of your time because you'll have to learn about two companies and two or more product lines. Plus, there are likely to be scheduling problems, such as both companies planning a big event on the same weekend. If you want to represent multiple companies, look for opportunities that are compatible with the Internet. Representing more than one company is easier when you can do the marketing and sales, and even the training, online. In Chapter 14, we tell you more about Internet-driven opportunities.

Selecting a dessert isn't nearly as serious as making a decision about your future in network marketing, and selecting a network marketing company isn't nearly as much fun as picking out a piece of dessert. The two processes are very similar, however, up to a point. With dessert, whether you choose wisely or poorly, you're almost certain to have a gain. With network marketing, if you don't choose wisely, you run a risk of having a loss — a loss of money, self-esteem, benefits, and perhaps even reputation.

When you get started in network marketing, you could be making a lifelong decision without even knowing it. Thousands of people through the years join a company part-time only to discover after a few years that they want to make networking their career. Should that happen to you, you'll be glad that you spent time evaluating the opportunities in network marketing. Choosing a company before you've investigated all the options isn't necessarily wrong. In fact, that's the way most people get involved in network marketing. They let someone else make this decision for them. However, it's not unusual to hear about networkers who have failed repeatedly, and others who have jumped from company to company to company, oftentimes crossing industries in search of an opportunity worthy of their time, money, and reputation.

To help you make a wise decision about your future in network marketing, we devote this chapter and the four that follow to evaluating critical elements of network marketing, including opportunities, management teams, products/services, and compensation plans. In this chapter, we discuss the types of industries that rely on network marketing to distribute their products and services, and we provide some benchmarks to help you decide which industry appeals to you. We also help you save yourself from a turnover rate that approaches 100 percent!

Network marketing companies come and go, but with few exceptions, industries tend to be permanent. If you decide that networking is what you want to do for the rest of your life, selecting an industry where you'll feel comfortable and have the opportunity to build your expertise is even more important. Even if you change companies down the road, if the industry appeals to you, you'll have a better chance of achieving the personal and professional goals that define an exciting and rewarding career.

Industries That Use Network Marketing: Profitability and Reputability

Contrary to what you may have heard, network marketing is *not* an industry. Rather, many industries *use* network marketing as a system for distributing their products and services.

Also contrary to what you may have heard, network marketing is broader than merely those companies that sell "lotions and potions." As you can see in this chapter, many different industries are at work in network marketing, and one or more of them is likely to attract you. Variety is the spice of life, the saying goes, and for that reason, you'll find certain industries more appealing than others.

Almost every industry can use network marketing, and some experts believe that eventually most industries will. The simpler the product or service, the better, because it's easier to teach a large and often international network of distributors how to market and sell it. However, even complex products and services, such as investments and business loans, are already using network marketing.

The Direct Selling Association (www.dsa.org) categorizes the industries that use network marketing under five major headings:

- ✔ **Home/family care products,** including cookware, cutlery, and cleaning products
- ✔ **Personal care products,** including cosmetics, jewelry, and skin care
- ✔ **Service/miscellaneous/other,** including telecommunications, training, and Internet services
- ✔ **Wellness products,** including weight loss, vitamins, and nutritional supplements
- ✔ **Leisure/educational products,** including books, toys, and games

While you're considering the industry that you'd like to represent as a network marketer, give some thought to the profitability and reputation of various industries. Some industries, owing to the products and services they offer, generate money faster than others, especially if they have a unique product or service. However, be careful of fads — products and services that exist today but are gone in a short period of time when no one wants them anymore. Also, products and services that earn a lot of money quickly could be prone to media inquiry and investigation by regulators who are charged with protecting consumers from fraud. Even if the product or service is legitimate, negative publicity could diminish future sales. Following are several thoughts to consider as you mull over the various industries available to network marketers.

Realizing that some industries are more profitable than others

Numerous variables determine profitability in business — management, marketing, sales, timing, and so on — and that's why certain industries generate more profit than others. However, after counting the factor of highly motivated and well-trained distributors, profit in network marketing is a function of the products and services that are marketed and sold. For example, "Any product or service that the baby boom market wants to buy is likely to create a hot industry in network marketing," says Travis Bond, vice president of sales and marketing for 2021 Interactive, a company that provides computer resources to network marketing companies. Therefore, industries that promote quality of life, family life, health, antiaging, and nutrition could be big moneymakers.

How about diet products? For sure! "Everyone is looking for a diet that will work," explains Clifton Jolley, president of Advent Communications, a 20-year-old, Dallas-based consultancy that advises direct sales companies, including network marketing firms. "Diets work well in network marketing," he continues, "because eight out of ten people who don't need to lose weight think they do! That means virtually everyone is a customer."

And how sweet it is when you find an industry that captivates a huge market that recognizes the value of your products and services. Not only can you make a difference in the lives of your customers, but you also have the luxury of serving the same customers month after month. (We explain why that's so important in Chapter 8.)

Clifton says that predicting which industries will become hot and remain hot is difficult. He explains, "I thought long distance had peaked by 1991, and then along came Excel Communications and created a huge market. Several years later, Excel had annual revenues in excess of $1.5 billion in the U.S. . . . And look at water filters. They sat on the shelves of hardware stores for half a century and few people bought them. But then in the 1980s, National Sales Associates educated consumers about water filtration, and within a few years, the company was selling a third of all the water filters in the United States! . . . You can't always predict these outcomes."

Ranking the industry classifications by sales

The Direct Selling Association's Web site lists network marketing's five industry classifications by the percentage of retail revenues they generated in 1999, when sales exceeded $24.5 billion in the United States! (You can check www.dsa.org for more recent numbers.) Here are the DSA's findings (also shown in the accompanying figure):

✔ At the top of the list, the home/family care products classification generated 33 percent of network marketing's 1999 U.S. retail sales.

✔ Personal care products ranked second with 24 percent of sales.

✔ Services/miscellaneous/other claimed 17.9 percent of sales.

✔ Wellness products accounted for 17.8 percent of sales.

✔ Leisure/educational products rounded out the listing with 6.4 percent, or slightly more than $1.5 billion in sales.

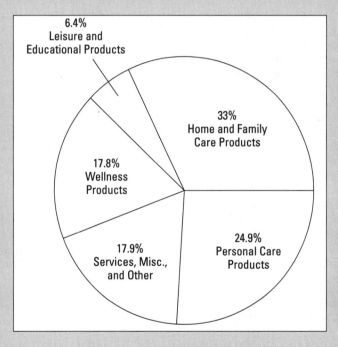

6.4%
Leisure and
Educational Products

33%
Home and Family
Care Products

17.8%
Wellness
Products

24.9%
Personal Care
Products

17.9%
Services, Misc.,
and Other

Be careful! "Hot" doesn't necessarily translate to "long term." Fads are often described as hot, and they frequently cool off just about the time sales really get going. When the bottom falls out of a market or an industry, the results can be devastating to the network marketer who spent countless hours building a business around a hot product or service. Before you commit your valuable time and talent in network marketing, do all that you can to evaluate the longevity of the industry. How do you do that? Read about the industry — every industry includes a number of trade publications. Ask questions of experts within the industry and seek the predictions of analysts who follow the industry that appeals to you.

Watching out for industries that are prone to investigations

You can probably assume that Big Brother is watching the network marketing companies. In spite of the fact that network marketing is a legitimate form of business, any company that uses network marketing is asking for federal and state agencies, including the Federal Trade Commission (www.ftc.gov), the Food and Drug Administration (www.fda.gov), and state attorneys general (find your state's attorney general's office at www.naag.org), to keep an eye on it. At least that's the way it is in the United States. Watchdog organizations, such as the media, and consumer protection agencies such as the Better Business Bureau (www.bbb.org), also closely follow the activities of network marketing companies. We're not complaining. A watchful eye is warranted. It can protect not only consumers but also legitimate network marketing companies and their distributors.

Industries that include companies and operators that make outrageous claims about their products and services — unfortunately, that describes more than a fair share — can expect regulatory intervention. And where the regulators discover illegal activity, they'll move quickly to shut down a business. The net effect will shake up an industry, and it can destroy a market overnight.

"Watch for the red flags," advises Travis Bond. "Some companies and some distributors create a bad situation for themselves and their industry by making hyped-up claims about their products. 'We have the cure for cancer,' 'Our product adds years to your life,' and similar unsubstantiated claims are asking for trouble. Where that kind of hype occurs, there's probably a regulator not far behind." Steer clear of these situations.

Getting help from the Better Business Bureau

Point your Web browser to www.bbb.com/alerts/ for Alerts & News Releases from the Better Business Bureau. This organization helps consumers, as well as businesses, make informed decisions about the current marketplace. The Alerts and News page posts "time-sensitive and newsworthy" information, while the Library (www.bbb.com/library/index.asp) contains general-interest publications for both consumers and businesses.

BBB Alerts are considered "urgent warnings" that notify the public about fraudulent business scams.

Obtaining government information: Big Brother doesn't snoop and tell

It would be convenient if federal and state government agencies posted the names of all the network marketing companies they were investigating on a Web site, but it wouldn't be fair. Not all investigations lead to government intervention. Besides, Big Brother would rather keep things quiet until all the goods are gathered and the case is closed. At that point, if the company is found to be fraudulent, it's toast.

Government agencies can offer you a limited form of help in your investigation of network marketing industries and companies. Point your browser to www.ftc.gov, the Web site of the Federal Trade Commission (FTC), and you'll find several reports that pertain to network marketing. Read through the FTC's Frequently Asked Questions, and you'll discover, among other things, that no federal or state agency or private organization will tell you whether a company is legitimate or whether it operates in good faith. These organizations can, however, tell you whether they've received consumer complaints about a company. Unfortunately, the operators of fly-by-night business opportunities know how these organizations work, so they frequently change their company name and location so there's never a record of consumer complaints. Where there's a scam, there's a way!

You also may find information about how much of an eye your state keeps on network marketing. We visited the Texas attorney general's Web site at www.oag.state.tx.us/Brochure/busop.html and found out that network marketing companies usually don't fall under the guidelines of the Texas Business Opportunity Act. Therefore, the companies are not required to register with the secretary of state or comply with state disclosure requirements for businesses! What's the situation in *your* state? Visit the Web site of your state's attorney general for the details. You'll find a link to the states' attorneys general through the National Association of Attorneys General at www.naag.org.

In Texas, you're pretty much on your own when making decisions about network marketing. (We're still big on independence here!) And that's the way it ought to be. There's nothing wrong with a state office or an independent agency offering you a helping hand. But for your own protection, conduct your investigation as though your reputation depended on it. Because in the final analysis, it does.

Inquiring about consumer complaints

If you want information about consumer complaints, the Federal Trade Commission will help you get it, but only if you make your request in writing.

The FTC will check to see whether complaints have been received not only in Washington but also in its ten regional offices. Now there's a good use of your tax dollars!

To request information, address your letter to

Freedom of Information Act Request
Federal Trade Commission
Washington, DC 20580

How to Research Network Marketing Opportunities and Avoid Becoming a Turnover Statistic

No one really knows for sure, but network marketing leaders and consultants say that at least nine of every ten people who join a network marketing company quit or fail within the first 90 days. Even though no one can prove that statistic, no one we talked to denies it.

Why is the turnover so high? Why do people invest money and time only to quit or fail?

One reason is the manner in which most people get into network marketing. They don't do it proactively; they do it passively. They allow their involvement in network marketing to be *done to* them! Instead of looking for a network marketing opportunity that matches their interests and perhaps their financial status, they give someone else permission to make this decision for them. They wait until someone invites them to a meeting or hands them an audiotape, and then — often with less than an hour's investigation — they join a company.

You know why this phenomenon occurs? It's because people make buying decisions with their emotions first and their intellect second. That's okay when all you're doing is picking out a piece of dessert. But it's not okay when you're investing money, followed by your time, talent, and reputation.

ZIG SAYS

We're optimistic that the commonsense, tell-it-like-it-is approach we take in this book will, over a period of time, help people make better decisions and reduce turnover in the profession. If that happens, we will be more than pleased!

Your first step in the direction of making a wise network marketing decision is to proactively seek out as many opportunities as time and patience allow. With more than 1,000 U.S.-based network marketing companies to select from (and fewer in other countries), you have a lot of work to do. But here are several ideas to help you quickly move this process into high gear.

Ask your relatives and friends what they know

Network marketing isn't a topic of discussion in most households (not yet, anyway), but that doesn't mean your relatives and friends aren't aware of opportunities. No doubt some of these folks have been invited to an opportunity meeting or have been given an audiotape. Bring up the subject of network marketing at your next family get-together or during an outing with a group of friends. Bolster yourself, because you're likely to hear some disparaging remarks. But the opportunity that your Uncle George wouldn't even look at and called "some pyramid scheme" may turn out to be your ticket to success. Don't be afraid. Go ahead and ask, "Have any of you heard about (company or product name)?" If you're expecting the worst, don't say why you want to know. You're just making conversation.

Do you Yahoo? The Web lists countless opportunities

Is there anything that *can't* be found on the World Wide Web? Network marketing, or MLM, companies are there by the scores. While writing this chapter, our search on www.yahoo.com for "MLM" turned up 93,598 matches. On www.goto.com, the number jumped to 94,169 matches. Most employees don't have enough vacation time to click through all those Web pages. We're not suggesting that you even try. However, you can reduce the numbers by narrowing the search. Searching for "U.S. companies+MLM" turned up only 159 pages on Yahoo! That's a manageable number, which you can further reduce by using advanced search options. Surfing the Web is a good way to discover network marketing opportunities.

More people seem to be familiar with the term "multi-level marketing," or MLM, than they are with the more recent term: "network marketing." However, the terms are used interchangeably, and "network marketing" is now in vogue. When asking or looking for information about network marketing, you may get more responses if you use "MLM."

Check out the media

Your local daily newspaper probably includes advertisements placed by network marketers in search of prospective investors. Look under Business Opportunities. *USA Today, The Wall Street Journal,* and other national newspapers carry similar ads, as do city business periodicals, such as the *Dallas Business Journal.* By responding to these offers, you'll receive invitations to opportunity meetings at local hotels, or you'll be offered audiotapes that describe the opportunities. At this point, go to all the meetings you can and listen to every tape . . . but keep your wits about you! It's too early for you to jump into one of these opportunities.

You'll also find numerous publications that are dedicated to network marketing. They include not only articles but also ads from network marketers. Here are three of the most popular publications:

- *Network Marketing Lifestyles* is sold on major newsstands, or you can subscribe online at www.nmlifestyles.com. This bimonthly magazine captures the personality of network marketers and provides in-depth features about trends and ideas that impact networkers.

- *Upline* is a bimonthly educational and informational journal that continues to win praise from network marketers around the globe. Visit www.upline.com for subscription information, as well as to review past issues.

- *Money Maker's Monthly* bills itself as "the international industry journal for network marketing." It's full of ads and editorials. Details are at www.moneymakersmonthly.com.

Contact trade associations

The following two trade associations list network marketing companies and also provide articles, special reports, and information about events and activities related to the industry:

- **Direct Selling Association (DSA),** based in Washington, D.C., posts a list of its members at www.dsa.org. The only drawback is that fewer than 200 of the 1,000-plus network marketing companies belong to the association. On the other hand, not all companies qualify for membership. No one "buys" a DSA membership; a company has to earn membership by complying with the DSA's stringent Code of Values, which is posted at the association's Web site. DSA requires applicants to undergo a yearlong review before membership is awarded. During that time, the association inspects the applicant's business and marketing plans, product

materials, and corporate policies. Some companies balk at DSA's requirement for members to repurchase marketable materials at 90 percent of
their original cost within 12 months of purchase by a distributor. That
requirement, however, minimizes the amount of money that distributors
risk when they join a DSA member company. Membership doesn't necessarily mean that a company is any more trustworthy or secure than non-
member companies.

✔ **Multi-Level Marketing International Association,** based in Irvine, California,
posts its members at www.mlmia.com. MLMIA is a small operation with
few members. However, links to network marketing experts, including
lawyers and consultants, can be found through the MLMIA Web site.

Get the scoop from consultants

All the consultants quoted throughout this book are excellent resources
about network marketing, or they wouldn't be in the book! Perhaps the best
known of these consultants is Michael Sheffield, president of Sheffield
Resource Network in Tempe, Arizona. His agency helps as many as 40 companies get started in network marketing every year, so if you want to know
what's new, he's the man to contact. His Web site is at www.sheffieldnet.
com. You'll also be in good hands with Ken Rudd, president of Premier
Systems, Inc., in Melbourne, Florida. Ken's experience is vast — he's built and
sold downlines, he's trained networkers internationally, he's been the CEO of
a publicly traded network marketing company, and now he spends most of
his time as a consultant. You can contact Ken at OKRudd@aol.com.

Questions to Ask Before You Join a Network Marketing Organization

At the end of each of the next four chapters are questions you need to ask
yourself before you become a distributor of a network marketing company.
These questions are relevant to each chapter's topic. We include a list of
questions to ask on the Cheat Sheet at the front of this book as well.

If you like the answers you get when you complete these questions, you most
probably have found the network marketing company that is right for you. By
following the suggestions in this book and by doing your homework, you
should be able to select a network marketing company that meets your personal and professional criteria. Unfortunately, due to the nature of the industry, we have to add this caveat: *There are no guarantees!*

Network marketing advantage:
It offers *real* job security

When you're in network marketing, there's no need to worry about your future. "Will I or won't I have a job tomorrow?" That's a question you never have to ask. If the economy takes a turn for the worse, or if the company you're representing falters, you don't have to worry about your future. There are endless opportunities available and they exist in most parts of the world.

Real security is achieved when you sponsor, train, and inspire your sales organization or downline. Today, with the Internet and other communications tools at your disposal, a few minutes each day or a few hours each month will keep you in touch with the leaders of your organization. This enables you to not only maintain a remarkable residual income, but in many cases to increase that residual income. Having hundreds — even thousands — of people, each contributing to your income through their productivity, represents real security.

Chapter 5

Evaluating Network Marketing Companies

*A*fter you identify the industry and perhaps several network marketing opportunities that interest you, your next step is to investigate the specific companies that appeal to you. This chapter shows you how to get the information you need to make a good decision about joining a company.

Doing the Right Thing by Doing Your Research

Most people who become network marketers skip doing research before investing in a company. A reason for this lies in the fact that most people who become networkers are looking only for a part-time opportunity. Consequently, they don't see the sense of spending days or weeks investigating a company that will ask them to invest less than $500, and often less than $100, to get started. Now you know why so many networkers don't succeed, or why they lose interest after a few days or weeks!

"I would be amazed if 1 percent of the people who decided to get involved in network marketing said that they had researched the company first. That's just not the way it happens," says Russ Noland, a former real estate agent in Houston, Texas, and now, after ten years in the business, one of Excel Communications' top associates with a downline that numbers in the thousands.

This inattention to network marketing research isn't a U.S. phenomenon, either. Across the Atlantic in England, Gavin Scott agrees with Russ. Since 1992, Gavin has been an associate of Kleeneze, a company that sells hundreds of consumer products by catalog. "Common sense tells you that before you join a company you should do some research, but more than 95 percent of the people don't do it," Gavin explains. "They simply take their sponsor's word for it."

"One of the reasons this industry has had some image problems is that new distributors rarely investigate these companies before starting," says Michael Sheffield, a well-known consultant among network marketing companies. "Prospective associates should ask questions and make companies answer their questions to their satisfaction. But most would-be associates don't know what questions to ask or how to do the due diligence. As a result, they rely on their sponsor's or their company's credibility, and that's frequently not sufficient. It is the associate's responsibility to have all the facts so that they can make educated decisions before they invest. Ultimately it's a matter of 'buyer beware.'"

Doris Wood, president emeritus of the Multi-Level Marketing International Association and a 35-year veteran of network marketing, offers this advice to would-be network marketers: "There's really no substitute for some hard-nosed investigation. Remember, you are going to be living and breathing your networking experience for a long time. Due diligence on the part of the company, the management, and your sponsor pays off. It can bring you peace of mind, added financial security, and many new friendships."

Do the research! It gives you an edge that just may make the difference between a lackluster beginning and an exciting career in network marketing.

"When you join a network marketing company, you are investing more than just your money. You are investing your reputation with your closest friends and relatives. Can you put a price on that?" asks Travis Bond, vice president of sales and marketing for 2021 Interactive, a company that supplies computer services to network marketing companies. "Make a good decision before you join a company. You can replace money, but you can't replace your reputation."

Looking Beyond the Logo

If a company offered you a job, you probably would want to know something about that company before you agreed to become an employee. In fact, provided you had the time and the opportunity, you would probably look at several companies before you decided to join one of them. Depending on your talents, desires, interests, and needs, you may have a long list of criteria that you would want to apply to a prospective employer. After all, you will probably spend many hours, and perhaps years, at that job, so you'd want to be sure to select a company that showed a reasonably good chance of meeting your specific needs as an employee. For example, you might look for a company that pays a certain income and provides specific benefits. You might want a company that's known for integrity and character. You may also consider it important to select a company that has a vision for the future and a mission that appeals to you personally. Of course, you'll probably prefer a company that is strong financially and has a proven track record.

If all these criteria are important when you're looking for a job, is there any reason they wouldn't be important when you're looking for an opportunity to build a business? Even if you're planning to work only part-time in network marketing, you have numerous criteria to consider before making a decision to join a company. What should you want to know about the company? The critical points for evaluation are the following:

- ✔ Ownership, financial status, and philosophy
- ✔ The management team
- ✔ Products/services
- ✔ The compensation plan

In this chapter, we focus on ownership, financial status, and philosophy. We discuss the other topics in the following three chapters, respectively.

With more than 1,000 network marketing companies in existence in the U.S. today and new companies developing rapidly, you can't possibly keep abreast of them all. With the exception of a few consultants and attorneys who have a vested interest in knowing as much as possible about these companies, there's not a one-stop source that you can tap into for information. You can usually get whatever information you want to know, but be prepared to ask multiple sources.

Predicting the company's future by examining its past

There are no guarantees that a network marketing company will remain in business, but there are no guarantees that traditional companies will remain in business, either. However, looking at where a company has been is a good way to predict where the company is going. Nutrition for Life International's Tom Paredes suggests that before you join a company, you compare it to the survivors in the industry. "Network marketing is more than half a century old, and during that time," says Tom, "15,000 network marketing companies legally opened their doors for business. Of those, only 30 lasted more than 10 years. Study some of those companies [that survived]. Then, if you're not joining one of those companies, find out what the company you're considering has in common with these survivors. That will give you a good indication of the company's strength, as well as its prospects for remaining in business."

Among network marketing executives and government regulators, attorney Jeffrey A. Babener is a recognized authority in network marketing law. During the past 20 years, his clients have included Excel Communications, Nikken, Avon, Body Wise, New Vision, USANA, Melaleuca, Discovery Toys, and many others. His Web site (www.mlmlegal.com) provides a storehouse of articles, news releases, publications, and information about network marketing. To help you evaluate network marketing companies, Jeffrey offers these suggestions:

- ✔ Get as much information as you can about the company. Look at the number of years in business, the areas where it operates, the number of distributors, gross sales, and much more. Conducting this research requires some digging, but it will be well worth your time.

- ✔ Read business and trade publications such as *Entrepreneur, Business Start-Ups, Network Marketing Lifestyles,* and others that report on specific companies.

- ✔ Ask the person who presents the business opportunity to you to provide you with the names and telephone numbers of other distributors, as well as former distributors you can contact. Also ask to be introduced to retail customers. Talk to as many people as you can about the company (see "Talking to the right people" later in this chapter).

- ✔ Contact the attorney general's office in your state or the state where the company is headquartered, and ask whether any red flags have been raised about the company (see Chapter 4 for more information on this subject).

- ✔ Call your area Better Business Bureau and ask whether any complaints have been filed about the company (see Chapter 4).

- ✔ Find out whether the company is a member of industry associations such as the Direct Selling Association (www.dsa.org) and the Multi-Level Marketing International Association (www.mlmia.com). These organizations have adopted standards for their members (see Chapter 4).

- ✔ Attend one of the company's business opportunity meetings and a company training session, if possible, so that you can ask questions, talk to others in attendance, and gauge the company's professionalism.

Obviously, you may come across some exceptions to this concept of choosing a reliable company with a solid background. For example, you may be convinced in your own mind that a new start-up company offers more growth possibilities and promotion advancements than does an older, more established one, especially if you have some knowledge of the company's principles. I have a friend, for example, who, after years of "chasing the rainbow," had an opportunity to join a new company that offered exciting products and a good plan for the future. He was excited about the possibilities and had faith through personal knowledge of the men and women who were running the company, so he cast his lot with them.

Less than five years later, he was able to retire very comfortably on a nest egg that will serve him in the years to come. With reasonably prudent expenditures, regardless of how he lives, he will have that income until the day of his death. So the exception is one of judgment and of being willing to stake your claim for the future based on a conviction that what you're doing is on solid ground because of the high character of the individuals and the quality of the products combined with the game plan the company has developed for success.

Talking to the right people

Before deciding to join a company, interview as many people as possible who are connected to the company. Your list should include owners, officers, managers, employees, and even vendors who sell products or services to the company.

If you do nothing else, interview the people who are most likely to know how the company really operates, what it stands for, and how it treats its customers. Who are these people? The distributors, of course.

Before you agree to join a company, ask the person who introduced you to the company to refer you to a dozen (or more) distributors you can interview by phone or in person. Ask for names of individuals with backgrounds similar to your own. For example, if you're a schoolteacher, a nurse, an engineer, or a pastor (yes, many clergymen are network marketers), explain that you want to talk to people who share your career interests. Also, ask to speak to two or three people who joined the company and quit. Interview them and then talk to their sponsors. Every story has two sides — and sometimes three. Be objective. Remember, you can find good sponsors in bad companies and bad sponsors in good companies.

Now here's a list of questions to ask both current and former distributors:

- ✔ Why did you decide to join this company?
- ✔ How much money did you spend before you started earning money?
- ✔ Is it reasonable to expect to succeed working this opportunity on a part-time basis?
- ✔ How valuable is the company's training?
- ✔ What do you like or dislike about the company's products or services?
- ✔ How do you rate the company's customer service performance?
- ✔ What three things do you like most about the company?
- ✔ What three things do you like least about the company?
- ✔ What's the company's mission, and how well does the company support its mission?

✔ What are the strengths and weaknesses of the company's management team?

✔ Can you explain the compensation plan to me?

✔ Are the products or services priced fairly, or competitively?

✔ Are you required to purchase inventory?

✔ Given your knowledge about the company and your experience, would you join this company again?

This is by no means a comprehensive list — you can probably think of many other good questions to ask. The topics covered by these questions, which in total comprise various aspects of evaluating companies that utilize network marketing, are discussed later in this chapter or in other chapters in Part II of this book. The answers to these questions will move you well on your way to making an informed decision about a particular company. Also, you can request a copy of John Hayes's special report: The Network Marketing Checklist. It's free and you can get it by sending mail to info@hayesworldwide.com.

Discovering Who Owns the Company

Although Jay Van Andel and Rich De Vos launched Amway on a financial shoestring in 1949, working at first out of a garage, launching a network marketing company now takes big money. Michael Sheffield, a consultant who has advised more than 3,000 network marketing companies, says that launching a company takes a minimum of $250,000, and much more to sustain the business. "Network marketing has become a 'get-rich-slow' business," he explains, "and the reality is that a company that wants to compete in today's environment will need between $500,000 and $1 million in capitalization with backup sources to remain viable."

So where's the bank? Who's funding the company (or companies) that you're evaluating? Is it an individual, a group of investors, an organization, or an institution? Any one or a combination of these answers could be satisfactory. What matters is that you know *who's* behind the business and that their values, interests, and principles match up with your own.

In certain instances, getting this information may not be easy, but that doesn't mean you shouldn't ask outright, "Who owns this company?" Most network marketing companies are privately owned, and they may not reveal this information. Of course, that may prompt you to ask yourself the question, "What do you have to hide?" If they won't tell you the names of the people or person who owns the business, you're probably not going to get other important information, either. Most network marketing companies nowadays practice full disclosure.

You can't make a good deal with a bad person. You may do well initially, but before it is all over, that bad person is going to cause grief, pain, and headaches.

When you're evaluating a network marketing company, the owner's heart may be more important than any other factor. "The only thing you can really evaluate about a network marketing company is what's in the owner's heart," says Tom "Big Al" Schreiter, an industry trainer, author, and part-owner of Nutrition for Life International. "When things get tough in a network marketing company, the owner will do one of two things: Take the money and run, or dig in and make it work." How do you find out what's in the owner's heart? "Unfortunately," continues Big Al, "it's not easy. But you can ask long-time distributors, employees, and company vendors." If you're looking at a start-up company, however, it won't have long-time distributors and employees to ask. In that event, find out where the owner worked before or whether he or she owned a company before. Then find someone who knows the owner and ask your questions.

Determining the Company's Financial Situation

The best way to evaluate a company's financial condition is to look at its most recent financial statement. But in most cases, that's not a document you're likely to get your hands on, unless the company is publicly owned. In that event, you can gather financial data via the Internet or possibly from a brokerage house. Publicly traded companies often post their financial information on their Web sites. Privately owned companies are often squeamish about handing out this information. Nonetheless, ask for it!

"Do they need to make money this week to stay in business?" That's the question "Tremendous" Bill Pike says he would want answered if he ever looked at another network marketing company. The likelihood of that happening is slim: Bill is the highest paid distributor with Youngevity, a company that sells antiaging products that aim to "cleanse, burn, build, and beautify."

"Here's the key to evaluating a company," Bill says. "The public company is forced to publish a record of its performance. The law requires it. If a non-public company won't give you similar information, move on! What are they hiding?"

Other questions to research are

- ✔ What is the company's debt load?
- ✔ Does the company have a good credit rating?

The answers to these questions may help you decide whether to become involved with the company.

Checking up on a company's owners

Dayle Maloney was very nervous about joining Consumer Express, the forerunner of Nutrition for Life International. He had spent several years building a successful downline numbering more than 8,000 people with another organization, but one day that company closed its doors for good. "Dishonesty and bad management destroyed the company," says Dayle. Many of the people in his downline were angry, and even though he had nothing to do with the company's demise, some members of his downline held him responsible. Two threatened his life because they were devastated by the sudden loss of income!

It was a sad period in Dayle's life, but Dayle's life was full of sad stories. He contracted polio as a teenager and had to fight his way back to good health. He and his bride were evicted from an apartment because he couldn't come up with $425 for rent, and he accumulated debt in excess of $350,000 before joining a network marketing company, a "foolish move," many people told him. But network marketing was exactly what Dayle needed to prosper, and just as he was on his way to financial freedom, the company collapsed!

Dayle Maloney knew there wasn't anything wrong with network marketing. He just needed to find the right company. But now he decided to take his time and investigate his options before committing himself, and the remnants of his downline, to a new company. "Between April and June of 1985," Dayle recalls, "I looked at 50 different network marketing companies."

He was pretty sure he had found the right one when he discovered Consumer Express in Lake Charles, Louisiana. The company was only nine months old at the time. "My number one priority was to find honest management," Dayle explains, "and before I agreed to join Consumer Express, I went to Lake Charles to meet the owners and check them out. Lake Charles is a small place, so I walked around town and asked people about the founders, and I was impressed by what I heard. People who knew them said they were honest." Dayle looked the owners in the eye and asked for their assurance that they would remain in business, ship products on time, and pay their distributors on time. The owners said they would, of course, and even though he knew there were no guarantees, he believed them.

Within three or four months of joining Consumer Express, Dayle Maloney became the company's number one distributor! He's been in that position for more than 15 years, and today there are more than 40,000 people worldwide in Dayle's downline. Retirement isn't part of his plans, though. In 1998, he wrote a book, _I Could Have Quit $7,000,000.00 Ago,_ in which he explains his journey in network marketing. Dayle turned 65 in 2000 and continues to spend up to 70 hours a week working in his business. "I don't think about the money," he says, "I'm touching lives, and the lives I touch are touching other lives, and they are touching still more lives . . . how could you ever stop working a business like this?"

Estimating how deeply the company is entrenched in the proverbial debt hole

Rarely are network marketing companies debt-free. But that's okay. It's better for a company to carry some debt than to risk running out of money. After the money is gone, the company usually goes belly-up. Problems occur when companies are heavily in debt and can't generate enough revenue to keep the business stable. Unfortunately, unless the company is publicly owned, you're not likely to know whether the company is carrying too much debt. You could, however, check with the company's vendors by asking, "Is the company paying your invoices on time?" Businesses frequently call one another to check up on a company's payment history. If the company is not paying in a timely fashion, money could be tight, or the company may need much of it to pay off debts. If you find out that the company does have a poor payment history, you should probably wonder whether it will pay your commissions on time.

Does the company have a good credit rating?

Although vendors who sell products to the company may share information with you about the company's payment history, you can also contact Dun & Bradstreet (www.dnb.com) and purchase a credit rating report for the company. Dun & Bradstreet relies on government sources, banks, trade associations, financial institutions, customers, and employees of the company to gather information about the company. You can buy this information in a D&B Report. A Business Background Report, which doesn't include the company's credit information but provides basic research, sells for less than $25. A Credit Scoring Report, which includes credit risk scores and average dollar amounts extended to the company by other firms, costs about $100.

Before you spend this money, however, keep your total investment in mind. How much does it cost to join the network marketing company? Probably less than $100, and at most $500.

"I was once with a company that generated $100,000,000 in volume in its second year of business," recalls Bill Pike. "They went out of business because the owners did not understand the value of a dollar. They ran the company from a cash point of view. That's why it's important to know the financial status of the business and to be sure that the owner or managers are business people first, and not just salesmen!"

If a company doesn't want to provide you with its financial data, you're not totally at a loss. "Take a look at how they run the business," advises Dayle Maloney. "The first company that I belonged to had lavish parties and spent money foolishly. At first, it may have looked like they had a lot of money, but that wasn't the case. When I joined my present company, they didn't give me their financial statements, but I made a point of looking at how they ran the business. They kept their overhead low, and they admitted that they did not have a lot of money. However, they had conservative fiscal policies that helped them stretch the money they had, and that's one of the reasons they're still in business after 16 years."

Knowing the Company's Philosophy

Money — whether in the form of corporate profits or big paychecks and benefits for distributors — is not a good enough reason for a company to exist, or for you to join the company. Never forget that it's called "netWORK marketing." You're going to work hard to build a successful business. Unlike what happens in a job or a traditional business, you may work hard for just a few years in network marketing before you generate a lifetime of residual income, but make no mistake about it: You *will* work hard if you want to succeed.

That said, think for a moment about what will influence you to work hard, possibly harder than you've ever worked before. Do you think it would help if you were excited every day about the business, the people in it, the products and services, and your customers? Wouldn't it be great if you were personally motivated to do the best possible job? Would it help to know that your work transcends money — that it could be responsible for helping people change their lives for the better?

We're guessing that you said yes to all those questions. Therefore, once you know that a company's ownership consists of people you respect and possibly even admire and you feel confident that the company is fiscally responsible, you must examine the company's ideology.

Finding out the company's vision

What's the company's mission? If it's simply to make a lot of money, it might achieve that mission, but the company won't last long. Not one of the people we interviewed for this book said that money was their sole motivation for working hard in network marketing. Most of them said that money motivated them when they first started their businesses — usually because they didn't *have* any money — but once they made money, often more money than they believed possible, including a fine residual income, money stopped being a factor. People who become leaders in network marketing look to the mission for their daily excitement and motivation.

Network marketers must be in sync with the company's mission. "Make certain the mission is consistent with your principles and values," advises Jim Bruce, a Pompano Beach, Florida–based distributor with the Small Business Club of America (SBCA), which markets a package of benefits — for instance, legal services, motor club services, and so forth — to small and home-based businesses. "Any inconsistencies between the company's mission and your own values will demotivate you," he continues. "Desire to improve one's life is the key to success in network marketing, and if you're not comfortable with the company's mission, you'll gradually lose your motivation. Choose a company with a mission that gets you excited and is consistent with your values."

You need to have a mission and a code of ethics by which you operate. Furthermore, you need to follow that mission and the principles upon which you have built your life. When you're deciding to join a network marketing company or to bring someone into your sales organization, make sure your principles remain intact. Don't sacrifice your principles!

Many years ago, during a difficult time, we offered an executive position to a gentleman who had a fabulous track record. He sold us on the idea that he was seeking a small company where he could have an impact. We disagreed about a few things philosophically, and some questions about his character should have raised red flags. However, his track record in the business world had been so phenomenal that we quieted those fears and invited him to come aboard. For several months, he had us snowed. Then, as the truth surfaced, we discovered that we had invited a problem creator and not a problem solver to join us. We parted company, sadder but wiser, and then got busy solving the problems he left behind. This experience simply reinforces the adage, "You can't make a good deal with a bad person." So when you're choosing your network, look at management (see Chapter 6) and the company philosophy very carefully. Make sure that it is a fit.

Reading the company's policies and procedures

You should expect a legitimate and professional network marketing company to operate by a set of policies and procedures. Generally speaking, these rules are intended to protect the distributors and the longevity of the company. Before you join a company, however, know what the rules say, and if you don't like them or can't live with them, find another company. In addition, find out whether the rules are merely window dressing, perhaps to appease regulators, or whether the company actually enforces them. Ask the company for recent examples of enforcement of its policies. Ask your sponsor for examples, too.

Don't discount intuition

In some circumstances, you will be unable to get all the factual questions answered. In the early days of our company (which was many years ago), we didn't have the sophisticated approaches of today's technology, and yet the evaluation of personnel was very important. I used a reasonably simple method: When I was considering someone for a position, I arranged a luncheon with the individual and his or her mate, and I brought my wife and oldest daughter. If all were not available, I interviewed the candidate in my office and had my wife and daughter drop in to meet and chat. At the conclusion, my wife, daughter, and I had a private discussion. If both of my "consultants" agreed

that the candidate was a good fit, we offered the position. If both agreed that the interviewee was not a fit and either of them did not feel right about it, we didn't offer the position.

I'll be the first to acknowledge that my candidate evaluation process was not scientific. But in 100 percent of the cases when I overrode both my wife and my daughter, I lived to regret the decision. Some call it "intuition," and some call it "a feeling," but most women seem to be better at it than we men. That's one reason to have your spouse (if you're married) fully on the team if you're considering a future in network marketing.

Given the image problems that may sometimes shadow even the best network marketing companies, avoid a company that doesn't put any teeth into its policies and procedures. "In Nutrition for Life, if a distributor hurts other people or does something to jeopardize the stability of the company, that distributor will be terminated," says top performer Tom Paredes. "A company must protect the dream for all of its distributors."

Questions You Should Ask Before Joining a Network Marketing Organization

Evaluating network marketing companies requires time, patience, and the fortitude to do your homework without giving in too soon and joining a company. This chapter thoroughly prepares you to conduct this evaluation. Now, here are several questions that you should answer during your investigation:

- Is the company mission-driven or "get-rich-quick" motivated?
- Does its corporate philosophy fit your personal philosophy?
- Do you feel comfortable around the people who own and operate the company?
- Would the company's opportunity give you a real chance to make a positive difference in the lives of those you sponsor into the business?

✔ Do you feel good about the company's long-term future?

✔ If you were looking for a job, would you go to work for this company?

✔ Does the local Better Business Bureau have a file of unresolved claims against the company?

✔ Are you willing to accept personal responsibility for your actions, whether they result in success or lack of success?

✔ If you succeed with this company, would you have more of the things money will buy and all the things money won't buy?

ZIG SAYS

Network marketing advantage: Your territory has no boundaries

In traditional selling, you may be assigned a specific territory. You're obligated to sell within that territory and never to go outside of the territory. Such a relationship is fraught with problems and discouragement. For example, if you develop a big customer who moves to another territory, too bad for you. Or, if new businesses are developing or moving into your territory, your company may decide to hire another sales person and let her share your territory. Under such an arrangement, there's not much incentive for developing business outside of your territory and that's detrimental to everyone concerned.

Network marketing doesn't abide by territorial boundaries. Your territory is *everywhere*.

Since your territory is *everywhere*, this means that the economy is always good in some areas and bad in others. If the economy is good, your retail sales will be good; if the economy is bad, people will be looking for opportunities to earn additional income — which means your recruiting efforts will pay off. Either way, you win in network marketing.

Chapter 6

Evaluating a Company's Management Team

In This Chapter

▶ Knowing what to look for in a management team

▶ Checking out the company's leaders and top distributors

▶ Sizing up the experience of the management team

▶ Making sure the company has strong, ethical, caring leadership

ZIG SAYS

The perfect example of my version of the Golden Rule (also discussed in Chapter 11), which I express in the phrase, "You can have everything in life you want if you will just help enough other people get what they want," is network marketing. The only way you can succeed in network marketing is by sponsoring, training, and inspiring those you bring into the business and teaching them how to teach others so that they become successful. The reality is you don't build business — you build people, and people build business. The better you teach and inspire your people, the more successful they will be — and the more successful you will be.

In all of business, there may not be a more complicated role than that of the management team in network marketing. A company can't prosper without an enthusiastic and competent management team. But in network marketing, there's a rub: The most enthusiastic and competent management teams understand that they have to work hard only to become transparent.

How so? Because the glory in network marketing belongs to the field, to the distributors who market and sell the company's products and services. The management team — in spite of its ideas, its training expertise, its creation of professional sales materials, its research and development, and endless hours devoted to building a system and enforcing policies for the good of the company — remains behind the scenes, all but forgotten. Until something goes wrong! Then without a doubt the problem is the fault of the management team. The best of these teams shove pride and ego aside and dig in to fix the problem, to repair the damages, and ultimately to do the only thing that's required of them: help the distributors succeed without claiming victory themselves.

Network marketing managers are a special breed of people, and the expanding population of network marketing companies has created tremendous demand for them. Every company strives to recruit and retain the elite among these managers while simultaneously assembling a team that will work together harmoniously to serve the needs of the distributors. Assembling such a team is not a simple achievement. It's also not inexpensive: Many of these executives command well-rounded compensation packages.

Important as it is, the management team is usually overlooked by the tens of thousands of people who join network marketing companies every year. The product, the service, the company name, and sometimes the people in the upline receive all the attention, and the management team — the engine that every distributor needs — is simply taken for granted. The oversight often proves to be a serious mistake. If the engine doesn't purr, the machine won't produce, regardless of how impressive it appears.

For these reasons, we recommend that you evaluate the management team before you join a network marketing company. This chapter shows you how.

As network marketing matures as a profession, keep in mind that making comparative studies is easier today than it ever was before. Research may not tell the entire story, but most network marketers we interviewed think it's worth conducting. So do I! There's no substitute for doing your homework before you invest in any business opportunity.

Knowing How to Recognize a Good Management Team

You can take several steps to find out about the management of the network marketing organization you're exploring to see whether you want that organization to have a place in your future.

Network marketing consultant Michael Sheffield has helped pull together countless management teams for network marketing companies. Here's a list of steps he says you can take to help you determine whether a network marketing management team is designed for success:

- ✓ Interview corporate executives before joining the company, or — if that's impossible — at least talk to successful distributors and ask for their thoughts.

- ✓ Make sure that one or more of the executives have experience in network marketing.

> ✔ Be sure that the management team includes experts who are involved in areas of administration, financial management, distribution, and commissioning software.

> ✔ Ask whether the company hires professional consultants to help in areas of weakness. If the answer is no, how does the company know the areas in which it needs to improve?

Getting to Know the Management Team

Network marketing companies are *not* created equal: Some have cultivated better management teams than others; some have no management team at all, but rather one or two individuals who are pretending to be a company. Before investing your money and latching onto what you hope will be a rising star, find out who's really behind the company. Who are the executives? What are their responsibilities? And how well do they handle those responsibilities? You should be able to get answers to those questions simply by visiting a company's Web site, or by calling the company and asking for it. Any company that fails or hesitates to offer this information is suspect, and you may be better off continuing your search.

"If you believe in and are comfortable with the way the company is run, you will be more effective in promoting the opportunity," says Jim Bruce, who's built several large network marketing organizations since the early 1980s. "Get a sense for the management team before you join the company. The people are the most critical element contributing to the success of many businesses. Try to meet them in person, but if you can't, at least call them on the telephone and ask them questions about their interests within the company, their priorities, and what they are doing on a regular basis to help the company fulfill its mission statement. Evaluate whether the mission is just talk or is based in action."

When you contact existing distributors, ask them: How good is the management team? Are there weaknesses of any significance? Who's cooperative and who isn't? Does the team look out for its own interests or the interests of the distributor network? Overall, would you rate the management team's performance as excellent, good, or poor? Perhaps the most important question to ask is this: If I need help from a member of the management team, can I depend on getting it? Some distributors may not be forthcoming with answers to these questions, or they may hesitate to speak negatively about the management team. That's why you need to speak to more than just one or two distributors. Speak to at least half a dozen, or more if possible.

A management team can make or break a company, says James Davis — a former high-powered real estate agent in Hardy, Arkansas — and now one of the most successful associates of Horizons Interactive, which sells products and services for 125 stores via Internet malls. See James's Web site at `www.jdavis.com`. "The leader of your company is the cornerstone of your business foundation. When you begin to evaluate the management team, start with the president and learn as much about him or her as you can. Spend some time and some money to get the facts."

"The evaluation of the corporate staff is one of the most important elements in determining which company you want to represent," says Jeff Roberti, who was a waiter before he found network marketing. "Ultimately, I would search for a team that has a proven background. I believe a network marketing background is helpful, but I'd also look for significant financial stability for the company. When I joined NSA [National Safety Associates — though the company goes solely by NSA], one of the major reasons was because I met the president and founder, and I believed in his vision and his ability to run a successful network marketing company. What also impressed me was that the president had surrounded himself with a team of leaders in the corporate office. It takes a team to make a successful network marketing company, not just an individual."

Commitment to integrity

Doing the right thing goes a long way in building a sales organization, and it's particularly important in network marketing. Many people remain skeptical of this profession and the people who operate within it. The last thing you want to do is align with a company that isn't committed to integrity. Yes, every company will say that integrity is important, but before you sign any agreements or pay any amount of money, you want to be sure that the management team of the company you plan to join is aboveboard. You want confirmation that they have a reputation for doing the right thing.

James Davis of Horizons Interactive suggests calling the Better Business Bureau to ask whether complaints have been filed against the company and says, "A good leader will be proud of the fact that if there were any complaints against the company, they settled them amicably." Of course, if there's a long list of complaints, be careful. The company may be honest, but it might not be smart! Otherwise it wouldn't get itself into trouble so often.

You can also ask existing distributors as well as the company's vendors about their experiences with the company's leadership. Go to the top of an organization to ask questions of distributors because those at the top are likely to know the management team best due to their length of affiliation with the company. As for vendors, if they're not being paid by the company, they usually won't hesitate to say so. It's a small world when it comes to network marketing, so you won't have to ask too many distributors or vendors before you get the story on a particular company or its leadership team.

James Davis concludes, "Integrity and honesty are paramount here. This is your future. Invest in it before you commit yourself to it."

Management "must be committed to quality and integrity and must have a genuine concern for the company's associates," maintains Michael Sheffield. "They may not be able to do everything, but they must recognize that their primary responsibility is to serve the customer, the men and the women who are representing the company in the field."

It takes more than one or two to make a team

There's no law that says a network marketing company must include a president plus senior executives to oversee operations, marketing, sales, compliance, and distributor support. However, if one or two people are trying to manage all those responsibilities, either the company's ownership doesn't plan to attract many distributors — thus one or two people can handle the workload — or the company is undercapitalized and can't afford the necessary personnel. Either scenario spells disaster!

Along with the major areas of responsibility listed earlier, a network marketing company requires a lot of support from additional staff members. Technology is wonderful, but there's still no good substitute for a live voice answering the phone, whether it's at the reception desk, in distributor support, or in customer service. Companies need numerous people to process paperwork from new and existing distributors, schedule product shipments, and answer an endless variety of questions that distributors and customers ask every day.

In addition, network marketing companies need people to staff the accounting and information systems departments. Most network marketers seem to be reasonable people . . . until their commission checks don't arrive! Who's responsible for reviewing sales commission reports and issuing the checks? Today, a computer program processes these details, but even computers are temperamental and need attention. Has the company employed the appropriate personnel to manage the technology and information processing that's required of an expanding network marketing company?

Successful teams work together

After you're satisfied that a company employs a management team that's large enough to handle responsibilities at the corporate office, the next step is to find out whether the team works together. Dan Gaub, who scrutinized Market America before he joined the company in 1995, says that you can size up the compatibility of the management team in two ways: "Go to the corporate office and watch them for a day or two. Look at how they interact. Or go to an event that's sponsored by the company and watch how the executives work with each other." Set up interviews with the management team prior to visiting their offices. Go to lunch with one or two executives. Don't overlook the support staff — those folks tend to know *everything*. By spending some time at the desk of an assistant or with a receptionist, you can pick up some good insight. Explain that you're looking for a company that you can trust and a management team that will be interested in helping you succeed. Ask for examples of how the team works together.

"The very first Market America convention that I attended," says Dan, "I showed up early at the meeting room to get a good seat. Two of the company's vice presidents were making sure that the chairs were lined up and that other details had been handled. I asked if I could help them, and they said, 'No, you paid for a ticket. You're here to learn.' I learned a lot from that one statement alone. Real leaders just do what they have to do."

A good management team looks to the future

Louise Adrian, a distributor of candles for Party Lite Gifts in Vancouver, British Columbia, and a ten-year industry veteran, adds yet something else to look for in a management team: "Is it always searching for new products? If so, that's the mark of a progressive management team, and that's important to know. You want a management team that's always looking for what's new, what's better, and what's next."

Internet company management issues you may encounter

There is a type of network marketing scenario that doesn't need a lot of staff support. Today, one or two executives can manage a network marketing company that is Internet dependent and doesn't ship products. These companies sell services via the Internet, and they're usually found only on the Internet. The companies often don't encourage live interaction by telephone, but rather, they handle as many issues as possible by e-mail correspondence or via their Web sites, where they post answers to Frequently Asked Questions (FAQs). These high-tech, low-touch opportunities appeal to many people, and many similar companies will exist in the future.

Although there's no reason to believe Internet companies are any less viable than non-Internet-driven companies, you should still proceed cautiously. If you're not Internet savvy, make sure that you can get the help you may need to succeed with one of these companies. Oftentimes the company's management — usually the founder of the concept — expects you to be familiar with Internet jargon and systems. If you're not, you may find it extremely frustrating to get your business off the ground without some high-touch help!

The management team should support these positions

Attorney Jeffrey Babener, one of the most prominent network marketing legal advisers in the United States, suggests that you look for a management team that supports the following principles:

- **High-quality products:** Businesses can't afford to skimp when it comes to product quality or the value of services. You should be eager to buy the company's products and services yourself, even if you aren't a member of the company. You should expect the products and services to be priced fairly and to include a buyback agreement. The management team should enthusiastically promote and protect these issues.

- **No earnings representations:** If members of the management team tell you how wealthy you'll become after you join them and their company, turn in the opposite direction and run! Neither the management team nor the marketing and training materials they produce should make claims about specific income potential.

- **An emphasis on retail sales:** A management team that's more interested in getting you to purchase products and services than

in helping you sell products and services to consumers who are not associates of the company is misguided.

- **No inventory requirements:** Beware of the management team that talks about the "minimum purchase requirement" or "inventory requirements" that you must buy simply to become a distributor. After you join the network, there will likely be minimum activity requirements for you to remain a qualified associate.

- **A buyback policy:** The management team should support the policy of buying back resalable inventory and sales kits from distributors who decide to terminate their relationship with the company.

- **Timely sales commissions:** Some companies pay sales commissions weekly, others monthly. The schedule isn't nearly as important as knowing that the management team is squarely behind the timely payment of commissions.

Management teams that support these principles are clearly on the side of the distributors and also within the bounds of network marketing law.

In days gone by, a company could introduce a product such as soap, water filters, or a vitamin package and nearly make a career of selling that single product without much, or even any, competition. But not anymore. A company can get the jump on the competition by introducing a new product, but that advantage doesn't last long. That explains why there are so many "me, too" or copycat products and services in the marketplace. Companies move faster than ever, and once they hear about a new product, they'll get their hands on it and figure out if they want to make one just like it. Competition is good, no doubt about that, and it's fierce in network marketing. Consequently, the best network marketing companies are always on the lookout for new products and services. As a distributor, you probably won't have the time, money, contacts, or knowledge to seek out new product lines or to test new ideas for services. But research and development is one of the benefits of joining a network marketing company. Research and development is the management team's job.

Make sure to join a company where research and development gets plenty of attention. When you're asking questions of the management team, find out who's in charge of research and development. Spend time with that executive or management team, if possible.

Having "Been There, Done That" Is a Good Thing

Whether it comes from the network marketing arena or business in general, experience enhances every management team. When possible, join a company whose management team includes members with business and management experience, as well as network marketing experience in the field.

Business and management experience

Almost anyone can start a network marketing company today, and thousands try every year. Unfortunately, most of these start-ups fail. Why? Oftentimes it's a lack of business and management expertise. Because of the excitement that network marketing companies generate, and due to the fact that a network marketing company can recruit a huge sales organization worldwide in just a matter of months, or a couple of years, many people are attracted to the profession. It looks so easy! What do you need to start a network marketing company? Capital, a product or a service, a compensation plan, and a Web site! Someone who's good at selling can raise the money to get started, find a good product or service, copy another company's pay plan, build a Web site, and voilà, they're in business. All too often, it happens just that way in the age of cyberspace. But then the troubles begin. Either the company doesn't catch on and it flops immediately, or it catches on like wildfire and flops after a couple of years. In either case, the failure comes about because there is no management team or the management team really doesn't understand how to build a viable business.

Todd Falcone, an associate with the Internet-driven company ProSTEP, which offers services such as lead generation to network marketers, says he believes that the management team "must have a successful track record in business, with a strong understanding of the economy and current business trends to allow them to position the company for growth and to redirect the company, if necessary. As corporate leaders, they must be able to lead their employees. Network marketing is a people business from top to bottom. Weak management will lead to poor customer service and quality control issues, and either can ultimately break the company."

"Tremendous" Bill Pike maintains that business acumen is important. In fact, Bill — a Dallas-based leader in the Youngevity organization, which sells a variety of health and wellness products — thinks it's far more important than network marketing experience. "It's management experience that counts. The person without a network marketing background can get someone [with that experience] to head up the marketing. But the executive without management experience can have the best field force in the world and fail. I'd want to know that the company president has experience managing a company. Then I'd like to be sure he surrounds himself with the best talent."

Network marketing experience in the field

Besides experience in the business field, many network marketing experts strongly believe that management should have field experience. "It's . . . important for the management team to have network marketing experience," says Todd Falcone. "Otherwise it could be a nightmare if the executives don't understand the industry. If they've not worked in the field, they can't begin to comprehend what their distributors are going through on a daily basis. The managers who have network marketing experience will be able to empathize with the field and provide valuable insight from their personal experiences. I don't think they should just have network marketing experience. . . . I think it should be *very successful* network marketing experience."

"If they have network marketing experience, then they have walked in our shoes," says Louise Adrian. Louise says that if members of the management team have not been in the field, relating to the company's distributors will be difficult. "If they don't have field experience," she continues, "I'd want to know if they have an advisory team from the field. And do they listen to that team?"

Calling on the Pros When They're Needed

The best management team in network marketing won't be able to answer every question or solve every challenge that occurs in the development of a dynamic business. It's unreasonable to expect a company to employ full-time executives who can handle every detail that pops up in the operation of a network marketing business. For one thing, most companies can't afford the payroll to retain those personnel. For another, there aren't enough talented executives to go around. Also, the need is not always great enough to keep certain specialists on the payroll full-time.

Nowadays, however, there's an expanding pool of talent available to network marketing companies through consulting firms and other professional organizations. The Direct Selling Association (www.dsa.org), as well as the Multi-Level Marketing International Association (www.mlmia.org), maintains lists of suppliers and vendors who specialize in network marketing.

Before you join a network marketing company, ask its executives and top distributors to identify the company's areas of weakness. Needs vary from company to company. One, for example, may be weak in the area of software management, while another requires assistance in distribution. Just about every company today struggles to keep abreast of the changes and opportunities created by Internet technology. Some companies need help in international development; others struggle with training and sales issues. Whatever the need, specialists can fill in the gaps. Make sure that the company you decide to join isn't so arrogant as to think it doesn't need professional assistance from time to time. Find out who the company calls on in times of special need. If possible, speak with some of these individuals about the company's viability.

Commitment to Employees: Attitude, Ethics, and Quality

The best network marketing companies understand the importance of rewarding and respecting their employees. You want to be sure to join one of those companies! A company that treats its employees well also treats its distributors well. Look for a company that boasts about its employees. Conversely, look for a company whose employees speak highly of its management team. That's where you're likely to find people who maintain positive attitudes, who believe in doing what's right for the company, the distributors, and customers, and who enjoy a quality of life at work that motivates them to do their very best.

Remember that every business has two groups of customers: the internal customers and the external customers. The way you treat your internal customers has a major bearing on how they, in turn, treat your external customers. When you treat your people with courtesy and respect, the tendency is for them to treat their customers the same way.

Management needs to know its people. What employees want and what employers think employees want are sometimes miles apart. The number one desire of employees is to have interesting work; the number two desire is for appreciation expressed for the work they've done; and number three is the feeling of being in on things. The beautiful thing about network marketing is that it is tailor-made to meet these desires.

"If the management team can focus on the needs of their distributors instead of seeing the distributors as expendable, then the likelihood of that team supporting the development of a distributor's business increases significantly," says Jeff Roberti, the NSA associate mentioned earlier in this chapter.

A passionate management team has the right attitude

Life's accomplishments are controlled by attitude and, as a result, a network marketing company rises and falls by the attitude of its management team. If the management team consists of executives who maintain positive mental attitudes, you can bet that they're passionate about their work. Furthermore, they will *respond* rather than *react* to the challenges and problems they face in the development of the business. Responding is much more intelligent and satisfying to everyone concerned than reacting. Besides, network marketers, like people in general, are inclined to cooperate with managers who respond to their ideas, suggestions, and even their occasional bad behavior! They'll withdraw, however, and challenge a reactive management team. Consequently, you want to find a management team that recognizes the value of the right attitude!

In times of difficulty — and there's never been a network marketing company that didn't run into some difficulties — it is up to the management team to guide the company. That's when attitude and passion really count. Therefore, look for these qualities in the management team before you agree to join a company.

Fairness and equal opportunity: hallmarks of a good management team

An effective management team sings from the same hymnal. In other words, it delivers the same message to *all* the distributors. If managers play favorites, or if they provide special help or treatment for one person and not for all, they create an unhealthy environment. "Find a management team that delivers one voice," advises Louise Adrian. "If the management team plays politics, stay clear of that company."

"You're looking to associate with ethical people," says Tim Sales, trainer for network marketers and producer of the training video "Brilliant Compensation" (www.brilliantcompensation.com). "Ethical people focus on helping you spend more time with your family [achieve a balanced success], rather than hyping how much money you're going to make if you join their company. Ethical people do what they say, and when they talk about numbers, they don't exaggerate or contradict themselves. Watch for the little things. These are good indicators of ethics and truth."

You'll want to favor a company that's committed to equal opportunities for all people, not just because it's the law but because it's the mark of a quality organization. As you visit with the management team and with distributors and vendors, ask for examples of how the company is committed to equal opportunity employment.

Network marketing is an equal opportunity structure. Many of the solid companies are either already international or are moving in that direction, and you will work with men and women of all races, creeds, and colors. In my life, the five people who had the greatest impact on me were all women. Three Native Americans had a huge impact on my life — one on my sales career, one on my speaking career, and one on my spiritual walk. An elderly African American lady is the reason I'm a Christian, my closest friend is Jewish, my daughter-in-law is from Campeche, Mexico, and our director of training and international operations is from India. I shudder to think what I would have missed out on had I been racist or sexist. Discrimination is not only immoral and illegal; it's not smart, because you will miss out on great people who could be a real asset to your organization.

Questions to Ask Yourself After Doing Your Research

Before you take that final leap of faith by signing an agreement and paying money to join a company, take the time to recap what you've learned about the management team. Following you'll find a list of questions that will help you zero in on many of the topics that we've discussed or introduced in this chapter.

- ✔ Would the integrity of the company's leaders inspire you to follow them?
- ✔ Is the leadership team mission-driven or "get-rich-quick" motivated?
- ✔ Does the corporate philosophy fit your personal philosophy?
- ✔ Would you feel comfortable working with this management team?
- ✔ Do the company's employees, distributors, and vendors speak highly of the management team?

Chapter 7

Evaluating a Company's Products and Services

- -

In This Chapter

▶ Discovering what and to whom you'd like to sell

▶ Considering marketability issues

▶ Getting the details about the marketplace, present and future

▶ Assessing the quality of a company's products and services

▶ Finding out about the training you'll need

▶ Looking at product delivery

- -

*H*ere's a myth that we want to dispel immediately: "Network marketing is so 'hot' that the product really doesn't matter. Build a sales organization of mission-driven people, and they can sell anything!"

Not so! "That kind of thinking," says Clifton Jolley, Ph.D., former university professor and long-time adviser to network marketing companies, "turns this industry into a scam. Network marketing has always been based on charismatic products, and when you're evaluating products, you must constantly ask yourself, Is the product dynamic? Or unique? Is it something I can get excited about personally? Do I want to become a product of this product? If not, find another opportunity."

I certainly agree with Dr. Jolley, who is president of Advent Communications in Dallas, Texas. As a matter of fact, from time to time in interviews, the statement has been made to me, "I understand you could sell anything to anybody." My response has always been, "No, that is definitely not true. You just described a con artist." A con artist has no concept of moral values and looks out only for himself or herself.

The truly professional salesperson, the one who can build a business, maintain customers, and enjoy a less stressful life, is one who would never dream of selling anything he or she didn't completely believe in. This type of salesperson is convinced that the customer is the bigger winner of the two, and he or she can transmit this conviction to the customer. This ability is particularly important in network marketing because, especially in the past, people have bought into the myth that quality and integrity are not important. They're not just important — they're critical.

In our company, we believe that you must become a product of the product — that you have to be the right kind of person and do the right thing. By becoming a product of the product, in many cases, you will become the right kind of person. As an example, by listening to motivational audiotapes, you can improve your personal level of motivation. By using nutritional supplements, you can improve your energy and overall health. By becoming a product of these and other products, you increase your chances of enjoying all the benefits that life — and your network marketing company — has to offer.

Here's an entire chapter to help you evaluate products and services so that you can make good decisions about their marketability, as well as about your desire to represent and sell them.

Deciding What You'd Like to Sell

Whether you decide to sell a product or a service — or in some companies, both — you want to be sure that your enthusiasm for whatever you sell is genuine. Here's a good test: Do you use the product or service yourself? If not, maybe you're not sold on it.

Lee Lemons, for instance, spent 13 years with IBM as a systems engineer. At age 40, earning $50,000 a year, he experienced what he says was a midlife crisis. "The money was good at IBM," he says, "but I wanted something more, and I decided I had to make a move." Lee wanted a business of his own, and he found it once he heard about Excel Communications, which markets long-distance services. "I liked Excel right away because it was a service, it sold something that people need, and Excel could save them money. That all made sense to me. I started full-time with Excel in August 1991." Within 90 days, Lee had recruited 100 distributors into his organization. Today, he remains one of Excel's top earners.

From Vancouver, British Columbia, Louise Adrian, an independent consultant of Party Lite Gifts, says, "Before I got started in the business, it was important for me to believe in the products that I'd be selling." Party Lite sells fine candles and home décor accessories. "Our products are something special," says Louise. "You can't find them in stores. I fell in love with them myself, and that's why it's so easy for me to sell them to my friends and to their friends." Party Lite sells its products via in-home parties and personal shopping appointments.

"Any consumer product or service is fair game for network marketing companies," says network marketing attorney Jeffrey Babener in Portland, Oregon. "In the past, the industry was dominated by cosmetics, nutritional and personal care, and home cleaning products. Not anymore. It has become evident that anything and everything can be sold by network marketers, including services. Today, discount buying services are popular, teachers and parents are experiencing great success marketing educational toys, and home and personal security products are booming as well."

Jeffrey adds that if a product benefits from demonstration, explanation, or personal testimony, then it is an excellent candidate for network marketing. Once they're excited about a product or service, network marketers share their enthusiasm with their families, social contacts, and coworkers. "Sales are often made from one friend to another," he says, "and credibility is very important."

Sitting in a chair was all Trish Schwenkler did to get interested in her own network marketing business. For ten years, this homemaker and mother suffered with severe back discomfort. She had visited physical therapists and orthopedic surgeons, but no one could help her much. Most years, she spent at least $1,000 just on medical bills and acupuncture hoping to get some relief. What a surprise when she visited a friend's home and sat on a magnetic chair pad developed by Nikken. "What *is* this?" she wanted to know. She felt some relief upon sitting.

The friend invited Trish and her husband to test a bed and back pad, also sold by Nikken. Trish couldn't believe the difference — she was used to sleeping on the floor. This experience occurred in 1993. Trish immediately purchased products from Nikken, and she couldn't help thinking about the business. Today, Trish and Bob Schwenkler are members of Nikken's millionaire club, living in Boise, Idaho — just seven years after she sat on that chair! In this case, as in so many others, the product made the difference.

Deciding to Whom You'd Like to Sell

Who are the customers who buy these products and services? Describe them. More importantly, are these customers the kind of people you know, or want to know, or can get to know? For example, if the customers are primarily baby boomers — which they will be for most network marketing companies, at least for the first quarter of this century — is that a market you can penetrate? If most of the customers are female, or most are mothers or homemakers, will you enjoy pursuing these markets? If the products sell primarily to blue-collar customers, will they respond to you? If the service sells to white-collar customers or corporate America, can you see yourself successfully working in that market?

These are important questions to answer for your own psyche and peace of mind, but you should consider your familiarity and compatibility with the customer base for another reason. You're not going to get rich your first few months in network marketing — this is a "get-rich-slow" profession. In fact, depending on the amount of time you devote to the business and your effectiveness, you may take a year to break even financially or to begin earning more money than what it costs you to pay for the products or services that you purchase for yourself or your family.

Consequently, in the early months of your networking career, when doubt and fear try to become your constant companions, your commission checks probably won't be impressive enough to keep you committed to the business. But here's what will: fun! If you like the people you meet in network marketing — your fellow distributors in the business as well as your customers — then you're more likely to continue working the business. When you're not having fun and when the work is hard and sometimes discouraging, you're not likely to want a long-term future in network marketing.

Most of the people who join the Zig Ziglar Network do so because they want to make a difference in their lives and in the lives of other people. As a matter of fact, our mission is to be the difference maker in the personal, family, and professional lives of enough people to make a positive difference in the world. We do appeal to those people who are "missionary minded," who really do want to make a difference in the lives of others. A friend of mine, Gary Billions, who is that kind of guy, was still a little bit surprised to discover just how important and significant that is. That's the main thrust of his activities — he loves what he's doing and is cashing his checks and looking forward to even bigger ones. But the mission is what makes the difference in many people's lives. Some of them have even said, "If there was no money involved, I wouldn't stop doing this under any circumstances." Network marketing is not only fun but also personally gratifying.

Two of the most gratifying things in the profession are letters of thanks that people get and the joy they receive as a result of watching others grow and achieve success in their lives — in every area, we might add.

Marketability Issues to Consider

Deciding which products or services to represent and sell is a major decision for network marketers. Aside from the quality and integrity of the product or service, you want to sell something that's highly consumable. That way, you can sell it repeatedly — once a month, or more often if possible. Without repeat sales, your commission checks may be too small or too infrequent to justify your marketing and sales efforts.

You also want to consider the value of any product or service that you decide to represent. Will the value be obvious to the consumer? Or will you have to convince your prospective customers that the value exists? If the benefits of your product or service are not easily recognizable or understood by your customers, then it will be more difficult to make sales. Ideally, look for products or services that almost sell themselves. For example, millions of people already understand and accept the value of consuming nutritional products, vitamins, and weight management products. Millions of people buy these products in the United States every month. The benefits are well known. If you decide to sell these products, you won't have to create a market by convincing people that your products serve a purpose. You'll only have to explain why *your* products are better than all the other products on the market.

The following information will help you choose wisely about which products or services to sell.

Purchasing repetitively: Consumption rules!

"Is it a product (or service) that people will buy repeatedly, month after month?" Answer that question before you get too familiar with a product or service. As a network marketer, you're looking for the opportunity to sell something once to a customer who will continue buying the same product or service every month for years to come. You make the sale once, and every month thereafter the customer needs to purchase additional products or services — no matter whether they're supplements, weight management products, a waterless car wash, laundry detergent, long-distance service, or legal services. You earn a commission with every purchase! As long as the customer continues buying the product or service, you get paid. The more you sell, the more the customer buys, and the more you earn.

The consumption rate is inadequate if the product isn't something the customer will buy repetitively or if it's not one of a line of products the customer is likely to buy all or most of over a period of time. Because *consumption rules* in network marketing, you want to find a company where you can invest your time and money in products and services that people will purchase repetitively. Of course, a company's product mix is likely to include some products that will be consumed monthly and others that will be purchased only occasionally. That's acceptable as long as the company's consumable products generate earnings that you find satisfying.

Not everyone appreciates the repetitive sale, and over the course of your network marketing career, you may face criticism for it. Some who look down on network marketing say this sales approach is a trap. They say you're duping customers into robotically making purchases they don't need. Nonsense. People *do* need these products and services. Buying them automatically month after month saves them time and money. Let your customers know that you buy and use the products and services repeatedly yourself. (And be sure you do!) Customers of network marketing companies are almost always adults. They shouldn't continue buying something month after month if they don't use it or need it.

"If the product or service isn't consumable, then it's not going to provide solid residual income," says Jim Bruce, the Pompano Beach, Florida–based distributor of the Small Business Club of America (www.savewin.com), which markets products and services to small businesses. "I want to spend my time promoting a product or service that I believe in and people will continue to order. That gives me an opportunity to build relationships with customers, and that usually leads to even more sales."

Evaluating whether the benefits are obvious to the buyers

Surveys by Packaged Facts, Inc., a market research firm, reveal that more than half of the U.S. adult population uses dietary supplements. Americans spend about $7 billion annually on these products! The benefits of dietary supplements are obvious to millions of consumers. However, the expansion of this huge market depends greatly on consumer education. Not every adult understands the value of enzymes or the dangers of free radicals in the human body. After they're educated, even more consumers may want to buy dietary supplements.

And so it goes for every product or service. If the benefits of using a product or service aren't obvious or desirable, it's probably going to be hard to sell. Everyone understands the concept of saving money — that's a benefit. Thus, low-fee long-distance service doesn't take much explanation. However, not everyone grasps the benefits of a product like prepaid legal services. Creating buyers in that market takes some education, but once they hear the benefits, lots of people want to subscribe to the service and pay a monthly or annual fee.

Look for products and services that people use with frequency. The more obvious the benefits, the better. If you think that you'll have to *convince* people to use the product or service and resell them month after month, find something else to sell! Thousands of products and services are available to network marketers.

Making sure you can demonstrate the benefits of the products or services

People won't necessarily believe what you say, but they'll believe what you do! You can tell people that nutritional supplements are good for their health, but they'll believe you only when they have evidence that you use supplements and that you and others have benefited.

You can tell people that a baking stone will keep crescent rolls from turning black on the bottom when they bake them, or you can go into their home and *show* them. Cooking demonstrations are a major part of the marketing plan at The Pampered Chef. In fact, all the party plan network marketing companies use demonstrations to market and sell their products.

You have a huge marketing advantage when you can easily demonstrate a product. The waterless car wash sold by Enviro-Tech International is a good example. "Squirting is a major part of our marketing plan," explains Kamie Downen in Honolulu. Squirting? It's not a Hawaiian ritual; it's a 30-second product demonstration. Kamie says, "Three times a day we look for opportunities to squirt our waterless car wash on a dirty car or truck. Of course, we ask for permission first. Then we squirt, buff, and wipe it off! And the product sells itself because it works. People are amazed at how quickly the product removes all kinds of dirt from their vehicles. By doing these demonstrations every day, we can move a lot of our product."

Sizing up the market

Most of the time, the bigger the market, the better. Need for a product or service does not a market make. The need may be intense, but if the need is shared by only a small group of people, the market for the product or service may be too small. Small markets do not create sufficient opportunities for sales, and skimpy sales generate skimpy commission checks! That's not good. Therefore, look for large and expanding markets not only because bigger is better, but because once a real market is discovered, the competition will follow. But that's okay. Many of the richest folks in network marketing earned their fortunes by capturing just a tiny percentage of a huge market.

While you're considering network marketing companies and having discussions with the management team or your prospective upline, don't be shy about asking for proof of a market's size. How big is it? Where is it? In other words, get the demographics for that market.

Using the Internet to size up a market

Countless Web sites track consumer markets worldwide, and by visiting them, you can gather and view statistical data, as well as read analyses of various markets. Here are some Web sites that you may find helpful:

- ✔ **U.S. Census Bureau:** www.census.gov. The preeminent collector and provider of data about the people and economy of the United States.

- ✔ **U.S. Department of Education:** www.ed.gov. The latest research findings, statistics, and information on education.

- ✔ **U.S. Bureau of Labor Statistics:** www.bls.gov. The principal fact-finding agency for the U.S. government in the broad field of labor economics and statistics. The BLS collects, processes, analyzes, and disseminates statistical data.

- ✔ *American Demographics* **magazine:** www.demographics.com. This publication provides consumer insights, trends, and analyses as well as examples of real-world marketing success stories.

- ✔ **The Right Site:** www.easidemographics.com. Offers free, easy-to-use demographic reports generated from U.S. census data.

Getting researchers to do the work for you

Webhelp.com (www.webhelp.com) invites you to submit questions to a Web Wizard who will seek the answers for you. A similar service is at www.askjeeves.com.

We asked Webhelp.com, "To what degree will the market for weight loss supplements expand or contract in the USA?" Anisley (Web Wizards don't use last names) found several articles that not only addressed the size of the market but also provided helpful information about specific weight loss supplements, as well as Food and Drug Administration (FDA) regulations for such products.

Anisley's research also turned up this tidbit of information from *Nutraceuticals World*: 1998 marked the first year that Americans spent more on services than on material items, demonstrating the trend to increase personal satisfaction and enjoyment. The quest for an extended quality of life will motivate consumers to purchase more of the products that can help them realize this goal.

If you don't have ready access to the World Wide Web, you can always visit the library for information. Remember the library? Research librarians are happy to help you track down information about a particular market. By the way, don't be surprised if *they* use the Web to call up your answers!

Considering additional market factors

Although learning as much as you can about the size of a marketplace is important, keep in mind that size isn't everything. The ultimate success or failure of a product or service depends on additional factors, including the following:

- **The package:** The name of the product or service and the product size, weight, color, look — and possibly even its smell! — must all appeal to the consumers within the marketplace, or they won't buy it.

- **Positioning:** A product or service has to appeal to the emotional needs of the marketplace. Even if they don't ask this question directly, consumers want to know, "Why do I *need* it?" The marketing efforts behind the product or service must explain why they need it. Similarly, the answer to this question is important: "Why do I need it *now*?"

- **Timing:** When and where is the product or service available? In the age of the Internet, as well as instant gratification, consumers want everything *now*. If they have to wait, most of the time they won't purchase the product.

- **Information:** Better-educated consumers tend to ask many questions before they make a purchase. Providing answers to consumers expertly and quickly, such as via a Web site or by telephone, is paramount.

- **Results:** The service needs to *deliver* — the product must live up to its promises. Failure in either category means the marketplace won't continue buying and consuming.

Tracking the Market: Where Did That Market Go?

Have you ever fallen in love with a product that suddenly disappeared from stores for no apparent reason or was discontinued because it was no longer fashionable or couldn't be mass-produced? Or what about a service that you thought was terrific, but its market was limited to big cities, or small towns, or only certain classes of people, and therefore it wasn't readily available? These are the types of products and services that you want to avoid, if possible, when choosing a network marketing opportunity.

Markets come and markets go, and keeping up with them is the job of your corporate office. Market tracking isn't a discipline that you'll have time (or necessarily the expertise) to worry about. But someone must! Ask the company's management team for proof that its products and services will continue to enjoy a large and expanding market. If they can't give you proof, look for another company!

Why? Consider this scenario:

Phone cards allow you to prepurchase long-distance service. When these cards were first introduced, they were the rage in network marketing. Sales were "incredibly successful," recalls Dr. Clifton Jolley. Network marketers created the marketplace for the phone card. But then one day, almost as quickly as the market appeared, it disappeared, at least for network marketers. "Network marketers popularized the phone card," explains Clifton, "so much so that it became a traditional retail item." A commodity! As a result, the price of these cards was deflated, negatively affecting network marketing.

"Any product that experiences a deflated price probably doesn't have much of a future in network marketing," says Travis Bond, vice president of sales and marketing at 2021 Interactive. Dr. Jolley adds, "The traditional retail marketplace oftentimes can sell a product, especially a low ticket item, for less money than can network marketers. Once the phone card became a commodity, consumers could buy it at every 7-Eleven, every Wal-Mart, every Eckerd Drugs. That doesn't mean some companies aren't still selling the phone cards," he says, "but they're not the big lead product they once were."

Want another example? Thigh creme. Not so many years ago, thigh creme was a product that female consumers *had* to have, even if it cost $49.95. Now they can buy it at Sam's Club for less than $15 a tube.

"There are products that will bring a market to an end in this industry," continues Clifton Jolley. "Often they begin as 'fringe' products, not something the mainstream wants to buy, but then enthusiastic network marketers create a groundswell for the product and presto! . . . suddenly the product is in the Sharper Image catalog. We'll see more of this happening in the future."

Many times when network marketers create a market, they then move a product into the mainstream through stores and retail outlets, but in most cases those are the lower-priced products. However, the interesting thing now is that many of the traditional companies market their products either directly or indirectly through network marketing companies. Organizations such as Coca-Cola, MCI, Pro Bass, and many other companies are following that process. This certainly is a tribute to the concepts and identifies many of the advantages that network marketing has — namely, that we can reach a diverse market with just a fraction of the costs that some of the companies encounter with massive advertising. In our own company, for example, we often can offer our traditional products at the same price and, in several cases, at lower prices. Score one for network marketing!

Exclusive products and services help ensure the future of a market. If the customer can't get the product anywhere but from you, or if the service comes with a brand name that adds credibility and authority, you're in the proverbial "high cotton!" Of course, demand must exist for even exclusive products and services to maintain and expand a market.

Threats that challenge the market

Anything can happen in business; there are never any guarantees. Most crises are impossible to predict. Products can be tainted without the knowledge of a network marketing company or its distributors. Some people may misuse a product, purposely or not. If a research study suddenly shows that a product or service is harmful, the market for the product or service will vanish. The media, the public, and the government, for reasons that may or may not be legitimate, can snuff out a market overnight, and sometimes a company, too.

We agree that fraudulent or deceitful companies should be shut down. But, unfortunately, companies operating with a high level of integrity can also be destroyed. You need to be aware that the threats are real, and they can be devastating.

By 1970, Amway's product line included more than 200 items, and that year the company's annual retail sales revenue exceeded $100 million. Impressive! The U.S. government thought so, too, only the government wasn't so sure that Amway was a legal operation. For most of the 1970s, Amway was investigated by the Federal Trade Commission. Most network marketing companies would not have survived the intense scrutiny. The cost of the legal proceedings alone would have sunk many companies. But Amway held its ground, and all of network marketing owes that company a debt of gratitude for its courage. In 1979, the FTC finally published its "Opinion and Final Order" regarding Amway. Not only did the FTC rule that Amway's multilevel marketing structure was legal and proper, but it also said the company was the benchmark for other network marketing organizations. In summary (as reported by *Network Marketing Lifestyles* magazine), the FTC said that Amway "injected a vigorous new competitive presence into a highly concentrated market."

Sensitive and controversial products are prone to investigation. "Nutritional products are a concern to regulators," reports Dr. Clifton Jolley, "so they are more suspect than other products or services. The attorneys general, the Federal Trade Commission, and the FDA all share an interest in the oversight of these products. More often, however, I think that what gets investigated are the sales strategies that some companies use to promote these products!" See Chapter 4 for more information about regulatory agencies and network marketing.

Avoiding fraudulent products

Sooner or later, by one force or another, products that perpetrate a fraud on the public won't survive. You're wise to avoid them altogether. The National Council Against Health Fraud says that bogus products can often be identified by the types of claims made in their labeling, advertising, and promotional literature. Possible indicators of fraud include the following:

✔ Claims that the product is a "secret cure." Terms such as "breakthrough," "magical," "miracle cure," and "new discovery" are suspect.

✔ Pseudomedical jargon, such as "detoxify," "purify," and "rejuvenate" to describe a product's effects. These words are vague and difficult to measure. They make it easier for a company to claim success for its product even if it's not true.

✔ Stating that a product has met the approval of scientific examinations, but a list of references isn't available or the references are out-of-date.

✔ Accusations that the medical profession, drug companies, and the government are suppressing information about the product.

Using common sense: Can the product deliver on its promises?

You don't have to be a professional marketer to make good decisions about products and services. However, you do have to be careful not to be misled by a network marketing company or recruiter that puts a spin on the company's products and services when in fact the market for these goods has not been established. In this profession, it's easy to make claims and remain "technically" within the bounds of the law, so let your common sense prevail regarding these claims. A network marketing company may imply that it has discovered the cure for cancer, but what's the likelihood that a company could keep such a discovery all to itself? Or keep it out of the hands of the huge pharmaceutical firms? We hope there will someday be a cure for cancer, but we doubt that any one network marketing company will have such a product all to itself.

"Use your common sense so that you don't get lured into a deal by false or misleading claims," advises Todd Smith, who represents Rexall Showcase International, which markets weight management products, homeopathic medicines, personal care products, nutritional supplements, and water filtration systems. "Be aware that anyone can make claims, but look for the *real* need and demand for the product being offered, and then look deep in your heart and ask if the product makes sense."

Wild product claims not only hurt the image of the network marketing profession, but they also lessen a company's credibility and could even destroy the company. Stay away from companies or distributors that encourage misleading, false, or hyped-up claims about their products and services.

"People want a safe, natural alternative to drugs, and that's valid," comments Todd Smith. "But is there any research supporting that the company's claims are true? Even after ten years in this industry, I'm more aware of the spin put on certain products, and when you ask for documentation and statistics, you don't get any. That's a red flag." Even when documentation exists, Todd urges people to look into it. "If a study comes from a credible university, not just a doctor, or from a medical clinic, then you ought to be able to verify it."

There's No Substitute for Quality

If a company skimps on quality, the owner may have a gland problem, as in "greedy glands." Chances are, the company was established to line the owner's pockets instead of truly helping customers. Sooner or later, inferior products fail. Network marketing truly is a "copycat" profession. As soon as a company promotes its latest product to the world via a Web site, a dozen other companies are likely to develop a similar product. However, oftentimes the original product is the only one that will stand up to a quality test. Avoid any company that doesn't invest in the quality of its products and services. You can evaluate the quality of products or services by making sure that they are guaranteed and have been tested and approved.

Making sure the products or services are guaranteed

What happens when customers say that the product doesn't work or the service is ineffective and they want their money back? The best network marketing companies publish a return policy. Their products and services are guaranteed, and they return the customer's money, no questions asked. That's the mark of a trustworthy company. Make sure that the company you plan to join guarantees its products and services. Ask to see the return policy in writing!

Looking into product safety

Ask a company's management team, "How can I be sure your products are safe?" You can bet that consumers want to know about safety. They certainly will ask questions about supplements and weight management tablets before they ingest them. Parents will probe for safety issues about educational toys before they give them to their children, and understandably so. Find out about the company's safety procedures. Look for evidence of government or independent agencies that test and approve the products. Don't simply accept the company's word about safety precautions. If possible, talk to the manufacturer and ask for information about product testing, reliability, and safety. It would be rare for a network marketing company not to make this information available to distributors and consumers.

"Natural doesn't necessarily mean *safe,"* advises Elizabeth Yetley, Ph.D., of the FDA's Office of Special Nutritionals. "Think of poisonous mushrooms, they're natural." If you're not sure about a product, you probably won't feel comfortable marketing it. Get all the details the company has available, and if you need more information, visit the FDA's Web site at www.fda.gov.

How Much Training Is Required to Learn about the Products or Services?

In network marketing, the simpler the product or service, the better. Distributors and buyers of these products or services don't have the patience to endure elaborate training programs. And if people need any special equipment or skill, either to find out about the products or services or to use them — well, excuse our informality — *that ain't gonna work*. However, you should reasonably expect that you'll need *some* product training.

Getting your training by phone or fax

Most network marketing companies train via the telephone. Every weeknight, managers and leaders of network marketing companies conduct thousands of conference calls. As few as 2 or as many as 150 networkers may be hooked up to any one of these conference calls. Ask for a published list of these calls, and you're likely to find all the educational opportunities you'll need to get started in the business.

Fax on Demand (FOD) is another training opportunity that's initiated by phone. You can pick up your phone, dial a company's FOD number (most companies have one), and request information for specific products and services. Within a few minutes, the documentation will be sent to your fax machine. Yes, you either need access to a fax machine, or you must have fax software on your computer to make FOD work.

Getting your training online

A company's Web site, which usually includes details about products and services, is another source for product training. Some of this training is in audio or video format, which you can play on your computer. Demonstrations of product sales, including questions that prospects will ask and the appropriate answers, are frequently captured on video so that distributors can return to the Web site repeatedly to learn the presentation and sharpen their skills. This technique makes training easy and fun.

Getting your training in the car

The audiotape industry loves network marketing because just about every company produces training tapes and sells them (oftentimes at cost, or for a small profit) to their distributors. Typically these tapes cost $1 to $10 each. You can keep these tapes in your car and listen to them en route to a presentation to brush up on your product information.

The fascinating thing about the material you select to listen to in your car is that it's information that generally is not taught in formal education classes. For example, audiotapes can tell you how to build winning relationships, how to get up when you've been knocked down, and what qualities you need before you can expect to have balanced success. You can also find out exactly how to set your goals and reach them, and why you should have goals in the first place. Subjects like these are important, as evidenced by the fact that ten years after graduation, over 80 percent of college graduates earn their living in a field unrelated to their college major.

One of my favorite examples is Stephen Payne, a Native American from Bartlesville, Oklahoma, who got his GED (General Equivalency Diploma) at age 23 but in the last ten years has become proficient in seven foreign languages. He is now translating for his company in French and Spanish. He acquired over 90 percent of this information while listening to tapes in his car. In short, your car is a marvelous place to get a wonderful and career-advancing education.

Getting your training live

Perhaps the most exciting and effective way to learn about a product or service is to attend a live presentation. There's nothing like sitting in a room with your peers watching a professional trainer explain how a product or service delivers benefits. The interaction provides valuable reinforcement, and it's a pleasurable way to learn.

However, companies have a limit on the number of live training sessions that they can produce per year. These sessions are time-consuming and expensive, not only for the company but also for the distributors. Usually, these events are held in major cities where they can attract large numbers of people. Often, for the sake of convenience, the company will schedule training events in the city of its location, making it easier for the home office staff to be involved in the event (usually to work behind the scenes!). Distributors can expect to pay a fee — $50 to $150 and up — to attend these events. The fees help defray the company's expenses. Distributors also pay for their own travel, meals, and lodging. Rarely will a company underwrite these expenses — they're part of the distributor's cost of conducting business.

Delivering Products: Is It Your Responsibility?

After you sell a product or service, how will your customer get it? The preferred method, in all but a few instances, is direct shipment by the company. This saves you the hassle of storing products and then scheduling time to deliver them. However, some companies prefer their distributors to deliver the products. They see it as an opportunity for the distributor to demonstrate the product and sell the customer additional products.

Beware of companies that require you to stockpile products for resale. This concept is known as *front-loading,* and it can have disastrous results for a distributor. Network marketing history is replete with stories of distributors who were required to stockpile products as a requisite to joining a company. Many of these distributors got stuck with the inventory when they couldn't sell it, either because they weren't capable of selling it, or the market for the product disappeared, or the product wasn't salable. Oftentimes these distributors became disgruntled, understandably so, and filed complaints with state and federal agencies and organizations such as the Better Business Bureau. Consequently, regulators now investigate companies that force their distributors to maintain large supplies of inventory.

Measuring a company's success potential through its products and services

The products and services that a network marketing company offers ultimately determine the size and long-term success of its associates. One thing that everyone must clearly understand is that the products must be good and the service must be great. The salespersons — the associates — should definitely feel that the product is indispensable and that it is so good that they either could not or would not get along without it — it's a must on the list of products they use. When networkers have that kind of feeling, they can transfer that feeling to the prospect, and the prospect in turn transmits the feeling, need, and desire to his or her associates.

The reality is it takes a team to render good customer service. This team includes the shipping department, the finance department, the collection department, and, most important, those people who answer the questions and solve the problems when customers call in. When you combine a belief in the product (which has got to be good) and a follow-up service to satisfy customers, you have a winning combination. Just be sure to select a company whose products and services meet the needs of a massive consumer audience. And, of course, make sure that you appreciate and use the products and services, too.

Today, prudent network marketing companies follow what's become known as "the 70 Percent Rule." This rule wasn't ordained by legislators. It was included in the Federal Trade Commission's 1979 "Opinion and Final Order" regarding the Amway case, which we discussed several pages earlier. Basically, the 70 percent rule requires that distributors purchase inventory only after they have sold or used at least 70 percent of previously purchased inventory. This is a good way to protect distributors from risking too much in products that they won't be able to sell or use.

In some situations, however, keeping a supply of products available makes sense, particularly if you sell the products at seminars or in retail locations. Just don't overdo it. You don't want a garage full of products that you may not be able to sell.

Ultimately, your personal evaluation of the company's products and services determines whether you choose to look into that business further. If a company can't pass the products and services test, you don't need to invest more of your valuable time with it. The homework you do at this level helps you become the success you want to be.

Questions to Ask a Network Marketing Organization about Products, Services, and Training

Here's a list of questions about a company's products, services, and training that you should research before you become a distributor for that company:

- ✔ Does the company's product or service sell at retail? In other words, is there a market that's willing to purchase the product or service, or will you have to create the market? See "Sizing up the market" earlier in this chapter.

- ✔ Does the company's product line include a reasonable number of consumables?

- ✔ Does the company depend on glitz, glitter, and hype to sell its opportunity, or will the company and opportunity survive a factual examination of the claims made at company-sponsored opportunity meetings?

- ✔ Would the company's income and product claims pass muster with regulatory bodies, or do they sound too good to be true?

- ✔ Would the company's opportunity give you a real chance to make a positive difference in the lives of those you sponsor in the business?

- ✔ Does the company have a proven and effective training program to educate distributors about its products and services?

- ✔ Does the company want to load you up with products that you must sell before you can recoup your investment?

Chapter 8

Evaluating Your Opportunity to Make Money

*T*his may be the chapter you've been waiting to read. Or didn't you wait? It's okay if you jumped to this chapter first, because we know this is the question you really want answered: *How much money can I make?*

It's an important question and a fair question, and if you were applying for a job, it would be an easy question to answer. You'd either be compensated by the hour or on salary, and you would receive periodic raises and possibly bonus money. Year to year, you would have a clear idea of what you could earn, but unless you were being paid a commission relative to your performance, you would have very little, if any, ability to influence your compensation. Basically, someone above you — the boss — would determine your rate of pay, and you could take it or leave it.

In network marketing, the rules of compensation are entirely different. It's not a "take it or leave it" proposition. Instead, it's a "how much do you want to earn?" proposition. That's *not* to say it's a get-rich-quick proposition. (Many network marketers like to say it's a get-rich-slow proposition.) However, in network marketing, you *can* influence your compensation, and *you* determine your rate of pay within the boundaries of a compensation plan (or comp plan, for short). This chapter shows you how to evaluate compensation plans so that you can be sure your paycheck will reflect the time and energy you invest in the opportunity.

Defining a Compensation Plan

Nothing is more serious in network marketing than paying the distributors. Billions of dollars worldwide are paid out annually to nearly 35 million distributors! The document that controls the amount of money paid out is the compensation plan. It spells out the rules by which networkers get paid.

Network marketers earn money in a variety of ways — primarily by qualifying for commissions and bonuses — but the rules vary from company to company. For example, networkers who purchase products at wholesale and sell them at retail may earn the difference at one company, but not at another. Networkers who sponsor a distributor in their downline may earn a commission or a bonus, but it depends on their company's policy. Networkers earn bonus money by meeting certain criteria — for example, by recruiting a certain number of distributors or reaching preestablished levels of sales revenue. A promotion to a higher rank within the organization — for example, advancing from Consultant to Director, or from Gold Executive to Diamond Executive — almost always results in additional income, or at least a higher percentage of commission.

However, so far we've described only the window dressing of a comp plan. The *piece de resistance* is the section that describes how the distributors are paid on multiple levels, or paid for certain results achieved by their sales organization. That's how the dollars can add up to huge numbers over a period of time. In most (but not all) pay plans, distributors earn percentages, which can be as much as 25 percent, on sales generated by members of their downline. A downline is characterized by levels, and a payment percentage is assigned to each level, as shown in Figure 8-1. Sales generated on Level 1, for example, might pay a 15 percent commission; Levels 2 and 3 could pay a 10 percent commission; and Levels 4 and 5, a 5 percent commission. The depth of levels, and the percentages paid per level, vary by company, but the details can be found in your respective company's rules and regulations handbook or manual. One comp plan in particular, which we discuss later in this chapter, does not pay a percentage per level. Instead, it pays on the total sales volume generated by distributors in several levels.

That doesn't sound or look too complex, does it? But there's more, as you'll discover as you continue through this chapter.

"Compensation plans make the U.S. Tax Code look like a pamphlet!" says Tim Sales, trainer for network marketers and the producer of what he calls a "hype-free, educational video" called "Brilliant Compensation" (www.brilliantexchange.com). Tim says he wrote and produced the video to help individuals understand the brilliance of network marketing.

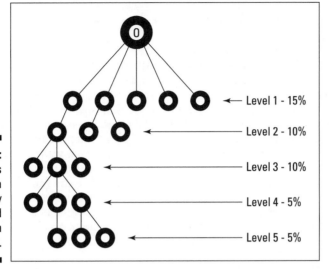

Figure 8-1:
A sales organization defined by levels and commission percentages.

Level 1 - 15%

Level 2 - 10%

Level 3 - 10%

Level 4 - 5%

Level 5 - 5%

Payday Was Never Like This Before

Everyone who works looks forward to payday, but two significant differences turn a network marketer's payday into an event that's almost always more exciting, and potentially more lucrative, than an employee's payday. First, network marketers earn residual income as opposed to linear income, so they get paid multiple times for the same transaction. (See Chapter 3 for a discussion of residual income.) Second, network marketers get paid not only for their own results but also for the results of their sales organization. These two differences are explained in more depth in the following sections.

Difference #1: Network marketers get paid repeatedly for the same transaction

An employee who works for one hour gets paid for that hour *one time.* A mechanic in a garage spends an hour repairing a car; he gets paid once for that hour. An accountant spends an hour working up her company's payroll; she gets paid once for that hour. A doctor spends an hour in the emergency room; she gets paid once for that hour. Network marketers are never paid by the hour, but if they were, they would get paid *repeatedly,* possibly every month for years, for the same hour's work.

How does that happen? Dayle Maloney, the most successful distributor at Nutrition for Life International and the author of *I Could Have Quit $7,000,000.00 Ago,* explains it perfectly.

"I knew my network marketing career wasn't going very well when I invited 30 people to my mother-in-law's home for an opportunity meeting and only two of them showed up! It was 1983," Dayle recalls, "and I was $350,000 in debt. Network marketing was my last hope. I needed it to work. But when only two people came to the meeting, my wife cried, my mother-in-law broke down, and I was nearly in tears. That first month I got a check for the grand sum of $5.60! . . . But here's the point no one should miss: That was only *one* check. Seventeen years later, I'm still getting paid for what I did that first month!" In other words, a network marketer gets paid *every time* the same retail customer or downline distributor purchases a product or service. Dayle sold a product *once* to his first customer, and even if he never spoke to that customer again, as long as she continued buying products or services, Dayle got paid.

Difference #2: Network marketers get paid for the results of their sales organization

Employees get paid only for the results they produce. Invest an hour, get paid for an hour. Even if an employee is on commission, earning a percentage of the sales she's responsible for making, she's still getting paid only for *her* results. Meanwhile, Jan Ruhe at Discovery Toys, Todd Smith at Rexall Showcase International, Russ Noland at Excel Communications, Louise Adrian at Party Lite Gifts, and millions of other network marketers are getting paid every month not only for *their* results but also for the results generated by the people in their downlines!

This is where the networker's payday *really* gets exciting. How would you like to get paid *every* month for the time invested by 5, 50, or 50,000 people? In a large sales organization, the distributors could be spread across the world, and you may not even know more than 1 percent of them. But, depending on your position in the company and the terms of your company's compensation plan, anytime one of the distributors purchases or sells a product or service from your company or recruits a new distributor, *you* earn a small percentage of the revenues generated. Even if you don't work that month, you still get paid — and handsomely!

"Five years ago," explains Todd Smith, a distributor with Rexall Showcase International, "I stopped recruiting new distributors. In nine years of network marketing, I only recruited 44 people, and I found 20 of them in my first month." Fortunately for Todd, he found the *right* people. His 44 recruits mushroomed into "several hundred thousand people" joining his downline. In year 2000, "well over 70,000 people internationally" remain active in Todd's downline. In Todd's first year as a networker, he earned $300,000. Nine years later, his career earnings exceeded $12 million!

Skeptics will say Todd's story is an anomaly, but we could fill this book with countless similar stories. People may even refute Todd's story, but anyone who understands geometric progressions realizes that the very same story could happen to them. Todd recruited 44 people, and even if each of them recruited only 5 people (some didn't recruit any, and some recruited 20, 30, 40, or more), that resulted in 220, who recruited 1,100, who recruited 5,500, who recruited 27,500 . . . and the progression continued into several tens of thousands of people.

It's unreasonable to think that all those people would succeed or that they would remain active in the business. However, numbers feed the success of your downline. The more people you attract into your sales organization, the more who are likely to remain. And so long as a good number of them sell products and services and recruit additional distributors, there's going to be a payday for you every month!

There's nothing quite like payday for a network marketer. Just ask Todd Falcone, who was a distributor with two different network marketing organizations before joining ProSTEP in 1995. ProSTEP (www.prostepinc.com) is an Internet-based network marketing company that provides support and training materials to networkers and also generates leads. "I like residual income," says Todd, who celebrated his 33rd birthday in 2000. "If I decide not to work for a day or so, or if my wife and I decide to travel, which is what we enjoy, then I don't have to worry about my paycheck. As long as my sales organization is out there working, I'll have a payday."

Staying wary of wild earnings claims

Attorney Jeffrey A. Babener points out that "a legitimate network marketing company should not make earnings representations unless those representations are based on a track record." For example, if a company representative says that you can make a certain level of income by working the opportunity so many hours a week, ask for proof of that statement. If there is no proof, look for another opportunity.

Distributors are notorious for making earnings representations, particularly in their sponsor mode. Professional network marketers refrain from making these claims, unless, of course, they're willing to back them up. If an intended sponsor tells you he's making an amount of money that sounds too good to be true, ask to see his paycheck. If he refuses, look for another sponsor or another company. On the other hand, if he can document his claims with W-2 forms or photocopies of his checks, that's a different story.

Todd quickly adds, however, that network marketing isn't about making a fortune. "Once I realized some financial success," he explains, "I was attracted by freedom. Network marketing isn't about the money; it's about *not* having a job. It's about being able to spend time with your family. I like the fact that I can get up when I want and take a day off when I want, or work really hard when I want. I can pay my bills and put some money in the bank. There's peace of mind in that." Todd pauses and says, "I will do whatever I have to do to make sure that I don't ever have to go back to a traditional job."

Recognizing the Major Compensation Plans

Compensation plans may not have been any less complex several years ago, but they were easier to categorize than they are today. That's because companies today are adapting hybrid plans. They're combining the best features of two or three plans, and the results have been advantageous for both distributors and the companies. In addition, as regulators have cracked down on the network marketing profession, companies have shunned the more controversial plans.

Should you decide to join a network marketing company, here are the names that you're most likely to hear:

- The Binary plan
- The Unilevel plan
- The Stairstep Breakaway plan
- The Forced Matrix plan

Each of these plans is discussed in this section, along with some explanation of their pluses and minuses.

No two compensation plans are alike. Two companies can each use a Unilevel plan, but those plans can be vastly different in the way that they reward and pay the distributors. There are no standard rules and regulations for plans. A company can create a plan that's unique to its organization and revise the plan whenever the need or desire arises. Most of the network marketers interviewed for this book said they did not immediately understand their company's comp plan. In fact, Michael Sheffield, a prominent network marketing consultant, says, "Most networkers cannot explain their own company's comp plan. These plans are the most misunderstood aspect of network marketing."

You may not understand your company's comp plan at first, either, but don't panic. "When I looked at Excel's comp plan," recalls Russ Noland, who gave up a lucrative career in real estate to become a networker in 1990, "it looked like a cross between Einstein's theory and I Ching. I didn't understand it. I thought I saw some money there, but I wasn't sure how it worked. But I understood that if I could recruit three people and help them recruit three, I was going to get a percentage of everyone's business. That made sense to me." Russ continues, "If you are just getting started and you try to make sense of the compensation plan, you are going to suffer 'analysis paralysis.' You might never get started as a result."

That said, here is some information that will help you recognize the various comp plans and at least begin to understand how they work.

Binary plans

If you remember that *binary* means two, then it's easy to identify this plan. You sponsor two people, and they sponsor two people, and so it goes. The two people you sponsor will be placed on your *frontline,* which means they will be on your first level (refer to Figure 8-1). Your downline builds under these two people, each of whom represents a "leg" of your organization. As you sponsor additional people, you're forced to place them in one of your legs, and they may be many levels below you. Figure 8-2 is a representation of a Binary plan.

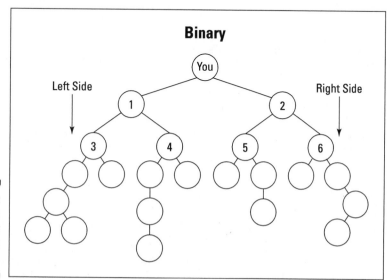

Figure 8-2:
A diagram
of a Binary
plan in
action.

"This can be a good plan in the right circumstances," says Ken Rudd, who has observed numerous plans as a former distributor and a former director of a publicly held network marketing company and as a CEO of yet another. The Binary plan usually pays distributors weekly, and it encourages people to work together because, as we explain later in this section, they get paid by generating specific amounts of sales revenue. "Many people have been able to earn huge money very quickly because they're handsomely rewarded for recruiting" in a Binary, says Ken. "However, that's also the plan's downfall. You need sales of products and/or services to create longevity for a company in network marketing. The Binary tends to attract people who want to make quick money, and those people don't last very long."

The "quick money" quality of the Binary has also created an atmosphere of suspicion among regulators who watch multi-level marketing pay plans. "The Binary had its unfortunate origins in the early 1990s in fraudulent gold coin programs," explains attorney Jeffrey Babener, author of *Network Marketing: What You Should Know* (Legaline Publications, 2000). "By the end of the 1990s, and after many legal challenges, the Binary was not in great favor." Still, several companies continue to use the Binary, and it's difficult for any company to drop one plan and switch to another.

The major downfall of the plan is balance. A Binary requires the sales volume in a distributor's two legs to balance in order for the distributor to be eligible to earn a commission. The plan might specify that a commission of $100 will be paid when each leg reaches at least $1,200 in sales revenue. However, one leg may develop slowly or not at all — possibly because the distributors aren't working the business or aren't working hard enough or effectively — while the other leg develops quickly and turns into what networkers call a "runaway leg." If the distributors in the first leg generate $1,000 of sales revenue while the distributors in the second leg generate $10,000 of sales revenue, the distributor at the top will not qualify for a commission. "The required balancing of sales volume means that hard work might yield no payoff," says Jeff.

In spite of the "quick money" appeal of the Binary and its simplicity, experts say that its future is limited. The time has come and gone for the Binary, Jeff says, and very few network marketing companies will begin using this plan after the year 2000.

Unilevel plans

On the flip side of the Binary plan is the Unilevel plan. "It's really the opposite of the Binary in many ways," explains Ken Rudd. "The Binary is heavily front-end loaded, meaning that it pays well when you recruit new distributors, but it's weak on the back-end residuals. The Unilevel pays on multiple levels — for example, 5 percent of each level." Most Unilevels stop at seven levels simply because the more levels in the plan, the more money the company has to pay out, or the smaller the percentages it can afford to pay per level.

What's impressive about the Unilevel is that it's possible to make as much money from the bottom level of the sales organization as from the top level. That's only true, however, if the commission percentages are equal for each level — that is, each level pays 5 percent. In some Unilevels, one or more levels will pay higher percentages. (See Figure 8-3.)

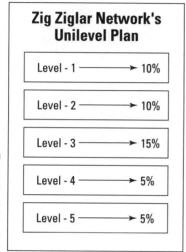

Zig Ziglar Network's Unilevel Plan

Level - 1 ⟶	10%
Level - 2 ⟶	10%
Level - 3 ⟶	15%
Level - 4 ⟶	5%
Level - 5 ⟶	5%

Figure 8-3: Zig Ziglar Network's Unilevel plan.

The compensation plan for the Zig Ziglar Network (ZZN) includes a Unilevel, and it demonstrates how a company can get creative with this pay plan. We use the Unilevel in conjunction with several features that enhance the plan so that it appeals to full-time as well as part-time networkers. The Unilevel portion of our plan pays 10 percent on levels 1 and 2, 15 percent on level 3, and 5 percent on levels 4 and 5. I bet you're wondering why we would pay 15 percent on the third level. It's because we want to encourage our associates to reach down into their downlines and help as many people below them as possible. Those extra percentages on level 3 provide a good incentive for our associates.

Before you can make big money with a pure Unilevel — one that does not include enhanced components such as generational bonuses, which we explain momentarily — you'll need several thousand people in your organization. "The Unilevel is fair and democratic," explains Ken Rudd, "but it's also socialistic. It cuts up the money to share it with everyone, and consequently it takes longer to make a lot of money."

One advantage of the Unilevel plan is that it can (but, depending on the company, doesn't always) pay generational bonuses. That is, it can pay a bonus on a specific group of people — a generation — in the downline. Here's how it works. You rise to the rank of Director, and then you help a distributor below you — the level doesn't matter — qualify for Director, too. When that distributor becomes a Director, everyone under that distributor forms a generation. You can earn an additional bonus — 5 percent is a common number — on the sales volume of that generation. You were already earning a percentage of sales by those people in the generation who fell within the first five levels of your downline. But now you're also earning a bonus on the sales volume produced by the generation.

Now it gets trickier! If a distributor between you and the Director below you becomes a Director, you now have two generations under you. Each Director's downline forms a generation, but the depth of a generation is blocked by the next Director in the downline. That's not a negative; it's a positive, because now the Director at the top — in this case, you — can earn a bonus on the first generation as well as the second generation, and however many generations may follow. As the number of generations increases and the generations themselves become larger (because new distributors are being recruited), the bonus money becomes significant.

"A generation could extend for a hundred levels of depth or more before there's another Director," explains consultant Michael Sheffield. "Career-oriented network marketers love that concept because they can make the majority of their money from generational bonuses."

Stairstep Breakaway plans

Think of an ascending staircase and pretend that each step is a different rank in the comp plan's hierarchy. The bottom rank might be Sales Executive, and the top rank National Director, and in between there are several other ranks or titles. Each rank is assigned a percentage, which denotes the discount or percentage rebate from the company, that the distributors at that rank are entitled to earn on their purchases from the company. In Figure 8-4, for example, a Sales Executive can purchase product at a 20 percent discount, while a National Director is entitled to a discount of 40 percent. The more the distributor buys, and the more the people under him buy, the faster he moves up the ranks. Promotions are based on a distributor's ability to build a certain number of legs — usually more than four but less than ten — in his downline, and for the total sales volume of the downline. When a distributor reaches the top of the hierarchy, he earns the right to "break away" from his sponsor. At that point, everyone under the distributor is considered a generation, and now his sponsor will earn a bonus on the group sales of the generation. A sponsor may have numerous distributors who break away and form generations. Figure 8-4 shows that each generation pays a 5 percent bonus, but that's not a standard; the percentage can vary from company to company.

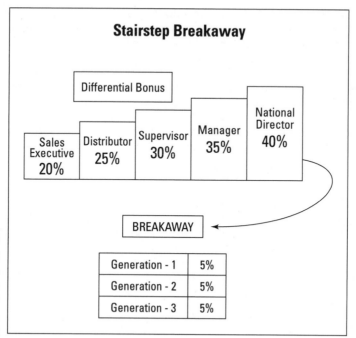

Figure 8-4:
The
Stairstep
Breakaway
plan.

There are two potential problems with a Stairstep Breakaway. First, it can be "front-end loaded," meaning that a distributor may be required to purchase a large quantity of product, costing a considerable amount of money — several thousand dollars — to join the company. "Front-end loading has created a negative reputation for network marketing in general," explains Bill Porter, a veteran networker and a leader in the Zig Ziglar Network. "People sometimes end up with a garage full of products they can't sell after they join a company that uses the Stairstep Breakaway." As a result, federal and state regulators frown on front-end loading. To minimize this scrutiny, many companies now cap the amount of the initial product order at $1,000 or less.

The second potential problem, according to Bill, is that the distributor at the top of the staircase may not be eager to see the people under her earn promotions. The distributor at the top may earn more money by keeping people under her than she does when they break away. "Personally," explains Bill, "I don't want to build a leg of my organization just to see it spun off, resulting in a financial loss." Michael Sheffield points out that some companies solve this problem by establishing a bonus percentage for a breakaway that is equal to or greater than the percentage earned in the stairstep prior to the breakaway.

The payout in a Stairstep Breakaway can be large and attractive. "An aggressive distributor can sell a $20,000 package (of products or services) to someone and earn $5,000," explains Ken Rudd. "That's a lot easier to do [for some people] than to build a sales organization over a longer period of time and earn a commission that amounts to $700 or a $1,000 a month," as would be the case with a pure Unilevel. However, selling large packages of products or services that end up sitting in a distributor's garage or basement reflects poorly on the profession and must be avoided.

Many of network marketing's best-known companies use the Stairstep Breakaway. "It's the oldest and predominant compensation plan," says attorney and author Jeffrey Babener. However, according to Michael Sheffield, most new companies opt for simplifying the Stairstep Breakaway and requiring lower qualifications for earning bonuses.

Forced Matrix plans

The objective of the Forced Matrix is to recruit a distributor for each available space in the matrix, and when each space is occupied the distributor starts building a new matrix. For example, if you're building a 3 x 5 Forced Matrix, as shown in Figure 8-5, each space in the matrix is an opportunity for you and the distributors above you to recruit new distributors. As the new distributors join the organization, they're automatically assigned to a space by a computer program that's especially designed to build Forced Matrix plans.

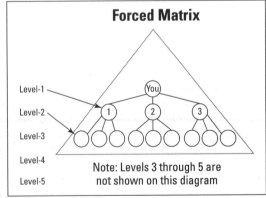

Figure 8-5:
An example
of a 3 x 5
Forced
Matrix plan.

Proponents of the Forced Matrix say they like the plan because a distributor anticipates that other members of the sales organization will create "spill over" to help fill the open spaces or even fill the spaces for them. In other words, as more senior distributors recruit new members, those members are placed in open spaces that are under the less-senior distributors. However, opponents say that's precisely what's wrong with the plan. "There's a lot of sizzle to selling this type of plan," says Ken Rudd. Distributors are led to believe that once they recruit a few people, they can depend on the organization to fill in all the open spaces. Bill Porter adds, "Distributors are led to believe they can sit back and let the organization do the work while they collect money and enjoy the beach!"

"The Forced Matrix creates a 'something for nothing' philosophy," explains Michael Sheffield. "A lot of people join with unrealistic expectations that never develop." That's because people who are attracted by a "something for nothing" philosophy tend to be lazy, or they don't do any work. "They were told they wouldn't have to do anything," adds Ken Rudd. "The computer would fill up their matrix." But that usually doesn't happen.

Even when distributors do their jobs and recruit new distributors, the plan has its drawbacks. An enrolling distributor has no control over the placement of new distributors. Plus, the matrix is limited by width and by depth. For example, a 3 x 5 matrix is limited to three legs and five levels. That means the distributor's income is limited by the size of the matrix.

This is not to say, however, that the Forced Matrix doesn't have a future. Some companies prefer it because it's easy to attract new distributors and it forces them to build an organization within a defined grid. It's particularly popular among Internet marketing and affiliate programs. Used in concert with other plans, or enhanced by other pay plan components, the Forced Matrix can be an attractive compensation method.

Considering Compensation Plans

As you consider compensation plans, keep this in mind: Any one or a combination of these plans can be used to build an exciting, dynamic, and long-term network marketing company. Your job is to ask questions about the plan before you join the company so that you can determine whether you can make money in return for your efforts. The easiest way to do that may be to ask existing distributors about the strengths and weaknesses of the pay plan. "The bottom line," says Louise Adrian, an independent consultant with Party Lite Gifts, "is how much am I going to earn, how quickly am I going to earn it, and do I feel I can do what's required?"

Evaluate compensation plans thoroughly. Look at several so that you have a good basis for comparison, and never, never sign on with an organization until you have evaluated that company on the basis of integrity and reputation.

Explaining how network marketing works: The Mama Ziglar Network

In the Zig Ziglar Network, we have developed a system of explaining network marketing in a way so simple, and yet so complete and honest, that our people tell us they can learn it in a matter of minutes. I call this the "Mama Ziglar Network," shown in the accompanying figure. My mother had 12 children, 11 of whom survived to adulthood. She had these children over a span of roughly 25 years, and she gave birth to her children one at a time with one exception, when she gave birth to twins. In network marketing, I believe it's wise to give birth to your network children — your distributors — one or two at a time. Then you inspire, train, and develop them to repeat the process. The better you

prepare your first level, the better they will prepare, teach, and train the second level and so forth.

In my mother's case, those 11 children produced 40 grandchildren. It's safe to say that my mother could never have had 40 children, but what she did was produce some producers. Just like in network marketing, all of the children she produced did not produce exactly as she did. In short, none of her children had 12 children. By way of example, one of her children had three children, but those three children produced 14 great-grandchildren. That will happen in your network, too. You'll have several "children" who will produce even more "grandchildren."

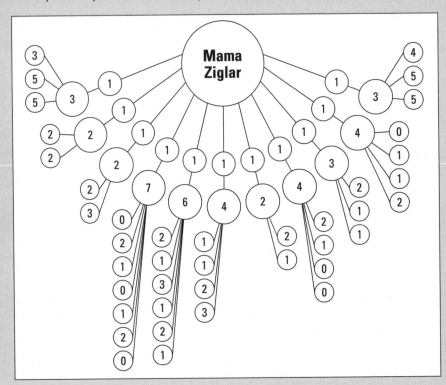

However, let me point out that one of my mother's children produced seven children, but those seven produced only six great-grandchildren. Actually, three of her grandchildren produced no great-grandchildren. One died in infancy, and the other two died before they could have children of their own. The same thing will happen in your organization. You will sponsor some who will do phenomenally well, others who won't do anything, and still others who will do a moderate job.

My mother was disappointed that some of her children and grandchildren did not produce more children. You will be disappointed in some of your "children," "grandchildren," and even "great-grandchildren," but that's part of network marketing. Just remember that if you sponsor, train, and develop them, they are more likely to be more productive.

Now the good news is this: My mother's 40 grandchildren produced 73 great-grandchildren, and who knows how many great-great- and great-great-great-grandchildren they will produce. That's the beauty of network marketing!

It took my mother more than 20 years to have her first grandchild, and an additional 20 years to have her first great-grandchild. In a matter of weeks or months in network marketing, you can have "children," "grandchildren," "great-grandchildren," and who knows how many

down the line? Even though the Zig Ziglar Network was only begun in early 2000, some of our distributors already have organizations that are 15 levels deep. In short, network marketing is exciting, and you can build an organization very quickly if you have a good plan and are willing to work that plan.

One more point: Here's the way we explain our compensation plan at ZZN. (I share with you only what we do in the Unilevel phase and won't get into the enrollment or generational bonuses.) If you look at the figure of the Mama Ziglar Network, you will see that Mama Ziglar had 11 frontline, or level 1, sponsors — her 11 children. Over a period of time in ZZN, you would probably have 11 on your frontline, too. Each month our computer program computes what 10 percent of your frontline's total sales volume amounts to, and then the computer issues you a check for that amount. We also pay 10 percent on the production of the 40 "grandchildren" in the Mama Ziglar example. On level 3, where there are 73 "great-grandchildren," the computer calculates the volume of production, and we send you a check for 15 percent of that volume. We then pay 5 percent of the volume of the next two levels. In short, when you look at the chart and look at the figures, you can easily figure out that network marketing really is quite simple and can be very rewarding.

Seeking a Balanced Compensation Plan

"More than anything," advises Ken Rudd, president of Premier Systems, Inc., a network marketing consulting firm based in Melbourne, Florida, "you want to be sure the compensation plan is balanced." That is, the plan should create opportunities for both full-time and part-time network marketers to succeed financially.

This section discusses the guidelines that help you recognize a balanced compensation plan.

A balanced compensation plan does the following:

- Pays the distributors fairly
- Allots reasonable purchase volumes so the distributors can easily remain active in the organization
- Rewards new distributors so that they can begin to make money quickly
- Offers features to distributors who work part-time
- Provides bonuses and substantial percentages for seasoned full-time distributors to maintain their loyalty to the company

Paying the distributors fairly

A balanced plan pays a *fair allocation* of sales revenues to the distributors. What's a fair allocation? It depends on whether the company is selling a product or a service, and even then it depends on the actual cost of each product or service. Speaking generally, Ken Rudd says, "A fair allocation is 40 percent to 50 percent of the company's total revenues. A company can't pay much more than 55 percent of its revenues to the distributors without strangling itself financially." However, some service companies may be able to pay out as much as 80 percent and still remain profitable. But anything less than 40 percent of revenues isn't fair. A company that pays out too small of a percentage won't motivate the distributors over a long period of time because they won't be able to earn enough money.

When you're evaluating companies, ask the management team to tell you the percentage of sales that's paid to the distributors.

Keeping product volume requirements within a reasonable range

Network marketing companies require distributors to maintain a certain level of monthly product volume to be considered active within the organization. Inactive distributors do not qualify for commission and bonus money, so this is an important consideration.

Typically, distributors need to spend $50 to $150 per month for products or services for resale to retail customers and/or personal consumption to satisfy the product volume requirement that entitles them to receive bonuses. Be careful, however. The price paid for a product or service may not be equal to the product volume assigned to the product or service by the company. Each company determines the product volume of its products and services, and commissions — *don't miss this!* — are calculated on product volume (or what some companies may call bonus volume) and not necessarily on sales volume.

For example, a product that sells to a distributor for $100 may be assigned a $75 product volume. Why? It's usually related to the margin, or markup, in the sale price of the product or service. The smaller the profit generated by the sale of the product, the less money that's available for the company to pay out to the distributors. The company assigns a product volume to the product or service, and hopefully does so reasonably. Otherwise, distributors could be required to spend large sums of money just to earn a high enough level of product volume to maintain their active status. In those cases, the comp plan is not a good one.

Use your company's autoship plan so that you don't forget to meet your monthly product volume requirement. Almost every network marketing company offers an autoship plan to its distributors, as well as to its retail customers. An *autoship* is a standing order. When you sign up for an autoship plan, you authorize the company to ship a specific order to you monthly and to continue doing so until you either change the order or terminate the plan. For example, you decide to purchase a monthly supply of nutritional products and vitamins from your company. As a matter of convenience, you can request this order on autoship so that you don't have to place the order month after month, 12 times a year. As much as you may appreciate that convenience, you may value the autoship option all the more because it's a good way to make sure you satisfy the monthly product volume requirement and thereby keep your active status. Imagine that you're expecting a check for $300 or $3,000 or even more at the end of a particular month, and it's not until after the month is over that you remember you forgot to place an order for that month! Sadly, without meeting the product volume, you're considered an inactive distributor, and you won't get a check for that month. You ·can reclaim active status by placing an order for the current month, but the previous month's commission and bonus money are lost forever. This has happened to many a sorrowful distributor. Don't let it happen to you.

Helping new distributors earn money fast

"Does the plan reward people who are just getting started in business?" Ken Rudd asks. If not, it's not a good plan. "The key to success in network marketing is to help a new distributor earn $300 to $500 within the first 90 days." Someone who earns that much money in a short period of time won't easily give it up. That's enough money to make a lifestyle change, such as paying for a new home or saving for a vacation. Once people make lifestyle changes, they usually don't quit. A good plan accommodates these people by rewarding them for making retail sales and recruiting new distributors.

Before investing in Nutrition for Life International, Dayle Maloney, the company's top earner, said he looked at 50 network marketing opportunities. "In each case, I was looking for one thing in particular," he explains. "Did the compensation plan take care of the 'little guy'?" Dayle describes the "little guy" as the person who is only looking to earn $500 a month. "Gosh, there's a place for them in network marketing," he says. "Not everybody comes into this business with multimillion-dollar dreams. A good compensation plan has to include these folks, too, or the business won't survive."

Creating a home for the part-time majority

"A balanced plan includes a legitimate opportunity for people who want to work part-time," explains Ken Rudd. Good compensation for part-timers is key because they make up the majority of the organization, solidly filling in the middle ground between newcomers and higher-ups. New distributors come and go rapidly, and senior distributors are highly paid, but they may be sitting back and enjoying the fruits of their labors. They're content to live off the productivity of their downlines. "The largest group in any network marketing company will be the people in the middle," Ken comments. "They'll require a pay plan that rewards them for their efforts and includes a lot of recognition as they earn their promotions. It's possible that these folks may convert to full-time distributors, but most of them will never work more than part-time."

Ken points out that a company of all generals and no privates doesn't have much of a future. "You need the leaders to recruit, to create the critical mass for your products and services, and to train," he says. "But you need the privates to build the company's infrastructure. The veterans won't be on board forever, and the part-timers are needed to replace them. Consequently, the compensation plan has to include features that will keep both of them happy."

Slapping golden handcuffs on seasoned distributors

Residual earnings in a network marketing compensation plan have to be large enough to attract and keep a professional networker committed to the company. The professional networker is the one who works full-time and teaches others how to succeed in the business. "After a while," says Ken Rudd, "the full-time networker won't have as much time to recruit. He or she will be busy training the downline. This is when it's important for the comp plan to pay this person 5 percent to 8 percent of revenues six or seven levels deep." Plus, the plan must include bonus opportunities and other features, such as a car payment or mortgage payment plan. Anything less won't capture the loyalty of professional network marketers. And that's not a good plan.

An ideal compensation plan rewards leaders by giving them a share of the company's annual revenues. Even a small percentage — 1 to 2 percent — can result, over time, in a huge chunk of money. People can't easily walk away from that size of a reward. That's why it's called slapping on the golden handcuffs!

A good compensation plan should afford you a good opportunity to make a reasonable sum of money fairly early and an unreasonable (that is, very large) amount of money later. However, if money is the only thing the plan offers, I encourage you to be wary of it, simply because it means there will be very little growth opportunity. Some people will end up holding the short end of the stick, with a finite amount of money and no room for growth.

Evaluating Compensation Plans

We don't expect you to join a network marketing company and blindly accept the compensation plan — even though that's precisely what happens most of the time. People get excited about the products, the services, and the opportunity to escape their jobs, and they overlook the comp plan. Although we think that's a mistake, we also think it's a mistake to refuse to get involved with a network marketing company until you're intimately familiar with the plan.

Dr. Clifton Jolley, a network marketing consultant in Dallas, Texas, says, "What you need to know about the compensation plan is: How much money am I going to make . . . what will I have to do to make it . . . and is it fair compensation for the work I'll have to do? In my point of view, that's the sensible way to examine a plan."

Network marketing veteran and trainer Tim Sales says, "I suggest you go from the product up to figure out how much money you'll earn. Ask these questions: If I sell the product, how much money do I get? How many of these products do I have to sell to earn $3,000 (or whatever amount you desire)? How much do I earn when I recruit a new distributor? How much money does the average distributor spend monthly (the company can answer that question for you), and what percentage of that money will I earn from my downline? . . . Answers to these questions will give you a sense of whether or not you can make any money."

Try not to think too much about making a fortune in network marketing, at least not until you've had some experience. Tom Paredes, who has become a millionaire as a distributor for Nutrition for Life International, advises: "Why worry about earning big paychecks? The average American earns $30,000 a year. So $500 a month will make a big difference in their lives. Everyone says they want to make more than that, and you can, but why worry about it when you're just getting started? You're not going to make big dollars overnight. When I started, I didn't focus on becoming a millionaire. I had more realistic dreams . . . like buying a new couch, a new car, and other material things that I just didn't have. A lot of people are anxious to dig into the compensation plan to find out how much it pays, when there are more important issues to be concerned about. I don't even explain the compensation plan when I invite people into my organization. If a company is fair and reasonable, it's going to have a good compensation plan."

We think Jim Bruce is right when he says that most people won't truly understand the compensation plan until they've experienced it. Jim is an associate with the Small Business Club of America. He continues, "When you get promoted, when you get paid, when you can look at your check and understand why you earned that amount of money, then you'll begin to understand the plan."

Jim cautions, "If the person who's recruiting you talks primarily about the compensation plan and little about the company's products or services, ask yourself, 'Is the product or service of good value, and would I buy it if there were no income opportunity with it?' Be wary of opportunities sold primarily on the basis of their financial compensation. Consider value offered to the customer."

Questions to ask about a company's compensation plan

Mike Cheves and Nick Gasaway are authorities on compensation plans. They're also associates of the Zig Ziglar Network. They suggest that you ask the following questions about a company's compensation plan to help you decide whether it will be good for you:

✔ **Do you get paid just for recruiting people or for recruiting people who buy a product or service?** If the plan pays just for recruiting, beware! It's probably a pyramid scheme. "Recruiting people who don't purchase a product or service is really dangerous," explains Mike. "Regulators look closely at those deals and move quickly to shut them down."

✔ **Do you have to spend $100 to earn $50 in personal volume?** (See the section "Keeping product volume requirements within a reasonable range," earlier in this chapter.)

Your personal volume (PV) — reflecting the amount of money you spend each month on the company's products or services — determines your status in the company's pay plan. Fall short on PV credits in any given month, and you may lose a big chunk, if not all, of your income, or not qualify for a bonus. Companies assign different values to different products and services, so ask for clarification. You don't want to get stuck paying large amounts of money to the company just so you can earn enough PV to qualify for a bonus that may not even cover the amount of money you spent that month!

✔ **Are time and effort proportionate to the money you can earn?** "Make no mistake about this," advises Nick. "You must be ready to devote time and effort to your downline to help the members succeed. A productive downline needs to be trained and encouraged — that's the role of the sponsor. But if you spend the time in this role, will you be rewarded financially?" Discuss this issue with existing distributors; they'll tell you whether training your downline is worth your time.

✔ **Does the pay plan compress so that product volume rolls up when a distributor doesn't qualify for a paycheck?** If a distributor under you doesn't qualify for commission in a particular month — maybe because his PV was too low, and he's inactive for the month — your commission check will be less by what would have been your share of that distributor's volume. Doesn't seem fair, does it? You only earn commission on the product volume of a finite number of levels, and if there's no volume on one of those levels, you lose money, even though you had no control over the situation. But no distributor gets paid on the volume of an inactive distributor. In fact, the company can keep whatever commission would have been paid out on the inactive distributor's product volume.

However, when there's an inactive distributor, a good pay plan automatically compresses and "rolls up" the next distributor by one position. By doing so, all the distributors above the inactive distributor earn a commission for what otherwise would have been a level with no volume. That next distributor's product volume carries forward, and the distributors above the inactive distributor are paid commission on that volume. The replacement product volume could be equal to, lower than, or higher than the inactive distributor's volume. Even if it's lower, it's better to get commission on some volume than no commission at all. And if the volume is higher, no one will complain — except, perhaps, the inactive distributor who earned no money that month!

"Look for a compensation plan that compresses the volume," says Mike, "so that everyone who's active can get paid the maximum amount of money."

✔ **How often does the company include special incentives in its pay plan?** "Incentive plans motivate distributors to sell more products and services during certain times of the year or during the holidays," explains Nick. "They also help increase sales levels during normally slow periods. Does the company periodically offer these plans?" You can find out by asking the company's leadership.

✔ **Do you understand what you need to do to get promoted in the organization?** Mike recommends that you draw an organizational chart so that you can easily see what you have to do to get promoted. "How many people will you need in your downline, and where should they be placed to maximize your opportunities for promotion? If it looks too hard to achieve the top tiers of the promotion schedule, it probably is. Ask existing distributors or members of the company's management team to tell you how many people have earned the top titles. If it's only a few and the company has been in business for several years, you might want to look elsewhere."

Although you need to do as much analysis of a company's compensation plan as possible, ultimately you will have to take a leap of faith and become a distributor. That's why we urge you to make sure that you believe in the product or service that you're going to sell. On the chance that the compensation doesn't develop the way it was promised or anticipated, at least you'll never have to spend a sleepless night worrying that you sold something inferior.

Questions You Should Ask Before You Join a Network Marketing Organization

As one last safeguard to help you understand the compensation plan of the company that you're considering, and as a means of ascertaining that the compensation plan will reward you fairly and adequately for your investment of time and money, seek answers to these questions before you join a company:

- ✔ Does the company tell you in understandable terms what volume of activity you must maintain in order to receive the residual income — commissions and any bonuses — from your downline?

- ✔ Do you expect the company or your upline to recruit people into your downline or to do your work for you?

- ✔ Has your intended sponsor or any other member of the company told you how much money you can earn by joining the company? If so, are you satisfied that he or she substantiated these claims?

- ✔ If you're planning to work part-time, does the compensation plan include features that will be attractive to you?

- ✔ If you're planning to work full-time and make a career of network marketing, does the compensation plan include features that will interest you for the long-term?

Part III
Signing Up and Setting Up for Success

The 5th Wave   By Rich Tennant

"I think Dick Foster should head up that new network marketing initiative. He's got the vision, the drive, and let's face it—that big white hat doesn't hurt either."

In this part . . .

*O*nce you've decided that network marketing belongs in your future, and you've joined a company and become a distributor, you don't want to miss a step as you prepare to get fully engaged in the business. Yes, this *is* a business. Hobbyists, please look elsewhere!

Network marketing demands your attentiveness to details such as legal requirements and accounting procedures. You will want to be sure your business meets all local and state licensing regulations. You will also want to organize your business financially so that it satisfies all pertinent tax codes; there's no sense making a lot of money just to pay it out to the tax collectors! Consequently, we suggest you discuss your business plans with key advisors and, again, we tell you how to proceed.

Early in your business, it's important for you, as well as those you sponsor, to get a quick start. The fact is: most people who get into network marketing quit! However, those who earn just a few hundred dollars a month are very likely to remain in business over a long period of time. So plan on getting a quick start, and learn how to help your new recruits get a quick start. Through training and preparation you can do it — and we show you how in this part of the book.

Chapter 9

Organizing Your Business

• •

In This Chapter

▶ Protecting your business by operating it as a business

▶ Consulting with professional advisors

▶ Partnering up: the pros and cons

▶ Doing business from home

▶ Getting help from the corporate office and your upline

• •

"**W**ait a minute," you say, "I've never owned a business before and I don't know the first thing about how to structure one. Do I need an attorney? Should I register my company with the state or my county? Am I going to be scrutinized by the Internal Revenue Service? So far I like what I hear about starting my own network marketing business, but what am I getting into legally?"

Relax! Operating a business isn't as complicated as it may seem. This chapter includes the major steps that you need to consider, with the help of several experts, including a business lawyer and a financial adviser, to set up your business for success. But don't jump to any conclusions; we are *not* providing business advice. Before you start your business, we urge you to consult with your own legal and financial advisers!

Network Marketing Is Not a Hobby

Whether you plan to work 6 hours or 60 hours a week as a network marketer, treating your business like a hobby is a mistake. Do you know anyone who's made money from a hobby? Once in a while it may happen, but it doesn't happen in network marketing. We're all for hobbies. They're great tension breakers, and they serve a purpose in our lives, but a hobby is not supposed to be a moneymaking proposition. If it is, it's no longer a hobby, and the Internal Revenue Service (IRS) will be the first to tell you so!

"If you plan to take advantage of the tax treatment of your network marketing business, it has to be a real business," says Jeffrey A. Babener, a Portland, Oregon–based attorney who advises network marketing companies and practitioners nationwide. The IRS says that if you're going to claim business expenses as a network marketer, then you must engage in the business as a for-profit enterprise.

The IRS uses two tests to determine whether your enterprise is a hobby or a business. First, the revenue collectors expect you to make a profit in three of five years in business. Second, you must be able to demonstrate that you are engaged in the business so that you can make a profit. "The IRS is looking to see whether or not you carry on the business in a businesslike manner," explains Jeffrey. Among other criteria, the IRS considers the time and effort you put into the business, the degree to which you depend on income from the business, and whether or not you have developed expertise in the business. (That last criterion makes a good argument for attending company training sessions.)

Bottom line: When you become a network marketer, get fully engaged in the activity of building a business!

Setting Up Your Business

The time to seek professional advice from a business attorney and an accountant is shortly before you join a network marketing company. If you already have a business attorney and an accountant, you may be tempted to skip this section of the book. However, the following paragraphs include information specific to network marketing that you will find useful.

There are several ways to structure a business entity, and no one way is right for everyone. Only your accountant and your attorney can help you make the best decisions. However, by reading the information that follows and becoming educated about your options, you can save yourself time and money when you meet with your professional advisers.

Selecting a business attorney

Just because you're going to spend only a few hundred dollars (or less) to join a network marketing company, don't assume that you won't need an attorney. Chances are, you'll *rarely* need an attorney, but it's a good idea to know one and to have consulted with him or her before you launch your business.

Select an attorney who is knowledgeable about business opportunities, and preferably one who has advised network marketers. How do you find these attorneys? Ask your sponsor for referrals. In the age of the Internet, you do not have to rely on a local attorney, but if a local attorney is your preference, then ask local members of your organization for recommendations.

Don't be intimidated by attorneys, and don't assume that they're all out to take advantage of you. Pick up the phone and call an attorney, or perhaps make your initial inquiry by e-mail. Explain that you're starting a network marketing business. Ask the attorney to tell you about experiences he or she has had with network marketing companies or business opportunities.

Ask the attorney how much he or she charges. You may be surprised. The attorney may advise you by phone or e-mail and charge a minimal fee. On the other hand, depending on the business format that you select and your personal situation (we discuss those issues a bit later), you may need to buy several hours of an attorney's time.

Selecting an accountant

Before you get too far down the road in your new business, consult with an accountant. Once again, look for a professional who is experienced with business opportunities, preferably network marketing companies. You may find just the accountant you're looking for through the Century Small Business Solutions Web site (`www.centurysmallbiz.com`) or the American Express Small Business Web site (`www.americanexpress.com`). Many of the business advisers in these two name-brand companies are familiar with network marketing opportunities. Because they serve small businesses, these advisers are usually well-versed in home-based businesses, too, which we discuss in more detail later in this chapter.

Accounting services are extremely competitive, and as with any other service, you get what you pay for. Contact accountants just the way you contact attorneys. Ask about their fees. Often, the initial consultation is free. You will need the ongoing services of an accountant as you build your business. If you're working the business part-time, you may need your accountant only a couple of times during the year; but if network marketing is your full-time occupation, it's smart to keep your accountant in the loop every month.

"When I started my network marketing business," explains Priscilla Harrison of Greensboro, North Carolina, "I didn't have a clue how to keep my books or how to set up my home-based business." Priscilla's husband, an airline captain who earned a substantial income, insisted that his wife consult with an accountant at the outset of her business. "When you're only working part-time, as I was at first," explains Priscilla, "and you're not making a lot of money, you don't give much thought about tracking your expenses or filing taxes. But based on my husband's advice, I immediately contacted an accountant."

It was a good thing, too. Priscilla worked full-time as a dental hygienist, her 20-year occupation, and devoted 15 to 20 additional hours a week to her network marketing business. Today, Priscilla is a full-time distributor of Starlight, which markets a variety of health and wellness products. She relies on her accountant more than ever these days — at the time of our interview, her commission check had jumped to $42,000 a month! Priscilla's accountant also introduced her to an investment adviser who set up three accounts for her: one for retirement, another for investing, and a third for taxes. "Every month, I automatically deduct money from my checking account for my investment account and my tax account. The automatic deductions force me to save and to have the money I need to pay my quarterly taxes. I pay into my retirement account once a year. These accounts have removed a lot of stress from my business, and they help me make money!"

Choosing the business format that makes sense for you

You can operate your business as a sole proprietorship, or you may decide to file for incorporation. Setting up a sole proprietorship is easy, whereas filing for incorporation is complex and costly. However, these are issues that you must discuss with your attorney and accountant. You need to consider your personal financial situation, your tax obligations, and certain other business matters when choosing a business format, and your professional advisers are prepared to guide you.

In the early stages of building their businesses, before they're making a lot of money, most network marketers choose to operate as sole proprietors. Unlike the process of incorporation, there are few formalities, if any, to setting up a sole proprietorship. Plus, it's inexpensive. The only requirement is that you comply with state and local licensing laws. Your attorney or accountant can advise you about any such laws.

If you plan to operate your business under a name other than your own — for example, Over the Top Enterprises — then you'll be required to file a fictitious business name registration at your courthouse. It's not a big deal. It's usually a one-page form. You list the name of your new business, show evidence that you're who you say you are (a birth certificate will do), and pay the clerk of courts a small fee, and you're ready to conduct business. If you plan to open a checking account in the name of your business and apply for a business credit card, the bank will ask to see the fictitious name registration form.

Making a case for liability insurance

Joe and Blake Gecinger, a father and son accounting team within the Century Small Business Solutions franchise network, represent Priscilla Harrison, the successful Starlight distributor mentioned earlier in this chapter. Joe was once a network marketer, so he's intimately familiar with the concept. "We want to make certain that we do everything possible to help protect the personal assets of our clients," explains Joe, "and that means we've got to consider more than the business format. A network marketing company usually indemnifies its distributors from lawsuits that may pop up now and then. But that won't necessarily prevent a client from being named in a lawsuit. Extricating yourself from a lawsuit or building your defense can be costly. That's why we recommend liability insurance to our clients. We also encourage them to discuss their liabilities with their attorneys."

Sole proprietorship is the most popular option among network marketers, but it's important for you to understand that as a sole proprietor you are personally liable for your business. You place your personal assets and wealth at risk with this option. When you file Articles of Incorporation, you establish a separate legal and tax entity that provides you with limited liability benefits and a different schedule of taxation. An incorporated business minimizes your risks. The details are complex, and you should rely on your professional advisers for guidance.

Disseminating information is one of the greatest services performed by the United States government, and if you know your way around the Web, getting your hands on all types of information related to starting and developing a business is easy. You really don't have to look any further than the home page of the U.S. Small Business Administration: www.sba.gov. From the SBA's home page, click on the Starting link, and then on Startup Kit. The SBA provides a comprehensive resource guide, free for the downloading, that provides pages of details about establishing your business.

All 50 states in the United States regulate businesses, although some are more protective than others. Want to know what your state requires of a new business? You can also access the home pages of all 50 states from www.sba.gov.

Going into Business with a Partner

Husbands and wives, fathers and daughters, brothers-in-law and sisters-in-law — you find these and many other partnerships in network marketing. The word *partnership* is used loosely in network marketing, as it is in traditional business. Basically, it's a term that describes two or more people who work together to build a business. The implication is that the partners share responsibility for the business, as well as ownership. When the business generates a profit, the partners share the money. When the business generates tax liability, the partners share the expense. However, not all partnerships work that way. There's no one law that governs partnerships, at least not in the United States. People can call themselves partners without filing any legal paperwork. They can decide among themselves who owns what percentage of the business, and they're free to determine how the profits will be divided or the expenses shared. Husbands and wives may not give their business partnership a second thought. It's an extension of an already legally binding marriage. Unfortunately, however, not all partnerships work out, and when a dispute arises and the partners cannot resolve it, they start asking: Who owns what? Who's responsible for what? At that point, it may be too late to resolve any difference amicably. Therefore, it's a good idea to formalize partnerships with a legal agreement prepared by a business attorney.

Many partnerships work extremely well; others work initially and then fall apart. If you go into business with one or more partners, make sure that you're fully aware of the advantages and disadvantages of your relationship. Here are some important questions for you to consider and answer:

- ✔ Do you own an equal share of the partnership, or does one partner control the business? The controlling partner can make decisions that you may not like. As equal partners, you can make decisions together.

- ✔ What are your responsibilities? Do they differ from your partner's responsibilities? Sometimes partners divide responsibilities. For example, one oversees sales, another marketing, another operations, and so on. Know who's responsible for every facet of the business.

- ✔ What happens if you don't get along and you decide to end your relationship? Can one partner buy out the other? It's probably too late to answer these questions amicably in the midst of a dispute. That's why it's better to decide at the outset of the business relationship how to terminate the relationship.

- ✔ Are you free to start over again in the same business? You are unless you agreed otherwise. Many partnership agreements include a non-compete clause. Again, check this out with your business attorney.

Partnerships, even among family members, can be tricky, so if you plan to be involved in one, or you already are, think carefully about the ramifications. Your local library includes numerous books on the subject of partnerships. Reading one or more of them may be helpful even before you consult with a business attorney.

Teamwork is critical, particularly in a close relationship in which you have two people working a business, such as husband and wife or two friends. My friend and mentor Fred Smith says that you never really get to know people until you have financial dealings with them. I believe he's right.

In my own life, my wife and I are on the same page. I can tell you without hesitation that if it were not for the parts she brings to the team, my career would not be even close to where it is today. Yes, that harmony is important.

A good partnership is like a symphony orchestra. If each musician were allowed to play whatever notes he or she chose, you would not have harmony — you would have noise. But when the conductor steps up to the podium and raises the baton, all the musicians get into the ready position. When he or she brings the baton down, indicating the time to start, beautiful music results. That's what a partnership should make — the equivalent of beautiful music as two people work together.

Jimmy and Carol Bishop are a dynamic husband and wife team who have been partners in network marketing since 1986. Fun-loving and energetic, this twosome from Waxahachie, Texas, says network marketing is a great way to build a business and develop new relationships. Even so, they've been through some emotional ups and downs. Fortunately, when one was down, the other was up, and that's how they've helped each other through the tough times.

One sweltering summer day, Jimmy called Carol from a phone booth and told her to write down a telephone number. "Why?" she wanted to know. Jimmy explained that he saw the number on a business card that posed the question, "Are you sick and tired of being sick and tired?" Carol recalls that Jimmy was "just flat sick" because he had been working in 105-degree Texas heat, delivering furniture for their family business of 30 years. Carol, on the other hand, wasn't sick and tired at all. "I had a nice cushiony job in our air-conditioned office, so I wasn't really interested in that phone number."

When they called the number, a Nu Skin representative invited them to a business meeting in Dallas, about a half-hour drive up the highway. "We met a lot of people who seemed very excited about their products and their business, and I liked what I saw," Carol recalls. Suddenly she was interested. "I'm the kind of person who doesn't want anything getting by me!" But when Jimmy discovered that he and Carol were at a network marketing meeting, he wasn't so excited anymore. Carol persuaded Jimmy to work the business with her, and he did, but only half-heartedly. After six months, they quit. Jimmy explains, "I just didn't understand networking at the time."

Four years later, Jimmy understood what he was missing after he and Carol attended an Amway meeting. "That's where we both caught the dream of network marketing," explains Carol. For several years in the early 1990s, the Bishops built a successful Amway business, but then one day Carol pooped out. Jimmy found her in the living room one evening when he thought she was getting ready to join him at a presentation that he was going to make for a couple of Amway prospects. "Jimmy was dressed in his blue suit," Carol remembers, "and he thought I would be dressed up, too. But I was leveraged out! Jimmy asked if I was ready, and I said, 'Yes, I'm ready to sit down in the living room and watch a movie . . . and Jimmy, I'm not doing network marketing anymore.' Poor Jimmy worked the business alone for a while, but then he quit, too."

Once Carol said "no more network marketing," she held on to those words as tightly as she could, even when her daughter joined Excel Communications. "She wanted us to go to a meeting with her," says Carol, "and Jimmy was all for it, but I wouldn't do it because I know network marketing is like a malady. Once you got it, you got it!" Well, Carol *had* it; she just didn't know it. With some coaxing from Jimmy, the twosome attended an Excel meeting, and they became distributors in that organization and repeated their earlier success.

Today, Jimmy and Carol Bishop are founding associates of the Zig Ziglar Network, and they've never agreed with each other more about their commitment to network marketing. "We feel very fortunate for all the training we've received in the last 15 years," says Carol, "because it got us ready for what Zig Ziglar has offered us. We love network marketing, and I doubt that either one of us would ever give up on it again." Jimmy smiles in agreement!

Defining the key elements of a successful partnership

"There is always strength in numbers," advises Jeff Roberti, a Florida-based network marketer who has built two huge organizations, first for Herbalife, where he earned $100,000 annually when he was just 21, and since 1987, for NSA, where he has amassed a fortune as one of the company's leaders. "I have partnerships in all areas of my life," Jeff explains, "and I like partnerships because they provide an opportunity to focus on helping other people get what they want from life, which in turn helps me get what I want." Jeff readily admits, however, that partnerships don't always work. "They're not for everyone," he says, "and if you're going to get into one, make sure certain key elements exist." What are those key elements? Jeff lists them as follows:

✓ **A clear understanding between the partners:** Who's responsible for doing what in the business?

✓ **Acceptance of each other's outcomes and responsibilities:** Partnerships are no fun if one partner is blaming the other partner all the time or if one partner steps on the other partner's toes.

✓ **Tremendous communication:** Partners need to know what each party is thinking, planning, and dreaming. If you were in business on your own, you wouldn't have to verbalize as much. But in a partnership, you need to explain what you're doing before you do it.

✓ **Similar values and character traits:** Like-minded people succeed in partnerships. It's good to have different and complementary skill sets, but you must trust each other and like each other before you can form a loyalty bond.

Considering the talents of the partners

Building a network marketing business — or any business, for that matter — requires a variety of talents, and few people begin a business career with all of those talents intact. Selling, for example, is a talent that takes practice. So is marketing. Understanding the financial side of the business is another talent. Most people need to develop at least one or more of these talents, and that's why a partnership can be a huge advantage. Partners can rely on each other's strengths to make up for their own weaknesses.

Bob Schwenkler is an engineer by training, and his wife, Trish, is a former housewife who had a bad back until she discovered the Nikken network marketing company in 1983. Since then, the Schwenklers, who live in Boise, Idaho, have built a sales organization of 20,000 people. They are Royal Diamonds with Nikken, which means that they are only one level away from the very top of the business. It also means that they earn more than $1 million annually!

But this is a success story that would never have come to life if Trish had listened to "Negative Bob." He thought it was fine for his wife to buy the Nikken products that helped her aching back — a backpad and a bed to begin with — but when she wanted to get more products to share with others as part of Nikken's business opportunity, his advice was, "Don't."

"I'm glad she didn't listen to me!" says Bob, who's been committed full-time to Nikken for several years.

During our interview, Bob repeatedly mentioned that Trish built the business. She sponsored people far and wide, and in fact, at the time of the interview, she was on the road training the people in her downline. "We're a little different than many couples who are in network marketing," Bob explained. "Oftentimes, it's the man who's out on the road and the woman who's left behind to tend to the details. But I'm the engineer! I'm better at the details, like handling the phone calls and providing our distributor network with information on our Web site and writing our newsletter. Trish does what she does best, and I do what I do best."

By considering each other's talents, Bob and Trish find it easy to make their partnership work. You may, too, if you follow their example.

Agreeing to disagree

Some days, even in the best of times, partners do not agree. It's just human nature. Network marketing is a high-energy business. Getting excited about networking is easy, especially when things are going well, when products are moving, when the downline is growing and succeeding, and when the paychecks are getting fatter! Conversely, when things are going wrong, getting depressed is just as easy. Then one partner decides that if such and such were the case, the business could prosper, but another partner disagrees. Who's right? Frankly, what difference does it make? If the partners don't agree and they allow their differences to come between them, the business doesn't have a future.

So what do you do? From day one in your partnership, you should agree to disagree. For example, suppose that you and a friend form a partnership. You're responsible for sponsoring and training the people in your downline, and your partner is responsible for the behind-the-scenes, detail-oriented work. You agree not to cross into each other's area of responsibility. At one of your planning meetings, your partner says that she wants to buy a new computer program to manage the company's finances. You don't think the business needs a new computer program because the old one seems to be working just fine. However, because you're not involved in managing the company's finances, you don't make an issue of it. You may state your opinion, but that's as far as you take it. You've agreed to disagree.

Of course, it's not always so simple. On occasion, partners disagree philosophically, or they disagree about major issues, such as how to reinvest money in the company or when to personally withdraw profits. Once again, if you've agreed to disagree, you may save your partnership. Until you both agree on a major issue, don't make changes. The downside of such an agreement is that you must be willing to live by the decision. If you're not able to, then a breakup is inevitable.

Even then, you will have saved yourself a lot of heartache and legal positioning if you agreed to the terms of your breakup in advance of forming the relationship. We don't believe in premarital contracts, but business relationships are not necessarily bound forever, or until death ends the partnership. In business, planning for the downside is prudent, especially when the business is unpredictable.

In a good partnership, when the partners disagree, they're basically disagreeing on a procedure and not on a principle or philosophy. That's the reason you need to be very careful about the people with whom you form partnerships. You can compromise on procedure, but principles and philosophy are entirely different. Above all things, explore to make sure that philosophically and principally you and your partner are together. You can work out the other details in most cases.

Working from Home

Millions of people work from home in countries throughout the world. And they are often the envy of people who have to dress up every morning and dodge traffic to get to work. Lee Lemons is a network marketer who works from his 7,200-square-foot home in a gated community of Desoto, Texas. Because Lee sold long-distance phone services as a distributor for Excel Communications, people used to call him "the phone man." Now that he's successful and earning large commissions, he's the one having fun. "Lots of mornings I tease the doctors and other professionals who live in our community," he says. "I stand at the gate in my jogging clothes and wave as they're rushing off to work."

Network marketing is the type of business that can be operated from any city, large or small. The marketplace is geographically unlimited, because the primary way to reach the market is by phone, and now via the Internet. Consequently, you can set your work hours to accommodate your family's schedule — or any other schedule. Talk about doing things the way you like to do them — network marketing offers you that opportunity, particularly when it comes to setting up your work environment.

By establishing a work environment and a routine, you're likely to take your business more seriously. Plus, you're demonstrating to others — family members, neighbors, occasional visitors, and don't forget the IRS — that you really do have a business and not a hobby. Establishing your daily routine, setting a work schedule, and having the tools available to conduct your business efficiently, such as tracking your expenses and income, all contribute to a productive work environment. Following are some points for you to consider about working from home. See Chapter 10 for additional information about physically setting up your home office.

Running a business from home

Attorney Jeffrey Babener, who writes extensively about network marketing laws and regulations, offers some suggestions for running a business from home. You can read more on this topic at Jeffrey's Web site: www.mlmlegal.com.

Select a name carefully. You get only one chance to make a first impression. The name of your business is what most people see or hear first. Think about the name before you select one — be sure that it is descriptive and easy to remember.

Open a checking account. If you're serious about your business, you need a separate business account. You need the account for tax purposes, but opening an account is also visible evidence of your commitment and decision to go into business for yourself.

Apply for a sales tax license, if necessary. If you purchase products at wholesale and sell them to retail customers, and *you* collect the money as opposed to your company collecting the money (which is rarely the case), you may be required to pay sales taxes. If you're required to pay the sales taxes, you need to apply for a sales tax license. That's usually a simple process that involves filling out a form or two. To be on the safe side, verify the regulations for your state with your accountant.

Organize your paperwork. Buy a box of file folders from your office supply store. Set up separate files for Prospects, Sales, Follow-Up, Tax Info, Expense Receipts, and so on. Doing so will help you organize your business.

Establishing your daily routine

It's important to establish a daily routine when working from home. It may seem elementary, but developing a business-like attitude is easier if you stick to a daily schedule. When you're working from home and on your own, there's no one to check up on you, no one to nag you to make phone calls or complete projects, and no one to assist you, either! Set a schedule and live by it. Doing so is the easiest way to discipline yourself for success while working from home.

After you establish your work hours, respect them. If you plan to be at your desk (or the kitchen table, if that's where you work) at 9 a.m., show up on time. When it's time to quit for the day, quit! God didn't create us to work *all* the time.

ZIG SAYS

Setting a schedule and falling into your rhythm

My professional career as a salesman started in the cookware industry, where we sold heavy-duty, waterless cookware on a direct sales basis. The first two and a half years were a real struggle; financially, we were in hot water all the time. Then P. C. Merrell, a visiting supervisor who spoke at a training session I attended, persuaded me that I should go to work every day at exactly the same time, regardless of what time I finished the night before. He said, "The time you set is not important, but that you have a time and adhere to it strictly every day is critical."

Because it was often 11 or 12 o'clock at night when I got home, I didn't feel a compulsion to get up too early the next morning because I needed a certain amount of rest to be effective. From that point on, that's exactly what I did.

Interestingly enough, I don't ever remember looking forward to knocking on the first door at 9 a.m. Or, for that matter, the second, third, or fourth door. But by the fifth door, I was warming up to the occasion and starting to look forward to the next door.

The previous year, my success had been minimal. That year, though, with the simple adjustment in procedure — combined with an entirely different and more confident attitude that Mr. Merrell had imparted to me — I finished number two in the nation out of over 7,000 salespeople and had the best promotion the company had to offer. The next year I was the highest-paid field manager in the United States.

The major part of this success came from the fact that my consistency dramatically improved. I don't remember a single week I finished in the top 20 in sales or a single month when I finished in the top 20; but at the end of the year, I was number two in sales in the country because I had no blank weeks. Every week produced business.

That end result is what you'll find in network marketing when you discipline yourself to follow a schedule.

You'll find that much of your work is repetitive from day to day: reading and listening to tapes to motivate and educate yourself about your business and products; calling prospects to attract them to your business; calling existing customers to refill orders and tell them about additional products; *calling more prospects;* answering correspondence from your customers, the people in your upline and your downline, and the corporate office; *calling more prospects;* conducting three-way conference calls with members of your downline or upline; *calling more prospects;* participating in company conference calls; *calling more prospects* . . . and don't forget to schedule time for lunch and a break now and then.

Use your break time for a trip to the post office or your local mail center to send audio- or videotapes to prospects who asked to receive them. Also, use your break time for things you need to get done — picking up the kids at school, dropping off the laundry at the dry cleaner's, getting the oil changed in the car, for instance. Working at home allows you this flexibility. Hey, if you want to, you can even drive a friend to the airport. Just make sure that your breaks don't consume your day because the best way to build your business, as you've probably figured out by now, is to *call more prospects!*

"The hardest part of building a house is digging the hole, doing the grunt work, and getting the dirt out of the way so you can build a foundation," explains Starlight International distributor Priscilla Harrison. "The same is true of network marketing. Knowing where to spend your time, and with whom, is a challenge." Get rid of that challenge by knowing how to identify your leaders and scheduling your work every day!

Overcoming loneliness

Loneliness is a major complaint among people who work from home, especially if they formerly worked in an environment where they were constantly surrounded by people. "It *is* lonely," says Louise Adrian, a ten-year veteran of Party Lite Gifts in Canada. "But when you build a network marketing business, you work with your team or sales organization, and you'll soon find that you are around people who are much more positive than the people you were around before. And with the Internet, connections are endless."

Louise created a support group in Vancouver, British Columbia, consisting of seven women from seven different home party plan companies. "We're all in the middle management tiers of our companies," she explains, "and we meet monthly for lunch to talk about a different business topic. Sponsoring is a good topic, for example, and when we discuss it, we bring our training materials, and we talk about what works for us, and then we go back to our own teams and share that information. It's fabulous!" Louise says the members do not try to sponsor each other — that is, sell their business opportunities to each other — but they do buy each other's products. "We're best customers to each other, and we learn a lot from each other."

For those who feel lonely working from home, or who desire more social interaction as network marketers, Louise suggests: "Put out feelers and ask who else is selling products in your area. Bring those people together, and you'll have a great support network."

Convincing others that you still have a job

The bane of a home office is that people think you don't have a job! "Hi, John," comes the friendly phone call, "we need a ride to the airport tomorrow at 10 a.m. and since you don't go to work, we're wondering if you can help us out."

What do you do? Help a friend and possibly hurt your business? Or say no and possibly hurt a friend? The first thing you should do is explain to your friends, family, and relatives that even though you're at home every day, you really *do* have a job. Your hours are 9 a.m. to 5 p.m., or 6 p.m. to 9 p.m., or whatever you desire. And during those hours, you're just as busy and committed as they are when they go to work!

After your neighbors discover that you're at home during the day, they tend to drop in for coffee or ask if you'll watch their children until *they* get home from work. You just can't do it, and the sooner you make it known that you *work* at home, the better.

Most people who work at home are confronted with an ongoing problem: Their friends and relatives think they no longer have jobs. When Julie Norman, my daughter, agreed to be the editor for my newspaper column and books, she was confronted with that problem constantly. Because of the kind of person she is, if anyone asked for her help, she found it extraordinarily difficult to say no. As a result, she sometimes found herself working all night to make certain that we met our deadlines. Obviously, this sort of situation does not lead to long-term health, happiness, and, for that matter, productivity. It didn't work for her, and it won't work for you, either.

So what is the solution? When someone approaches you on the premise that, because you don't have a job, she would appreciate your help, your response should be a very pleasant and friendly, "Oh, but I do have a job. As a matter of fact, it's the best job I've ever had because it's my own business. I'm having more fun working, and I'm actually going to have more money, and I'll be helping more people in the process."

You may recognize this response as the first step to getting that person into the business as well, but even if that doesn't happen, it will help you to establish that, yes, you do have a job. In fact, it's more than just a job; it's your own business! You should use this response from the moment you start working from your home. It's amazing, but the word spreads very quickly that, yes, you are working, and that cuts off many requests.

Obviously, if you would leave an office job to help a friend or a family member who has an emergency, you would do the same thing now. You are still a loving, concerned, and caring friend or relative. But establishing specific work hours and spending a certain amount of time working every week are essential. Otherwise, you will become what we call a *wandering generality,* when you need to become a *meaningful specific* if you're going to be successful in your network marketing business.

I'll be the first to recognize the fact that many habits are difficult to break. A neighbor who, for some time, has been periodically dropping in unannounced at 10:30 a.m. for a long cup of coffee will have to be discouraged in a pleasant but friendly way. The first time it happens after you've set your schedule, invite her to come in; then explain that you have a deadline and will have only 15 minutes to visit. Then at the end of the 15 minutes, say, "I'm sorry, but I have a commitment that I must meet, and I have to get busy doing that." Then stand up to clearly signal that the visit is over. If your neighbor or relative repeats the process the next day, this time say, "I'd love to do this, but I'm so excited about my work and feel so much responsibility to meet my deadline, I'll have to pass this time. Tell you what I'll do. I'll give you a call when we can get back together, and I won't be in such a rush."

Of course, you need to understand that you can't work all the time. I don't believe we were put here to be one-track, one-direction people. You still must look after the other things in your personal and family life. Just remember to always be courteous and pleasant, and chances are pretty good that the day will come when your neighbor, friend, or relative will be curious enough to ask what's so important that you're so committed to getting it done. I believe you'll find this approach will work. My daughter did.

Tracking income and expenses

Network marketing is a business, not a hobby, and you may need to prove that it's a business to your friendly tax collector!

Get used to tracking your income and expenses. Income is a lot easier to track than expenses. Even when your commission check amounts to tens of thousands of dollars a month, it still arrives only once a month, or at most, once a week. At the end of the calendar year, your corporate office will send you a Form 1099 that documents (for you, the IRS, your state, and even your city government) the amount of gross income you received for the year.

No matter how big or small the earnings, reducing the taxable income to as small an amount as possible is prudent. If you want to keep all the income that you are legally allowed, make a habit of tracking your expenses *every day*. Use a journal or a software program and consult with your accountant.

Making bookkeeping easy

"I don't know about bookkeeping or accounting, and I never had to track expenses before," says Melynda Lilly, a Fort Worth, Texas, representative of Discovery Toys, which markets toys through home parties. "There are some things that I didn't even know I could deduct as an expense. For example, I look through the newspaper for certain kinds of ads, so I write off the expense of paying for the newspaper. My mileage is a deduction because I'm dropping off catalogs and driving to parties that I conduct. Since my business is in my home, I write off a portion of the utility bills. Since I'm in the toy business, I can write off some of the gifts that we give . . . and I would not have known about these expenses except for my CPA. I just collect the receipts, give them to her, and she takes it from there."

Similarly, Priscilla Harrison in Greensboro, North Carolina, says she knew nothing about tracking expenses, but her accountant showed her what to do, using a manual system. "I track my expenses faithfully," says Priscilla, adding that it takes her about 30 minutes a month to report her expenses to her accountant. Although numerous software programs are available for expense tracking (you can find out about them wherever computer software is sold), Priscilla says, "I just track my expenses on a spreadsheet provided by my accountant, and he puts everything on the computer. I keep an envelope in the back of my business planner, and that's where I store receipts and stubs, and then I categorize the expenses monthly before I give them to my accountant. There's not much to do, but I'd have a tax nightmare if I didn't do it!"

Relying on Your Corporate Office for Assistance

When you join a network marketing company, you're in business for yourself, but not by yourself. In other words, a corporate office is willing and able to assist you. Plus, there are people in your upline to help you, too. Make good use of these resources. Don't reinvent the wheel! A good corporate office has developed a system to help you succeed in your business. Use that system!

The system should include marketing materials, sales aids, and a variety of tools such as audio- and videotapes to help you get started quickly and to sustain your business. If you don't understand how to use the tools or if you're not clear about any aspect of your business, call distributor support at the corporate office or ask the people in your upline. Network marketing is all about people helping people. You can't do it all alone, and no one expects you to. Help is available, and using it is important.

Chapter 10

Knowing What to Do After You Sign Up

In This Chapter

▶ Preparing to hit the ground running with your new business

▶ Looking over your company's starter kit

▶ Spreading the word about your business

▶ Dealing with the "dream snatchers"

*Y*ou've selected the network marketing company of your choice, printed the company's application from its Web site, filled in the application — including your credit card number — signed it, and faxed or mailed it to the company. Now you're excited! This is your chance at the American Dream, and you can't wait to get started. Problem is, you have to wait for your starter kit, including the distributor's manual and training materials, to arrive by mail. That could take a week or more. Meanwhile, what do you do?

Perhaps your sponsor, who recruited you and led you to the company's Web site, has already listed numerous suggestions about what you can do to get started. Or the company's Web site may include a page that explains how to spend your time while you're waiting for your starter kit. If we just swung and missed twice, don't worry, because we're about to hit a home run. With the help of several network marketing experts, we tell you what you can do — both before and after you receive your starter kit — to get a running start in your network marketing business.

Preparing Yourself and Your Surroundings for Business

You *should* be excited because you're now part of a huge, vibrant profession that gives you the freedom to control your future. Where you go from here and the speed at which you progress are entirely your decision. Whether you're planning to earn a few hundred dollars a month for extra spending money or several thousand dollars a week to support your family and build your retirement fund, network marketing is a marvelous vehicle. You have no boss to answer to, no sales and marketing boundaries, no office politics, no commuting, no old boys' network, no Monday morning staff meetings, and no waiting for a slot to open before you can get promoted. Network marketing levels the playing field and lays all the opportunities at your feet from the moment you sign an application to join a company!

Okay, come back down here. You're so happy you're floating. Freedom does that to people. But as good as it is, network marketing doesn't do the work for you. You can make plenty of money, but getting your hands on it depends on your planting your feet firmly in your network marketing activity. You no longer have a boss to tell you what to do and when to do it. As Oxyfresh leader Connie Dugan says, "This is a volunteer army. You're not an employee anymore." (Oxyfresh sells personal health products, including many that are marketed to dentists.)

If you're going to succeed in this new business, you're the one who's going to make it happen. Here's what you need to do before receiving your starter kit:

- ✔ Set goals
- ✔ Create a vision
- ✔ Familiarize yourself with the company's Web site
- ✔ Study and master network marketing skills
- ✔ Organize your environment

Planning your success through goals

Maybe you've already set your goals, both for your business and for your personal life. If you have, now's the time to review and refine them and to set a plan of action for completing them. If you haven't, get busy right away and spend at least a couple of days working on your goals. Once your starter kit arrives, you'll be busy absorbing the details of your business. Take advantage of the time you have now to create your future on paper. Map out your path to success by answering these questions, for example:

- ✔ What do I want for my family and myself?
- ✔ How will my business help me get what I want?

After you commit your goals to paper, distinguish between short-range and long-range goals. Reading *Network Marketing For Dummies* is a short-range goal. Building a sales organization of thousands in a network marketing business is a long-range goal. Keep the range of your goals in mind as you begin to work on them. You're not going to accomplish a long-range goal, which could require years, in a short-range time frame, which may mean a week or less.

After you identify your goals, list the benefits that you'll receive when you achieve each goal. Psychologically, this list helps strengthen your commitment to complete the goal. The more you want a benefit of a goal, the more you're likely to stay committed, even when you don't feel like it or when you face certain obstacles.

Next, identify the obstacles that stand between you and the completion of each goal. What could possibly keep you from successfully claiming this goal in your life? Could it be a lack of money? A lack of discipline? A lack of education or know-how? Would you need to improve certain skills? For every obstacle, there's a solution. Take time to think about those solutions. If you need more education or better skills, you could read a book on the subject, listen to tapes, watch a video, enroll in a seminar, or maybe hire a personal coach. Write the solutions to your obstacles on paper. Once you see them, black on white, you start to believe them.

Finally, write an action plan to complete each goal. What will you have to do, day by day or week by week, to accomplish the goal? Make a personal commitment to follow your action plan. Use a calendar or planner and schedule your action plan a week at a time. Doing so will enable you to accomplish your goals.

When Lee Lemons gave up a $50,000-a-year job with IBM to build a network marketing organization with Excel Communications, which markets long-distance phone service, his first goal was to replace his income. "I set a goal to recruit 100 representatives within 90 days," Lee recalls, and then I set a second goal to earn $100,000 within a year of joining the company." Lee explains how he followed Zig's advice to commit his goals to paper and then develop an action plan. "I knew what I had to do," says Lee. "I had to talk to prospects *every* day for 90 days. I held opportunity meetings twice a day at 10 a.m. and 7 p.m. Sometimes I squeezed in a third meeting. I knew how many hours I had to put in each week to generate the prospects who I needed to talk to so that I could hit my goal. I had no time to waste." Nor did he. Lee fulfilled both of his goals and also won a contest that he hadn't anticipated. He joined Excel in August 1991. That fall, the company sponsored a contest that was based on finding three new representatives, then helping them find three, helping those three find three, and so on. In December of that year, Lee was responsible for the highest number of recruits, and he won the contest. "The reward was a Lincoln or a Cadillac to drive for a year, courtesy of Excel," Lee explains. However, instead of the car, he asked for the money. "We had a baby on the way, and I needed cash," he admits. For the next 12 months, Excel paid him the cash that was intended for the car payment: $900 a month. "Write down your goals," Lee says, "and that's when you will begin to believe that you can achieve them. That's the first step. Next, figure out what you've got to do to reach the goal and then make it happen."

Goal setting is featured in Zig's *Strategies for Success,* produced by Ziglar Training Systems. This product is available in audio and video formats, as well as on CD, and it includes a workbook to step you through the entire process of planning your success. You can read more about *Strategies for Success* at www.zigziglar.com.

People who set goals

- ✔ Are bringing their future into the present so they can do something about it now.

- ✔ Clearly understand that if they don't plan their time, someone else will take their time. (Surely you have noticed that people with nothing to do generally want to do it with you!)

- ✔ Do so because they recognize that they get twice as much done on the day before they go on vacation as they do on a normal day. Reason: The night before, they plan their day and prioritize it. If planning one day can have such a huge impact on your productivity, think what a planned goals program would do for your life.

- ✔ Earn more money. Dave Jensen, Chief Administrative Officer of the Crump Institute for Biological Imaging and Department of Pharmacology at UCLA, conducted a study and learned that those people from many walks of life who had a balanced goals program earned an average of $7,411 per month. People without a goals program earned an average of $3,397 per month. Those with goals programs were also happier and healthier and got along better with the folks at home.

- ✔ Can focus on what they have determined are the really important things in life. A goals program can help people change from being a "wandering generality" to a "meaningful specific."

Connie Dugan of Oxyfresh explains why associating your goals with your commitment to your network marketing business is critical. "It's the 'no' factor," she says. "It's rejection. If you talk to 30 people, only 3 may be interested in what you're selling. Twenty-seven no's is a lot of rejection. If you don't have goals that relate to succeeding in your business, then it's easy to quit."

Catching the vision for your business

It's important to envision your role in life and then figure out your direction and focus based on your vision. Similarly, you need to understand where you're headed with your business. What do you see happening in five, ten, twenty years? Where will this business lead you? What will you accomplish as a result of your business? Record the answers to these questions on paper, preferably in a place where you can review them and refine them as the years go by.

Uncovering your motives

Jack Maitland, a former NFL star and a member of the Baltimore Colts team that won Super Bowl V, is now a leader in the Nikken organization, selling magnetics as well as health and wellness products. "An undecided heart is the biggest reason for failure in network marketing," maintains Jack. "You can't be wishy-washy. You have to decide: Do you want to be a wholesale buyer of your company's products, or are you interested in the business opportunity?"

If you make the decision to work the business, then Jack says you need a plan of action, and it doesn't matter whether you're going to work part-time or full-time. If you don't plan to succeed, you probably won't.

By creating a vision for your business, you'll help yourself make future decisions. Prioritizing your work is easier when you have a clear picture of where you want to go.

If you let somebody else row your boat, they're going to take it where *they* want it to go, not where *you* want it to go.

Connie Dugan spends much of her time helping the people she sponsors in Oxyfresh to create a vision for their business. "It's a good way to help people get motivated," Connie explains. "Once you're in the business, it's rare that someone will call you and bug you to do what you know you need to do yourself. If you're not self-motivated, that's a problem. Writing a vision helps. But ultimately, self-motivation comes from within each of us."

Becoming familiar with the company's Web site

Almost every network marketing company posts a Web site that includes detailed information about the company's mission, vision, products, services, compensation plan, and policies and procedures. Go to the site, download the information, and study it. Pay particular attention to the information about the company's products and/or services. Why are they valuable? What benefits do they provide? How do they differ from the products and services offered by other companies? Who buys these products and services and why? Look for testimonials from satisfied customers. Become familiar with the products you're going to sell. Buy them and use them. Also, dig into the company's compensation plan. Find out how you earn money and study the criteria for getting promoted. Much of this information will be repeated in your starter kit, but until your kit arrives, this is a sure way of learning how to make the most of your new business.

Mastering the skills of a successful network marketer

Alphabetically, the activities of reading, listening, and watching do not appear before leading, but Jan Ruhe, network marketer extraordinaire, says it best: "Leaders are readers." Jan was a single mom in Dallas, Texas, carrying a load of debt when she joined Discovery Toys in 1980. Once she saw what network marketing could do for her, she borrowed $250 to order her starter kit and got busy right away. "Book by book, seminar by seminar, sermon by sermon, video by video, audiotape by audiotape," she explains, "I began transforming into a woman who was not going to be denied. I wanted the lifestyle of a successful network marketer." Today, after more than 20 years with Discovery Toys, Jan is a happily married millionaire, living with her husband in Aspen, Colorado.

Now's the time to become a student again — a subject we touch upon throughout this book. In fact, as a network marketer, you're always a student. You need many skills to succeed, including sales, networking, telemarketing, goal setting, and much more. Use this time to brush up on these skills; study them on your own or attend a seminar.

Many products have been produced in recent years to help network marketers build their businesses. *Upline* magazine produces a catalog that offers a variety of books, tapes, videos, and software. For more information, visit www.upline.com or call 877-898-8882. Your public library may have some of these products, too.

Becoming a student of network marketing

Attending training seminars and listening to tapes are valuable aids to helping you build your network marketing business. "It wasn't long [after joining Discovery Toys] that I discovered Tom Hopkins [one of America's leading sales trainers]," explains Jan Ruhe, the top-ranked distributor in her company. "I became a student, and I took my three children to his seminars, just as I took them to a local church to hear Zig Ziglar speak in Dallas. Then I discovered Jim Rohn [another leading speaker and trainer], and I took my children to hear him, too. Information from these three men molded me into who I am today. Jim's philosophy of 'Why not you?' and 'Why not now?' rang in my ears over and over. Tom's sales closing techniques worked for me beyond belief. Zig's lesson about helping others achieve their dreams and putting others before me was exactly what I needed to hear. This training eventually changed me and allowed me to become a leader."

Organizing your work environment

You need a place to work. It doesn't need to be elaborate, and you don't need to go outside the home. A corner of a bedroom, or a table in the basement may be suitable (but see the warning later in this section). Wherever you've set up your computer is an ideal spot.

You can even work from the kitchen table. Many network marketers get started by using a cardboard box to store their forms, supplies, workbooks, and Rolodex. They carry the box from room to room, setting up their office wherever it's most convenient on a given day. Yes, it's nice to have privacy, to have an office with a view, a huge desk, and filing cabinets. But that's all window dressing. You don't need any of it to succeed as a network marketer. Once you're successful and you have money to spend, you can formalize your office. In fact, if you work hard and hit it big, after a few years you may be able to build your dream house with your own luxurious office. Thousands of network marketers have already done so.

Be aware of IRS requirements. According to attorney Jeffrey Babener, who writes extensively about network marketing laws and regulations, your office should be an area — preferably a separate room or rooms — used exclusively for business; otherwise, you can't legitimately claim a portion of your home's square footage as a business expense. Also, Jeffrey recommends that you consider foot traffic, noise, telephone lines, lighting, and windows. Will your office be protected from pets and children? It would be a shame to arrive at your desk one morning to find your important paperwork transformed into your child's artwork! Jeffrey's Web site, www.mlmlegal.com, offers other suggestions for starting up a home business.

Privacy is important, especially while you're using the telephone, and that's what you can expect to be doing much of the time. You'll be listening to conference calls conducted by your corporate office, training sessions conducted by the people in your upline, and eventually three-way calls — you listen while someone in your upline makes a sales presentation to a prospect. Conference calls usually occur in the early evening, but training sessions and three-ways calls can be scheduled at any time of the day.

Working from home may be a challenge if you're used to working in a corporate environment. The support services that you may have relied on at the office aren't likely to be at home. Copying machines, fax machines, laser printers, a well-stocked supplies cabinet, and people to fetch things are all part of the corporate world but not usually the home. Therefore, you'll need some equipment and basic supplies, including the following:

- ✓ **Audiotapes and videotapes:** Some companies provide tapes that you can mail to prospective customers. Your starter kit may include several of these tapes, but you'll need more. The people in your upline can advise you about how to place an order.

- ✓ **Business cards and company stationery:** People in your upline can tell you how to order these supplies. Don't wait to order them; you want to be ready to go when your starter kit arrives.

- ✓ **Calendar:** Be prepared to schedule appointments for telephone calls with your prospects as well as with members of your upline and downline. Remember to jot down the dates of training sessions, conference calls, and so on. The distributor's manual, which is part of your starter kit, often comes with a calendar.

- ✓ **Computer and printer:** They aren't requirements, but getting along without them makes the work more difficult. You should have access to word processing software and a contact management or database program for lead tracking. An e-mail account is also very useful because your corporate office, as well as the people in your upline and downline, will want to communicate with you via e-mail. If you can't start out with these tools, buy them as soon as possible.

- ✓ **Fax machine:** Optional, but useful. If you have a computer, you can install fax software.

- ✓ **Miscellaneous supplies:** You'll need pens, paper, a stapler, a calculator, and file folders. The Rolodex seems to be losing out to contact management software, such as ACT!, but some people prefer to spin the wheel of their Rolodex when they need to find a name or number quickly.

- ✓ **Notebook:** A three-ring binder with dividers is perfect. You can use it for a variety of purposes, including tracking your marketing activities, goal setting, and notetaking during training sessions and seminars.

- ✓ **Telephone:** A portable phone is fine, but there's no substitute for quality. If you're buying a phone, get one with a mute button — for conference calls and three-way calls — and a speaker phone. Also, once you get busy, you'll probably want to use a headset, so make sure that the phone will accommodate one. Many a network marketer won't leave home without a cell phone. They use it to network with the people in their upline and downline, as well as to speak with prospects, while their kids are at music lessons or while they're in line at the grocery store. You can make better use of your time with a cell phone, but please, don't dial and drive!

"Disorganization is a huge challenge for the new network marketer," explains Connie Dugan of Oxyfresh. That's why it's smart to be prepared to hit the ground running in your business. "If you're out collecting business cards and writing information on Post-it Notes and you don't have a follow-up system, you're dead in the water," Connie continues. "If you lose names and numbers or you don't call people back after you said you would, you will lose credibility. There's no room for procrastination in this business."

Working with children at home

Even when their children are infants or toddlers, moms are attracted to network marketing because they can build their businesses from home. The opportunity to stay home is more than enough incentive for most moms to figure out how to work with children at home. Plenty of working moms and single parents have done it in network marketing. Ask the people in your upline; chances are, they know someone who can offer you some advice.

If you have small children at home, figure out how to work around their needs and schedules.

Maybe you can trade child care with someone in your neighborhood or hire a babysitter for an hour a day. Married moms, of course, may be able to work in the evenings when dad is home to watch the children.

If your children are older, perhaps you can work while they are occupied with homework, a favorite toy, a game, or an educational video for a half hour at a time while you work. A cell phone gives you additional portability to do several things at once.

"When you're just getting started, you learn to depend on yourself for everything," says Louise Adrian, a Vancouver, British Columbia–based distributor of Party Lite Gifts. Louise worked in the medical industry but gave up her job to raise her children. "Then, after you've made some progress and your business is building, you can hire a teenager from the neighborhood to help you with the data entry and the paperwork. Or call the local high school and ask who's looking for a job. Some school programs require the students to get work experience. Of course, once your own children become teenagers, they can help, too."

Communicating with your sponsor

Your sponsor wants you to get a running start in the business because his or her success depends on your success. You're never alone in network marketing, and that's one of the profession's strengths. If your sponsor doesn't communicate with you during the time you're waiting on the arrival of the starter kit, don't be shy. Call your sponsor! Find out whether there are local meetings you can attend or conference calls that you can join. Ask your sponsor to meet you for coffee so that you can begin to get answers to your questions. Sponsors respond generously to enthusiasm, so be sure to show yours.

Connie Dugan, a leading Oxyfresh distributor, suggests, "Establish a mutually agreeable business partnership with your sponsor. Treat your sponsor like a mentor."

Understanding the Company's System

At last, your starter kit is sitting on the kitchen counter, waiting to be opened! Having followed our pre-starter kit game plan, you're ahead of the learning curve. Open your kit, and you'll probably find an introductory letter from your company with instructions about how to proceed. "Follow your company's written guidelines on how to get started," advises Connie Dugan. "Don't get too creative or reinvent the wheel." As reinforcement, we list our post-starter kit suggestions here:

- ✔ Familiarize yourself with the starter kit.
- ✔ Bone up on the fast-start plan.

Somewhere between signing the company's distributor application and receiving your starter kit, you're likely to feel overwhelmed, if not uncertain, about what you've done. Don't worry — these feelings are normal! You may start thinking that there's too much you don't know and you have too much to learn. Remember: Networking is all about working together. You have colleagues in an upline to help you, as well as support staff at your corporate office. No one expects you to master the distributor's manual overnight. You may also start thinking that you made a mistake: Going into business isn't for you. That's called buyer's remorse. Push those negative thoughts out of your mind. Thousands of people in network marketing can truthfully say, "If I did it, anyone can!"

Getting familiar with the kit

Familiarizing yourself with everything in your starter kit may take several days, but spending time reading it is important. Here are several suggestions:

- ✔ Don't skip over the policies and procedures material; you need to know the company's rules. Violating certain rules will result in the termination of your relationship with the company. Know how to keep yourself in good standing.

- ✔ Schedule extra time to read the company's compensation plan. Understand how and when you get paid and how you qualify for promotions. See Chapter 8 for information about compensation plans.

- ✔ Study all product information. You want to know as much as possible about your products and services before selling them. Try to anticipate the questions that your prospects will ask you about your products, and be sure that you know the answers.

✔ Practice the product and business opportunity presentations. Your kit probably includes sample scripts that you can study. Your success as a network marketer depends to some degree on your ability to make strong presentations.

✔ Make a list of questions while you're reading the manual or listening to or viewing tapes. Your company's Web site may include a Frequently Asked Questions (FAQ) section where you may be able to find the answers to these questions. For any that remain unanswered or unclear, call your sponsor and set a time to go over the information.

✔ Read all product brochures before you start handing them out to prospects. Likewise, your kit may include a brochure about your business opportunity. Staple your business card to these brochures so that your prospects know how to contact you.

✔ Schedule time to study any audio or video training programs included in your kit. Most companies include at least one or two of these programs.

Training is always important to network marketers. You can never get enough of it! At the Zig Ziglar Network (www.zigziglarnetwork.com), we've based our reputation on quality training products for our associates. As an example, our starter kit includes "Networking for Significance," a 12-set audio package, and "Networking for Success," a training program that includes an audiotape, a videotape, and a workbook. We also include two of my books: *Success For Dummies* (IDG Books Worldwide, Inc.) and *Over the Top* (Thomas Nelson Publishers), and we include a copy of *Network Marketing For Dummies*. These are the minimal training tools that our associates need to get started on a path to success.

Beginning with the fast-start plan

Almost every starter kit includes a program to help you get a quick start in your business. This program may be called the Quick Start Plan, the Jump Start Plan, the Fast Track Plan, or one of many other titles. Look for this program, read it, and follow through right away.

As an example, here's a condensed version of the FastStart Action Plan contained in the Zig Ziglar Network (ZZN) associate's manual:

✔ List 20 people you know who may want to discover ways to improve their lifestyles and their lives. (Chapter 14 of this book goes into detail about how to develop your initial list of people to contact.)

✔ Sign-up for the ZZN Unified Messenging Service so you can be kept up-to-date on training, product development, and meetings in your area.

- ✔ Order business cards and stationery, as well as marketing tools including brochures, videos, and so on.

- ✔ Attend two events such as opportunity meetings in your area, conference calls, or individually scheduled meetings with your sponsor.

- ✔ Host two presentations where you or your sponsor can present the company's products and services or the business opportunity. These presentations can be conducted by phone or informally in your home.

Party Lite Gifts recommends that new distributors get started with six in-home parties to earn their starter kits and build momentum. "We work closely with new consultants to get their first six shows on the calendar," explains Louise Adrian in Vancouver, British Columbia. "That's when the business takes off, and that's how our consultants set themselves up for success. They will start making money right away from those shows."

- ✔ Learn the simple and easy-to-use ZZN Opportunity Presentation. Practice it and watch how your sponsor uses it.

"Duplication is the name of the game," explains Jon Miller of Body Wise International. "This is a monkey-see, monkey-do industry." In network marketing parlance, you may recall that duplication is the act of following your sponsor's lead, or following the company's proven system for success. Don't reinvent the wheel — just duplicate the actions and efforts of those who are already successful in the business.

Taking responsibility for another's success

Seasoned networker Dan Gaub of Yakima, Washington, has his own quick-start program that he introduces to the people he sponsors in Market America.

"Networking has always been about helping others," he says. "When a person takes responsibility for another's success by leading rather than herding, success develops much faster." Here's how Dan leads his "partners" in Market America:

"We form a game plan. I ask, 'Where do you want to be?' and 'What are you looking for in a home business?' Then we need to get six to ten customers, and we need to interview six to ten people who may want to become partners in our business."

Dan monitors progress on a monthly basis, "adjusting where needed." He makes it a point never to sign up a partner who isn't committed to the business. He can tell who's committed and who's not by their actions. Those who attend opportunity and training meetings, listen to the company's audiotapes, and study the company's Web site are committed. These are the folks who, as Zig says, "become a product of the product."

Getting the Word Out

Tell somebody about your business! "Start talking," says Connie Dugan. "After all, it's word-of-mouth advertising that you'll get paid for."

Pick up the phone and call a friend. Walk down the street and talk to a neighbor. Connect to the Internet and send an e-mail to the people you know. Talk to the person behind the checkout counter at the supermarket or to the man who sells you produce. Use your bubbling energy to spread the word about your new business. Chapter 14 includes plenty of ideas about how to spread the word.

"Network marketing is a matter of building relationships," says Jon Miller. "Maybe six days or six weeks from now, you'll be friends with someone who will want to hear more about your business opportunity. It's because of your relationship that they will be open to it."

Even if you don't feel that you've absorbed everything you need to know about your products or your business opportunity, step out into the real world and tell people what you're doing. Some of these people may want to join you or at least become a customer of your products or services. If nothing else, they should at least congratulate you for becoming a business owner.

As soon as you tell the first person about your business, you're on your way! You may not make a sale immediately, or even for a couple of weeks, but you're on your way, regardless. If you continue following the system that your company has designed for your success, the first sale will come, and it will be followed by many more.

"You Can't Be Serious . . . Can You?"

Before we go any further, we better warn you about the "dream snatchers" who will torment you as soon as you say you're going to join a network marketing company. You may have met some of these folks already because there are more of them than there are of us. They're not evil people; they're well-intentioned, and they'll tell you that they're looking out for *your* best interests when they advise you not to join a network marketing company. At first they'll laugh it off: "Oh, you can't be serious!" they'll say, thinking that perhaps you're joking. If you persist, they'll come on stronger: "They're all pyramid schemes, and all you're going to do is lose your money! You're not that foolish, are you?" If you don't yield to their advice, they'll turn to ridicule.

Lee Lemons knows that drill. After he resigned his position with IBM in 1991 to join Excel Communications, which markets long-distance telephone service, some of his friends were sure he had lost his mind. He gave up a $50,000-a-year salary and 13 years seniority for what? "Here comes the telephone man," Lee's friends used to tease him. The fun didn't last long, however. Within two years, working full-time as a network marketer with Excel, Lee doubled the salary he had given up at IBM. Then he moved his family into a big home in a gated community just south of Dallas, Texas. Now when Lee's friends see him, they say, "Here comes *the man*."

Lee laughs about it now. "Before I made the money," he says, "there was a stigma attached to my profession. But now my friends know the score. In two to five years as a network marketer, you can make more money than you would earn in 30 to 40 years working for someone else."

Even when you're a successful network marketer, the dream snatchers will still be gunning for you. Colleen Zade gave up a full-time job to stay at home with her infant daughter, and later she became a part-time network marketer with Epicure Selections, a Canadian-based firm whose independent consultants sell gourmet spice blends and cooking utensils at home parties. Colleen, who says "it feels great to make more than most professionals," explains that occasionally she still runs into people with condescending attitudes about her profession. "They think that women who sell at home parties can't get 'real jobs,' but I wouldn't change places with any of them. I love what I do," Colleen continues. "I get paid better than they do, and I don't consider what I do to be work! If someone really gets negative, I just tell them about my paycheck and about how many hours I work a week and explain that I can be with my family and still earn that much money. They usually ask for my business card!" In July 2000, Colleen reached the top level of her company's pay plan.

"There will always be skeptics about network marketing," says Jeff Roberti, a waiter-turned-network marketer in Florida. When he was 21, he was earning more than $100,000 annually with Herbalife. "I learned early to stay focused on my dreams and goals and not get caught up in negative thinking. If more people were educated about network marketing and what it could do for them, the skeptics would diminish over time. Network marketing has grown into a very successful economic model throughout the world, and it's more accepted today than at any time in the past." *Yes, but just try telling that to the dream snatchers!*

We often wonder why some people want to rain on somebody else's parade. Oftentimes it's the people they should be encouraging. Why is this? Number one, many times the criticizer or dream snatcher has heard just bits and pieces of information from various sources, put it all together, and said, "The whole deal is bad." It reminds me somewhat of the little fellow who visited his elderly grandfather after school, only to find grandfather sound asleep. The youngster took Limburger cheese and quietly and carefully spread some on grandpa's upper lip, right into his mustache. When the grandfather awoke, he scratched his head and said, "Something doesn't smell good — it must be the sofa." As he stepped into another room, the odor followed. After a few minutes, grandpa announced, "I think the whole world stinks!"

Unfortunately, some people heard about one person who got involved in network marketing and lost money or worked hard and didn't accomplish anything, so they judge the entire profession on that basis. Try to be tolerant of those people. They need your sympathy — they don't need your attention or for you to listen to their voices of doom.

The second reason many people are so critical of network marketing is that they're honestly and sincerely concerned about you — but it's misguided concern. They can't picture themselves getting into network marketing and becoming successful, so they naturally can't see you taking that step and becoming successful.

So how do you handle this situation? First of all, I encourage you to agree with them. "You know, you're probably right. It might not be a good deal. But it looks good to me, and I've already signed up. But I haven't done much yet, so I would consider it a real favor if you would go with me to the next meeting or accompany me to talk with my sponsor and express your concerns to him. Please listen carefully, because if it's not a good deal, I certainly don't want to be in it!"

Don't be surprised if your friend refuses to go, hiding behind the lame old excuse, "It would just be a waste of my time, and I don't want to see you waste your time." If this person really is a friend and open-minded (you know, some people are so narrow-minded they can see through a keyhole with both eyes at the same time!), he or she will go with you and then undoubtedly tell you why "it is not really that bad . . . as a matter of fact, it's really good!"

If this particular approach doesn't work, I encourage you to remember that everyone is entitled to his or her own opinion — but no one is entitled to the wrong facts. So what you need to do is have facts at your disposal so that you can simply say, "Well, you know, your opinion is apparently pretty well set, but I base mine on some facts because I was open-minded enough to listen . . . and it's the wisest thing I've ever done. Why don't you listen and see what your opinion will be after you've heard the facts? After all, I just talked with a young mother of three who has been in the business only six months, but she's been able not only to spend more time with her children but also to provide for them in a much better way. So it can't be all bad. Besides that, there have been no layoffs with this company since they went into business, and from what I hear, in the corporate world, layoffs happen regularly."

Open their minds with facts, but always remember that your own attitude is yours — and it's yours to keep. You do that by simply remembering that failure is an event, not a person, yesterday really did end last night, and today is a brand new day. In the meantime, keep listening to the tapes, reading the books, attending the meetings, and listening to your sponsor and others in your upline who are doing well. You won't have all the answers the first day, but over a period of time, you'll get them. Your sponsor and others in your upline probably have the answers you need at this point. Don't listen to those who know nothing but have strong opinions. As a matter of fact, they generally express them "with the confidence that often goes with ignorance."

In Chapter 4, we discuss the high rate of turnover in network marketing. You don't need a lot of money to get started in this business, and as a result, people frequently walk away from their investment without knowing what they're giving up. These people never really got started. They lost interest, or they were discouraged by a family member or friend. Protect yourself from the turnover rate. Remain positive about your future in network marketing. Getting started right away may be the best defense against quitting.

A former skeptic discovers that "these people don't have horns!"

A couple of years ago, a small group of college professors and network marketing executives huddled at the University of Texas-El Paso (UTEP) to consider establishing university-level curricula around the subject of network marketing. "The academics were skeptical and wary," recalls Dr. Frank Hoy, dean of UTEP's School of Business and a longtime proponent of network marketing as a college-level subject. They weren't convinced that the topic of network marketing belonged in a university curriculum, or that it merited a course of its own.

The conference helped educate the college professors, and more than one of them thought it would be possible to teach a network marketing course at their universities in the near future. But the most telling observation came from an associate professor of management from Baylor University. "My idea used to be that [network marketers] were people who made you want to shower after you were around them. . . . But hey," confirmed Dr. Ray Bagby, "these people don't have horns!" Dr. Bagby said that his perception changed after meeting with the network marketers at the UTEP conference. Since learning more about the benefits of network marketing and the success of companies and individuals who are engaged in the profession, he has encouraged more research on the topic of network marketing.

Chapter 11

Sponsoring, Training, and Motivating People in Your Downline

*O*ne of the most enticing features about network marketing is that you're in control of your own business. Neither bosses nor employees can tell you what you can or can't do. No one can lay you off, transfer you, or tell you to work more or fewer hours. Your territory can't be reassigned or downsized, and product lines won't be taken away from you and given to a coworker. With the exception of corporate rules and regulations, which rarely include any surprises, *all authority* rests with you. The time of day or night that you work, the marketing tools that you use, the product mix that you sell, the people you sponsor, and how and when you train them — *all* of it is up to you. There's only one caveat: The ultimate success of your business is also up to you!

But even that caveat isn't anything to fret about, because network marketing consists of both a downline and an upline that ideally interact with each other. That's another enticing feature.

In network marketing terminology, a *downline* consists of the distributors you agree to sponsor. These are your team members, and they make up your sales organization. Downlines are organized horizontally by "legs" and vertically by "levels" (see Figure 8–1 in Chapter 8). You earn residual income based on the performance of the people in your downline. An *upline* consists of the distributors who are positioned above you. Your upline earns residual income based on your performance, as well as the performance of your downline.

To *sponsor* a distributor means to train and support that distributor. Sponsors are in the business of duplication. They show their distributors what they need to do and to accomplish so that they can become successful network marketers. Then, by coaching, advising, instructing, and encouraging, they empower the distributors to begin building their own organizations.

Your ability to sponsor, train, and motivate the people in your downline improves when your upline is dedicated to helping you succeed. Sometimes, however, because of circumstances that range from lack of interest to periodic health problems to personality clashes, an upline is ineffective. Such an occurrence is unfortunate, but you must be prepared for it, and you will be if you follow the ideas and suggestions we provide in this chapter.

Three Reasons Why Building a Downline Is Important

In network marketing, the downline, or the sales organization, is the heart of your business. Excitement, energy, and action emanate from those in the downline. For that matter, so does your money! This is the group that can make you wealthy. Plus, this is the group whose friendships will give you years and years of satisfaction and contentment. Here are several reasons why building a downline is important.

✔ **A downline is your key to residual income and eventual wealth.** As the distributors in your downline generate revenue by recruiting new distributors and selling products and services, you earn a commission! The more productive your downline, the more money you earn. Plus, the more people in your downline, the more diversified is your income.

Rather than depending only on yourself for income, a downline provides the security of multiple revenue streams. Jan Ruhe, the most successful associate in Discovery Toys, which sells educational toys for children, says, "I'd rather earn 10 percent of many people doing a little bit than 100 percent of what I can do myself."

✔ **A downline generates synergy, and synergy creates momentum.** "It's the mastermind formula," says James Davis, a network marketer with the Internet-based company Horizons Interactive. "Having two or more brains working in harmony towards a common goal, that's real power." When you have dozens, hundreds, even thousands of people sharing your opportunity, selling your products and services, your business kicks into high gear, and then your income and your security are multiplied.

✔ **With a downline, you have OPT — other people's time.** Maybe you've heard of OPM — other people's money. A downline gives you the benefit of other people's time, which is far more valuable. "When you build a downline of 100 people who work 7 to 10 hours per week," continues James Davis, "you are earning an income from 700 to 1,000 hours a week of effort. That's significant!"

Jan Ruhe calls this phenomenon SWIS: Sales While I Sleep. "While I'm sleeping, eating, vacationing, the checks keep coming in," she explains. "It's fantastic to reap these rewards."

Deciding Whom to Recruit for Your Downline

Top network marketers will tell you this: Don't prejudge when it comes to recruiting distributors for your downline. "I have watched ordinary people become extraordinary after working with me for three to six months," explains Jan Ruhe. "It's not who *you* recruit and sponsor that builds your business . . . it's who *they* recruit and sponsor."

That advice makes sense, but Jan and other leaders admit they're attracted to certain types of people more so than others, as we explain in the following two sections.

Identifying good candidates for your downline

Your product line may be better suited to certain types of individuals than others, creating an opportunity for you to look for candidates in certain professions. For example, teachers may be well suited for demonstrating products in front of a group or at home parties, whereas medical professionals, including doctors and chiropractors, may be more interested in selling nutritional products.

James Davis sits at his computer most of the day selling thousands of products from his Internet mall at www.jdavis.com. His specialty, however, is arranging loans online for small business owners. It just so happens that his clients often make great candidates for his business. "I look for successful business professionals who are very busy, but time starved," James clarifies. "I feel they would love the time freedom that network marketing provides. I particularly look for sales professionals whose incomes would stop if they stopped working. Like real estate and insurance agents. I was an award-winning real estate agent before a stroke forced me into network marketing. So I feel I can relate to these candidates and attract them to my business."

Jan Ruhe is less interested in specific professions than in personality traits. She says, "I like digital people, the bottom-line types. I like the auditories who talk a lot, and the kinesthetics who feel deeply passionate, as well as the visual people who can see the big picture." Overall, when Jan looks for candidates, she says she keeps the acronym STEAM in mind. That helps to remind her that she's looking for salespeople, teachers/trainers, enthusiastic people, attitudes that are positive, and money people, meaning people who want to earn an extra income.

Basically, everyone you meet is a potential candidate for your business, and you shouldn't hesitate to tell all of them what you do. Even when you're an experienced network marketer, be careful not to allow your perceptions to stop you from talking to everyone about your business. Those who aren't interested will let you know soon enough!

Looking for "powerhouse associates"

Some people, because of their skills and personalities or because of circumstances, can make a big splash in network marketing within days or weeks of joining an organization. Go-getters, those bold, confident people who step into elevators and start telling the captivated audience about their products, or closers, the people who have a natural ability to close sales with little effort, can begin building downlines even before they've finished reading their distributor's manual. And Webmasters, who attract millions of visitors to their sites every week, are beautifully positioned to start making sales without the need to prepare or to generate leads. Potential powerhouse associates are attractive because they have the ability to move quickly and to build organizations of their own in record time.

"Most networkers gain a lion's share of their income from half a dozen key associates," explains James Davis. But he cautions that finding those key associates isn't predictable. People don't walk around wearing signs that say "Powerhouse Associate." Concentrate on recruiting first and let the powerhouse associates reveal themselves in time.

On occasion, leaders of large downline organizations move their entire downline to another company. Perhaps they're looking for a new opportunity with a better compensation plan. Or maybe they've had a disagreement with their corporate office. Such a move can look pretty good if you're on the receiving end of this big downline. But keep in mind: What goes around comes around. "I know a lot of people have tried to recruit people who will bring their networks to another opportunity," says Jan Ruhe, "but I don't want them. If they will do that [move their downline] to their organization, they will probably do it to mine. It's too painful to lose 300 people in a month."

Protect yourself by building your downline wide for financial independence, and wide and deep for security. In other words, build several legs in your downline and build the levels deep. If you built only one leg, or you built a few legs but only a couple of levels deep, that could be dangerous to your organization. What if your big moneymaker quits? Or what if several of your top associates break away and join another company? You would have to start building all over again. (See Chapters 14 and 15 for more on the subjects of recruiting and prospecting.)

Training Your Distributors to Shine

James Davis points out that recruiting distributors is a lot like digging for diamonds, even if the associate shows all the signs of becoming a leader. "If you were to go to Crater of Diamonds State Park, not far from where I live in Arkansas, and hunt for diamonds, you wouldn't just walk out into the field and pick up a diamond," relates James. "You would have to dig for hours, maybe days, then sort through the dirt and gravel, and with some luck you might find a diamond. But even when you do, you'll still have to polish it up to make it shine." In other words, all distributors need to be trained.

"When you recruit distributors into your downline, your work is just beginning," insists Carol Bishop of Waxahachie, Texas. She and her husband, Jimmy, have been associates in several network marketing companies and most recently joined the Zig Ziglar Network. "You have to train your associates to duplicate what you do. You have to lead and guide and teach them," Carol continues. "Train your associates to be a TEAM, which means Together Everyone Achieves More. That's the only way to make the big money in this industry, and it's a way to have a lot of fun, too!"

The next several sections reveal a system that you can use to train your distributors so that they will shine.

Introducing Zig's golden rule philosophy for success

Millions of people have heard or read my golden rule philosophy:

You can have everything in life you want if you will just help enough other people get what they want.

People who live and work by that philosophy know that it's powerful, and given the opportunity, they will train others to follow the same philosophy. Network marketers especially embrace the philosophy because it's the epitome of every network marketing organization. Only by helping other people, including distributors and retail customers, can a network marketer succeed. You can't do it all by yourself in network marketing. First, you wouldn't reach many people. Second, you wouldn't make much money. And third, it would be lonely! When you recruit a group of people, introduce them to the Golden Rule. When you do, you'll be committing to help them reach their goals, and then, you can't help but reach your own goals, too.

Even before the Zig Ziglar Network existed, Jimmy and Carol Bishop incorporated Zig's Golden Rule in their training system. "We teach everyone to take their eyes off themselves," says Jimmy, "and focus on their associates. We don't want to be stars in our company; we want to be star builders. By focusing on our associates, we find out what they want out of life, what will cause them to make sacrifices and reach for something bigger or greater in their lives. And then we purposely help them work towards their dreams. People with dreams are willing to fight for what they want. And when we're all focused on our associates and their dreams, rather than on our own dreams, that's when our team members come together, they get excited, they build momentum, and things start happening."

Carol Bishop says that she and Jimmy didn't understand Zig's Golden Rule when they first started in network marketing, but once they incorporated it into their training, they saw its value, particularly in building a downline consisting of hundreds of distributors or more. The philosophy is the glue that keeps an organization together and working hard. "Once you build a team that looks out for each other," Carol says, "it starts growing all by itself because the word gets out that your organization is achieving goals. You can't stop a team like that!"

When it comes to Zig Ziglar's Golden Rule, no one knows how it works better than Jan Ruhe. A divorced mother raising three children, Jan had a dream to become a millionaire. One Saturday in the early 1980s she visited a church in Dallas, Texas, to hear Zig Ziglar speak. "What Zig said that morning," says Jan, "is the reason why I'm a millionaire today. When he said, 'You can have everything in life you want if you will just help enough other people get what they want,' I shifted my mission away from what I wanted at that moment in time, and I focused on helping other people achieve their dreams. It worked! I am a walking testimonial of Zig's philosophy."

Getting 'em all to become products of the product

You might call people who try to sell you a product that they themselves don't buy or use a hypocrite, and in network marketing, hypocrites stick out like spines on a porcupine. They may jab you once or twice, but by their example, they force people to run away from them. They struggle to convince people of their sincerity, and they find it nearly impossible to persuade people to do what they themselves are not willing to do.

Therefore, to become a leader in network marketing, you and your distributors must each become a product of your product. (See Chapter 7 for more on this subject.) That means before you can train a distributor, you need to buy and use the products and services that your company sells. Experience the health benefits of your nutritional line of products. See for yourself the savings that you can achieve by using your company's long-distance services or utilities. Be prepared to talk from personal experience about the quality of your products or the effectiveness of your services. By personally understanding how your products and services work, you become more credible. Then you can inspire by example and train from experience.

It's equally important to show your distributors that you're a student of the training materials that your company provides. Absorb everything you can about your industry, its products and services, and how to represent them. Attend the meetings sponsored by your company and by other leaders within the company. Get involved. Be seen. When you do, you'll become a walking billboard for everything that's good about network marketing and your specific company. And when that happens, your performance will take on a life of its own. You'll begin attracting people to your organization simply because they want to be associated with a leader. While other distributors struggle to build a business, you'll have a hard time keeping up with the people who want to join your organization and be trained by you. They'll want to *be* like you, so when you tell them to become a product of the product, they will.

Atticus Killough began dabbling in network marketing in the mid-1990s in Dallas, Texas, but for several years he earned only a few hundred dollars a month, mostly because he was not a product of the product. Without the benefit of a strong upline to train him, he was ineffective. In addition, he says that he spent too much time listening to discouraging comments from people around him who had never made a dime in network marketing. The hypocrisy of training a distributor to become successful when he couldn't claim success himself prevented him from building a productive downline. Consequently, he clung to his corporate job, where he was a "cubicle convict."

Finally, after a lot of searching, he had a breakthrough. "It happened when I started seriously listening to audiotapes," he says. "I constantly listened to educational and motivational tapes, including those from all the network marketing gurus. That's what changed my mindset about how to make this business work. I had to do that for myself before I could do it for anyone else. I used to think all the positive attitude stuff was mumbo jumbo, but when I put it into my own head, the network marketing business changed for me, and it allowed me to help others." By working several Web-powered network marketing ventures part-time (see www.atticuskillough.com), Atticus was able to earn nearly a six-figure income by the year 2000.

Setting a training schedule

As soon as you recruit distributors, explain how you and perhaps other members of the distributor's upline will train them. Set the training schedule and emphasize the importance of participating in every training session. You may decide to train distributors one-on-one, or you may want to speak to several of them at the same time, either in person or by telephone. The number of sessions needed to train a distributor depends on many variables, including the length of the sessions, the background, interest, and cooperation of the distributor, and the complexity of the products or services being sold.

The goal of your training program is *duplication,* a term widely used in network marketing circles. You want your new distributors to be able to duplicate what you and other leaders do so that they, too, can be successful.

Ray Gebauer, a Mannatech distributor based in Bellevue, Washington, says he thinks that achieving duplication in training isn't enough. "What we really want to do is empower people because then they will see the big picture and they will start to believe in themselves and in their ability to succeed in network marketing."

Here's how Jimmy and Carol Bishop of the Zig Ziglar Network establish a training program for their new associates: "Early in our relationship with the associate, we get out our calendars and we schedule training time. We do most of our training by phone because our associates are all over the country. Any associate who wants to work with us will commit to spend ten hours a week in training for as long as it takes for them to be able to duplicate what we do. That's how they'll be successful.

"In our first couple of training sessions, we learn about their dreams and goals, and we get them to write them on paper. Then we explain the Zig Ziglar FastStart Plan to them. This plan gives them just a few things to do so that they'll be ready to start working their business as soon as they learn about the opportunity and our products. The plan includes ordering business cards and stationery, ordering the marketing tools they'll need, such as brochures and audiotapes, and attending corporate-sponsored training events as soon as possible. We also want them to start reading their associate's manual, spend 30 minutes a day reading Zig's materials, and listen to one of Zig's tapes each day.

"In the second week, we ask the associates if they want to get promoted and start climbing up the ladder of success within our organization. Of course they do! So then we explain how the compensation plan works and how they can qualify to reach the different levels of success, such as director, executive director, and all the way up to platinum director.

"Next, we help them identify their warm market. We help them make a list of 200 names of people they can contact, but we don't come up with all the names in one session. We act as a memory jogger for them, and over a period of time, they will come up with 200 names. Then we select the top 20 names on that list, and we show them how to contact them and what to say. We show them how to continuously add to the list so they always have people to call."

Your *warm market* consists of the people you know or who know you. Family, friends, neighbors, and everyone they may refer to you make up your warm market. Anyone outside your warm market is in the *cold market.* See Chapter 14 for more on this topic.

"We don't expect an associate to know what to say when they talk to a prospect about our business, so we show them. While we're both on the phone, we call their prospects for them. (This is called a three-way call.) The associate introduces us as partners in a new business opportunity, and then we take over from there. Basically, we're allowing the associate to learn a phone script that they will be able to use comfortably when they start talking to prospects on their own. We don't do a sales presentation. We don't feel we have to do that. We explain the opportunity with a lot of enthusiasm; we ask if the prospect would be interested in joining us; and then we wait for the prospect to ask questions. Answering questions is pretty easy, and we can have a lot of fun doing it. All during these calls, we're teaching our associate how to use phone etiquette and how to be effective. If the prospect says, 'Yes, I want to join!' we bring the person on board. If the person says he's not interested, we simply dial the next phone number and start the process all over again.

"After several weeks, our associates are ready to go on their own. But they also know that anytime they need help, all they have to do is call and get on our schedule. We work with the willing! We can't outgive our people, because the rewards keep coming back to us."

Motivating Distributors for the Long Term

Your passion and commitment for your business are two of the best ways for you to encourage your distributors to continue working hard to build their businesses. Unfortunately, that's not enough to keep them committed for the long term. Joining a network marketing company is easy — almost everyone can afford it — and conversely, it's easy to quit. When your distributors begin to face the inevitable frustrations and setbacks that every network marketer encounters, they may want to quit. That's why you, their leader, must stay in touch with them and help them through challenging times. They need to feel good about themselves and their decision to become network marketers. And they need to see results. This section presents some ways to encourage the members of your downline to stay involved for the long haul.

Motivating by money

Help your distributors make a sale or sponsor another new distributor as quickly as possible. The easiest way to do so is by using the three-way call. The people whom you contact on these calls usually belong to your distributor's warm market. Chances are good that one of these people will buy or join. Nothing is more exciting for a new distributor than the first sale or first sponsored distributor! Do everything in your power to bring it about early in the relationship.

In an attempt to help a distributor earn money faster, and as a strategy to increase the depth of the associate's downline, leaders frequently place their own personal recruits under their distributors. Aside from the money the distributor will earn from this recruit — perhaps for 10, 20, or more years — this act gives the distributor a tremendous boost of confidence (see also "Motivating by praise" later in this section). "I have tried to place people under every single one of my first-level leaders," explains Jan Ruhe, "and I have found that it is a great gift for them. I wish someone had done it for me!" Jan explains that she looks in her downline for people who can sell Discovery Toys' products before she places a new recruit under them. "I look for someone who can sell at least $300 of product a month. That's not much. If they can move product, then I have a conversation with them that goes like this: 'Hi, this is Jan Ruhe, and today is your lucky day! I see that you can move our products. How would you like to start building a business and become a leader in my organization?' Then I lay out the expectations. Trust me, this works. I have some of the finest leaders in network marketing worldwide today because of this strategy."

 ZIG SAYS

Distributors who earn even a small amount of money within the first 30 days of starting their network marketing business are likely to stick with it. Most people who become network marketers are not looking to make millions of dollars. They hope to make enough money to cover a car payment or a house payment, or to earn a little extra for their family's enjoyment. They may get only a $50 or $100 check in that first month of operation, but that may be all they need to see the big picture. If they hope to make $400 or $800 extra per month, that first check will motivate them to stay in the business.

Motivating through mission

To retain distributors and motivate them to become proactive in the business, it's important to sell them on more than the company or the company's products and services. "The only thing that works," says Ray Gebauer, one of Mannatech's most successful representatives, "is to sell them on mission.

The sooner you can enroll someone in a mission, where they see they're part of a worthy cause, where they can feel like a hero, the better your chances of keeping them excited and committed to their business. It doesn't do a lot of good to sign up people unless you enroll them in the company's mission."

Nowadays, perhaps more than ever in our history, people want to feel that their work is meaningful. Few people are interested in a job anymore. They want to make a difference in someone's life, perhaps their own, perhaps a family member's, and almost certainly their customer's. The search for significance and the desire to be part of it explain why so many people, experienced network marketers as well as newcomers, have joined the Zig Ziglar Network (ZZN).

"Our company's mission," says Tom Ziglar, Zig's son and the president of ZZN, "is to be the difference maker in the personal, family, and professional lives of enough people to make a positive difference in the world." That's more than just a statement, asserts Tom. Anyone who knows much about Zig Ziglar knows that's been his personal mission for more than three decades. "Ever since we announced ZZN in January 2000 and gave people the opportunity to participate in Zig's mission, our phones have not stopped ringing. People frequently tell us, 'I've never been involved in a multi-level marketing company before, and I never thought I would be. But if I can share Zig's mission with other people, count me in.'" These people are more motivated by mission than they are by anything else.

ZIG SAYS

Network marketing advantage: Training is at the heart of the business

In traditional business I've had owners and managers ask me, "Why should I train my people and then lose them?" It is frequently true that the better you train and develop your people in traditional business, the more likely you are to lose them because they often start their own companies. But that's not the way it works in network marketing. The more effectively you train, develop, and help the people in your downline, the more likely they are to stay with you because they are already building their own business. Bottom line: The better you train and encourage your people, the more likely they are to stay with you.

Training opportunities abound in network marketing. While network-marketing companies frequently sponsor regional and national training programs, individual leaders within a company will also invest time to train and develop distributors. Much of this training occurs by telephone, and it's at little or no cost to the distributors.

Motivating by praise

When you praise distributors, you give them hope, and hope is the foundational quality for all change, according to psychiatrist Alfred Adler. We all hope that tomorrow will be just as good, if not better than today. Author John Maxwell says, "When there's hope in the present, there's power in the future." When you praise your distributors, you give them a feeling of hope, and that's when exciting things can happen in a network marketing business. Also remember that encouragement is the fuel on which hope runs.

Become a "good finder," beginning right now. Make it a practice to find good in other people and circumstances. When you do, be sure to verbalize your findings. Tell people what you like about them. If you're working on goal setting with them and you admire their ambition, tell them so. If you're listening to one of their first business presentations, tell them what you liked. In times of doubt or disappointment, look for the good and share it with your associates. You'll be amazed at the results. First, your people will appreciate your encouraging words of praise. But also, *your* attitude will change for the better!

"I believe in you" are the four most important words in network marketing, according to Doug Firebaugh, a former associate in National Safety Associates (NSA), known for its water treatment systems, and now a trainer of network marketers. "To motivate your downline, you have to build their belief system," he continues. "Your associates need to know that they can succeed in this business . . . and as their leader, you have to build rock-solid belief in them. You do that through constant encouragement and praise."

Six ideas to motivate the people in your downline

Trainer Doug Firebaugh, president of PassionFire International based in Louisville, Kentucky, offers these ideas for motivating the people in your downline:

✔ Recognize your associates publicly. When you're on a conference call with a group of your associates or when you're sending the group a message by e-mail, publicly praise your associates for even their small attempts to get their business started.

✔ Work with your associates one-on-one. Personal attention is a motivating factor. People thrive on it, and it makes them feel like they're adding value to the organization.

✔ Be accessible! Many of the superstars in this industry are not accessible. A leader whom you can reach on the phone or by e-mail creates a feeling of confidence among associates.

✔ Arrange special events for your associates. Buy tickets for your leaders to hear people like Zig Ziglar, Jim Rohn, and others who have something important to say to network marketers. Join your leaders at these events. Doing so is an incredible bonding experience. Anytime you can get your group together, do something to celebrate the victories in your organization. If you can't do it in person, get everyone on the phone.

✔ Send handwritten notes. Say things like "I believe in you!" and "You're going to the top!" Write it on thank-you cards and send them to your associates. Nowadays handwritten notes are unexpected, and when you receive one, you know it's personal, and it was directed to you.

✔ Use personal audiocassette recordings. Get a ten-minute cassette and record a message to an associate. Tell her that you're proud of her because of her accomplishments, and you just want her to know how much you appreciate her. Then take an appropriate passage from one of Zig's books and read it on the tape. Preface it by saying, "Here's something I think is just for you." Your associate will listen to that tape over and over. It's not just motivating; it's a belief-building factor.

You can use many other ideas to motivate your team. Whatever you do, be sincere. Also, use words of praise and motivation to help your associates stretch their talents. "Everyone has a comfort zone," says Doug, "and you don't want them to get comfortable in it. Praising them for something well done is a way to motivate them to take the next step forward."

Part IV

Sales and Marketing Skills to Help You Build Your Business

The 5th Wave   By Rich Tennant

"I've been working on my network marketing business over 80 hours a week for the past two years and it hasn't bothered me OR my wife, whats-her-name."

In this part . . .

The people who understand that network marketing is a relationship business — *not* a sales business — and who focus on building and maintaining relationships are the people who succeed in this profession. New millionaires are created every week in network marketing, but not one succeeded in a legitimate business without building relationships. Whether you're hoping to earn a little extra money each month or you're planning on making a fortune, go out and build relationships.

By building relationships, you will attract customers, both those who will buy your products and services and those who will join you in business. You can use the phone, the mail, the Internet, face-to-face meetings, and a variety of other media to build relationships with customers, and we show you how professional network marketers do it all in this part of the book.

Customers remain loyal to network marketers who take the time to build relationships with them. And in business, nothing is more valuable than a loyal customer!

Chapter 12

Know Thy Customer

*B*efore you discover how to attract and keep customers in your network marketing business, you need to explore a few fundamental principles about customers. For a number of reasons, not everyone will become your customer, so you have to start looking for them in the right places. The sooner you discover how to recognize potential customers, attract them to your business, and keep them buying from you, the sooner you can build a satisfying and profitable network marketing business.

Determining Your Most Valuable Asset as a Network Marketer

Ask a half-dozen network marketers: "What's your most valuable asset as a business owner?" and you're likely to get a half-dozen different answers. They may give one of the following responses:

- ✔ "My personality. I'm outgoing."
- ✔ "My persistence. I never give up."
- ✔ "My attitude. It's always positive."
- ✔ "My sales skills. I'm a closer."
- ✔ "My products. They're outstanding!"
- ✔ "My marketing materials. People love 'em."

All of these are valuable assets, but all of them combined do not add up to a satisfying and profitable business, and that's the objective you want to achieve as a network marketer. Therefore, it's important to understand that the most valuable asset of *any* business is the customer! Profits aren't generated by marketing materials, sales skills, persistence, or any other attribute of the business or the business owner. You don't derive long-term satisfaction from these attributes, either. Only customers generate profits and satisfaction.

For that reason, you need to understand who your customers are in business. As a network marketer, you have two types of customers: *retail customers,* those who buy your products and services, and *downline customers,* the distributors who join your organization to build a business of their own. We discuss both types of customers in this chapter.

Creating Customers

You can find lots of ideas about how to attract customers in Chapters 14 through 17. In this chapter, our focus is on understanding why creating customers is so important.

The only reason to be in business is to create customers and keep them buying from you. Of course, you want to make a profit, and hopefully you have a mission to fulfill, but nothing happens in a business until someone sells something to someone else, and does so repeatedly. That's creating a customer.

Dan Gaub, 41, understood the importance of creating a customer from day one when he joined Market America in 1995. He's now one of only 40 directors nationwide in that company, which sells approximately $150 million in nutritional, home care, and personal products annually. He's also become financially independent.

"I don't think of someone who purchases from me once as a customer," Dan maintains. "I'm looking for repeat business. I look for what a customer can produce over a period of at least three to four years. I have customers who have been with me from the very first week I started. I've sold products to more than 900 people, but I have 400 customers who make up my customer base, and in an average month each one puts $37 a month into my pocket. That's a pretty good business!"

It's also a great testimony for the value of creating a customer.

Unfortunately, many network marketers spend a great deal of time on tasks other than creating customers. They spend time on busywork: asking questions they've asked before, reading product literature for the umpteenth time, filling out paperwork, talking on the phone, and cleaning up their offices. A year goes by and they haven't built a customer base, or they've built a very thin one.

Savvy network marketers understand that a fat customer base (comprised of both retail customers and downline distributors) produces residual income, and residual income provides financial freedom and security. Furthermore, savvy network marketers realize that when it's time to sell the business and retire or build another business, the fat, residual-income-producing customer base attracts the highest purchase price.

"Without customers, you don't have a business," says James Davis, a star networker at Horizons Interactive, which sells all kinds of products from Web sites. "Your customer *is* your business." James's downline extends to all 50 states, 4 countries, and numerous other territories. As a result of a stroke in 1994, just six months into his network marketing career, James lost most of his eyesight and the ability to drive a car. After an 18-month recovery, he started building his marketing business from home in Hardy, Arkansas, population 540. "Network marketers think their product is their business, but it's not," declares James. "You've got to have good products that people will like and buy, and you've got to have a good company behind you that will pay you when you make a sale, but you don't have anything until you build a customer base. You gotta roll up your sleeves and take care of your customers: solve their problems and answer their questions. Make 'em feel like somebody cares about 'em. When you've got customers, that's when you've got a business. And that's something that's very valuable."

Identifying Your Customers

Who is a customer? Network marketing attracts several kinds of customers, and they all require you to treat them like *they* want to be treated — not necessarily like you think they want to be treated. Study them and learn their likes and dislikes. Remember, you can have everything in life you want if you will just help enough other people get what they want. Take that approach, and you will build a permanent customer base.

Philosophically, the customer hierarchy looks like this:

- You
- Familial customer
- Affiliate customer
- Prospective customer
- First-time customer
- Long-term customer

The following sections talk about each type of customer.

The #1 customer: You

You're the most important customer in your network marketing business. If the business doesn't serve you, make you happy, fulfill your dreams, help you earn the money you rightfully deserve, or sell products and services that you would buy yourself, then what good is the business? If the business doesn't satisfy you, why would it satisfy any other customer? Sooner or later, dissatisfied customers go away — *and that includes you.* If you're a dissatisfied customer of your own business, how can you transfer positive feelings to your prospects? Believing is a prerequisite to succeeding.

The familial customer

Right behind you in the customer hierarchy is your family. Families deserve to be kept informed about the business, even if they're not directly involved in it. The business must satisfy them, too! If the business doesn't meet the family's needs, the business will eventually suffer, and the family member who operates the business may become an unwelcome guest at home.

Network marketing is a blessing for families who like to work together. Most network marketing organizations include family members who are distributors. Perhaps the wife launches the new enterprise. When her husband sees how well she's doing, he may get involved, too.

Many married couples quit their jobs, sometimes giving up careers to devote themselves full-time to network marketing. They get their parents involved, as well as aunts and uncles. They bring their children into the business, and before long it's a family affair. There's no better way to keep the familial customer informed than to involve them in the business. In addition, with one more thing in common, the family often becomes even closer and more supportive of one another. They also can pinch-hit when circumstances interfere or change, and they call on each other to temporarily carry the ball for them, thus assuring continuity of action.

Affiliate customers

Your affiliate customers are the people who work with you. Members of your downline, usually called *distributors,* are affiliate customers. If the business doesn't help them feel good about their work and their lives, they will not remain involved with the business for very long. In sales terminology, their benefits must exceed the price, or they will invest elsewhere their time, and the money you spent training them.

Downline is a term that describes your sales organization. As you recruit and sponsor (that is, train) distributors, they become members of your downline.

You will discover that your downline customers can require a tremendous amount of your time, especially when they're first getting started. They need to learn what you know about how the business operates, including how to identify and sponsor their own distributors. They also need to understand the business's products and services, as well as how to market and sell them.

Time invested in helping your distributors is well worth it because as customers, your distributors are valuable assets. You earn residual income from the future sales by these folks and from the sales of each of *their* downlines. When you sponsor a member into your downline, you're accepting an awesome responsibility. Without knowing what motivates your distributors and what their goals and life aspirations are, you can't help them succeed. If they don't succeed, they're out, and you've invested time and money to sponsor and train them for little or no reward. Befriend your distributors and help them get what they want from their network marketing activity because it's the *only* way you will build a satisfying, profitable network organization.

Prospective customers

There are two types of prospective customers in network marketing:

- ✔ **Retail customers** consume the products and services you sell. Their only interest, at least initially, is in using your products and services month after month.
- ✔ **Downline distributors** are interested in building their own businesses.

Distributors are really two customers in one. First, they are downline customers, and they rely on you for guidance as they build their business. Second, they are consumers and resellers of your company's products and services. Although they should use the products and services personally, they also market and sell products and services to their own customers. As distributors, they can purchase from the company at wholesale and sell at retail prices.

After they've purchased products and services for several months, retail customers often decide that they want to become distributors. They're likely to succeed rather quickly because they have already realized the value of the products and, in all probability, have told their families and close friends about the benefits they're enjoying from them. As a result, they can enthusiastically and effectively begin marketing and selling them.

Prospecting for these two types of customers is an ongoing responsibility for a network marketer, and we tell you how to prospect in Chapter 14. Suffice it to say that network marketers must carefully cultivate their own lists of prospective customers. Anyone who is interested in starting a network marketing business or purchasing the company's products and services can be added to the prospective customer list. Keep in mind that prospective customers need to know how the business, or its products and services, will benefit them. Not everyone becomes a customer the first time he or she hears about a network marketing company or a new product.

Network marketers must always remember their competition. Other network marketers may be vying for the attention of the same prospective customers you are pursuing, just like various retailers compete for the same customers. Just because you contacted a prospect once doesn't mean that a competitor hasn't contacted the same prospect several times and even treated the prospect to some sample products.

Always ask yourself this question: "Would my prospects say that I'm more effectively selling the benefits of my products and showing more interest in them than my competitors?" If not, they're not your prospective customers, and you are definitely a "suspect" in their book!

First-time customers

First-time customers present the greatest opportunity because, with proper service and personal interest, you can build a relationship with them, and they become long-term customers and friends (see the following section, "Long-term customers"). When you show those first-time buyers how your business can satisfy their wants and needs and that you care about them, they become permanent customers and encourage their friends and families to do business with you as well. That's why there's no such thing as a "little" or insignificant sale — *if* you properly service the customer.

Long-term customers

Last but not least are the long-term customers. Distributors who consistently work the business, whether full-time or part-time, are long-term customers. They fulfill their responsibilities to you, to themselves, and to their own customer base. Retail consumers who are loyal and faithful to you and your business and who buy products and services only from you and not your competitors are long-term customers, too. In terms of generating profit for your business, long-term customers are obviously the most valuable to you, and that's why you should work at building relationships with them.

The potential of your customers

As a network marketer, you must never overlook or underestimate the potential of your customers, be they family members, affiliates, prospects, or long-term customers. Unlike traditional marketers, who typically sell a product or service and not a business opportunity, you are selling both! That long-term customer who has been purchasing your services since the first week you announced your network marketing business may call one day and say, "I think I want to do what you do. Can you help me get started?" This dual opportunity presents a terrific advantage for network marketers. Just like traditional marketers, you will spend money to attract customers to your business, but unlike traditional marketers who are looking only for retail buyers, you're looking for customers who could become distributors once they're convinced that the products are really good and once they're made aware of the income and security opportunities that network marketing offers. That's exciting!

Long-term customers sometimes become friends and confidants, particularly when they experience the benefits of doing business with you. You can count on them to help you build your business, and they usually do so cheerfully because in network marketing they're building their own business as well. However, you must understand that long-term customers aren't created overnight. They require your willingness to be of service to them, your attentiveness to details, and your concern for their desires. *Make them feel important — because they are.* When you can count more long-term customers in your business than first-time customers, you're on your way to becoming a wealthy individual — in friends *and* finances.

Giving the Best Customers the Best Experience

Business really gets exciting — and profitable — when you understand the value of your customer base and you cultivate and then evaluate your customers so that you can treat them appropriately. Some customers are more cooperative, appreciative, and faithful than others, and being able to differentiate them is important. Only then can you determine how to cultivate the "right" customers for your business.

Rank has its privileges

Say that you have two retail clients, Bert and Bart, who've each been buying from you for three years. Bert spends an average of $100 a month purchasing your products. He's a likable guy. He refers you to his friends and occasionally helps you recruit associates into your downline. Whenever your company introduces a new product, you call Bert, and he buys it. He'll try almost anything at least once. What a customer! During the holidays, you always invite Bert to dinner, plus you give him a gift.

Bart, on the other hand, grudgingly spends $110 a month. With Bart, you feel like you earn every penny of your commission, and more. Anytime Bart calls your office, you cringe. He calls at least once a month to place an order and twice a month to complain. He frequently runs out of products and then wants an order sent overnight — at your expense.

You hesitate to introduce new products to Bart because he always says the price is too high, and unless you negotiate with him, he won't buy them anyway. As for referrals, he's never given you one, in spite of your frequent requests. Even though Bart spends $110 a month, he's a drain on you personally, and on your business financially. If you didn't have to spend time with Bart, you could sell more to other good customers like Bert. Bart's extra $10 a month isn't worth it. In fact, he's costing you money, especially when you have to mail products to him overnight at your expense. Even so, during the holidays, you invite Bart to dinner, along with your other customers. You give him a gift, too, although it's occurred to you that he doesn't really deserve it.

If we asked you why you invite Bart to dinner, you might say, "I never know when someone will decide to join my organization, although I'm not sure I'd really want Bart in my downline! However, he's one of my customers, and I treat all my customers the same."

Should you treat all customers equally?

"Sure I do. Doesn't everyone?" you might ask.

No! And neither should you.

Yes, laws require the equal treatment of people, but such laws are intended to protect our basic rights as human beings. A dinner invitation, a gift, or even a greeting card is *not* a basic right. The fact is, you do not have to do for all customers what you do for one customer. But make sure to give your best customers the best experience!

Fly on almost any major airline, and you'll immediately understand this issue. The most frequent flyers get special attention, including upgrades to first class, where they get even *more* special attention. The airlines — and nowadays many other businesses — realize that some customers are more valuable than other customers and deserve to be treated differently.

This is one lesson that network marketer Dan Gaub in Yakima, Washington, didn't have to learn. "I have always done a good job of knowing my customers. I track their purchases. When a customer has purchased $2,500 with me, I give them a lifetime 10 percent discount. If a customer buys $250 of products from me at one time, I give them an immediate 10 percent discount.

These are not company policies. These are *my* policies." By tracking his customers' purchases, Dan knows that his personal policies pay off. To those who buy the most, he gives the most, and in turn, they continue buying more from him.

The customer is not always right

"Wait a minute, now," you could be saying. "I've been taught that the customer is *always* right."

We've heard that saying for eons in traditional businesses. If a customer wants to buy your product six to a package, you'd better sell it six to a package. If the customer wants service on Tuesday, you'd better be available on Tuesday. If not, you're wrong, and the customer is right. At least that's what we've been told.

But what if you can't or don't want to sell product in packages of six? And what if you have openings only on Wednesdays because you don't work on Tuesdays? Don't you have some rights, too?

Indeed you do! You're not in business to meet unreasonable demands. You're in business to fulfill your goals and make a profit. At the minimum, you're in business to feel satisfied about what you do. You can't accomplish these goals by trying to be everything to everybody. And you shouldn't, especially if you want to build a satisfying and profitable network marketing business. This is all the more reason to pursue the right customers!

Imagine if your business attracted more customers like Bart than like Bert. Too many of the wrong customers zap all the fun out of your business. Even if you're making money and you feel like you're doing some good, you will eventually become so dissatisfied that you won't be able to sustain your business. You'll want out, at any price!

"When I speak with a prospect, I say, 'How can I help you?' I'm not a salesman, I solve problems," explains Dan Gaub. "I want to hear about the prospect and the prospect's problem so that I can make sure if I invest my time as a service manager or a customer manager, there will be value for both of us. I want to be sure there's a need for my product and that I will get paid. If I do business with a customer and later discover the customer is not right for me, I thank them for their business, but I tell them they would probably be happier doing business with someone else. This could open the door of communication and could lead to turning an unsatisfactory relationship into a winning one for both parties."

The good news is that by recognizing that some customers are more valuable than others and that some are better suited than others for your business, you can stop trying to be everything to everyone. If you have a customer like Bart, you can stop catering to his idiosyncrasies. While you refrain from being rude, you can persuade Bart to do business on *your* terms and not his. Bart will either become a "right" customer or decide on his own to go elsewhere. Either way, once you stop wasting time with Bart, you'll have more time to spend with your more valuable customers. You'll also have time to attract new customers who will make your business more satisfying and profitable.

The most valuable customers are the right customers for your business. They're the distributors who do their homework, attend meetings, and talk to prospects about their business every day. They're retail customers who happily spend their money because they appreciate your products and services. They're also considerate of your time. Once you know where to find these customers and how to attract and keep them loyal to your business (we discuss these issues in Chapters 16, 17, and 20), you can eliminate, or at least minimize, the "wrong" customers who seem to delight in disrupting your business and taking away all your fun, not to mention your satisfaction and profits.

Chapter 13

Determining a Customer's Value

*H*ow much is a customer worth? Good question.

Everyone who owns a business — network marketing or otherwise — ought to know the answer. If you don't know how much a customer is worth, how can you tell which customers are more valuable than others? Unfortunately, many business owners can't, but network marketers should.

Without knowing the value of a customer, you can't know whether you're making or losing money on that customer. For example, if attracting a new customer costs you $25, you ought to know when that money will be returned to you through the customer's purchases. Until that point, you've lost money. If the customer generates a $10 commission for you but never buys again, you're out $15 forever! You'd better hope that customer returns and generates another commission or two for you. Of course, if the customer's first purchase generates a $50 commission, you're way ahead. If you can earn a monthly $50 commission from this customer and the customer continues buying from you for five to ten years or even more, then you've gained a valuable business asset.

Remember that a customer is much more than a dollar sign, however. Also remember that you can have everything in life you want if you will just help enough other people get what they want. If the products you sell fill a need, there's no limit to what that customer's value can be. The leads they will give you alone can be extraordinarily valuable.

ZIG SAYS

Satisfied customers provide more than money

Many years ago, when I was a rookie salesman just getting started in selling heavy-duty waterless cookware, we lived in Lancaster, South Carolina. I had the good fortune to meet Mrs. Will Hendrix, the wife of the postmaster. She had owned a set of our cookware for over 30 years, cooked in it every day, and had an outstanding reputation as the best cook in town. She loved her set of cookware and allowed me to host a dinner party at her home. She invited eight couples who all attended, and I cooked the meal in her old set instead of using my new set to prove its durability and lifetime quality. That night, I didn't give much of a sales talk. As a matter of fact, Mrs. Hendrix did the sales talk — and all eight couples bought as a result of that satisfied customer.

During the next two years, whenever I hit a sales slump, I drove by and visited with Mrs. Hendrix. She had more or less "adopted" me and treated me like a son. Without fail, when I dropped in for a visit she had "just yesterday" or "just today" cooked a special dish, and she raved about how good it tasted, thanks to her set of cookware. I always left there charged up, and the sales slump was frequently broken. In short, that one customer was an invaluable asset. Your satisfied customers can do the same for you: They can motivate you and give you the leads to sell other people on your product.

Calculating the Cost of Acquiring a Customer

Business owners who don't know the value of a customer also don't know the cost of a customer. That's not good, because acquiring a customer almost always comes with a price. Even before you calculate the value of a customer, it's a good idea to calculate the cost of acquiring one customer.

Customers are rarely free. If you place an advertisement in a newspaper to generate customers, the ad costs money. If you subscribe to a phone service that automatically answers calls from the people who respond to your ad, and you also subscribe to a fax-on-demand service that transmits materials to your prospects, there's more cost. If your prospects call you, or you call them, and they ask for a brochure, an audiotape, a videotape, or all three, you just added more cost. If you maintain a Web site that provides information about your business, that's even more cost.

Don't forget to figure in the less-obvious costs. For example, your company probably sells videotapes that you can use for marketing purposes. Suppose that one tape costs only $1. Don't forget that you have to enclose the tape in a mailing envelope, label the envelope, and affix postage. More costs. You'll probably want to include a note, a business card, or perhaps a letter with the tape. More costs. And don't forget about your time — that's worth something, too.

Generating one lead and providing information to that lead may cost you a few dollars or many dollars. What's important is that you know the price you're paying to acquire a customer.

You can minimize your customer acquisition costs by prospecting for customers in your warm market. If you continuously expand your warm market by asking for referrals, you can keep your customer acquisition costs low — but still not free. Walking across the street to sell a neighbor a product or to recruit the neighbor for your downline doesn't cost a cent — until the neighbor asks for information and you hand over some brochures and a marketing video. Granted, the effort may not cost more than a few dollars and 15 minutes of your time, but it's an expense. In business, tracking every expense is an important part of the job.

To keep your marketing costs as low as possible, always ask for referrals. If your prospect says, "Thanks, but I'm not interested," you just smile and say, "Who do you know who *might* be interested?" Constantly keep a list of referrals — names and phone numbers — and work the list. Open the conversation with something like "Hello, Mary, you don't know me, but our neighbor, Janice, said you might have an interest in a product that I represent." Get the idea? This really simple technique will save you a lot of money.

Tracking leads and evaluating their costs

From the outset of your business, make it a habit to track the source of every lead. When prospects call or e-mail you to request information about your business opportunity or your products or services, ask them, "How did you hear about me?"

If, for example, you purchased a list of prospects and mailed those prospects a letter or a product brochure, or you faxed or e-mailed them a message, you need to evaluate the return on your investment. Similarly, if you placed an advertisement in a newspaper or exhibited your business at a trade show, you want to know whether the money you invested was worthwhile. That way, you'll know whether to repeat this activity in the future.

If you use e-mail to prospect for customers, you can find our thoughts about spamming in Chapter 14. For now, suffice it to say that we are against it and encourage you never to do it.

You can track lead sources in a couple of ways, and you have to decide which method is best for you. Your first option is the manual method, and it's an easy system to follow. All you need is a notepad and a pen. Down the left side of the notepad, list all the marketing activities you're currently using — for example, direct mail, newspaper ad, radio ad, expo, e-mail promotion, fax promotion, and so on. Across the top of the notepad, make two columns: Leads and Customers. The following is an example.

Marketing Activity	Leads	Customers
Radio ad		
Newspaper ad		
Fax promotion		
Expo		
Referral		

Always add "Referral" to your Marketing Activity list. Hopefully you'll receive a lot of referrals because they cost the least money!

Every time a prospect contacts you, ask, "How did you hear about me?" and place a tick mark next to the appropriate lead source. Every month or every quarter, add up the tick marks for each source. The results will be enlightening. You may discover, for example, that your direct-mail campaign produced the majority of leads and your e-mail promotion produced the fewest. That's good information. However, it's incomplete information. The tick marks represent only the number of *leads* generated, not the number of customers acquired. Therefore, you need to track which of the leads you converted to customers.

When you process a new customer application or a customer order, make note of the lead source. Then return to your notepad and put a tick mark across from the appropriate source. When you add up the tick marks for both leads and customers, you have an accurate record of how many customers each source generated.

Now divide the number of customers into the cost of the marketing activity to get a good estimate of the price you're paying per customer. For example, if you paid $200 for a newspaper ad and it generated 20 leads, your cost per lead is $10. However, if you convert only two of those leads to customers, then the price you paid per customer is $100 — plus the cost of brochures, tapes, postage, and so on.

Now you have to ask the question: Is it worth paying $100 to get one customer? You can't answer that question until you calculate the value of a customer, which we're about to show you how to do.

Instead of tracking your leads and customers manually, you can use a computer and any one of the popular spreadsheet programs, such as Microsoft Excel. A computer is the preferred method. You can set up a spreadsheet to track the sources of customers by marketing activities, just as we suggest that you do manually.

Determining a customer's potential as an investment

Looking at customer acquisition as an investment in your business is a good idea. How much you're willing to pay for a customer should be relative to the value of the customer. While factoring in the probability that some of your customers will become distributors, so their value will be much greater, the Customer Lifetime Value exercise (see the following section) shows you how much a retail customer is worth. If, on average, a customer generates $25 a month in commission money for you, would you be willing to spend $25, $50, $100, or more for that customer? If you knew that, on average, a customer would generate a $25 commission check for you every month for 60 or more months (a total of $1,500), you would be delighted to invest $100 or more to acquire that customer — it's a good investment. Of course, you should discuss this business decision with the people in your upline.

Network marketer James Davis of Arkansas knows his numbers. "If I spend $100 for a customer, it's a good deal," he says, "because I look for a long-term relationship. I take action so that I can keep that customer for life. If that customer generates a $20 or $30 commission check for me every month, that's an investment I'll make every day!"

The cost of a customer is not the same as the cost of a lead. You may convert one of 10 leads, or one of 20 leads, into customers. If a lead costs you $5 and you need ten leads to get one customer, then your cost per customer is $50.

Determining the Value of a Retail Customer

A network marketer serves two types of customers: the retail customer, who buys products or services, and the downline distributor, who buys products or services, sells products or services, and also sells the business opportunity. This section shows you how to calculate the value of a retail customer; later in this chapter, you can find out how to calculate the value of a distributor.

The Retail Customer Lifetime Value Chart in Table 13-1 demonstrates how you can turn a "small" sale into a "big — really big" sale, and how you can do it time and time again for as long as you decide to operate your business. Simply fill in the right-hand column as best you can, based on the realities of your business.

If your business is just getting started, you won't be able to complete this chart with figures based on your actual experiences. In that event, you may want to collaborate with a colleague, such as a member of your upline, and use your colleague's numbers to get an idea of how it works in your own company.

Table 13-1	Retail Customer Lifetime Value	
Average commission earned per customer per transaction:	A.	_____
Number of commissions earned per customer annually:	B.	_____
Annual commissions earned per customer (A × B):	C.	_____
Number of years customer buys from you:	D.	_____
Customer lifetime value (C × D):	E.	_____

The Retail Customer Lifetime Value Chart demonstrates the value of the average customer. When you attract the right customer to begin with and keep that customer loyal to your business, the financial relationship and personal satisfaction rewards can be amazing.

Calculating the average commission per retail customer

You begin filling out the Customer Lifetime Value Chart by calculating the following:

> Average commission earned
> per customer per transaction: A. _____

To arrive at this number, first calculate the average value of a single sale in your business. To do so, divide the gross annual sales (the total sales revenue generated by your company for a specific period of time, typically one year) by the number of sales, or transactions. After a couple months of doing this, redo the chart and calculate *your* average sale and revenue; your average will differ from the company average. It could be higher or lower.

> Gross annual sales revenue ÷ Number of sales = Average value of a sale

For example, if your business generated annual sales of $80,000 (this number can vary enormously) and you made 1,380 sales during the year, the average value of a sale equals $57.97.

> $80,000 ÷ 1,380 = $57.97 per sale

For the sake of this example, say that the average value of a sale is $30. If you earn a 20 percent commission on sales, then your average commission equals $6. So enter $6 on line A.

Average commission earned
per customer per transaction: A. ___$6___

Note: Average sale can be — and in most cases is — much higher.

Calculating the annual number of commissions per retail customer

Next, calculate the number of commissions earned *per customer* annually, as shown in the following excerpt from the Customer Lifetime Value Chart:

Number of commissions earned
per customer annually: B. _____

In other words, how many times in a year (or any other specified period) does the customer buy from you? Or how many times a year will you earn a commission from the customer? Calculating this number is easy if all your customers are on a monthly autoship program (see the glossary for an explanation of *autoship*) so that each customer makes 12 purchases annually. Write the number 12 on line B.

Number of commissions earned
per customer annually: B. ___12___

Although a customer may occasionally place an additional order, 12 times a year is a reasonable number to use when your customers are on autoship. In fact, most network marketing companies are designed so that customers purchase at least once a month. Even when customers are not on autoship, if you're doing your job as a network marketer, your customers are likely to place an order once a month.

Calculating the annual commissions earned per retail customer

To calculate annual commissions earned per customer, multiply A × B, or in this example, $6 × $12. The total is $72, and that's the number to enter on line C.

Annual commissions earned
per customer (A × B):   C. ___$72___

Determining how long a retail customer remains a customer

Next, estimate how long a customer will remain your customer:

Number of years customer buys from you: D. _____

Before arriving at an estimation, you have several factors to consider. This is one area in which network marketing holds a distinct advantage over traditional businesses, especially businesses that are bound geographically or that operate from a retail location. In today's mobile society, customers come and go. They tend to buy from businesses located within a 3- to 5-mile radius of their home or office. If they move across town, across the state, or out of state, they'll find a new dry cleaner, a new supermarket, a new hair salon, new restaurants, and so forth.

In network marketing, on the other hand, if you've done a good job and turned customers into clients, they'll continue buying from you even after they've moved several times. Because most network marketing companies ship directly to the customer, relieving the distributor of those responsibilities, distance and location are seldom issues. As a result, a network marketer can keep a customer as long as the networker remains in business, or for the customer's lifetime.

But not every customer remains a customer forever. Some customers are fickle. They like to experiment, so they buy from several different companies and show no loyalty to anyone. Some customers become dissatisfied, and even though they never complain, they switch suppliers. Also, competition steals some customers, even after they've been buying from the same business for many years. Circumstances such as a customer's sudden financial difficulty, illness, and a variety of other factors can disrupt or end a customer's patronage.

In service industries, which include nearly every network marketing organization, it's estimated that a customer remains a customer for approximately seven to ten years. To be conservative, and to acknowledge a high turnover rate in network marketing, we suggest that you write the number 7 on line D. Again, over time you can track these numbers for your business and complete this chart with more meaningful numbers.

Number of years customer buys from you: D. ___7___

If the average customer continues to buy for seven years and generates $72 annually in commission money, then the customer's lifetime value is $504 ($72 × 7). Record that amount on line E.

Customer lifetime value (C × D): E. ___$504___

Death shortens the customer cycle

Of course, nothing ends a customer relationship more abruptly than death. And it's been estimated that, on average, a business loses up to 3 percent of its customer base annually to death. Frederick Reichheld, author of *The Loyalty Effect*

and director of Bain & Company, a strategy consulting firm with offices worldwide, found that the average business loses 10 to 30 percent of its customer base annually!

Granted, prices are likely to increase during those seven years, but we won't complicate this exercise by factoring in those increases. If you continue your relationship with the same customer for seven years, you'll earn at least $504 in commission money. That may not seem like much, but we'll reserve comment until a little later in this chapter. What you've done so far is turn a $6 commission into $504.

Calculating a retail customer's Maximized Lifetime Value

There's yet another level of value to be added to this calculation. We call it the *Maximized* Customer Lifetime Value, shown in Table 13-2.

Table 13-2	Maximized Customer Lifetime Value	
Number of customer referrals annually:		F. _____
Percentage of referrals who become customers:		G. _____
Total number of customers from referrals (F × G):		H. _____
Lifetime value of commissions from referrals (E × H):		I. _____
Maximized Customer Lifetime Value (E + I):		J. _____

First address line F:

Number of customer referrals annually: F. _____

The greatest compliment that any network marketer — or any business owner — can receive from a customer is a referral. When customers refer you or your products, they're saying that they're not only satisfied in doing business with you, but they're willing to vouch for you! You might think of these customers as cheerleaders for you and your business. They love to share their experiences with family, friends, colleagues, and anyone they meet who expresses a need for what you sell. Cheerleader customers often do such a good job of referring you to prospective customers that you don't have to sell the prospects on the benefits of your products; the prospects are sold by the time they call you. All you have to do is take the order!

However, don't be too confident or presumptive. Make sure to test the waters for the sale at least casually. Give your prospect some of the details and ask him whether the person who referred him told him about their marvelous benefits. Then you can ask, "So I assume you're seeking the same satisfaction that your friend has found?" In all probability, he is going to say yes. When he does, the sale is made.

So how many referrals will each of your customers generate for you annually? The answer depends on a number of variables. First, how well are you doing your job? Are you taking care of your customers? Are you solving their problems and making them feel good? Are you creating cheerleader customers? If you are, you'll get a certain number of referrals without even asking for them. However, if your current customers don't volunteer prospects, you should ask whether they have friends or family who would like to enjoy the same benefits.

Some good customers aren't likely to become cheerleaders, however, no matter how much attention you give them and how much they love your service and products. These customers tend to be more reserved. They may need a little encouragement to refer business your way. They'll generate referrals for you, but only if you ask them. If you offer them an incentive, such as a financial reward or a free product, they'll often make it a point to help you find new customers.

As you build your network marketing business, you'll discover that some customers generate a half-dozen or more referrals annually, others don't contribute any, and the majority generate two or three. So write the number 2 on line F.

> Number of customer referrals annually: F. ____2____

A referral frequently results in a sale, but in network marketing, as in life, there's no such thing as a sure thing. A referral may be weak, or the prospect could have no interest. Sometimes the network marketer doesn't respond fast enough or responds with poor sales skills. So to be safe, say that 75 percent of referrals become new customers. Write 75 percent on line G.

> Percentage of referrals who become customers: G. ____75%____

Now multiply the number of referrals annually by the percentage of referrals who become customers. In this case, $2 \times 75\%$ equals 1.5 customers. That's the number to record on line H.

Total number of customers from referrals: H. ____1.5____

What's 0.5 of a customer? You can't have half a customer! But statistics do strange things. If that 0.5 of a customer bothers you, look at this way: Every two years you gain three new customers via referrals. Or go ahead and do what the statisticians say to do — round up the number. In this case, it's 2. If you really want to avoid statistically dividing people, learn to sell 100 percent of your referrals!

You can calculate the lifetime value of commissions from referrals by multiplying Customer Lifetime Value ($504) by the number of referred customers (1.5). In this example, the total is $756. In other words, during the average customer lifetime of seven years, 1.5 customers will generate $756 in additional revenue.

Lifetime value of commissions
from referrals $(E \times H)$:   I. ____$756____

Add the original lifetime value of a customer ($504) to the value of referred business ($756) and the sum is the *Maximized* Customer Lifetime Value, which in this example is $1,260! And that's how you turn $6 — and a lot of consistent, smart, effective work and customer service — into $1,260.

But There's More: Making Customers Distributors

By now, it should be obvious that you can do a lot of figuring, conjecturing, and projecting about what happens in network marketing. However, putting figures on paper and making them sound good doesn't necessarily make them so. The reality is that if you do a good job with your customers, you will keep them around for a long time, and they will refer you to other people. When you start adding the benefits that the customer receives along the way and the benefits that you receive by offering them quality products at a fair price, you create a win/win situation.

As I mentioned early in this chapter, the real benefit comes when those customers become distributors. That's the secret of having good customer service and good products. That's the way you build business; that's the way you build an organization, residual income, financial security, and a host of other things. I can't overstate the importance of having quality customers and bringing them into the business at some point if they so desire.

Enrollment bonuses

When you recruit a distributor, your company may reward you with an enrollment bonus or commission. But because this is a one-time payment, the Customer Lifetime Value calculation does not include bonus compensation. Nonetheless, bonus money adds up quickly, and you may not want to join a company that doesn't pay liberal enrollment bonuses.

Incidentally, your customers who are senior citizens have children and grandchildren. Many times, 60- and 70-year-olds (or even older) want to join the organization so that they not only get the preferred customer discounts but also can supply members of their families with products at a reduced price. When they realize how much fun it is to work with their children and grandchildren, many of them will easily persuade others to join the network. The possibilities are endless. That's why establishing good, repeat business with retail sales can be so significant.

Remember that the most successful people in network marketing, and the ones who build income, are those who retail products *and* recruit people and build a downline. So in the following section, fill in the Customer Lifetime Value chart again, this time by using numbers from a downline customer, or distributor.

Determining the Value of a Downline Customer

The Downline Customer Lifetime Value Chart in Table 13-3 follows the same procedures that you complete for the retail customer.

Table 13-3	Downline Customer Lifetime Value
Average commission earned per customer per transaction:	A. _____
Number of commissions earned per customer annually:	B. _____
Annual commissions earned per customer (A × B):	C. _____
Number of years customer buys from you:	D. _____
Customer Lifetime Value (C × D):	E. _____

Calculating the average commission per distributor

The first calculation asks for the average commission earned per distributor per transaction. The rate of commission may depend on the distributor's position in your downline. Is this distributor on your first level or lower? Depending on your company's compensation plan, a first-level distributor may generate a 10 percent commission, whereas a fifth-level distributor may produce a lesser amount, perhaps 5 percent.

For the sake of this exercise, assume that the distributor is first level, or what network marketers call your *frontline,* and the commission rate is 10 percent. Also assume that the value of an average sale is $100. Therefore, the average commission earned per first-level distributor per transaction is $10 ($100 × 10%).

> Average commission earned
> per distributor per transaction: A. ___$10___

Calculating the annual number of commissions per distributor

The number of commissions earned per distributor annually is the same as the number of transactions this distributor handles in a year. (You're not counting individual customers now. One customer may purchase multiple times in a year, accounting for multiple transactions.) Assume that the distributor processes 800 transactions annually.

> Number of commissions earned
> per distributor annually: B. ___800___

In that event, the annual number of commissions earned from this distributor is $8,000 (800 × $10). Keep in mind that you may have three, four, or more frontline distributors, each generating $8,000 a year for you.

> Annual commissions earned per distributor: C. ___$8,000___

Calculating distributor longevity

If a frontline distributor remains in your downline for just five years,

> Number of years customer buys from you: D. ___5___

the lifetime value of this one distributor will be $40,000 ($8,000 × 5)!

Customer Lifetime Value (C × D):   E. $40,000

Chances are, distributors who generate that much money for you, and more for themselves, will stay in your downline indefinitely, which means that over the long haul they can be very valuable to you because they're doing well and enjoying many benefits.

So far, we've looked only at the income from the frontline distributors. You're also going to earn money from your second, third, fourth, and maybe deeper levels of your downline. The depth of earnings in your downline depends on your company's compensation plan.

ZIG SAYS

Again, we could project what the possible earnings would look like on paper, but unless you do the job and produce the results, on paper is the only place the money will be. But I hasten to add that many people, including those mentioned in this book, are doing *really* well financially — and otherwise.

Chapter 14

The Art of Prospecting

. . . .

In This Chapter

▶ Using a database to store information about prospects and customers

▶ Heating up warm and cold markets to find the best prospects

▶ Selling your business opportunity

▶ Getting on a fast track to prospecting

▶ Using various forms of communication to contact your prospects

▶ Representing your company professionally

. . . .

*N*ew network marketers are typically excited about their businesses until they start prospecting for distributors and retail customers. Up to this point, you've done everything by the book. You've evaluated the profession, matched yourself up with the best company, organized your workspace, and invested time to learn about your mission and the value of the company's products and services. Now it's time to make some money, and that requires attracting distributors and customers. Suddenly, and possibly for the first time in this new business, you experience fear. "How am I going to prospect successfully? . . . How do I get a distributor? Where do I find retail customers? . . . Who do I ask? . . . What do I say?"

Relax! We have the answers for you, most of them, anyway. In this chapter, we show you how to begin prospecting for people to buy your products and services, as well as to join you in business. Whether you plan to do your prospecting offline (that is, without the Internet) or online (using the Internet), you'll find plenty of help in this chapter.

Don't let fear zap all your enthusiasm for building a network marketing empire. It's important to safeguard your enthusiasm, and you can do so by remembering that FEAR is simply an acronym for **F**alse **E**vidence **A**ppearing **R**eal. There's little if any substance to the fear-inspired questions that pop up in a network marketer's mind when it's time to prospect for business. Sure, it's normal to feel anxious about taking this next step in the development of your business. But if you selected the right company, the answers to your questions already exist. The company, through its training programs, its leadership, and the people in your upline, will teach you *how* to prospect. Follow the system, and fear will first diminish and then go away.

First Things First: Setting Up a Database of Prospects

Before you start prospecting, set up a database to track pertinent information about your prospective distributors and customers. Until you do so, you're not ready to take this step in the development of your business. Typically, from the moment they join a company, network marketers start making notes of the people they want to approach to join their business or to buy their products or services. But by the time the network marketers are ready to start prospecting, the notes have disappeared or they're nowhere to be found. Making matters worse, the network marketers continue this process: jotting notes on slips of paper, grocery sacks, receipts, napkins, and the like. No, no, no! That's not what you want to do. You must have a database; whether you keep it manually or on your computer is up to you.

A database is the foundation for your marketing program. Without a database, you'll create chaos for yourself, and worse than that, you will miss many opportunities to attract and keep distributors and customers.

Use your database to track the following information about a prospective distributor and customer: name, mailing address, e-mail address, phone number, and notes about previous conversations with this prospect. Tracking the source of each lead is always helpful. How did you find this prospect, or how did he or she find you?

You can purchase a database software program at your favorite computer retail outlet or on the Internet. These programs automatically store and massage your data, making it easy for you to access it. If you're not using a computer, then you can build a manual database by using 3-x-5-inch index cards. Store the cards in a metal container or wrap a rubber band around them. Index the cards by date so that on any given date, you can quickly determine which prospect needs a follow-up contact that day. After you convert a prospect to a customer, transfer the data to a different color index card so that spotting your customers is easy. This method is the only way you can keep track of who's who and what needs to be done in your prospecting efforts.

Keeping your database on a computer makes business development a lot easier. It won't take you long to build a database of several hundred prospects. Manually maintaining a database that large is cumbersome, although that's what people did before computers. With a computer, however, the database software can reduce chaos and streamline your prospecting efforts.

Programs such as ACT! and Goldmine automatically sort and index your data. They also include mail-merge programs, making it easy for you to send follow-up letters to prospects, and provide a note-taking section where you can store information about each prospect. These programs provide many other features, including a To Do function that alerts you when it's time to follow up with a specific prospect. As soon as possible, start keeping your database in a software program!

In Chapter 17, we discuss lead generation programs that are available on the Internet. These programs usually include a database so that you don't have to use a separate program.

Making Two Decisions Now

Before you start prospecting, you need to decide on the wheres and the whats. Where will you look first for distributors and retail customers? Should you contact your family and friends or canvass your neighborhood? Or would it be better to advertise to generate leads? And then what do you sell to these prospects? Should you begin by offering your retail products or services? Or should you sell your business opportunity first? This section won't make these decisions for you, but it at least clarifies your options, leaving you to make the final decisions.

Any time you face a decision and you don't know how to proceed, your first call should be to your upline sponsor. What does your sponsor recommend? Where does he or she look for distributors or customers? What works for other distributors with skill sets and time commitments similar to yours? Also consider your compensation plan. Some plans make selling products more appealing than sponsoring. Depend on the people in your upline to help you evaluate your options before you make a decision.

Decide where to look first

Warm market versus cold market: Which do you want to pursue first? Or do you want to go after both simultaneously?

Your *warm market* consists of the people you know or who know you. Family, friends, neighbors, and anyone they may refer to you make up your warm market. Your *cold market,* on the other hand, consists of strangers and acquaintances.

The choice is important because prospecting can be discouraging, and your success in either market depends almost entirely on your attitude about that market. If you don't like meeting strangers, then you probably won't like cold calling — that is, telemarketing from a purchased list or knocking on home or office doors. Some people say cold calling is a tough way to start a business.

Conversely, if you would rather undergo root canal surgery than approach your family and friends, you're not likely to convert many of them to customers. If you don't know where to begin, or you're comfortable in either market, or you prefer variety, then go after both markets.

"The warm market is 'where it's at,'" says Hilton Johnson, founder of Florida-based MLM University and a trainer of many top network marketers. "If you want to be successful in this industry, you need a perpetual warm market. Do things that will increase the warm market by building trust and attracting people to your business. The great majority of people who come into network marketing do so because of a product or service experience. It's usually one that changed their life, or the life of someone they know. Unfortunately, most network marketers don't have an organized way of keeping track of their customers, so they rarely ever go back to them and try to sponsor them."

Network marketing trainer Doug Firebaugh of Louisville, Kentucky, is of the opposite opinion. He built a successful National Safety Associates (NSA) business by selling water purifiers to the cold market. "That's where I spent 90 percent of my time," he explains. "I could cold call all day long!" However, prior to NSA, Firebaugh had a career in selling investments by telephone. Cold calling is what he had to do. He admits, however, "My three strongest legs in NSA were people I knew."

Bottom line: There is no right answer. It's a personal decision, really. After you evaluate the pros and cons of each market and evaluate your feelings about these markets, you should be able to make a decision that's best for you.

If you discovered a gold mine in your backyard, who would you share it with first?

One of Mannatech's most successful distributors, Ray Gebauer of Bellevue, Washington, says that if you discover a gold mine in your backyard and you're going to give most of the gold away because it's more than you can use, who do you want to give it to first? Strangers who answer an ad that you place in the newspaper? Or family and friends, the people who know you and like you? "I'm a proponent of going to family and friends first," says Gebauer, who sells nutritional products as a Mannatech distributor. "If they're not ready for the opportunity, you build without them. But give them the first chance. If you can't sell to them, then I question whether you will be able to sell to strangers. If you don't want to sell to them, then you're with the wrong company, or you don't believe in the company. You have to believe. After you sell to your warm market, you can move to your cold market with greater success."

Decide what you will sell first

Retail sales versus sponsoring: What's your pleasure? Yes, you can do both simultaneously, but hear us out first. You may be able to kill two birds with one stone by selling products or services first and your business opportunity second. Oftentimes, after using a product or service, a retail customer will say to you, "I love this . . . how can I get into this business for myself?" At that point, you won't have to "sell" the business opportunity. You're just an order taker! You can go ahead and sign them up.

Seasoned marketers say that those who enjoy the most success, build the largest organizations, create the most residual income, and consistently earn the most money don't do it just by sponsoring distributors. They do it by enthusiastically and successfully selling their products and services. We suggest that you take the same approach.

In the last several years, 48-year-old Ray Gebauer has earned "several million dollars" as a Mannatech distributor. "Eighty percent of that income," Gebauer explains, "was earned from people who never sponsored anyone, but fell in love with our products. Some of these people, six months or a year or two from now, will say, 'I could really sell this stuff. It has changed my life.' Others get to that point within three or four days! But the point is, you don't make the majority of your money just by sponsoring people. It's important to sponsor, but you have to sell your product, too."

To have a successful business as a network marketer, you have to be the right kind of person and do the right thing in order to gain all that network marketing has to offer. In other words, before you can excel in selling your products, you must become a product of your product. Show people that you set goals, you attend meetings, you study the distributor's manual, and, most importantly, that you use the company's products and services.

Todd Smith earned more than $2 million in 1999 as a Rexall Showcase International distributor selling nutritional products. He did it, he says, as a result of focusing on product sales, not on selling business opportunities. "If you have a product that impacts lives in a positive way, then people can see how they can make money in your business. So I suggest you lead with your products, not the opportunity. There have been too many 'opportunities' through the years in network marketing. Those days are about over. People will be moved to get involved after they see the value of the product."

People aren't always looking for business opportunities or second jobs. They're not always interested in changing careers, and when they are, they're not likely to think of network marketing. However, people buy products and services every day. By selling them your products and services, you may trigger their interest in your business. Once they realize how you earn money, they may want to join you in business. At that point, you'll have the opportunity to sponsor them.

Sponsoring is the act of recruiting and mentoring distributors. You find them first, often by selling them your products and services, and then you teach them how to become successful in your business. These folks comprise your downline.

Anyone you sponsor should also be a retail customer. If they're not, their chances of succeeding in business are somewhere between slim and none, although on rare occasions it does happen. Their belief in the product or service is going to be minimal until they experience the benefits themselves.

The fastest way to succeed as a network marketer is to set an example. In network marketing, that's called *duplication.* Selling is a transference of feeling, and if you can make the new distributors feel about the product like you feel about the product, based on your personal experience with it, then they're going to want to have that feeling also and receive the benefits you have. People will do what they see you doing. If you are a product of the product, and you believe that your product or services are terrific and save money, your customers and associates are apt to believe you and do likewise. If you're a goal setter, your associates will see the value in setting goals. Successful network marketers lead by example, and as an associate, you must always set an example.

Sponsorship involves responsibility

Network marketers sometimes have the notion that they sponsored a distributor when they signed them up and took their money. "I sponsored someone last night," they say excitedly. Oh? Veteran marketers know that sponsorship doesn't happen in an hour or two. Sponsorship takes weeks and sometimes months of working with an associate and building a relationship. That is prerequisite to trust, which is the stabilizing factor in long-term associations.

As you build your network marketing business, sponsor only one or two distributors in the beginning. You can give them the personal attention they need, making sure that they attend meetings, get in on training sessions, or develop their list of warm prospects. They'll get involved in the products themselves, and they'll be sold on what they're doing and the opportunity they have to offer, both from a product benefit and a financial opportunity point of view.

You then proceed to help them sponsor one or two people to do exactly the same thing.

This approach gives you two significant early benefits:

- ✔ You feel that you're helping someone do something significant and contributing to your own financial well-being at the same time.

- ✔ If you bring someone into the business and that person, in turn, brings in someone else who does well, the one you directly sponsored will renew his or her efforts, and you are more certain of keeping him or her excited and locked into the business.

Remember the underlying philosophy that you can have everything in life you want if you will just help enough other people get what they want.

Keys to success

Rexall Showcase's successful associate Todd Smith, who markets health and nutritional products, says that his personal fast track to success in network marketing goes like this:

1. **Find out the fundamentals.**

   Certain things, if done correctly over time, produce great results. What are those things? Ask!

2. **Find out how to do the fundamentals.**

   Ask the people in your upline. Ask your company's leadership. Ask the most successful network marketers in the system.

3. **Go out and do those things, and work at getting better at doing them.**

   Much of what you must do is on-the-job training. You have to experiment. Learn what fits your personality. Get comfortable. Have fun. If it's not fun and/or exciting, you're not going to do it for very long.

When deciding which to focus on — selling products or sponsoring — you need to keep in mind that sponsoring is a serious commitment, much more so than selling products and services (although we don't say that to diminish the value of selling products and services). As a sponsor, you must foster the success of your distributors. These distributors will look to you for guidance and coaching, particularly when they're first getting started. You have to help them understand the value of your products and services, as well as how to make money in the business. In down times, they'll want you to pick them up. In up times, they'll need you to keep them on course.

Sponsoring distributors who commit to buying products and services is the best of both worlds. You maximize your prospecting efforts, and you teach your distributors the proper way to work their businesses.

Getting on the Fast Track to Prospecting

A good network marketing company provides its distributors with a Fast Track program. Different companies use different names for this program, but all the names imply that the distributors who follow this action plan will get a fast and successful start on building their businesses. Here are the steps we propose:

1. **Identify your warm market.**

2. **Ask for referrals.**

3. **Find sources of leads.**

4. **Contact your prospects.**

These steps are a proven method for business development. There are other ways to build a network marketing business quickly, and you should explore them, particularly if they're recommended by your sponsor.

If you're working your business part-time, say weekends only or two nights a week, that complicates matters all the more. Your prospects may not be available when you call. Therefore, be sure to include all your contact information on all marketing materials: business cards, letterhead, brochures, tapes, your Web site, and so on. Make it easy for your prospects to connect with you. Chapters 18 and 19 also provide information about how to connect with your prospects and sell them.

Identify your warm market

Identifying your warm market is one of the first steps in the action plan. You will be advised to sit down with a sheet of paper, flip open your address book or click open your personal database on the computer, and begin making a list of everyone you know, with addresses and phone numbers. Your goal: a list of 100 names.

At first, this request may sound intimidating, and it would be if you were asked to complete the list in an evening or a weekend. Instead, create this list over a period of time, possibly as long as a month or more. After all, you really need only a dozen names to get started in your network marketing business. Starting today with a dozen names, when your excitement is intense, is infinitely better than starting next month with 100 names. As my friend Lou Holtz, head football coach at the University of South Carolina, says, take the WIN approach: What's Important Now?

Prejudging anyone on your warm list by saying, "He won't be interested," or, "Not her, she's too successful already," could be a mistake. Record people's names and contact them anyway. You may be surprised at who's interested in your new business or your products and services. And even if they're not interested, they may know someone you should contact.

Ask for referrals

"One of the exciting things about network marketing," says Ray Gebauer, "is that you don't know who your family and friends know. They may refer you to someone who comes into your business and makes you a pile of money." So you approach Uncle Harry about your new business, and after listening to you, he says that he's not interested. You have two choices: Thank Uncle Harry and drop the subject, or thank Uncle Harry and ask him for a referral. Because Uncle Harry really does want to help you, he's going to think about his "circle of influence" — his friends, neighbors, and coworkers — and he's likely to give you a name or two.

Mind-joggers to identify your warm market

Just in case you're one of those folks who think that you don't know 100 people, let us help you.

Use these mind-joggers to create your warm market list:

Immediate family	Distant relatives	Neighbors
Coworkers	Church members	Accountant
Barber/Beautician	Attorney	Customers/Clients
Landscaper	Day care provider	Contractor
Doctors	Dentist	Gardener
Exercise instructor	Grocer	Gas station attendant
Insurance salesperson	Landlord	Interior decorator
Loan officer	Librarian	Little League coaches
Mail carrier	Pet groomer	Stockbroker
Salespeople	Tenants	Teachers
Cable repairperson	Veterinarian	Zookeeper

A referral is an extension of your warm market. When you contact Uncle Harry's friend, you're not total strangers. You both know Uncle Harry! That connection may be enough to get your foot in the door to present your business or your products and services. With any luck, Uncle Harry's friend says yes.

Just to be contrary, pretend that the friend says no. What are you going to do now? You're going to say thank you and ask for a referral! Never forget to ask for a referral. Each time you do so, you tap into another person's circle of influence. If five people in one week say no but each gives you one referral, you have five more people to approach next week. And so far, it hasn't cost you any money. Referrals are free! Keep working those referrals, and you'll find people who want to join your organization, as well as buy your products and services.

When you get referrals, contact them at the very earliest possible moment. Here's why: An amazing change in your own thinking takes place. If you have 10, 15, 20, or more prospects and you start shuffling the cards, trying to decide which ones to call on first, and then you add *more* names, confusion erupts. An interesting thing happens: As you review the names, for some reason you lose your enthusiasm for each name. If Uncle Harry gave you a lead today, call or see that lead today if humanly possible. Uncle Harry's excitement and willingness to share the name with you generates excitement within you. The sooner you can get to the prospect and share your excitement, the better that prospect is going to be as a prospect. Follow that approach throughout your network marketing career, and I can assure you that your results will be better than if you simply continued to add prospects with the intention of calling on them later.

As my friend Joe Sabah says, "You don't have to be great to start, but you've got to start to be great." The sooner you start, the sooner you follow through, and the more likely you are to be great sooner.

Find sources of leads

Along with identifying and extending your warm market, the people in your upline should be a good source of leads. If your upline sponsor is successful, he or she is unable to work all the leads he or she generates. Let it be known that you're interested in these leads, but don't expect to have them handed to you free. Generating leads is expensive, as we discuss in Chapter 13, so the people in your upline may charge a small fee per lead.

Before you get too ambitious about the number of leads you'll need, consider the number of hours that you can devote to your business. If you're working your business part-time, your warm market may be all you need to generate leads, especially if you remember to ask for referrals. On the other hand, your warm market may not be big enough, or you can't extend it fast enough, to keep yourself busy full-time. In that case, you'll appreciate the lead-generating marketing activities that we provide in Chapters 16 and 17, as well as the discussion later in this chapter about using the Internet to build your business.

Leads are "hot" for a limited time, and once they go "cold," you may never resurrect their interest. Work your leads in a timely fashion because a pile of leads can represent false security — and a waste of your money — or the pile could be your ticket to outstanding success!

Contact your prospects

One way or another, you and your prospect must have a meeting of the minds. You need to present your business, products, or services, and your prospect needs to understand what you sell, ask questions, establish rapport with you, and then decide whether to get involved.

The best approach is to meet face-to-face, as we explain in Chapter 16, but doing so is not always possible. As a network marketer, your sales territory has no boundaries. If you live in California and your prospect lives in Pennsylvania, you may never meet personally, at least not before connecting in other ways. This is another reason to pursue your warm market first. Even if geography or other circumstances keep you from sitting down with a relative or friend, at least you already know each other. Rapport already exists between the two of you, and that's an advantage in your prospecting efforts.

But even when you and your prospect live in the same city, a face-to-face meeting may not be your first opportunity to connect. Furthermore, until you are secure in your business and are capable of answering questions about your products and services without looking through your sales literature, you may not want to meet in person.

Here are some alternative means of contacting your prospects.

By telephone

After you advertise for prospects, your telephone will ring (we hope so, anyway), and a stranger will ask for information about how to get involved in your business. Or you have a list of prospects to call, names from your warm market, and the most expedient way to contact them is to pick up the phone and call them.

No matter how it happens, you're going to be nervous the first few times you talk to prospects by phone. It's like the first few times you called to ask for a date or the first few times you received such calls. Your heart skips a few beats, your tongue twists a word or two, and you never know what to say next or what the other party is going to ask next. But the nervousness is short-lived, and before long you can anticipate the questions or answers and handle these calls like a pro. You're able to laugh easily, establish rapport quickly, and represent yourself confidently. The more success you encounter, the easier it gets.

You'll soon discover that the telephone is your best friend in a network marketing business. It enables you to spread the word quickly and inexpensively. Plus, it provides instant gratification to your prospects. Some prospects are ready to start immediately in your business. Maybe they did a little homework before calling you. Or perhaps they've been thinking about joining a network marketing company, and suddenly there you are on the phone. All you need to do in these situations is answer a few questions, and your prospect will sign up over the phone. Some prospects would rather not wait to meet in person or to attend a meeting; they just want to get started.

Your lifetime of contacts with individuals in your personal, family, and professional lives provides you with a warm market of possible customers who may live 1,000 miles or more away. In cases like this, I encourage you to arrange for your sponsor to speak with your contacts, provided that sponsor has had enough experience to make the contact beneficial.

First, you call the warm prospect (your friend or family member) and briefly tell him or her that you're in a new business and that you're enormously excited about it. However, because some questions that you don't feel qualified to answer may come up, you would like to schedule a time for a conference call with you, your sponsor, and your friend. That way, you capitalize on the experience and expertise of the people in your upline, and you also let your friend know that you're excited about the business. But you also want your friend to realize that your business is so important to you that you don't want to provide incorrect or insufficient information. So for that reason, you're bringing in someone who has been successful in the business who can answer questions.

Numerous benefits go with this approach. You're listening to a successful network marketer handle the situation so that you receive valuable training, which puts you in a position to quickly start training your own people in your downline in the same manner. Initially, the best thing for you to do during these calls is to sit, listen, and take notes. Let your sponsor show you how to handle these calls. After several calls, your sponsor will invite you to take the lead while he or she listens. Following these calls, you and your sponsor can discuss specific aspects of the call, and soon you'll be ready to make calls on your own.

By fax

A fax machine works like a submarine when you're prospecting for customers. Suddenly it appears! A fax is not as intrusive as a telephone call, and it's a good icebreaker. With one sheet of paper, you can get your prospect's attention, and the prospect can either pay attention, and possibly contact you, or simply toss the information. You can load your own fax machine with numbers to dial, or you can use the many services that do this work for you. When faxing, keep your message brief and include your name and contact information so that an interested prospect can contact you.

In some states, sending a fax to someone who doesn't know you is illegal. Ask your attorney for advice if you're not familiar with the laws in your state. Also use common sense. Send faxes to your warm market, not the cold market. And if someone requests (more likely, demands!) to be removed from your list, honor that request. You don't need to make people mad at you before you've even had a chance to represent your business.

Fax-on-demand is another tool that network marketers frequently use. This technology enables you to store sheets of information in a fax machine so that your prospects can request it around the clock. When they call the fax-on-demand number, they're asked to enter their own fax number. In return, your fax-on-demand technology immediately transmits your information to the prospect's fax machine. Very impressive and effective! Ask your company's marketing department for more information about fax-on-demand. If you want to see how the technology works right now, call Zig Ziglar's fax-on-demand at 888-776-1113. Be prepared to enter your fax number when you call.

By mail

This isn't a discussion about direct mail; we cover that topic in Chapter 17. Say that a prospect calls you in response to an advertisement or via a referral and asks for information about your business opportunity. You want to return that phone call as quickly as possible, but this prospect wants to see or hear some information. Even before you return the call, you can address an envelope and send the prospect a brochure or an audio- or videotape that introduces your company. Include your fax-on-demand number, as well as your Web address. Drop your package in the mail and then call your prospect and tell him that it's on the way.

Some distributors insist on using overnight mail or Priority Mail. That's a judgment call you have to make. Mailing costs aren't cheap, but if your prospect is already demonstrating buying signs, the extra cost may be worth it.

Always keep a supply of your company's audio- and videotapes so that you can mail them or hand them out as appropriate. Every network marketing company produces these tapes, and your company can tell you how to purchase these and other marketing materials.

By e-mail

You can assume that your prospects are every bit as busy as you are, so connecting with them by phone may be difficult. That's all the more reason to use the mail, fax, and e-mail when possible. Chapter 17 contains much more information on e-mail and other Internet forms of communicating facts about your products, services, and opportunities to your prospects.

E-mail is the simplest form of marketing on the Internet. You can write a sizzling promotion — better yet, you can borrow an already proven promotion from someone in your upline — and with one click of the mouse, you can inform countless people worldwide about your products, services, and business opportunity. People who are interested in your message will respond to you, perhaps with questions, which beg further communication. This is a good way to educate your prospects and sort them. You'll soon know who's really interested and who's not.

Network marketing is a business built on relationships. Don't expect too much of your e-mail processor. E-mail is a cold form of communication. Use it to sort through your prospects and identify those who are interested in moving forward. E-mail helps you find an opportunity to build a relationship, but you'll probably have to use a warmer form of communication to further the relationship. Pick up the phone and call these prospects!

When you use faxes, mail, e-mail, or your Web site to promote your business, always include these questions: "What's the best day and time to contact you?" and "How do you prefer to be contacted: by mail, phone, fax, or e-mail?" Make note of these preferences in your database.

Being a Good Ambassador for Your Company

From the outset of developing your business, you must set the right tone or attitude. Prospects may not want to buy your products or services now, or they may not be interested in joining your downline. But circumstances change, and when they do, you'll want your prospects to feel comfortable about contacting you again. Whether they feel comfortable depends on how you treated them the first go-around. If you responded negatively or sarcastically when they told you that they didn't have a need for your product or service or they weren't interested in your business opportunity, they won't forget that about you, so you've probably lost a sale. Instead, try the following approach with your prospects. Emphasize your product knowledge and show concern for their needs. Listen to them instead of trying to talk them into a sale. Back off gracefully when they reject your offer, and suggest that they call you if circumstances change. With this sales approach, they just might call you back! In this section, we discuss how you can become a good ambassador for your company.

Do unto others . . .

As you look for prospects who may be interested in your business, not everyone will share your enthusiasm — and that includes your family and friends. But are they going to be offended? Only if you do something to offend them! A good rule to remember now is the one that says, "Do unto others as you would have them do unto you."

The following guidelines can keep you from looking like a self-centered, self-serving person rather than someone who genuinely wants to share a unique opportunity that will benefit the person you're talking with:

- **Don't misrepresent yourself or your business.** When you contact people with the intention of introducing them to your business, tell them what you're doing. Don't hide behind a dinner party or the guise of friends getting together just for the fun of it.

- **When prospects say that they're not interested, don't force the issue.** Smile, ask for a referral, and say nothing more about your business unless you're specifically asked.

- **Don't be pushy or insulting.** Persistent, yes, but not obnoxious. If a prospect smirks when you ask for an opportunity to talk about your business or belittles your business even before hearing about it, don't plan your retaliation. Some experience may motivate this very prospect to come knocking on your door at a later time, asking for the opportunity to join you in business.

✔ **Don't violate the rules of common decency.** Never use the telephone, the fax machine, or the Internet to pester people. Be proud enough of your business to ask them straight out: "Can we spend a few moments together so that I can show you how you can benefit from this business (or product or service)?"

Handle rejection positively

Prospects, whether they're in the warm market or the cold market, do not reject you personally. They simply refuse your business offer, whether it's for a product, a service, or a business opportunity. They would have refused the same offer from countless other people. Don't take it personally. Keep the following things in mind:

✔ Prospects don't always tell all, at least not immediately. They may really like your product or have an interest in joining you in business, but there's some reason why they can't, and they're not ready to tell you about it. Don't force it. Keep the door open for a future sale.

✔ Personalities do clash, and a simple personality difference may have caused a prospect to refuse your business offer.

✔ When people are rude and ornery, they're not that way (in most cases) to hurt you. They behave that way because they're hurting. There's something they need to deal with that has nothing to do with you or your offer. Whatever you do, don't respond in any manner but graciously. Who knows, your kindness may in fact change their decision, and they just may become the most productive member of your downline.

Remember, your prospect is not rejecting you personally. He/she is refusing your professional offer. Clearly understand this and you can leave with your confidence and self-image intact, ready to move on to your next call.

Don't be surprised if, two or three years down the road when your organization consists of hundreds or even thousands of distributors, you encounter the people who spurned you when you were just getting started, and they now say, "Well, it looks like I've waited too long; you have all the good people in the business already." Just remember: People who don't want to do something give you all kinds of excuses for not doing it. People who are ambitiously dissatisfied and want to make their mark in life find a way to do it. Continue to look for those people who fit the latter description.

Network marketing advantage: You can do it poorly and still master it

As you build your networking business, you need to remember that anything worth doing is worth doing poorly — until you can learn to do it well. This is true in every phase of life. Nobody starts out as an expert, and in network marketing chances are good that your first sales presentation will be a few steps away from professionalism, to put it mildly. For that matter, so will your second and third presentations. By the time you've given a half-dozen presentations your confidence will start to rise, and along with it your effectiveness and success rate. But initially you have to understand that you're going to have to do it poorly in order to get better at it.

One Sunday in church, a young mother brought her four children to my attention. They were little stair-steps, beautiful as dolls, impeccably dressed. The mother explained that I had given her permission to fail when she heard me say a couple of years earlier that anything worth doing is worth doing poorly — until you can learn to do it well. Initially, she refused to attempt to sew. Although her mother was a marvelous seamstress, the young woman's first efforts, to be honest, were sad — as were her second and third efforts. But two years later, there in front of me stood four little girls dressed in matching outfits that Nieman Marcus would have been delighted to feature in their show window. Yes, you've got to understand that anything worth doing is worth doing poorly!

In a traditional business, you may not get the chance to do things poorly, but in network marketing that's the way all of the champions started. Their first presentations were not smooth as glass, nor as effective as the professional presentations they do today. But had these achievers not started — poorly — they would not have become masters at the trade. Someday you'll fully appreciate the significance of starting poorly.

Chapter 15

When the Prospect Says Yes, You Shout... "Hallelujah!"

In This Chapter

▶ Giving everyone a chance to say yes

▶ Looking at "no" responses as future "yes" responses

▶ Understanding how continuous follow-up can lead to more "yes" responses

▶ Letting technology help with follow-up

▶ Securing "yes" responses by asking for help

As a network marketer, you will treasure the moments when prospective customers and distributors say yes. You ask whether they want to buy your product or service, or whether they want to build a business of their own with your support, and they say yes. When you hear the word *yes,* celebrate and make it a memorable event. Kiss your spouse, hug the kids, give the dog a biscuit, and shout "Hallelujah!"

Celebrating on those occasions when you hear the word *yes* serves an important psychological purpose. It's not just a confirmation of your good work; it's also a reminder that you have the skills and the ability to succeed as a network marketer. It reinforces your belief system, it adds to your reservoir of hope, and it prepares you to pick up the phone again, to knock on the next door, to dial in to the next conference call, or to conduct a conference call for the people in your downline.

The benefits of following up a sale with another call are obvious. You maintain the momentum you've already started. Not only that, but your confidence is higher, your excitement and enthusiasm are greater, your smile is broader, you're more friendly in your approach, and you're in the process of maintaining that momentum. By no means is this a time to relax and have a cup of coffee while you grin and beam about your success. An old saying recommends that you "strike while the iron is hot." To add to that, I say you can keep the iron hot if you keep on striking. Remember, if you really do have a legitimate product that solves problems and a legitimate opportunity that benefits people, your objective always should be more calls and more sales.

Celebrating your victories never gets old

"It's a great sense of achievement when some-one says yes to you," explains Nuala McDonald. She would know. Nuala is a leading networker in southern Ireland and an associate of Kleeneze, a catalog-based home shopping business. Since joining Kleeneze in 1995, Nuala has attracted hundreds of catalog customers, and her down-line exceeds 500 people. She's a Silver Senior Executive Distributor, meaning that she's only a couple of promotions away from the top of her company. But like most seasoned networkers, Nuala still celebrates when she hears a cus-tomer say yes.

"You feel good about yourself during these moments," explains Nuala. "Take time to appre-ciate them, because it involves hard work to build your business."

As a result, more people benefit from your product and your opportunity, and your family benefits from the additional sales. It truly is a win/win situation, so follow a sale with another sale by making that other call and making it immediately.

We want the word *yes* to ring repetitively in your ear as a network marketer, so this chapter shows you that repetition begets repetition. Building a suc-cessful network marketing business requires you to follow up with your prospects. *Repeatedly!* Rare are the occasions when you'll get a yes the first time you ask for the sale — though it does happen, as we explain in this chap-ter. Instead, you'll find that network marketing is very much a numbers game (meaning the more times you get up to bat, the better your odds of getting a home run), and if you want to hear yes, you have to be good at playing the game. Following are some of the rules.

Follow-up leads to success in network marketing. You need to take this fact to heart even before you start honing your marketing skills — which we'll dis-cuss in detail in Chapters 16, 17, 18, and 19.

Some People Are Just Waiting to Tell You Yes

A wise sales trainer once said, "Never make assumptions about your prospect."

Following that advice may take some practice, particularly when you're get-ting ready (or working up the nerve) to introduce your opportunity to your warm market — the people who know you. "Uncle Harry, he's got too much money to be interested in network marketing . . . and Cousin Cynthia is so well educated she'd never want to do something like this . . . my neighbor Bill is just too busy . . . and my friend Jo Ann is such a cynic, she'd just laugh at me."

Au contraire! Uncle Harry has a lot of money because he acts fast when he sees a good opportunity. Cousin Cynthia has been looking for a way out of her Ivory Tower. Bill is busy because he has a knack for getting a lot of work done in a short period of time, and he's always interested in a new business. Jo Ann dislikes her job, dislikes her boss, dislikes commuting, and would just love the opportunity to find *something* she could really enjoy doing.

What we're saying is that you can't be certain how anyone will respond to network marketing until you ask. Some people, due to circumstances unknown to you, are waiting to tell you yes. So don't judge them before you ask them. Give them a chance to say yes.

Choose the time and place carefully before you ask someone to take a look at your opportunity or to consider your products or services. If your friend is trying to meet a deadline, wait until his deadline has passed before you ask him to look at your compensation plan.

"Many people are just looking for something," says Melynda Lilly, a Fort Worth, Texas, representative with Discovery Toys, which sells unique and educational toys for children through in-home parties. "They're not happy, or they don't have a job, or they need more money, or they want a more flexible lifestyle . . . and if you show them that what you do is fun *and* lucrative, as well as simple, and you explain that you will help them succeed, what can they say except yes?"

Every "No" Is a Step Closer to a "Yes"

Another wise sales trainer once said, "Don't despair when someone tells you no. Be happy! You're one step closer to hearing someone tell you yes."

Successful network marketers expect every prospect to say yes, but they're prepared for the fact that most people are going to say no. Nuala McDonald of Ireland says, "As you play the numbers game, you immediately discover that the majority of people don't want to buy from you, or they don't want to be in business for themselves. Sometimes I wonder, 'How is it that everyone I show the business to doesn't jump at it? How could anyone not want to be involved in this business?'"

Sales trainer Hilton Johnson, who runs MLM University in Lauderdale-by-the-Sea, Florida, knows only too well about the numbers game, and he can show you how to play it as well as anyone. The problem is, neither he nor anyone else can tell you precisely how many numbers it'll take before you get a yes. That's something you may have to figure out for yourself. This much we know, however: The resulting numbers depend on your skill level, your perseverance, and your desire.

The numbers also depend on the market you contact. "The numbers in a cold market are dismal," says Hilton. "People will make 100 to 200 calls a week, and even when they connect with real prospects, the results are not very good. Someone did a study and found that he had to make 250 phone calls just to get one appointment! On the other hand, in the warm market, you might make a half-dozen calls and get an appointment. Where do you want to spend your time?"

Carol Bishop, a zany Zig Ziglar Network associate, loves to use catch phrases as part of her sales strategy. She eagerly approaches every presentation and her enthusiasm alone can almost close a sale. She never forgets, however, that she's playing a numbers game, and she doesn't have time to spare. When she encounters a prospect who can't make a decision, she'll often relieve the pressure by saying jestfully, "Tell me yes or tell me no, but tell me quick, I gotta go." She laughs, the prospect laughs, and they move on to discuss the next step, if there's going to be one. Carol is smart to use her personality to influence a sale.

Working Your Leads Repetitively

The one thing you don't want to do in a numbers game is run out of leads! That is, you need people to talk to about your products and services or your business opportunity. In Chapters 16 and 17 we explain how you can generate the numbers of leads needed to succeed in network marketing, but for now you need to understand how to get the most out of your sales efforts. By the way, we don't want you to think that the numbers game lessens the fact that network marketing is a relationship business. The numbers game is merely a method of determining who is and who isn't interested in developing a relationship with you. Some people will want to buy your products or services, some will want to join you in business, and some will want to do both. But many won't want any part of what you're selling, and that's okay. However, until you identify those people and avoid investing time in them, you won't make much progress as a network marketer. Playing the numbers game is time consuming, and it can be expensive, especially if you don't know how to play the game! Persistent follow-up is the key to success in the numbers game.

Too many networkers — often because they make assumptions — approach a prospect once, get turned down, and never approach the prospect again. Ouch! That's not the way a winner plays the numbers game. The act of following up, which creates top-of-mind awareness for your prospects, is an important strategy in your overall sales effort.

Kathy Smith, a leader in the Discovery Toys network, tells this story about her best friend, Renay Lawson:

"Renay was my first hostess," explains Kathy. "She invited her friends to her home for a Discovery Toys party. At that time, I spoke to Renay about joining me in business, but she was not interested. Every year thereafter I asked her again. Her answer was always the same: 'No.' Finally, the fifth year I asked her, she said, 'Where's the trip going this year?' Every year, our associates have the opportunity to qualify for a fantastic all-expenses paid trip, and Renay was aware that I had been on several of them. When I told her the trip was to Hawaii, she immediately said, 'Yes.' Renay earned that trip to Hawaii, and she's earned about another nine since then, one for each year she's been in the business."

My friend, John Nevin from Australia, was a part-time milk deliveryman several years ago when he got a part-time job selling World Book Encyclopedias. One evening, he called on a German couple who spoke very little English. They had had a baby when they were both well over 40 years old, and at age 50, they were more like grandparents than parents. John made the call after 9 p.m., and it was after midnight when he left with the sale. As he departed, the mother reached up and put her hand on John's shoulder, saying in her guttural, broken English, "Tank you, young man, for staying 'til we understand what you say . . . that these books will help our boy. Tank you, tank you, tank you."

When I heard the story, I understood there is a better word for persistence. It's "belief." If you really do believe that the product you sell or the opportunity you offer has enormous benefits for the prospect, you will persist. You will do it pleasantly and professionally, but you will do it with the right motive — and that's what makes the difference.

Follow Up Even When You'd Rather Not

In network marketing, follow-up separates the heavy hitters, that is, the big moneymakers, from the rest of the pack. Persistent, continuous follow-up is the only way to win the numbers game. In fact, if you don't follow up, you're not getting your money's worth out of your marketing budget. In that case, ask yourself whether you really ought to be spending any marketing dollars!

Most of the time, people won't make a decision about *anything* (especially an investment) until they've seen the opportunity repetitively and heard about it at least twice, and usually more often. Even then, they'll want time to consider it, think it through, discuss it with others, and so on. A marketing maxim says that prospects need to be contacted at least seven times before they'll make a purchasing decision. *Seven times!* Unfortunately, most networkers give up pursuit after they're turned down the first time by a prospect.

That's not the time to quit! Prospects are busier than ever, and they have more options and choices than ever. If you want them to make a choice in your favor, you'll have to work for it. *You have to follow up, even when you don't feel like it!*

Repetition cultivates relationships

Seasoned networkers understand the importance of cultivating relationships with prospects before converting them to customers or distributors. Repetitively following up with prospects is the best way to cultivate relationships. Unless a prospect says, "No, I'm definitely not interested, and don't contact me again," you should continue following up with that prospect. If you talked to the prospect on the telephone or in person and she said, "I'm not interested," or "It doesn't appeal to me right now," or "I've got to think about it," you can say, "Would it be all right if I follow up with you now and then in the event you change your mind?" In these circumstances it's likely the prospect will say yes. That's your invitation (maybe even an obligation, so far as your marketing budget is concerned) to set up a tickler file to remind you to follow up with those prospects. If you use a software program such as ACT! or Goldmine, the tickler file is built in for you. But you can also set up a manual tickler file by recording on a calendar the names and phone numbers of the prospects you're to call.

Once or twice a month — perhaps more often — follow up with your prospects. Remember: *Seven times!* And if they don't buy after seven times and they haven't contacted you to request that you stop sending them information (most won't, but some will), keep following up! You just never know when the prospects' circumstances will change, and they're ready for a business opportunity, or when something you say or send triggers a buying response for your product or service.

 Network marketing trainer Doug Firebaugh says, "If you truly show up for people in a caring way, put their interests ahead of yours, and send them information that would be of value to them, they'll keep coming back to you. Why? Because you have shown them value beyond the product or the opportunity. You've established a relationship."

Following up uncovers the seeds of discontent

By following up with prospects, you expose them to the many benefits of your opportunity, product, or service, and one or more of the benefits, at any time in the follow-up process, could address a prospect's need. The prospect may not have experienced that need the first time the two of you made contact; perhaps the need developed over time. Or maybe the mention of a particular benefit helped the prospect realize a certain need. These are the occasions that convert leads to sales. "Find the need," advises Jack Maitland, a Fort Lauderdale, Florida-based associate of Nikken, a marketer of wellness products. "Whether you're recruiting for new associates or you're selling products, the most important thing is to find your prospect's seed of discontent." The only way you can do that is to follow up continuously, until the prospect says yes or tells you, "I'm not interested. Don't contact me anymore."

Follow-up is the key to success

"It took me more than three years to understand how to be successful in network marketing," says Fred Raley, a part-time networker who represents several different companies, including Ameriplan USA and Melaleuca, which markets personal care and home care products. "It all boiled down to one thing: my ability and determination to follow up with prospects and with new customers and associates after their initial introduction to my product line. Why so long to a 'duh,' you might ask? Very simple. My trainers and mentors did not know how to follow up either!"

Fred points to a study conducted by the National Sales Executive Association to underscore the importance of follow-up in the sales process. The study found that 80 percent of sales occur between the fifth and the twelfth contact. Only 2 percent of sales are made on the first contact, 3 percent on the second, 5 percent on the third, and 10 percent on the fourth.

"Realizing that, don't you think it would be good to learn how to follow up?" Fred asks. "You've got to get your message in front of the prospect repeatedly over the course of time, from your initial introduction until he tells you to stop sending information. That may seem drastic, but who will be sending your prospect information if you're not? Guaranteed it will be someone else who will be there when the time is right for the prospect to buy, and you will have lost a sale

because you failed to continually stay in the prospect's face."

Should you say, "I don't have the time to do that"? Fred will say, "You must!"

He explains: "You can either follow up manually with pencil and paper records, or you can do it with some sort of database reminder system. Or you can let technology do it for you. I vote for letting technology do it for me!" (See "Using Technology to Do the Follow-up for You" later in this chapter.)

Fred says that since he started using computerized programs to generate leads and follow up, his mentors think he's a master salesman. "Wrong! I'm a master educator, and I use systems to do the work for me. I could never find the time to follow up with hundreds of prospects without automated systems."

Lest you think computerized programs will do all the work for you, Fred is quick to say they won't. "You can close another 20 percent or more of your leads with personal contact. People buy 'you' as much as they buy a product or service," he explains. "Personal contact makes you a real person instead of a simple e-mail address. Whether you're good on the phone or not, I recommend calling your prospects. Just strike up a conversation, answer their concerns, and you will be amazed at how many people respond positively to you."

"People buy for their own reasons, not our reasons," explains Jack, "and we don't always know what those reasons are. That's why it's important to think of yourself as a problem solver in network marketing. If I'm trying to sell you on the concept of making more money when you don't need to make more money, I haven't found your need. But if I discover that you have a bad back and I can show you how to alleviate that problem, there's a good chance you'll spend Monday night at a Wellness Program with me, and afterwards you will purchase my products!"

Following up triggers different emotions

"It's better than a job," you tell a prospect about your business opportunity, but the fact is, the prospect *loves* his job. "This product will save you time," you say to a prospect, and although time is important to her, it's not one of the major issues in her life. Just as important as uncovering the prospect's real need is triggering the emotions that capture the prospect's interest.

Saving time may not get your prospect excited, but when you follow up with a postcard from Maui, now you've struck a nerve! "I've always wanted to go to Hawaii," the prospect says to herself, "but I don't see any way of getting there on *my* salary." Bingo! Your postcard triggered the right "hot button" by portraying your business opportunity as the prospect's ticket to paradise. See Chapter 3 for more information about the importance of uncovering the prospect's hot buttons.

All people want the same things: to be happy, healthy, reasonably prosperous, and secure and to have friends, peace of mind, good family relationships, and hope. Each of these desires conjures up a variety of emotions. When you follow up with your prospects, show them how your products, services, and business opportunity provide solutions to these desires.

Following up works

When it comes to following up, the bottom line is that prospects need to hear your message again and again. "Something happens in their lives," says Nuala McDonald, Kleeneze distributor in Ireland, "and suddenly they are ready, whereas they weren't ready all the times you contacted them before. It's important to keep notes going to them, to ring them now and then, to send them updated information about your product, or send them a copy of your most recent commission check, or a testimonial from a common friend. Relate your story to them time after time. You can never give up on them."

That's the attitude of successful network marketers! They continue following up because they know that doing so works.

Following up is valuable, but experience tells us that only the most committed networkers do it. Why? Well, for one thing it requires discipline. You have to remember to implement the follow-up activities. Second, it requires patience. So many networkers want to have it all TNT — *today, not tomorrow.* Successful networkers understand that developing relationships takes time, and they're willing to continue playing the numbers game.

Six follow-up techniques you can use

Here are six follow-up techniques that you can use to give a prospect a gentle nudge to take another look at your offer. See Chapter 17 for additional ideas about using these and other techniques.

- ✔ **Send a letter.** Write a brief message thanking the prospect for his time on the phone or at a meeting. Enclose your business card, too.

- ✔ **Use postcards.** Network marketers love postcards because they're inexpensive to mail in any quantity, and they transport another gentle reminder to the prospect. As part of their marketing package, network marketing companies or a vendor of their choice will reproduce the postcards in bulk and sell them to distributors. For $100 you should be able to purchase at least 500 full-color postcards. You have to add the postage, of course, but that's a minor detail. Write a brief note on the back of each postcard and mail them to your prospects.

- ✔ **Send an e-mail.** Smart marketers ask prospects and customers for their e-mail addresses. Save these addresses in your database or card file. Keep your message brief and to the point. See "Using Technology to Do the Follow-up for You" later in this chapter for more information on this topic.

- ✔ **Mail an audio- or videotape.** Your network marketing company probably produces several marketing tapes specifically for follow-up purposes. A prospect who doesn't read your mail or respond to your phone calls may very well listen to or view a tape. Next thing you know, you get a call from the prospect wanting to know more about your product or offer. It happens all the time — but only to networkers who follow up! The cost of tapes varies from company to company. But as an example, the Zig Ziglar Network (ZZN) Opportunity video costs $1 in quantities of 100, while the ZZN Audio Catalog runs about 60 cents per 100.

- ✔ **Use brochures.** Prospects who like to see, touch, read, and re-read information about products and opportunities appreciate receiving brochures by mail or perhaps delivered personally to their home or office. Once again, look to your network marketing company or to its vendor to supply a variety of brochures. The ZZN Financial Opportunity brochure, as well as the product brochure, each cost $25 for a package of 100. Most companies produce these brochures in huge quantities so that they can be sold at or near cost to the distributors. All you have to do is buy the brochures and use them to follow up.

✔ **Place a phone call.** Every so often, call your prospects again. You say something like, "I wrote your name and number on my calendar for a follow-up call tonight, and I'm just checking in with you to see if you might like to hear more about my product or my business opportunity." If they're still not interested, take the opportunity once again to ask for permission to keep in touch with them.

You can use any of these follow-up techniques more than once with the same prospects, but spread them out so that you use them over a period of time. Plan to follow up with your prospects at least seven times within six months.

If after seven contacts you still get a "no," that doesn't mean it's a lost cause. Why are you getting the "no"? If the prospect tells you, "I have absolutely no interest in your business, and I never will," you can take that as a definite "no," at least for the time being. A lot can happen in a year or two!

But if the prospect says, "I appreciate your thinking of me so often, but I'm still not interested. I've got to take care of some family issues before I can consider anything," then that's a soft "no." In such a situation, continue following up with this prospect — perhaps once every four to six months, until you get a firm response, yes or no.

Avoid disappointment when someone tells you no. Don't forget that not everyone is interested in what you have to offer, and that's okay. Your job is to find out who is or who may be interested and then develop relationships with those people. When people say no, they're *not* rejecting you. They're merely saying, "It's not the right thing (product or opportunity) for me."

Melynda Lilly, a Discovery Toys representative, remembers how she worked for months to convert a particular prospect to an associate. "I knew she was interested," Melynda explains, "but at first she said she had to talk to her husband, and he was out of town. Then there was sickness in the family, and later it wasn't the right time. I kept following up with her, and finally she made the decision to join me in business. But then, everything she did bombed! She wasn't making sales, and she wasn't sponsoring new associates. In spite of that, she didn't give up, and she never had a negative thing to say about the business. I just kept encouraging her and congratulating her for a positive attitude. A year into the business, things started to click for her, and now she's sponsoring people, and her people are sponsoring, too." As Melynda knows so well, getting a prospect to make a decision takes time, and even then, it sometimes takes longer for the new associate to become productive. "In network marketing, you must have stickability. It takes time to build a business. Just start with three to five people and help them sponsor their first three to five people," says Melynda. "Follow-up is the key."

Using Technology to Do the Follow-up for You

The Internet and the World Wide Web are making it easier than ever for network marketers to stay in touch with their prospects. With a few strokes of the keyboard, a networker can send an e-mail message to multiple prospects in a nanosecond. The Web, with an increasing capacity to use technology such as audio and video streams, provides an attractive and consistent follow-up system. At its best, technology provides opportunities for networkers to let the computer do most of the follow-up work, as we explain in this section.

Autoresponders follow up 24/7 and never tire

An *autoresponder* is a technological enhancement that can be programmed to repeatedly send messages by e-mail, and it may be the best follow-up tool of all for network marketers. Using an autoresponder, a networker can rely on technology to send one message after another, spread only a few days or weeks apart, to the same prospects. After setting up the process by loading the e-mail addresses into a database and after scheduling the system to send specific messages on specific dates, the networker doesn't have to do a thing! Some networkers refer to this process as *dripping,* that is, sending little drops of information over time to the same prospects. Whether or not you like this term isn't the point. Technology makes it possible to follow up by dripping. You can usually get an autoresponder free from your Internet Service Provider (ISP). Also ask the members of your upline to advise you about using this technology.

Dripping is effective for two reasons: First, it leverages the distributor's time. It's like flying a plane on autopilot! Second, frequency of contact always yields a greater response and a higher rate of conversion from leads to sales. More follow-up results in more sales and more distributors in your downline.

Spamming — the act of sending unsolicited e-mail messages or sending messages to people who didn't ask you to contact them — is an abuse of the dripping process. If you spam, three things may happen to you, none of which is good! First, you'll destroy rather than build relationships with prospects. Every message you send by e-mail should include instructions about how the recipients can ask you to delete their e-mail addresses from your list so that no further messages will be sent to them. Always provide these instructions and honor all requests. Second, you'll risk losing your Internet access. If enough of your e-mail recipients complain to your ISP about your messages,

Succeeding with Internet technology

Internet technology provides systems that enhance but don't replace traditional marketing activities, and it's important to keep that in mind. "The Internet is no magic bullet that will vault a network marketing rookie to the top of a company's pay plan overnight," explains Atticus Killough, webmaster of FreeLeads.com, a self-replicating, lead-generation site for network marketers. "The telephone is still the most effective tool for network marketers, but anyone who's phone-shy can build a solid MLM business using e-mail, live chat software, and other tools that the Internet provides."

In order to succeed in network marketing by means of the Internet, it's important to get prospects to "opt in," a term meaning that the prospect asks to receive specific information, such as a newsletter, or an e-mail about a business opportunity or product. How do you do that? "Use traditional advertising methods to get people to your self-replicating or lead-generating Web site," explains Atticus, "and then offer your visitors something of value (that is, a free report, a newsletter, and so forth) in exchange for their names and e-mail addresses." Over a period of time you will have created a database of prospects. "That database," says Atticus, "can be turned into an MLM gold mine" by using Internet tools to follow up with the people on the list.

the ISP is likely to pull your Internet connection. Third, if your e-mail recipients complain to your company, you may be reprimanded by the company, and your distributorship could be terminated. For policy clarification, consult your company's Rules and Regulations, which are usually part of every distributor's manual. *Please don't spam!* See Chapter 17 for more information about the ills of spamming.

Web sites that follow up for you

The Web also makes it easier to follow up with prospects and to give them immediate access to information. Many network marketing companies offer self-replicating Web sites to their distributors. Here's how *self-replicating Web sites* work. A company creates a site that provides information about its business opportunity, products, and services. These sites use the latest technology so they can include audio sound clips and video. The company then invites its distributors to buy a self-replication of the site for a monthly fee that could range from $20 to $50, depending on the content and the technology that the distributor wants to include on the site. They're called self-replicating sites because the distributors can customize them to include their photographs and personal information, such as their phone number, e-mail address, and ground mailing address. The distributors don't need to reserve a separate Web domain because the sites piggyback on the company's Web address. Market-savvy distributors use self-replicating sites for these reasons:

✔ **Reliability of the content:** By providing the content for these Web sites, distributors are assured that the information they're disseminating to the public is accurate and up-to-date. When it's necessary or time to change the content of the pages, the company can do so automatically by updating the original site.

✔ **Unification:** By using a self-replicating site, distributors are all promoting the same message about their products and opportunity. No one needs to spend valuable time trying to gain a competitive edge over anyone else.

✔ **Consistency:** Unlike the human distributor, the Web site always looks the same, sounds the same (if it includes audio), and delivers a perfect presentation every time (except when there's a technological snafu).

✔ **Revenue generation:** If the sites are designed to accommodate e-commerce, they generate revenue without human intervention. Many of the sites accept applications from new distributors who can use their credit cards to pay the enrollment fees. Imagine waking up every morning and discovering that your Web site earned a few hundred dollars while you were sleeping! That scenario is not science fiction — it's happening today in many network marketing organizations.

Dual-purpose, self-replicating Web sites

Generic self-replicating Web sites (see the section "Web sites that follow up for you") provide dual purposes for the distributors who use them: These sites can be used to persistently follow up with prospects, and they can also be sold as business opportunities. A network marketer who signs up for one of these sites can earn additional money by referring people who also sign up for one of the sites. In fact, these sites include multilevel pay plans that can generate large monthly commissions for distributors.

Assume that an associate of ABC Network Marketing Company (a fictitious name made up for this example) buys a generic Web site, such as www.freeleads.com (a *real* site). As prospects who are interested in business ownership visit his site, the automated follow-up system within the site sends the prospects information about the ABC business opportunity. Some of these prospects, over time, will join ABC, and others will not. Whether or not a prospect joins ABC, the distributor can also program the freeleads.com automated follow-up system to send all or some of the prospects information about the freeleads.com business opportunity. Some of the prospects who join ABC will also buy a freeleads.com Web site because they plan to use it for lead generation and follow-up. Some of the prospects who passed on ABC, but who went on to become distributors of other network marketing companies, will also buy a freeleads.com Web site because they want to use it to generate leads and follow up with those prospects who are interested in their network marketing company. Of course, most of the prospects won't join either business opportunity. It's a numbers game, remember? However, the original ABC distributor wins when he recruits an ABC distributor into his downline, and/or when he recruits a freeleads.com distributor. He's building separate downlines in these two business opportunities and earning commissions from both companies.

If you want prospects to visit your site, you need to advertise your Web site address. How? By including it in all of your marketing programs, including direct mail, advertisements, radio spots, business cards and letterhead, and e-mail promotions. See Chapter 17 for more information about marketing.

If your company doesn't offer self-replicating sites, or even if it does, several Internet companies offer generic self-replicating sites specifically for network marketers. You may want to sign up for one (or more) of these sites, even if you also use a company-sponsored self-replicating site. The idea of using more than one is that you should be able to generate more leads. The following companies provide self-replicating sites: Recruitomatic.com, FreeLeads.com, WebenrollerSystem.com, and PCPowerSystem.com. See Chapter 17 for information about generating leads with self-replicating Web sites.

Asking for Help Is Another Way to Follow Up

Many people who might otherwise say no will say yes if you ask for their help. Melynda Lilly, a networker in Fort Worth, Texas, learned this lesson when she decided to pursue a new goal in her company, Discovery Toys.

"To achieve this goal," explains Melynda, "I had six weeks to sell $12,000 worth of product. Once I was clear on my goal, I decided to call everyone I knew, even businesses that had turned me down before and people who had been on my list for a year or more. I contacted them and told them about my goal. I explained that I needed their help. And I discovered that when you let people know what you're working for and you ask for their help, they're often willing to give it to you." Melynda's story is just another way of saying, "Don't give up on your prospects."

Melynda Lilly points out that when you contact people with a specific goal in mind, they may sense more excitement or urgency in your voice than when they heard from you previously. The new tone of voice may be all that's needed to get a "yes" when before you heard a "no."

John Hayes explains that for many years he was content as a customer of AT&T. "I wouldn't say that I was a happy customer, but I wasn't looking for a reason to change my long-distance provider. That kind of thing takes time, and it's a hassle, so even though I knew other companies were offering lower long-distance rates, I remained a customer of AT&T simply because I didn't want to bother with finding a new company, calling them, waiting to get through the customer service voice mail loops, and then having to fill out new paperwork."

All of that changed one day, however, when a friend called John and asked him to switch over to Excel. John told his friend, "I don't really care all that much about my long-distance provider. I just want to know that the service works, that it's dependable, and that it's reasonably priced. In addition to that, I *really* don't want to fill out a new contract. I have no time for it."

But then the friend pulled out all the stops and went for the sale. "I just started my business with Excel," he said. "I have been working at getting a customer for a couple of weeks, and so far, I've not had any success. I'd really appreciate it if you would consider becoming my first customer."

If John hadn't known better, he would have suspected his friend was making him feel guilty just for the sake of getting a sale. Then his friend added, "If you'll become my customer, I'll buy you lunch, I'll pay the $20 set-up fee, and I'll also fill out all your paperwork, and all you'll have to do is sign on the dotted line."

All of John's objections were nullified, plus he was going to get a free lunch out of the deal! "What really got to me," John explains, "is when this fellow asked for my help. How can you *not* help a friend? I had to say yes."

Following Up Keeps You from Giving Up

In network marketing, few words are sweeter than *yes*. However, getting to "yes" sometimes requires more persistence than you ever imagined, more follow-up than you thought was possible, and a lot of "no's."

But every leading networker will tell you that the secret to hearing the "yes" word is in the follow-up. It's a skill you must cultivate and practice throughout your career. Following up professionally and expertly, as we explain in this chapter, will keep you from giving up.

By following up and not giving up, more of your prospects will eventually say yes. Just don't forget to shout, "Hallelujah!"

Network marketing advantage: Sales have no limits

It's important in network marketing, and — for that matter — in sales, to understand that there is no such thing as a "little sale." Here's an example: For our 25th wedding anniversary, my wife gave me a beautiful set of cuff links. In 1971, shirts with French cuffs were not "in," and I tried unsuccessfully to find such a shirt so that I could wear those beautiful cuff links. On a trip into Iowa I was also seeking a white suit. A gentleman dressed in one told me he had gotten it from Glasgow Clothiers in Fort Madison. I went over the next day, bought the suit and a number of other items, and then asked Doyle Hoyer, the owner and manager of the store, if he had any shirts with French cuffs. His immediate response was, "No — but I can get them for you." I ordered the shirts.

About a month later Doyle called to ask if I had received the shirts and if I liked them. My response was an enthusiastic "I love them!" Because of Doyle Hoyer's interest in me and his concern for getting the French cuff shirts for me, I became not only a steady customer, but I also recommended him to countless other people. Neither of us has any way of knowing exactly how much business might have been generated

as a result of my use of him as an example in my seminars, as well as in my book, *Secrets of Closing the Sale,* but I am more than comfortable in saying that it was several hundred thousand dollars worth. Doyle Hoyer would have missed out on that much business — and I would have missed out on lots of good service — had he not taken that extra step and gotten those French cuff shirts for me.

Message: Treat every customer as if he or she is going to be the biggest customer you've ever had. If your retail customers are happy with the products you sell them, they will not only recommend them to their friends, but chances are excellent that they will want to join your downline, where their value to you can be incredible.

The amount of money a customer spends with you isn't the only factor to be considered in valuing customers, but it's a good place to start. Other important factors include your ability to relate to a customer, your compatibility with a customer's personality, and your enthusiasm for the customer — as well as the customer's enthusiasm for you and your business.

Chapter 16

Deciding On the Best Ways to Attract Customers

*L*et's get some customers! It's time to get down to business and figure out how you're going to attract customers so that you can both build a downline and sell your products and services. That's what marketing is all about.

Most people get the jitters just thinking about marketing — the process of converting leads to customers. To anyone who lacks marketing experience, this is one of the most intimidating aspects of building any business. "I don't think I can do it," people frequently say. Or: "How do I do it?" "*Can* I do it?" "What's it going to cost to do it?" These are the times when fear wraps its ugly arms around people and stops them dead in their tracks.

But look here: You can do it! We're convinced that you can, especially if you will claim that quality for yourself right now. Go ahead and say it: "I am becoming a marketing maven in my network marketing business." Frequently remind yourself of this ability. Why are we so certain that you can become a marketing maven when we don't even know if you have any background in marketing?

Because in network marketing, there's no one way, no right way, to generate leads and convert them to customers. You don't need special skills or special education to market effectively. You can use face-to-face conversation, the telephone, e-mail, a Web site, home parties, public meetings, seminars, direct mail, and numerous other nonthreatening, inexpensive marketing activities.

Traditional businesses are not as fortunate. They can't always afford the luxury of variety in their marketing programs. They're often forced to buy expensive television advertising to sell their products and services, and they almost always hire top-notch advertising agencies to handle this work for them at a cost of millions of dollars. Or they have to commit their marketing dollars to print advertising only, or radio commercials, or national billboards, or some combination of what can be very expensive media.

Such is not the case for network marketers. After you have made the initial investment to join a network marketing company, you can — with little or no money — begin generating leads and attracting customers. In addition, if you build your business on referrals, you will never be forced to spend large amounts of money on marketing.

Now here's another reason why we're certain that you can become a marketing maven in your network marketing business: You're embarking on a chapter of easy-to-grasp and easy-to-implement marketing recommendations.

Developing Your Personal Marketing Plan

As all successful marketers know, using marketing activities, techniques, and events that *you*, the marketer, enjoy is very important. Because variety is on your side, you probably won't have to use a marketing activity that you don't like, or one that you don't care to master. That's why it's important to develop a personal marketing plan that includes activities you enjoy utilizing and then to list the activities of your choice in a notebook. Otherwise, you may dread every day that you're a network marketer. If you can't work the marketing end of the business, success will elude you.

Selecting marketing activities you enjoy

Activities commonly used by network marketers include the following:

- In-home meetings, parties, and dinners
- Telephone conference calls
- Telemarketing
- Three-way telephone conversations
- Public opportunity meetings

> ✔ Face-to-face networking events
>
> ✔ Sampling, or giving away products
>
> ✔ Public speaking opportunities
>
> ✔ Trade shows, expositions, and fairs
>
> ✔ Direct mail: sending letters or postcards
>
> ✔ Sending e-mail and referencing Web sites

From the preceding list, select several activities that you want to include in your personal marketing plan. None of the activities requires special skills or experience. Once you know which activities you plan to use, make certain that the network marketing company you intend to join uses these activities effectively.

Don't join a network marketing company that requires its distributors to employ an activity that you would neither enjoy nor accept, or relies almost totally on a marketing activity that you wouldn't want to use.

Using a marketing notebook

Before going any further, start a personal marketing plan notebook. Use any kind of notebook or a three-ring binder with loose-leaf pages. Dedicate this notebook to your marketing activities. On the first page of your notebook write this headline:

Marketing Activities That I Will Use
to Build My Business
from (today's date) to (the date 90 days later)

Under the headline, list a maximum of six activities of choice to implement during the next 90 days. Don't overdo it! Eventually, you're likely to find the two or three activities that suit you best.

Next, devote one page of your notebook to each activity. So if you select in-home meetings, direct mail, and public speaking as your activities, dedicate one page of your notebook to each of these activities. Use these pages and date your notes so you can easily track your progress. Record what you did, when you did it, and what happened as a result. Also record what you will do differently the next time.

This note taking isn't an exact science, but there are several reasons for it. First, it's a reminder that you must take action to complete any activity. Second, it's a way of documenting what you did. Third, it's a reminder of what to do differently in the future.

Create one more page in your notebook and title it "Ideas." Actually, this may become an entire section of the notebook. Use the pages to record ideas that you pick up from distributors, either upline or downline. When you get together with distributors, either by phone, in teleconferences sponsored by your company, or at regional and national meetings, you will frequently hear good ideas. If you don't record them in your notebook, you're not likely to remember them for long.

Record all information related to your personal marketing plan in this notebook. After just a few months of tracking your progress, this notebook will become a valuable tool in the operation of your business.

One final point about developing a personal marketing plan. Never say never! Today you may not believe that you could ever stand up and speak to a group about a network marketing opportunity. Today you may not feel comfortable telling your best friends about the products and services your network marketing company sells. But every tomorrow is full of surprises. One day you may wake up ready to use a marketing activity that you had originally rejected. That's when you'll know it's time to revise and expand your personal marketing plan.

Dipping into Your Bag of Marketing Tools

A good network marketing company — the only kind you want to join — will provide you with a bag of marketing tools to help you attract and keep customers. These tools help you market your products and services, as well as your business opportunity, to prospects, and they facilitate the successful implementation of the marketing activities you plan to use.

Your network marketing company's start-up package should provide and describe many of these tools. This package is sent to all distributors upon joining the organization. If the start-up package doesn't describe the tools, they should be explained to distributors during teleconferences or face-to-face training programs.

The most common tools include brochures, audiocassettes, videotapes, CDs, telephone scripts, business cards and stationery, network-wide phone service, and Web sites. We discuss these tools in this section.

All these tools enhance a network marketer's opportunity for attracting and keeping customers. However, the tools are of no value without instructions for using them. You should expect your network marketing company's executives and trainers, as well as members of your upline, to show you how to use each of these tools.

Anticipate using a combination of these tools to attract and keep customers. For example, your initial contact with a prospect may be by phone, during which time you rely on the telemarketing scripts provided by your company so that you know what to say. During your phone conversation, you can invite the prospect to visit your Web site. By providing this experience, you may close the sale on the spot!

Or your initial contact with a prospect may occur at a networking party where you hand out a business card, a brochure, and an audiocassette, along with a recommendation to visit your Web site. You then follow up with the prospect by phone, answer some additional questions, and close the sale!

When we hear something, we forget it; when we see it, we remember. When we hear it, see it, and do it — we understand and take action that brings results. All three are necessary. The warmth, sincerity and affection of the human voice, combined with the vision in the eyes, along with the action that follows will produce remarkable results for you in network marketing.

Brochures

Visual people need to see something in print, such as a photograph of the product, before they buy. They want to read a description of how the product works (its features) or what it does (its benefits). They want the nitty-gritty about the business opportunity, and they're not satisfied just hearing the details from you. Thus, marketing brochures are extremely useful in the sales process. Some people like to review the brochures as a memory enhancer.

Upon joining a network marketing company, you're likely to receive several copies of each of the company's marketing brochures. Each company should have a product brochure (if not numerous product brochures), and definitely a brochure that describes the business opportunity. You can purchase additional brochures from the company.

Audiocassettes, videotapes, and CDs

Audiocassettes, videotapes, and CDs provide convenient ways to generate interest in products, services, and business opportunities. Many people listen to audiocassettes and CDs while driving to and from work. Meanwhile, videotapes are popular among visual prospects. They create a desire to know more! Your company's start-up kit will probably include at least one audiocassette or CD, and one videotape. You can purchase additional copies of these marketing tools, and you should always have a supply on hand.

Using brochures

Here are some suggestions about how to use brochures to present products and services, as well as your business opportunity. Most network marketing companies have several brochures available to distributors. Most likely, you'll have to purchase these brochures from the company.

✔ Remember that a brochure rarely makes a sale. At best, it's a supplement.

✔ Send brochures to existing customers, especially when you introduce a new product or service. Attach a note that says, "I think you'll love this new product. Should I order you a supply?"

✔ Mail brochures only when they're requested. Some marketers mail brochures to purchased mailing lists. Big mistake! Most people won't even open the mail.

✔ Use brochures in face-to-face meetings to show photographs or to emphasize details. Don't hand out brochures indiscriminately just because you have them. It's better to make your prospects ask to see a brochure, and then you can lead them through it. If they seem interested, give them the brochure. If not, save yourself the money.

✔ Attach your business card to the brochure, or stamp or imprint your name, address, telephone and fax numbers, e-mail address, and Web site on the back of the brochure so that your prospect can contact you.

✔ Don't become overly dependent on brochures. Some prospects need to see them before they can make a purchasing decision. However, many others simply pick up a brochure because it's available. When they get home, they toss the brochure in the trash. That's *your* money they're throwing away.

✔ Don't use a brochure for a crutch. Some salespeople think that they must have a brochure to be successful. Not true!

Telephone scripts

If you don't like using the telephone for marketing purposes, you might reconsider investing in a network marketing company. That's not to say you will initiate all your business by the telephone, but at some point in almost every sale, you *will* use the telephone. That's why your network marketing company is likely to give you a telemarketing workbook that includes sample scripts.

Network marketing companies use sample scripts for a variety of purposes. For example, one script may be designed to sell a particular product or product line. Another script can be used to invite people to your home or to a public meeting. And yet another script can assist you with hard-core telemarketing: calling strangers and inviting them to learn about your business opportunity. Studying these scripts is a good idea, even though you may decide not to use some of them. You can also adapt these scripts for face-to-face meetings as well as e-mail messages.

Business cards and stationery

Business cards are valuable tools at networking meetings, such as a Chamber of Commerce event. Well-designed business cards and stationery add to the professionalism of any business. And because network marketing is sometimes looked down upon as a business, these tools add legitimacy — especially for those customers and would-be prospects who like to see things in writing. Most network marketing companies make arrangements with a printer to sell authorized business cards and stationery to distributors.

Even if you don't plan to use direct mail as a marketing activity, you may frequently want to use stationery and envelopes imprinted with your network marketing company's logo and your personal contact information. You can use the stationery when you write letters of introduction, communicate with customers and vendors, and mail press releases to the local media.

Network-wide phone service

Good, frequent, and easy-to-access communication is the backbone of every successful network marketing company. The products may be fabulous, and the compensation plan may be the best ever created, but if the company doesn't communicate effectively with its distributors, you can bet that company won't exist for long. Network marketers may work independently, but they want to be kept informed.

Although e-mail continues to grow in importance as a communications tool, network marketing companies and their distributors still favor the good ol' telephone. As a result, most companies offer their distributors a third-party phone service that includes numerous features, the most useful being network-wide, instantaneous messaging. When the corporate office wants to get a message to every distributor, the message is recorded in the phone system, and with the push of a button or two, it's dispatched. The next time the distributors check their messages, they're made aware that the corporate office has left a message. Distributors who want to send messages to people in their downline can also use this feature.

The phone package may include other features, such as toll-free numbers and fax services. Because network marketing companies operate nationally and oftentimes internationally, network marketers are not restricted by geographic boundaries. You may begin your network marketing career in your local marketplace, but you may quickly broaden your prospecting to include people in distant cities and states. If you offer a toll-free number, these prospects and customers will appreciate the option of calling you or faxing you "on your quarter."

One problem with these phone packages: Not all distributors sign up for them. If your company offers such a package, we suggest that you subscribe. Otherwise, you may miss important communications.

Web sites

Nowadays, it's hard to imagine a network marketing company without a Web site. The site is particularly useful for providing services — for example, ordering products and downloading forms — to customers and distributors any time of the day or night, as well as sending information to prospects. The Web site address can be included on business cards and stationery and also promoted to prospects via e-mail, direct mail, the telephone, and other communications.

Many network marketing companies offer self-duplicating sites so that their distributors can personalize them with their photographs and contact information. While talking to a prospect by telephone, you can invite the prospect to connect to your Web site. Then you can point out various features and benefits of your products or business opportunity over the telephone. For much more information about these types of Web sites, see Chapter 15.

Getting Face to Face As Soon As You Can

In the early stages of developing your business, when you're still discovering how to use the marketing tools and sharpening the marketing saw, get in front of your prospects as soon as possible. Selling a business opportunity to a stranger by phone isn't easy. Selling vitamins and minerals, clothing, magnets, long-distance services, information, or any other product or service to a stranger by phone isn't any easier. The one exception may be weight loss products. People are often so desperate to lose weight that they'll buy these products with the hope that they're being led to a "magic pill." But, of course, as every reputable network marketing company knows, there ain't no such thing!

The best way to position yourself to close a sale, especially when you're just getting started and particularly if you don't have much sales experience, is to get face to face with your prospects in a selling environment. By *selling environment,* we don't necessarily mean the Chamber of Commerce networking party, nor do we mean you should market in the church, synagogue, or mosque, or an after-church social. You can use the following two types of marketing activities to *create* an effective selling environment, and we show you how to use them.

Inviting prospects to your home

The in-home meeting, a popular marketing activity, has been around since the beginning of network marketing. Unfortunately, this activity has turned many people against network marketing. By abusing this technique, overzealous network marketers tainted the industry's reputation. It's an image the industry still struggles to overcome today. Here's how it happened:

A friend called you and invited you to dinner. If you asked, "What's the occasion?" you were frequently told, "We just want to have some old friends over to get acquainted with some new friends — would you like to join us?" Of course, you may not have known the invitation was deceptive, or at least incomplete, until *after* dinner, when suddenly your host flipped on the television, popped in a video, and turned the evening into an "opportunity meeting" for a multi-level marketing concept. As a result, you were annoyed and felt betrayed, a friendship was strained, and multi-level marketing was damaged.

What a shame, because the in-home meeting, or party, can be, and for some marketers continues to be, a low-cost, enjoyable, and effective marketing activity. When you're nervous about making a presentation, being at home is all the more comforting. You can play the music of your choice in the background. You can serve coffee and comfort foods. Used properly, the in-home meeting often produces great results. It can be a positive and effective experience when there's no hidden agenda — "Come over because we're excited about a new business concept, and we want to introduce it to you."

Many network marketing companies continue to rely on these gatherings almost exclusively today. Marketers who sell home furnishings, kitchen products, and home decorations thrive in the home-party atmosphere. Other marketers sell wellness products, weight loss programs, vacation plans, and business opportunities in the home. This simple marketing activity requires absolutely no marketing acumen to use it successfully.

Organizing an in-home event — or for that matter, almost any other network marketing event — begins with a list of potential guests, or prospects. Here's where your List of 100 (from Chapter 14), your "warm market," comes into play. The people on this list know you, and hopefully like you and trust you. That's why this list is so valuable. Now it's time to call them and invite them to your home, one at a time or in small groups. You may discover that you not only enjoy this activity but are good at it, too.

Inviting your sponsor or people in your upline to the meeting may help you get through these early in-home meetings.

How to invite family and friends

Jack Maitland of Fort Lauderdale, Florida, is a Diamond distributor (meaning he's at the top of the company's compensation plan) with Nikken, a company that sells wellness products. Jack joined Nikken in 1996. His wife, daughter, and 80-year-old parents are also Nikken distributors. Jack is used to superstar status. He was drafted by the Baltimore Colts in 1970, and the next year he and his teammates won the National Football League's prized possession, the Super Bowl ring, when the Baltimore Colts won Super Bowl V. Here's how Jack handles inviting family and friends to look at his business. He doesn't always invite them to his home. Sometimes he asks them to meet him at a local coffee shop.

"I get a friend on the phone and I say, 'You and I go back a long way. I value your opinion. I'd like you to help me evaluate a business opportunity. I want you to give me some honest feedback.'

That's how to get face-to-face with your family and friends," he explains. "I don't have to ask them to buy anything. I want to hear their feedback. They'll either say they like it, or they don't. Either way, we're still going to be friends."

Does this approach only work for Super Bowl champions? Of course not. If your family and friends are interested in you and care about your welfare, they'll be willing to sit down with you and evaluate a business opportunity. And just in case you're thinking that this approach is a trick — *Jack's not really interested in the feedback, he just wants to get people to join him in business* — you're wrong. Network marketing is a relationship business. Successful network marketers realize that tricking someone into a business opportunity *never* works. If you're not sincere in network marketing, you're not likely to succeed.

Use the in-home marketing activity. Many successful network marketers say it's the best way to get started.

Inviting prospects to public opportunity meetings

Another good way to get started in network marketing is the public opportunity meeting, complete with music, motivational speeches, product testimonials, and an attractive display of the company's products. These events usually occur weekly at local hotels, and they're designed to attract existing distributors and their guests — the distributor's prospects. The meetings provide information (to both new distributors as well as prospects) and are intended to spark interest in the business opportunity. Public opportunity meetings last sixty to ninety minutes, but the individual questions and enrollment process can extend the time considerably.

Public opportunity meetings are successful for several reasons.

✔ Distributors who are not yet comfortable presenting the company's story, or who need more product information before making a presentation, attend the meeting for additional education.

✔ Frequently, the public opportunity meeting is followed by a training session for distributors. Prospects aren't invited to the training session unless they become distributors.

✔ Networking and socializing are important features of these meetings. New distributors mingle with experienced distributors and pick up ideas and techniques, as well as get encouragement, usually much needed in the early stages of a distributor's tenure with the company.

✔ The number of people attending the meeting usually generates enthusiasm for the products and for the business opportunity. The enthusiasm spreads to the guests as well as to the distributors.

✔ Some distributors rely almost exclusively on public opportunity meetings for recruiting purposes. They feel more comfortable selling when they're surrounded by friends.

At a public opportunity meeting, an experienced distributor, perhaps one who spends a lot of time training other distributors, delivers a brief presentation to provide an overview of the company. Then other distributors share their experiences with the company's products and services. When a network marketing company sells quality products, the products frequently produce positive results. Weight loss, relief from arthritis, increased energy, lower cholesterol levels, a better night's sleep, a better attitude, and more confidence are some of the common results discussed at these meetings.

Many times the testimonials are lively and animated, and occasionally they bring people to tears. That's not to imply that these stories are insincere or otherwise staged (though we're sure that happens). Imagine suffering from arthritis for years and then feeling better than ever after taking an all-natural product for several weeks. Or imagine battling your weight all your life, only to find help (notice we said help, and not magic) from a product that reduces your appetite and burns calories, too.

These are real results, and when people talk about them, you can bet they're going to be excited. These firsthand experiences motivate not only the distributors at the meeting but their guests, too. Suddenly everyone with a weight management problem wants to buy the company's products. And they can, just as soon as they place their orders.

The value of a public opportunity meeting

"Never underestimate the power of assembly," says Shawn Wheeland, president of Homebusiness.to.inc. in South Carolina. "There's power in numbers," he continues.

Wheeland says there's a science to the public opportunity meetings used by most network marketing companies. "You need high energy in these meetings, upbeat music, proper lighting, and people who can talk from the heart about the company's products. This is not *hype*," he emphasizes. "It's difficult to be a guest at one of these meetings where everyone is so excited and not feel your heart skip a beat or two. A company or a distributor can't create that highly motivated feeling with an audiotape or a brochure."

What's the secret of getting guests to these meetings?

"There's nothing secretive about it," Shawn explains. "You call people and complete a phone interview by asking probing questions and exploring their unwanted conditions. After you know what this person would do with some extra income or time, you then say to them: 'Based on your answers to my questions, I feel you qualify for the second part of our interview. I have scheduled a short program Tuesday night and I'd love to meet you and complete the interview. . . .' We can train people to do that! It's a lot easier than teaching people how to do their own face-to-face presentation. It's not hard to teach someone how to get a prospect out to a meeting."

Before the meeting ends, the guests are encouraged to get together with the distributor who invited them to the meeting. If you're that distributor, there may never be a better time to close the sale than now! The meeting did the hard work for you: It captured your prospect's attention, provided the necessary information, and even validated the products with testimonials. Now, everywhere in the room guests are meeting with distributors, and oftentimes checkbooks come out of pockets, and new distributors are enrolled. The selling environment hardly ever gets better than this. Your guest will be excited, motivated, and most likely ready to join forces with you, either as a distributor or as a retail customer of your products or services.

Relax. Someone in your upline or another distributor in the room can help you know what to say when you get together with your guest at the end of the meeting.

Shawn's explanation of how to get guests to opportunity meetings works only when it's delivered with sincerity. If your company's opportunity meetings are the type that pressure people into buying products and services or joining the business as a distributor, you'll only alienate your friends and prospects by using this type of invitation.

Network marketing is a relationship business. Trickery doesn't work. The moment you give a prospect reason to distrust you, you've lost the sale. You may also have lost a friend.

Chapter 17

Marketing Activities 101

. . . .

In This Chapter

▶ Relying on traditional print advertising

▶ Using the telephone to attract customers

▶ Creating a successful direct-mail campaign

▶ Speaking your way to a bigger business

▶ Making the best use of the Internet to build your business

. . . .

*Y*ou may not be comfortable marketing your product or your business opportunity in a face-to-face environment (as we discussed in Chapter 16) — at least not yet. Perhaps you need a little more time. Or maybe you just don't like crowds, or you think meetings are too time consuming. Whatever the reason, some network marketers simply prefer alternative marketing activities that don't include home or public meetings.

Hey, as the comedian Flip Wilson used to say, "Different strokes for different folks!" Fortunately, network marketers can choose from a variety of "different strokes." So many, in fact, that the choices tend to be confusing. It's not unusual for even an experienced distributor to feel lost or uncertain about how to use some of these tools. Some network marketing companies and sponsors are better than others at helping their distributors become effective in a variety of marketing activities.

The following sections help you make good decisions about your marketing plans. We make no claims about the success of these marketing activities, and by no means are these the only alternative activities available. We selected several of the less complex marketing activities and provided guidelines to help you make better decisions. We expect that you'll return to this chapter more than a few times.

Advertising in Newspapers and Magazines

When you're just getting started in network marketing, *if* you're going to buy advertising space to promote your business opportunity, we encourage you to start with small, local newspapers and magazines. Why the *if*? Frankly, advertising may not be the best way to build your business. Consult with the people in your upline on this issue before you commit to spend your money. If you've never placed ads before, it's not as easy as it looks, so don't try to do it by yourself. Get help from those in your upline and make certain you follow company guidelines.

Buying ad space

Assuming that your upline tells you that advertising works, start slowly and inexpensively, with a small community newspaper or a business magazine. A weekly newspaper is ideal. Get a copy, turn to the classified section, and read the ads under the heading Business Opportunities. Because you're offering a business opportunity — you're recruiting for distributors to join you in business — the newspaper or magazine places your ad under this heading.

You may find just a few or a lot of ads in the Business Opportunities listing. If there are a lot of ads, that could be a sign that this medium generates results for business opportunities. On the other hand, the appearance of only a few ads could mean the newspaper or magazine is waiting to be discovered.

Contact the advertising department by phone or online. Someone in the publication's ad department will help you place your ad and give you the rate information. Classified ads are usually sold by the line, and publications often have a three–line minimum. Lines are limited to a specific number of characters or words. You may even be required to buy the ad a minimum of three times, which, by the way, is a good idea. In fact, you should plan to advertise for at least seven weeks to give your message the appropriate exposure. People need to see the same ad over and over before they'll respond. Expect to sign a contract before your ad will be accepted for publication.

If you're thinking of advertising once just to test the market, please don't do that! Save your money until you can advertise multiple times. Successful advertisers know that the response to an ad tends to build over time. People generally need to see a message more than once before they'll respond to it, or remember to respond to it.

You can advertise wherever you want; you're not restricted to placing an ad in your community's weekly newspaper. If you know of a small newspaper several towns away from you, give it a try. After you've had some success with your ads and you have more money to spend, branch out to other newspapers in your state or across the country.

If starting small doesn't appeal to you, and you have surplus cash, then place your ad in the Sunday edition of a metropolitan newspaper or in your city's business journal. Thinking of something even bigger? Okay, several national newspapers and magazines promote business opportunities. You can find them on most newsstands or in an online search. Give 'em a try. Hey, it's only money, and after all, it's *your* money! You may even want to skip the classified section and buy a display ad. On the other hand, when you find out how much this costs, you may take our advice to start small and finish big!

Refraining from writing your own advertisements

This is not the time to reinvent the wheel. If advertising works for your company, then someone in your upline has already placed a successful company-approved ad. Get a copy of that ad and use it! Do not write your own advertising messages. Writing successful ads is an art, and you didn't start a network marketing business to become a copywriter, did you? Don't do it!

Similarly, don't allow the ad salesperson at the newspaper or magazine to write an ad for you. Stick with ads that are already proven to work. The salesperson's job is to sell you space in the publication, not write your ads.

Leveraging your money in an advertising co-op

If you're planning to spend money on advertising — whether for classifieds or display ads, and whether it's for newspapers, magazines, or radio stations — ask your upline about an advertising co-op. One of the great benefits of a network is buying power. On your own, you're limited to the amount of ad space you can buy, but if several distributors pool their money, they can afford larger ads and professional writers if needed.

Get ten or so like-minded people to each contribute $1,000 so that you have a substantial advertising fund. Usually, someone in the company starts a co-op by inviting other distributors to contribute money on a monthly or quarterly basis. Distributors decide for themselves whether they want to be involved. A company could have several co-ops. One co-op may specialize in radio advertising, another may buy display ads in national magazines, and another could be focused on buying space in trade publications that are targeted to specific kinds of people such as network marketers or realtors or Christians, and so forth. A co-op could also be involved in buying ads in a variety of media, even including billboards and postcard decks. Wherever there's an opportunity to advertise, there's an opportunity for a co-op.

If you're not the person running the co-op but you've chosen to participate, the best thing you can do is contribute your money and trust the leader to spend it wisely. Meanwhile, get ready to track your leads and turn prospects into distributors or retail customers.

Do some homework before you join a co-op. Ask the people in your upline about the history of any co-op that you're considering. If your upline includes the leader of the co-op, ask other distributors who have participated in the co-op about the results they received. If the results were positive, you may have to wait your turn to get into the co-op. Keep in mind that co-ops are not guaranteed. Things go wrong. Certain media pull results better than others, and even the same media do not respond similarly all the time. Even the best of co-ops has a flop now and then. Best advice: If you can't afford to advertise, it's better to wait until you can.

Ring, Ring: Use That Telephone

Opinions are mixed when it comes to telemarketing — some network marketers love it, and others dislike it — but we've never met a successful network marketer who didn't rely on the telephone to conduct business.

Chapters 11 and 14 provide information about your "warm market," which consists of family, friends, and associates — the people you know — as opposed to the "cold market," the people who are strangers to you. The discussion of telemarketing pros and cons that follows applies to both your warm and cold markets.

Pros and cons of telemarketing

Plan on using the telephone to build your network marketing business. As with most marketing activities, using the telephone comes with advantages and disadvantages.

Here are the pros of telemarketing:

- ✔ **No or little cost.** Much of the time you'll be calling people in your local area so telemarketing is economical to use.

- ✔ **Quick response time.** They're either interested or they're not; you'll know when you talk to them, and you won't have to wait for a response.

- ✔ **Faster than a flying finger.** You can make one call after another, just as quickly as your finger can punch or dial numbers.

- ✔ **Accommodates your schedule.** You can make telemarketing calls when it's convenient for you. However, don't call people when they're likely to be eating lunch or dinner. Don't call before 8 a.m. or after 9 p.m. Use common sense — are you calling people at a time when you would be receptive to taking a call?

- ✔ **It's repetitive.** Your company or the people in your upline can provide you with a telemarketing script. After you learn it, you'll use it over and over. Get a list of names and phone numbers and start dialing! Be careful not to read the script over the phone. Familiarize yourself with the script and then put it in your own words.

And here are the cons of telemarketing:

- ✔ **Getting connected can be difficult.** Nowadays, with caller identification and voice mail, anyone who doesn't want to talk to you doesn't have to!

- ✔ **Hearing isn't the same as seeing.** Visual people like to touch and feel a product before they buy it or possibly even understand it. Getting your point across may be difficult to do over the phone.

- ✔ **No's come easier.** Someone who might not tell you no in a face-to-face conversation may find it easier to say no over the phone.

"Most network marketers are afraid of what to say on the telephone when they're just starting to build a business," explains Shawn Wheeland, a former sheet metal mechanic at a nuclear power plant in South Carolina and now a six-figure-income distributor with NuCreations, Inc., which sells nutritional and weight management products, and president of Homebusiness.to.Inc. That's why Shawn offers Phone Reluctance Training to his affiliates. "I show people how to pick up the phone and do business," he says. "I teach them what to say to their friends, or how to interview strangers at www. homebusiness.to/online and then build relationships. It takes a little time for people to get the hang of it, but once they do, they can control their destiny, and they realize that telemarketing works."

Some distributors, however, never get the hang of it, or they never really like it. "Telemarketing is not a high relationship-oriented activity — it's more high tech than high touch — so some people steer clear of it," says Jon Miller in

London, Canada. He's been a distributor of Body Wise International since 1995, marketing the company's nutritional products. Jon says that a network marketer who doesn't have good telemarketing skills or who doesn't particularly like telemarketing needs to rely on a telemarketing script. "That way," he says, "very little will be left to guesswork or to raw talent."

Most network marketing companies provide their distributors with telemarketing scripts, but not all of them are effective. Joining a company with good scripts is important, particularly if you're not comfortable using the telephone. What do you do if your company doesn't have a good script? Find a seasoned distributor in the organization who will help you develop a script that complements your skills and gets results.

The diversity of opinions is one of the appealing attributes about network marketing. One networker will say something doesn't work, and another will tell you it does! That certainly goes for telemarketing, as evidenced by the discussions in this section. Hilton Johnson, founder of MLM University in Lauderdale-by-the-Sea, Florida, isn't a fan of telemarketing to a cold market — he says it's just too tough. On the other hand, Doug Firebaugh, MLM trainer extraordinaire, loves making those calls. Who's right? You won't know until you give telemarketing a try. If it works for you, it works!

With 40 years of direct sales experience, including 14 years in telemarketing and real estate, Hilton Johnson can show you how to use telemarketing successfully. However, he isn't encouraging about phoning a cold market.

"That's brutal," he says, "and most people can't cut it. It's like a prison sentence if all you do is call strangers on the telephone. If you make enough calls, things *will* happen, but making enough calls into a cold market is a problem. You'd have to make calls at the rate of thirty a day, seven days a week. There are people who do that, too, but you can make half a dozen calls in your warm market and get at least one or two appointments."

Of course, some people just don't like to work their warm market — they don't want to approach family and friends. "In that case," says Hilton, "you should do several marketing activities at the same time if you want to be successful. Use some telemarketing, do some advertising, schedule in-home meetings, take your guests to opportunity meetings, ask for referrals, and use e-mail. Everything adds up to success, providing you can keep up with all these activities."

Remember that the fear of loss is greater than the desire for gain. For that reason, be sure to point out during the presentation process what the prospect could lose by not becoming an associate. Example: "Mr. Prospect, I believe that one day you will say either 'I wish I had' or 'I'm glad I did.' Say yes, and you, your family, and your contacts can all win. Say no, and nobody wins."

Telemarketing etiquette

Remember that you're invading someone's time and privacy when you contact that person by phone. Don't abuse the technique — network marketing's reputation doesn't need any more sore points. Follow these guidelines:

- ✔ Use common sense. Be courteous on the phone.

- ✔ Ask for permission to talk. "Is this a good time for me to call you?"

- ✔ Don't call people before 8 a.m. or after 9 p.m.

- ✔ Don't call during the dinner hour or on holidays.

- ✔ Never argue, but never allow anyone to be abusive to you, either. Just thank them, hang up the phone, and move on.

- ✔ Like any form of marketing, telemarketing is all about building relationships. Listen to the prospect's point of view.

- ✔ Be flexible. Offer to send material via the mail, if desired. Or invite a prospect to a meeting, or to view your Web site. Some prospects won't like talking on the phone.

A cold-market "trench dog"

"I love it," Doug Firebaugh says about telemarketing to a cold market. He built a multi-million dollar international business with National Safety Associates International (NSA) before changing directions and becoming a network marketing coach two years ago. "I was a trench dog," Firebaugh says of himself. "I've made the 60,000 phone calls, attended the 2,400 seminars, and I've talked to the 8,000 people, and through my success I've learned that what I really like to do is help other people succeed in this industry."

As a network marketer, Firebaugh says he spent 90 percent of his time telemarketing to a cold market. "Most people are intimidated by the cold market," he explains, "but I can change their minds." He's writing a telemarketing training program called "Turning the Cold Market into the Gold Market" (see www.mlmleadership.com). Firebaugh teaches his students that cold calling is simply making friends over the phone. "These are friends you haven't met yet," he says. "And the next one you meet could be the superstar you've been looking for. The very next one could open the floodgates to success in your business, and if you don't make the call, what's that going to cost you?" Ah, there's the motivation: fear!

"That's right." says Firebaugh, "You work the cold market out of a fear of loss. It's incredibly easy to do. The cold market is huge, so it presents endless opportunities. Sure, there are people in the cold market who will be rude, and they'll hang up on you, but once you learn how to tap into the cold market, you may never want to do anything else. It's fast and it's fun, especially when you get results. That's how you make the big money in network marketing."

Want to read up on telemarketing? Try these books: *The Complete Handbook of All-Purpose Telemarketing Scripts* (Prentice Hall, 1990), by Barry Z. Masser, and *Cold Calling Techniques that Really Work!* (Adams Media Corporation, 1999), by Stephan Schiffman.

Unlike many of the other techniques available to network marketers, telemarketing can't be shoved aside altogether. Every successful distributor uses this technique at least part-time.

You've Got Direct Mail

Direct mail — the process of sending letters, postcards, and brochures by mail to elicit a response — affords you the opportunity to reach large numbers of people, including warm and cold markets. Along with or instead of printed materials, you can mail audio- and videotapes and product samples. A direct mail campaign requires a list of names and addresses — the people you want to reach — and a mailing piece, which includes an envelope and the contents, such as a letter or audiotape that presents the "offer" that you're trying to sell. Of course, you also need postage, as well as someone to stuff the envelopes and get them to the post office. Direct mail has both advantages and disadvantages.

The pros

Here are some of the benefits of using direct mail:

- **Reaches masses of people, fast.** Thousands of people can see your message all on the same day, or within several days, with direct mail. It's a fast way to spread your promotional message quickly. Telemarketing, by comparison, allows you to reach only one person at a time.

- **Doesn't intrude.** Direct mail arrives in the mailbox without interrupting anyone. The message is received when the recipient decides to open the envelope or package, play an audio- or videotape, or use the product sample.

- **Delivers a tangible item.** People who like to see and touch, rather than listen to a phone presentation, may respond faster and more favorably to direct mail after they've had an opportunity to read, re-read, and consider the offer. A product sample received in the mail and used successfully may result in an immediate call back with a request to order the product.

- **Teases for interest.** A well-written letter, a thought-provoking brochure, or a product sample that delivers immediate results may be the only way to get the attention of certain recipients. When you don't know who to call, or you can't reach them by phone because the secretary blocks your call, or you just can't get an answer, direct mail may be the answer. The mail might get the recipient to call you!

✔ **Saves time.** People tend to be busier than ever, so even if a recipient wants to talk to you, there may not be a good time to connect by phone. Direct mail saves the personal intervention and still delivers the message.

The cons

Here are some of the drawbacks of using direct mail:

✔ **Requires expertise.** Direct mail isn't easy to use successfully. Experts spend years studying and testing the details. Selecting the right word for a headline, including a particular phrase in a letter, choosing the right color for a brochure or postcard — each of these decisions and many others can make or break a mailing. Know what you're doing, or hook up with someone in your company who does.

✔ **Doesn't always get opened.** Lots of people think direct mail is junk mail. Frankly, a lot of it is! Your recipients must be willing to open your package. If they have no interest in your offer or don't like the look of your envelope or your postcard turns them off, your mail gets deposited in the wastebasket.

✔ **Costs money, sometimes too much money.** By the time you pay for the use of a mailing list (if you don't have your own), buy envelopes, pay to print or photocopy letters, buy tapes or brochures, spend your time or pay for someone's time to stuff the contents into the envelope, and then you buy postage, you may have $1 to $5 invested in each mailing piece. That's a lot of money when you're mailing hundreds or thousands of pieces at a time. It's really a lot of money if the mail doesn't get opened! (Don't do this, however, until you've sampled the market.)

Building a great mailing list

Your mailing list must be appropriate for your offer, and it must be fresh. You can develop a knock-'em-dead, creative, and expensive mailing piece, but if you send it to the wrong list, an outdated list, or an overworked list, the results will be dreadful. You just wasted all that money on your mailing piece.

Direct mail experts know the importance of spending money to rent a quality list from a list broker, a magazine, or a publishing company. (Ask the people in your upline to recommend a good source for list rentals.) Or they spend money to build their own list. The latter choice is preferable and almost always more effective. The problem is that it's time consuming and expensive.

You can build a list by advertising in newspapers, magazines, and other forms of media. This method involves a two-step approach:

1. You place a classified ad, say in your local newspaper or even a national trade publication, to invite interested people to call your toll-free number for free information. You might offer a free report, a booklet, or a videotape. Those who call should be asked to leave their name, address, and telephone number.

2. You mail the material that you promised to send.

If you represent a company headed by a celebrity or a well-known, highly respected company, a one line classified ad in a local newspaper can produce excellent results. For example: "Build Your Own Business With Zig Ziglar! Call now and we'll tell you how. 800-527-0306." As prospects respond to your advertisement, respond appropriately with a return call or by mailing information. Keep a record of all names and phone numbers that respond to your ad and store this information in a database so that you can use it again and again. Many people think that direct mail consists of mailing a brochure or a letter one time. That limited approach doesn't work. Direct mail has to be used repetitively, and it's important to reach the same list of people. A person often isn't interested the first or third time you send your mail. It's not unusual for people to respond only after they've heard from you a half-dozen times, and maybe even more.

As people's circumstances change — for example, they lose their job, or they desire more money — they may become more receptive to your offers. Unless, of course, your list isn't any good. If you don't get at least a few responses from your list per every 50 to 100 pieces mailed, your list may not be good. Or, your offer may not be good! Patience is a virtue in direct mail. You may get only a trickle of interest after you mail to the list one time, but the response may increase as you mail repetitively, or as you improve your offer.

Mailing an extraordinary offer

On the other hand, assume that your mailing list is fantastic. You created the list yourself, and it includes the names and addresses of people who expressed interest in a network marketing business. No name on the list is older than 90 days. If you mail an extraordinary offer to this list, the results of your campaign should be positive. But keep this in mind. Developing or renting a good mailing list is easier than creating a successful offer. A good offer includes numerous components: a strong headline, compelling sentences and paragraphs, easy-to-read text set off with subheads, and specific directions about how to respond, along with an emotional nudge to respond immediately. If you've never written an offer before, don't start now. It's too risky.

Besides, why reinvent the wheel? People in your upline or your company will have used direct mail successfully. Ask for their help and copy their offer! Many network marketing companies provide proven direct mail letters and postcards in their training programs. Use these materials if you decide to implement a direct mail campaign.

With a proven offer and the right list, your chances of succeeding in direct mail are very good. Many network marketers like the idea of mailing 100 letters a week. With just average results, those 100 letters may generate a half dozen leads a week. On the other hand, the right offer, mailed to a good list, may generate 10 to 20 or more leads a week. And that may be all the work that a network marketer, working part-time, can handle in a week.

 From Canada, Jon Miller, a health consultant (`www.ihacademy.com`) and Body Wise International distributor of nutritional products, says he believes it's important to keep a mailing small enough to personalize it. "Handwritten envelopes and handwritten notes generate better results," he explains. You may not have the time to mail 100 personalized letters a week. Even so, try mailing 25 personalized letters and see what happens. You may discover that fewer letters generates better results because of personalization. Experimentation is an important consideration in direct mail.

Jon says he isn't all that enthusiastic about using direct mail anymore. "I have to say direct mail has become a dinosaur in the age of the Internet," he explains. "Spending two to five dollars to send a letter and an audiotape to a prospect by mail isn't nearly so appealing when you can direct that prospect to your Web site. They can get more information on your site than you can fit into an envelope, and they can even listen to the tape online. I think network marketers will continue using direct mail, but I also think we'll be able to reduce the number of packets we send." Of course, not everyone is online, and among those who are online, many still appreciate receiving a direct mail package before visiting a Web site. In fact, your direct mail piece may be the catalyst that leads a prospect to your Web site.

The degree to which you use direct mail depends on a number of factors, but it begins with your own preferences. If you enjoy this marketing method, by all means use it! However, you can't just drop those letters in the mail and sit by the phone. You must — read that as *must* — continue your other networking activities, or your network marketing career will be very brief.

Speak Up! Speak Out! Speak Wherever You Can

"Oh no," we hear you saying. "I could never do that. I can't stand up and speak to strangers. The last thing in the world I want to do is give a speech. If I have to do that, I'm not getting into network marketing. I'd be scared to death to give a public speech."

Fair enough, but we think you *can* stand up and speak to strangers, and we think you will once you consider the ideas we present here. Many organizations are eager to hear what you have to say, and we can show you how to get comfortable in front of an audience with just a little practice and some encouragement. Plus, we tell you about a technique that allows you to speak to strangers by the telephone, so that you don't have to stand up in front of them!

But don't be so sure that you wouldn't enjoy getting up on the platform and speaking to a huge crowd of people. Give yourself a few months, maybe a year, with a good network marketing company — one that trains you how to give a speech — and you may never want to get off the platform!

I encourage you to practice and learn the skill of public speaking. The Toastmasters organization has chapters all over the country. Join one. You'll gain valuable experience *and* make lots of friends and build winning relationships, putting you in an ideal position to bring them into your organization. Yes, I know you may have a fear of public speaking, but consider this: As far as I have been able to discover, only three people have lost their lives in the process of public speaking. They are Arthur MacArthur, the father of General Douglas MacArthur, who died of a heart attack while on the dais addressing a reunion of his Civil War unit; Alben W. Barkley, former vice president of the United States, who died suddenly while making a speech; and a woman who was running for Justice of the Peace in a small New York town. Some estimates tell us that roughly 15 billion people have occupied the earth since Adam and Eve. That means the odds are five billion to one that you will survive your talk. Actually, it's more dangerous to take a bath than to make a public speech, as far as fatalities are concerned. A few butterflies indicate that you care about your audience. Experience will teach you how to get them in formation.

Speaking to organizations

Every community includes service organizations such as Rotary, the Optimist Club, and the Chamber of Commerce. They all need speakers! Call them to see whether they'll book you for a presentation, but be careful. Your purpose at that presentation is to practice speaking to people and to make friends, not to recruit or sell products to the members of the groups. If you do a good job, someone in that audience *may* approach you and ask for a business card or want more information about your business.

Offer to speak to these groups about a subject related to your business. Can you talk about sales, or marketing, or goal setting? Can you tell them how to set up a telemarketing program? Don't cross the line with these organizations. If they get the feeling that you showed up to "pitch them," you won't be invited back, and you're not likely to get a call from any of them.

Offer several of your products for door prizes. And when you give away your products, include a brochure about your business, along with your audiocassette or videotape. The organization may pass a hat (or a bowl) and ask each member to throw in a business card. At the end of the meeting, be sure you get those business cards! Take them home and contact these individuals by mail or phone to follow up on your presentation and ask if they have any interest in your products, services, or business opportunity. As long as you're not obnoxious in your follow-up techniques, no one should object to your contacting them. If they do, simply apologize and don't contact them in the future.

Teleconferencing your speech

David D'Arcangelo of San Diego, California, was already a successful speaker when he discovered network marketing and became a distributor of The People's Network (TPN), which was eventually sold to Pre-Paid Legal, a publicly traded network marketing company that sells legal services. David quickly realized that the fast track to a grand slam in network marketing required reaching masses of people. That's when he decided to organize a teleconferencing program.

Getting comfortable on stage

Here are a few simple public speaking tips:

- Prepare well.

- Make notes as reminders, but don't read your talk.

- Seek the eyes of a friendly face. Look at this person for a few seconds and then look into the eyes of another friendly face for a few seconds. This way, you're (in essence) speaking to one person, not to a group.

- Remember that virtually everyone there is pulling for you. Some will even be praying for you. Most will have already walked in your shoes, so empathy for you will be abundant.

- Remember also that everybody, initially, has stage fright. Some of the greatest speakers ever had to speak many times before they became proficient at speaking in public.

- Keep in mind that you are there to feed your audience, not to boost your own ego.

- Acquire a cassette recording of your talk and spend time analyzing it, concentrating first on what you did well and second on how you can improve.

These tips will be very helpful to you. In addition, other sources are available to help you hone your speaking skills. Many universities and community colleges offer courses for developing effective presentations. The Dale Carnegie Leadership Course is an excellent one, and Ziglar Training Systems offers a two-day Effective Business Presentations Seminar, during which we videotape several efforts. We consistently see a substantial difference between a student's first and last presentations. Take advantage of courses that teach how to communicate. They can and will make a difference in your network.

Teleconferencing utilizes video technology to broadcast your message to people who tune in to watch and listen to you. You can find teleconferencing services through the Yellow Pages, or you can go to Kinko's, as David did, to set up the program. He invited prospects in eight U.S. cities to visit their local Kinko's while his presentation was being broadcast. "For about $80," David explains, "I could rent an hour of broadcast time at Kinko's and tell my network marketing story to eight cities. That was a lot of fun!"

Anyone can use teleconferencing today. In fact, you may find it less intimidating to speak to a camera than to a live audience. However, until you have developed a downline of distributors who can help you recruit prospects in other cities, setting up a luncheon speech for 30 to 100 members of a local organization is less time-consuming!

We said that you don't have to use every available marketing activity. You probably won't succeed in network marketing if you don't use the telephone, but you surely can succeed without making a speech. However, we think you'd be missing a tremendous opportunity because few marketing activities are as exhilarating as speaking to a live audience. Come on, try it, at least!

You've Got E-Mail

E-mail is the simplest form of marketing on the Internet. You can write a sizzling promotion — better yet, you can borrow an already proven promotion from someone in your upline — and with one click of the mouse, you can inform countless people worldwide about your products, services, and business opportunity. People who are interested in your message will respond to you, perhaps with questions which beg further communication. This is a good way to educate your prospects and sort them. You'll soon know who's really interested and who's not.

Network marketing is a business built on relationships. Don't expect too much of your e-mail processor. E-mail is a cold form of communication. Use it to sort through your prospects and identify those who are interested in moving forward. E-mail helps you find an opportunity to build a relationship, but you'll probably have to use a warmer form of communication to further the relationship. Pick up the phone and call these prospects!

Thou shalt not spam

If you've spent any time at all on the Internet, then you probably know about *spamming,* the practice of sending unsolicited e-mail (we discussed this subject briefly in Chapter 15). This onerous practice is used by people who have absolutely no regard for *netiquette*, that is, the proper use of the Internet.

Spammers collect or buy e-mail addresses and send their messages to people they don't know, and people who mostly don't want to hear from them. Spammers clog cyberspace with untold numbers of messages that are at least annoying and at worst offensive. Pornographers may have been the first to use spamming, but now they have plenty of company. Unfortunately, network marketers are sometimes guilty, too.

Spamming may look benign, especially to those who believe *their* product is something *everyone* needs and wants to buy. And because these messages — commonly known as Internet "junk mail" — show up in everyone's mailbox, it's easy to think: *What's the harm? If all these people are doing it, why don't I give it a try, too? If it doesn't work, I won't do it again.* Big mistake!

Unless you know how to send your spam from an e-mail address that can't be easily tracked back to you (and what's the use of that if you're trying to convince people to build a business relationship with you?), you're probably going to get caught. And when it comes to spamming, Internet Service Providers do not look the other way. In fact, most of them employ people to detect spammers. If they track spam back to you, you're going to lose your Internet connection, possibly for a number of days. Spam a second time, and you'll probably lose your connection for good. Meanwhile, you've upset many of the people who received your message, and they'll write back and tell you a thing or two, neither of which you'll find pleasant. By the way, don't let anyone tell you that it's okay to send unsolicited e-mails as long as you explain in the e-mail how to unsubscribe from your list. The inclusion of that explanation does not make an unsolicited e-mail any less spam.

If you haven't already figured it out, spamming is a waste of your time and a risk to your credibility, as well as the credibility of your company. Our advice: Don't do it!

Thou shalt send thy neighbor legitimate e-mail

There *are* legitimate ways to use e-mail to promote network marketing. For example, you can send a message (or several, if the recipients will tolerate them) to the people who know you. Atticus Killough, a self-described "MLM (multi-level marketing) junkie" in Dallas, Texas, says he sends occasional announcements about his latest network marketing interests to family, friends, and business associates whose e-mail addresses are listed in his Address Book.

"I don't ask them to join the business," he explains, "and I don't try to sell them anything. I send them an announcement when I discover a new opportunity. 'Hello family and friends. I thought you might like to know about a terrific business opportunity I recently discovered. . . .' I explain a little bit about the business, and then I provide the Web site address. And that's all. Those who want to check it out will, and those who aren't interested just delete the message. Some people get back to me, but most don't. No one seems to mind, and if they did, I wouldn't send them the messages anymore."

You can also send e-mail to people who opt to receive your messages, or who e-mail you first. They may subscribe to a newsletter that you produce, a free report, or even a weekly or daily message of interest to them. You can promote all of these opportunities from your own Web site! Depending on your promotion skills and your advertising budget, you may build up an "opt-in" list that includes tens of thousands of readers worldwide. It's a privilege when strangers invite you to send them messages.

Use this opportunity to make friends online. Find out about the interests of your subscribers. Ask questions and invite feedback. If you take your time and offer thought-provoking messages, many of your readers will eventually want to know more about you and your business. When they start asking questions, you can step up the prospecting, and only then are you likely to find buyers. Move too fast, however, or take advantage of your readers, and you'll lose subscribers just as quickly as your Internet Service Provider can terminate your service.

A Web Site for Every Networker

Perhaps the greatest use of the Internet for network marketers comes with the World Wide Web. This technology provides nonstop lead generation and offers the promise of revenue generation 24/7. In Chapter 15, we discussed using technology in the form of autoresponders and self-replicating Web sites to help you follow up with prospects. Here we discuss self-replicating Web sites in terms of generating leads and explain some of the differences between company-sponsored sites and generic sites.

Company-sponsored self-replicating Web sites

Most network marketing companies offer their distributors self-replicating Web sites. These are replicas of the company's official Web site. Self-replicating Web sites make it possible for a network marketing company to control the flow of information online. By banning any site that's not a replica of the official company site, the corporate office can be sure that the information online is accurate.

Self-replicating Web sites contribute to a unified network marketing organization. When all the representatives have the same information, presented on a look-alike Web site, no one has to spend valuable time trying to gain a competitive edge over anyone else. These Web sites generate leads all hours of the day and night without getting tired or ever giving up. Unlike the human associate, the Web site always looks the same, sounds the same (if it includes sound), and delivers a perfect presentation every time (except when there's a technological snafu).

They generate revenue without human intervention, providing they've been designed to accommodate e-commerce. Many of these sites accept applications from new members who use their credit cards to pay for the enrollment fees. Imagine waking up every morning and discovering that your Web site earned a few hundred dollars while you were sleeping! That's not science fiction — it's happening today in many network marketing organizations.

Generic Web sites

These generic Web sites attract prospective distributors, and they can be used to schedule automated follow-up activity. However, unlike the company-sponsored sites, the generic sites are not designed to promote a specific business. Instead, they promote the opportunity to own a business, and they attract prospects who are looking for opportunities but who may not have a specific business in mind.

Once prospects visit your generic site, they are invited to enter their name and e-mail address so that you can send them information about your specific opportunity as well as your products and services. You can then program the site to send the prospects a series of personalized messages, which you write and load into the system. These messages will be delivered until a prospect either joins your business or tells you to stop sending information. To view samples of these sites, and for additional information about how to use them, visit www.freeleads.com/welcome.

"All we're doing is asking a person to raise his hand and say, 'I could be interested in my own business,'" explains Atticus Killough, a distributor of ProSTEP, a generic lead generator at www.prostepinc.com. "Those who provide their personal information are considered leads," Atticus continues. Once a company receives a lead, it's distributed to one or more network marketers who pay a monthly fee for lead generation. The networkers then follow up with the leads (see Chapter 15), offering information about the opportunity they represent and hopefully converting the leads to downline distributors.

According to Todd Falcone, a full-time associate with ProSTEP since 1997, "Ninety-nine percent of the people in ProSTEP do not sell the [ProSTEP's] business opportunity. They join ProSTEP for the leads, which they use to build another network marketing business. Maybe they introduce three or four new associates to the business in a year, but that's okay. It's a secondary opportunity for most network marketers.

Fred Raley, an avid Internet marketer in Montclair, Virginia, says his business doubled once he started using ProSTEP. He now subscribes to two lead-generating sources and receives more than 2,000 leads monthly. Fred is a distributor of Ameriplan USA, which markets discount dental, vision, prescription, and chiropractic health plans, and he represents other opportunities, too.

In addition to ProSTEP, www.prostepinc.com, www.Freeleads.com/welcome, and www.compensate.net also provide lead generation services.

If you sign up with a replicable Web site that promises to do lead generation for you, make sure the site doesn't practice spamming. See "Thou Shalt Not Spam" earlier in this chapter for more information about spamming.

Generating leads with generic Web sites

The secret to working with generic leads is to follow up with them frequently and consistently, according to both Atticus Killough and Fred Roley. The lead generation companies have automated that process, turning it into a no brainer. Atticus explains: "Once you receive a lead, the automated system will send the lead a half-dozen or more letters, spaced over a period of time [in other words, "dripping" — a word we introduced in Chapter 15]. You can control the content of the letters and the frequency of the mailings." Here's how Fred "drips" on his prospects: "The (lead generation) computer programs do all the sorting and most of the follow-up for me. I don't have a lot of time, so ProSTEP finds out who's interested in a business and who's not. In the first 30 days of receiving a lead, I'll send that lead ten to twelve messages to encourage them to visit my Web site for Ameriplan, or one of the other companies that I represent. The leads continue getting my messages for six to eight months, or until they remove themselves from the follow up system by unsubscribing.

When someone's interested specifically in Ameriplan, or one of my other products or businesses, I use another software program,

PostMaster.com, to send them a further set of automated, personalized messages giving them more information about the products, the company, our pay plan, etc. If they visit my Ameriplan site, I'll then contact them by phone to try to close the sale. It's really an efficient way to build my business. I only call people who want to join me."

When the follow-up process succeeds and a lead converts to a new distributor, Fred is happy. But he can get even happier! How is his new distributor going to generate leads? Fred has the solution: a lead-generating Web site! So now he has a chance to make a second sale to the same distributor. But then look what happens: As the new distributor begins to convert leads to Ameriplan, and to ProSTEP, Fred earns commissions off every sale. Now he's ecstatic!

"It just makes sense to use these lead-generation services," says Fred, who works a full-time job during the day and spends three to four hours an evening as a networker. "The services really boost my ego. I don't waste time cold calling, or pulling dead horses over the finish line to get them into my business. It's great working with motivated people."

Chapter 18

"But I Don't Want to Be a Salesperson!"

Few mothers have been known to tuck their youngsters into bed at night by whispering in their ear, "Mommy hopes you'll grow up to be a wonderful salesperson!"

The sales profession just doesn't get the respect it deserves. What a shame, too, because it's nearly impossible to get through life without selling something. In fact, everybody sells! Kids start selling before they're out of diapers. They sell their wants and desires to their parents, who often can't resist giving in to them! Teenagers sell themselves to good colleges and then to an employer (unless they discover network marketing). Adults are always selling. They sell new ideas to their spouses (like joining a network marketing company); they sell the building fund to members of their church; and they sell their kids on the value of brushing their teeth.

Selling is a natural part of our lives, and the truth is, most of us get to be pretty good at it. The world's greatest profession becomes a problem for many people only when their livelihood depends on selling. Suddenly flags go up, fears come out of the woodwork, and just the thought of selling leaves some people cold on the topic of network marketing. Well, now it's time to warm up to selling, and we're going to show you how as we present some sales basics in this chapter.

Selling: One of the World's Most Honorable Professions

From time to time in a job interview, a well-meaning interviewer makes the statement, "I understand that you can sell anybody anything." I quickly respond, "No, that is absolutely not true. What you're talking about is a con artist." A con artist, meaning he has no moral or ethical values, can learn a good sales talk, look at you with those baby blue eyes and a big smile on his face, and persuade you that what he is selling is the greatest thing ever, when in reality it might be pure junk. The professional salesperson, the one who builds a career, and works in the same company calling on the same people for lots of repeat sales, is the real professional. This type of person wouldn't dream of selling anything that he didn't fervently believe in.

To emphasize this point, here's a little routine I've used many times when conducting sales training sessions. While I understand that you may never have been in sales, the point is so important that I hope you read it with an open mind.

The first question I ask the audience is, "How many of you sell a pretty good product?" Hands go up all around the room.

Second question: "How many of you sell a really great product?" Again, hands go up all over the place.

Third question: "How many of you sell a product that solves a problem?" Again, hands go up.

Fourth question: "How many of you believe that you deserve a profit when you sell a product that solves a problem?" Hands go up again.

Fifth question: "How many of you believe you deserve two profits when you sell two products that solve two problems?" Hands go up.

Then I laughingly say (as the late Fred Herman would often say), "Don't misunderstand. I'm not trying to put words in your mouth, because that's not sanitary. But what you're really saying is, 'The more people I help solve problems, the more profit I deserve.'"

Sixth question: "How many of you have been selling for as long as a year or more?" Many hands go up.

Seventh question: "How many of you still have every dime of money that you've ever earned since you've been in the sales profession?" No hands go up.

Eighth question: "Then how many of you have customers who are still using and benefiting from what you sold them a year ago, two years ago, five years ago, ten years ago?" Hands go up all over the place.

Then the most important question of all: "Then who is the big winner — the salesperson or the customer?" I hear many voices say, "The customer." Then I ask my final question: "Then is the sales process something you do *to* someone, or *for* someone?" People are nodding their heads and murmuring, "It's something you do with or for somebody." Point made. Selling is an honorable profession.

I often say that outside of the ministry, it's more important for a salesperson to have high moral standards than any other profession because we are trained to persuade people to take action. We should be trained to persuade prospects to take action that is in their best interest. If you want to build a permanent network marketing business and develop considerable residual income, you want to take this concept very seriously and sell with integrity.

Selling requires training

As we've mentioned several times throughout this book, training will enhance your selling skills and you should pursue it. Jennifer Harper graduated from college with a degree in mechanical engineering, and before joining Henn Workshops, she spent seven years as an engineering consultant for insurance companies. "I don't know what you know about engineers," she explains, "but we are often not very exciting. We have very logical, calm, rational minds, and those qualities don't easily transfer to sales. When I first got started in network marketing, my gut approach to sales was to say: 'Here are the reasons why you should buy this: one, two, three. Here's the catalog. Now order!'"

That approach required a little work! And Jennifer quickly discovered two of the best ways network marketers can get some sales training.

✔ **From a sponsor:** "More than anything," says Jennifer, "my sponsor taught me about the personal skills that I didn't have. So I watched her, and then I learned what she did naturally. For example, I noticed how she leaned in to people when she talked to them about their order. I noticed that she never tried to sell anyone either our products or the business opportunity. And yet she had a way of casting a spell over the room with her warm personality. As she performed, I watched, and that's how I picked up what I was missing."

✔ **From tapes:** "As soon as I leave my house for a presentation," says Jennifer, "I pop a tape into my cassette player in the car, and I listen to it. Not only do the tapes provide training, but by the time I get to where I'm going, I'm really excited!" Most network marketing companies are high on using audiotapes and videotapes for training. By the way, if you need some great sales training tapes, we know where you can buy them! Try this Web site: www.zigziglar.com.

Here are two more sources of sales training:

✔ **From professionals:** "Tom Hopkins' (www.tomhopkins.com) sales training and boot camp put it all together for me," says Kathy Smith, a former English teacher who is on her way to becoming a Diamond distributor with Discovery Toys. When your company brings in a professional sales trainer, make sure you attend. Plus, look for these seminars in your local areas.

✔ **From private coaches:** When network marketers reach their peak, oftentimes they'll become trainers and coaches like Aspen, Colorado-based Jan Ruhe. She travels internationally and coaches members of her own downline as well as associates of other companies. Jan is an author of several network marketing training books available at www.janruhe.com. Two other well-known coaches are Hilton Johnson at MLM University in Florida, www.mlmu.com, and Louisville, Kentucky-based Doug Firebaugh at www.mlmleadership.com. Numerous quotes and tips from these coaches appear throughout *Network Marketing For Dummies*. Most coaches provide training via the telephone.

Several years ago, I served for two years as a visiting scholar at the University of Southern California. Actually, I was more like a visiting consultant. But while there, I leaned something fascinating — namely, that if you live in a metropolitan area and drive 12,000 miles a year, in three years' time, you can acquire the equivalent of two years of college education in your automobile.

I frequently tell people that when you listen to tapes, you never just "sit there to get there." You sit there learning things, and when you get there, you'll be a better-prepared person than you were when you left home.

I especially encourage people to listen to something inspirational as they travel to a presentation or a training session. They will arrive more inspired and excited about their job. On the way home, they can learn about building better relationships, how to be better husbands, wives, parents, and so on, and as a result, they arrive home inspired to do better at home than perhaps they otherwise would have had they carried the burdens of the job and the frustrations of the day with them.

Selling requires preparation

Even before you know how to sell, prepare to sell. That's what independent executive director Cathy Barber did in Canada. "First, I set a target. By the end of six months in business, I wanted to be a director in The Pampered Chef," she explains. "That meant I had to recruit five people into the business, and together we had to generate $5,000 in sales in one month." The target was a way for Cathy to prepare herself, and her family, for the amount of work she would have to do. "I needed to conduct 12 to 15 kitchen shows a month, which I was able to do. During November and December, I scheduled 20 kitchen shows each month," she recalls.

Cathy studied the company's sales presentation, and then, with no time to waste, she began conducting presentations. "Taking action is an important key," she explains. "Go out there and repeat the process over and over. Each presentation you make is good preparation for the next presentation." As it turned out, Cathy recruited 19 people in those first six months. "I was serious," she says. "But I figured, if I'm goin' to go for it, go big!"

Connie Dugan didn't know anything about selling products when she joined the Oxyfresh organization, which sells dental products, along with non-toxic wellness products for humans and pets. In 1990, when Connie started her business, she says she was "nervous" and "anxious" because she hadn't prepared herself for a career in sales or network marketing. For many years she was a dental hygienist, and then she ran her own temporary employment agency for the dental profession. "I made up my mind to get educated about selling," Connie explains. "I became a voracious reader. I listened to conference calls to hear how others were selling, and I attended leadership seminars. Gradually I began to design my own strategy, and that's how I recommend others prepare themselves for a career in this industry. If you know your weakness — if you're an introvert, for example, or you don't know how to break the ice to start a conversation — then prepare to learn what you need to know. At Oxyfresh, we provide models for people to work through their weaknesses." Today, Connie doesn't appear to have any weaknesses related to her sales abilities. Working from home on Daufuskie Island, South Carolina, she is one of the top ten producers in Oxyfresh. Her downline includes nearly 6,000 associates!

"Prepare yourself for success, and you will be successful in whatever you choose to do." That's the philosophy of Todd Smith, www.Rexall.com/ToddSmith who has built his business with Rexall Showcase International. "When people know that you're successful, they'll want to team up with you." No doubt this explains why more than 60 percent of the associates in Rexall Showcase International are members of Todd's downline.

Selling Is a Process, Not an Event

Selling isn't something you do *to* a customer; it's a process that you do *with* or *for* a customer. The sales process is simple. Anyone can learn it, and chances are that you're already using it. It's a process of asking questions so that you uncover a customer's needs. The more questions you ask, the more needs you uncover. The more needs you uncover, the more sales you can make!

Graphically, the process can be described by using the acronym BEST.

> B = Build trust.
>
> E = Examine the customer's needs.
>
> S = Sell the benefits.
>
> T = Take action by closing the sale.

Building trust

Look at selling this way: You're *not* selling a product or service. You're selling a relationship. Customers all want the same thing: trust and assurance that you and your company can provide solutions for their problems.

"You build relationships by giving your customer *value* beyond the product or service," explains trainer Doug Firebaugh. "Before you try to sell them anything, give them information that will help improve their life. The core of either a downline or a retail customer base is the relationships you have established with the people involved. All leaders understand this principle. The key is not how people feel about the product or service, as much as how they feel about you! Show value beyond the sale by putting their interests ahead of yours. Personalize your relationship, and you will create a loyal customer."

In network marketing, you're around people who are enthusiastic, highly motivated, and genuinely interested in others. One huge advantage of network marketing is the fact that you sincerely hope that each person you sponsor will know more people than you know, work harder than you work, become more successful than you, build a bigger organization than you build, and a host of other things. The reason is very simple: They're building their organization. They're not working *for* you; they're working *with* you. As a result of that, if they're building their organization, they're also building yours, but the relationship you enjoy with them is going to make a huge difference in every phase of your life.

Building relationships through network marketing

Many people won't admit it, especially in the beginning, but they join a network marketing organization because they see a chance to build relationships with other people. Check the records, and here is what you will find: If you're getting along well with the people who are important to you, almost regardless of your financial status or corporate position, you basically are a reasonably happy person. If you're not getting along well with the people who are important to you, it makes no difference how much money you have in the bank or how high on the totem pole you find yourself. You basically aren't very happy.

Unfortunately, we have more relationship problems in our society today than ever before in history. Today, nearly 100 percent of all counseling takes place as a result of relationship problems — husband/wife, parent/child, teacher/student, employer/employee, neighbor/neighbor, sibling/sibling, and so on. Many people notice that network marketers have a different approach to life. They're willing to help each other; they're close to each other. Relationships are the key to building a successful business — and a happy life.

What are some important but simple relationship tips you need to follow?

1. Be the kind of person who others can look up to and who never looks down on others.

2. Be aware, as Mary Kay Ash says, that all people have an invisible sign hanging around their neck that says, "Make me feel important." You do this by remembering and calling them by their name and saying something sincerely complimentary about them each time you have a legitimate opportunity to do so.

3. Note that if you go out in life looking for friends, they will be scarce. If you go out in life to be a friend, you'll find them everywhere, because what you send out is exactly what you get back.

4. Remember the basic principle of success in network marketing — namely, you can have everything in life you want if you will just help enough other people get what they want.

5. Read Dale Carnegie's old, but still very powerful, book, *How to Win Friends and Influence People.*

6. Watch the leaders in your network. Observe how they deal with other people and how they make others feel important by becoming good-finders and encouragers.

7. Learn from the ladies. Women are far more relationship-oriented than men. Watch how they interact with others.

Examining the customer's needs

In selling, using emotional logic is important if you want to sell more and have fewer cancellations. If you use emotion only, you will probably sell your product to many people, but the cancellation rate will be high. When they get home, their mates will talk them out of the business or encourage them to cancel the order for the product. If you use pure logic in attempting to make the sale, people aren't moved to take action, and as a result very little, if anything, happens. Combine emotion and logic, and you sell more today and it stays sold tomorrow.

Remember, we are emotional beings, despite what we say. For example, when the attendants on an airplane tell passengers to fasten their seat belts, I've never heard an argument about it. People just fasten their seat belts, no questions asked. But when automobile seat belt laws were enacted, everybody griped and complained and was very unhappy. Yet if you fasten your seat belt on the plane and it crashes from 30,000 feet, the seat belt isn't going to make any difference. However, if the automobile crashes while you're wearing your seat belt, chances improve by a three-to-one ratio that you not only will survive but also are far less likely to be seriously injured. So the objective is to get people excited about what you sell. Stories, examples, illustrations, and personal testimonies are helpful in reaching this goal.

In selling, you use logic when you ask questions. Approach your prospects as a friendly counselor, such as a physician or minister, gently asking probing, fact-finding questions to find out where they are, and where they want to go. After you know their answers, you can explain how your product or your business opportunity can be a solution to their problem. That way, you're involving the prospects emotionally but persuading them logically to take action. They buy initially, and when they get home, they have answers to the questions their mate or brother-in-law may ask.

By asking questions, you can easily encourage people to talk about their needs. "When I meet people — no matter where we are," says Kathy Smith in Nashville, Tennessee, "I ask a lot of questions and listen carefully to what I hear. There are so many ways to match up needs and interests in any network marketing business. I ask people about their work — many work full-time, and they'd rather work part-time — their personal growth, their interests in helping others. I find out a lot when I ask about their families. That's when people will share their true passions about life. To be successful in sales, you have to know what's going on with the prospect."

"Most people are too busy trying to build a business to create a business. The secret is to keep totally focused on what the prospect wants the company to bring into their lives," explains trainer Doug Firebaugh. "Too often we try to sell our products or our business opportunity for *our* reasons, and customers don't care about our reasons. They care about their own. Don't sell through your eyes. Sell through *their* eyes. Show them how they can achieve what they want, and in return, they will help you get what you want."

One of our favorite sales trainers is Bryan Flanagan of Ziglar Training Systems. He emphasizes the importance of asking open-ended questions when you're examining your customers' needs. Open-ended questions, as opposed to questions that require only a yes or no response, invite the customers to tell you their story and, ultimately, what they're seeking. Here are two examples of open-ended questions:

- ✔ "So, Jim, what are you doing these days?"
- ✔ "Mary, I heard you say that you want to spend more time with your family. What's keeping you from doing that?"

"Make sure you listen to people," says Oxyfresh distributor Connie Dugan. "If you listen, people will talk about their concerns for weight loss, their teeth, their need for more money, or their desire to travel more. Pay attention, so that you will be able to offer the right solution."

Selling the benefits

After you understand the customer's needs, you can introduce your products, services, or business opportunity. This is your time to demonstrate or explain how the benefits of what you're selling will solve the stated needs.

At this step in the process, you risk sounding like a salesperson and turning off your prospect or customer. But Connie Dugan says that's an easy mistake to avoid. "Listen. Pay attention. And when you hear your cue, that's when you respond," she explains. "For example, if someone tells me about a problem they're having with a pet, or gum disease, or their weight, I'll respond by saying 'I represent a company that manufactures a state-of-the-art product that specifically solves that problem. Is that something you would like to know about?'

"Asking for permission, rather than hammering the prospect with my information, is not threatening," continues Connie. "It's something you might do in a normal conversation. Once they give you permission to talk about your product, you know they're interested, and you take it from there. You can tell them about your product, or the business opportunity, right on the spot. Or you might want to lead them to a conference call, or to your Web site where there's more information. This isn't selling. This is a humanitarian gesture."

Interpreting the value of your product, service, or opportunity

Sales trainer Bryan Flanagan says that your job in selling is to communicate benefits, values, and advantages to your prospects and customers. He uses the Features Functions Benefits technique to teach this part of the sales process. Here's what he says:

"A feature is a part, trait, or characteristic of your product. If you're selling training materials, for example, a feature is that the product comes on a CD, or it's sold with a learner's guide.

The function explains what the feature does. The CD allows the buyer to listen to the training materials in the car or wherever there's a CD player. The learner's guide helps the buyer follow the training in a printed format.

The benefit is the advantage or the value of using the feature and function. The CD provides convenience and quality. The learner's guide reinforces the training information so that it can be recalled and implemented.

The benefit is the reason why the customer will buy, so it's the most important step in the sales process."

Taking action by closing the sale

The final step in the sales process is asking for the order. It would be nice if customers closed the sales themselves: "I'm sold! Here's my order." Sometimes it happens that way, but most of the time, you'll have to ask the customer to buy from you. And frequently, you'll have to ask them more than once. "People are busy," says Kathy Smith with Discovery Toys. "So it's important to follow up with them and make it easy for them to buy from you. Customers really do want to give you their repeat business, but you have to ask them." See Chapter 15 for more information about follow-up with your prospects and customers to secure more sales as well as to recruit more distributors for your downline.

One of the first things I learned when I entered the world of direct selling was that "you close early, you close often, and you close late." Part of that advice was good, but you must remember this: If you attempt to close by asking for the order before you have given the benefits (reasons) for buying, you come across like a high-pressure salesperson with the attitude of "I'm looking out for me. I want to make a sale for my benefit." In that case, the prospect is invariably going to say no. You would do the same thing under the same circumstances.

Once the prospect says no, then you have just built a barrier between you and the prospect. The proper time to ask for the order is when you have given a legitimate benefit and/or reason for the prospect to invest now, so that she can immediately start acquiring the benefits of your product or service. Lead off with your number one benefit, the thing that's likely to get a favorable yes to the question.

At this point, if the answer is no, remember that people will not *change their minds* but they will *make a new decision* based on new information, so at the first no, don't insist that they buy. If you do, you will irritate them and have less chance of eventually selling them. What you do is very simple: You give them another good benefit or reason for buying and then ask whether this benefit appeals to them. The answer is probably going to be yes. Then you can again ask when would be the best time for them to start enjoying these benefits.

Dr. Herb True, a psychologist at the University of Notre Dame, discovered that four percent of the salespeople earn 60 percent of the commissions, and interestingly enough, those four percent give the prospect five opportunities to buy. These opportunities may not all come during your first sitting with or exposure to the prospect, but over a period of time, the salesperson gives more and more reasons for making a yes decision, based on new information.

How can you tell when the customer is ready? Questions like these are always a good sign: (1) "How soon can I get your product?", (2) "How long does it take to learn how to sell these products?", (3) "What's it cost to get involved?", (4) "How much money can I make?"

Keep your closing technique simple by once again asking questions: "Why don't you give the product a try?" "How about if I write up an order and send you a supply of this product?" "You said you want to travel more and you want to work from home. Doesn't this sound like a good opportunity for you?"

Using the three-question close

A favorite closing technique among sales professionals is called the "three-question close." Here's how it works. Suppose that a prospect has told you he wants to earn additional income. You've heard at least one buying signal from the prospect. So now you ask these three questions, giving the prospect time to answer each one:

✔ "Can you see how this business will help you earn additional income?"

✔ "You're interested in earning additional income, aren't you?"

✔ "If you're ever going to start earning extra money, when would be the best time to begin?"

To that last question, you hope the prospect will respond, "Right now!" If you don't get that response, you may need to re-emphasize the benefits, or you may simply have to continue following up to close the sale.

Understanding Your Role in Sales

The selling profession offers you a variety of roles to play: counselor, teacher, motivator, coach, cheerleader, and investigator. You can play any one or all of these roles, depending on the circumstances and your personality. Using these roles is a good way to make the sales process more creative. These roles are important when you're selling products, services and your business opportunity. However, you can also rely on them when you mentor the members of your downline. The following list presents some situations in which these roles can be useful:

- **Counselor:** At any given time, people can be headed for, in the middle of, or coming out of a crisis. "If one of your downline associates is in the middle of a marital problem or a family problem, they may focus all of their energy on the problem and give up on their business," explains Cathy Barber, from The Pampered Chef. "That's when the counselor needs to step in and explain that the problem will be resolved, one way or another, but the business could be destroyed in the process. When people are down in the mud, it's hard for them to realize what they'll need when things clear up. That's when you have to help them see the future."

- **Teacher:** For many sales professionals, the role of teacher is a favorite. Jan Ruhe — who earns in excess of $500,000 annually and is the number one associate in Discovery Toys — is a good example. Almost everyone wants to know how Jan did it! She's more than willing to teach others how to follow in her footsteps. "I am a teacher/coach to thousands of people," she says. "I explain that if I can do it, so can they, and I'll show them how if they're serious about becoming a leader in network marketing."

"When you teach, make sure it's fun," advises Cathy Barber, who has studied successful network marketers throughout the industry. "I always include music and lots of fluff when I'm training my associates. We're adults in kids' bodies, so make sure to create an exciting environment."

- **Motivator:** Motivation is being ready to take action. You may have an distributor who knows everything it takes to become successful, but until your distributor acts on that knowledge, success will remain elusive. The same is true for your prospects and customers. They know what they need, but you may have to motivate them before they take action and buy your product.

When you understand that motivation gets you going but habit gets you there, you've taken a step toward understanding that if you make motivation a habit, you will get there more quickly and have more fun on the trip.

People do things for two reasons: the fear of loss and the desire for gain. Understand that the fear of loss is greater than the desire for gain.

Simple example: A good prospect whom you strongly feel could be successful in your network organization is reluctant to go ahead and make the decision to get started. You're convinced that he is sold on the product and the company and trusts you. Yet, for whatever reason, he is reluctant to take action now.

One good question you can ask is, "How would you feel if next week your best friend, the person you've been running through your mind as being one of the people you would immediately talk to, were to sign up with another friend — or even another company?" Sit quietly as the prospect considers the question and responds. The wheels will start to turn in his head, and he will imagine that very thing happening. He will even get a picture in his mind of all the people his friend might sponsor and the organization he would build. This is quite effective. Give it a try.

As a motivator, your role is to know which "hot button" to push for your prospects, customers, and associates.

- ✔ **Coach:** People who like to encourage others make great coaches in sales or any other profession. Bringing out the qualities of customers or associates and showing them how those qualities can serve them are the coach's jobs. "One of my team members in Discovery Toys is a single mom," says Kathy Smith, "and she sometimes has trouble seeing herself as a leader. But I know she's the most determined person in the world. She raised two sons to be upstanding Christians, and that takes a lot of backbone these days. I admire her for it, and when she's not sure she can do this business, I point out to her that I *know* she can do it based on what she's already done. If you can do what she's done with those boys, you can do anything! So many people have strengths, but they need these strengths pointed out to them."

- ✔ **Cheerleader:** When a retail customer tells you how your product solved a problem, that's a time to cheer! Your enthusiasm will likely keep that customer buying from you and going out and telling other people about your product.

  When an distributor tells you about making even a tiny sale or recruiting another distributor, that's a time to cheer! Enthusiasm is contagious. When you become known as a cheerleader, even the most timid customers and distributors will call to share good news with you. Why? Simply because they want someone to celebrate their victory.

  Insincerity neither builds nor maintains relationships. If people suspect that your cheerleading qualities are forced or manipulative, they'll avoid you. Always make sure that your enthusiasm is heartfelt.

- ✔ **Investigator:** Probing — listening and watching for clues — is an important attribute of the sales investigator. Cathy Barber of The Pampered Chef explains this role perfectly: "When I'm doing a demonstration in a kitchen, I can play the role of investigator by saying to one of the guests, 'Hi, I'm Cathy, and how do you know Sally, our hostess?' Or as I'm preparing the recipe, I might overhear someone say she just lost her job. My head turns immediately to that person, and I'll make a note to talk to her."

Cathy says she also plays the investigator when she's working with her team members. "You went from eight kitchen consultants to one. What happened? Why is your business turning upside down?"

By using the sales process and the roles that we explain in this chapter, you can start building your network marketing business today. Selling isn't easy, but in network marketing, it's a lot less threatening and difficult than many people believe. It really is just a matter of wanting to help people, and when that's your motivation, you can't help but succeed.

ZIG SAYS

Sometimes the customer is the salesperson!

In my early days in direct sales, we initially offered an outstanding set of cookware and later added fine china to our inventory. One night I conducted a demonstration in a home where I had cooked the meal and served the guests. In the process of cooking, I had a chance to explore the host's cabinets. Her cookware served as a mystery to me as to how she ever successfully cooked a meal. First, it was almost nonexistent; second, what she had was pitiful by anybody's standard. She desperately needed our beautiful, heavy-duty set of waterless cookware. I tried close after close; her response continued, "Can't afford it. Can't afford it. Can't afford it."

Somehow during the evening, the subject of fine china entered the conversation, and she asked me whether we carried fine china. I assured her we certainly did and said, "Let me get it for you." I ran out to the car and brought my china samples in, and the sale was already made. It was just a question of her picking out the pattern. The china cost more than the cookware. The difference? She really did have the money, but it wasn't for cookware — it was for what she wanted, which was fine china. Important lesson: Find out what the prospect really wants and show him how to get it. That want may be

additional income, or it may be a career opportunity. Maybe your prospect simply wants a washer-dryer combination. But always remember that the customer, in most cases, can buy what he or she really wants. Our job is to make them want it!

Because one thing we must all do is continuously prospect and ask for referrals, one evening after I had made my presentation to a lady and her husband, I was asking for referrals. In the process, I made the statement that I would deal with their friends and relatives in exactly the same manner I had dealt with them, pointing out that I hoped they had observed that I was not a high-pressure salesman. Her response amazed me and gave me many laughs and much pleasure. She said, "You sure are right about that! As a matter of fact, you are the nearest nothing to a salesman I think I've ever seen."

Now here's the really humorous part: She had just signed the order for everything our company sold, but she was right. I was not the salesperson. She bought — I did not sell. If you can create that kind of environment, you will sell more and build a bigger network of customers and associates.

Chapter 19

Taking Your Sales Skills to a Higher Level

. . . .

In This Chapter

▶ Establishing your customer's trust

▶ Turning the focus on the customer

▶ Knowing when to ask which questions

▶ Mastering two qualities that lead to more sales

▶ Handling objections likes a sales pro

. . . .

*I*f you plan to be a leader in network marketing and expect to "promote up" to the top level in your organization, make a lifetime commitment to mastering the sales process. Study it, practice it, and repeat the cycle. Be faithful to the process, and watch while the process goes to work for you!

After you're familiar with the basic sales techniques discussed in Chapter 18, you'll be ready to ratchet up your sales skills by a level or two. The basics are valuable, and you can build a good business by mastering them, but a deeper understanding of several additional principles may be all you need to take your business over the top.

"There's a gap in the network marketing industry," reports Hilton Johnson, the founder of MLM University. "People who join this industry usually do not have sufficient sales skills. Some companies, in fact, will say that sales skills aren't important, but that's often because they know selling scares people. Even with the most duplicative systems in network marketing, people need to be able to make a sales presentation if they want to succeed. It's not all that difficult, but it requires some education. We teach a low-key approach to selling, and oftentimes our students come back and say, 'Our company told us *what* to do, but you taught us *how* to do it.' People *can* learn to sell, regardless of their background, but not all network marketing companies necessarily teach enough on this subject."

Understanding Why People Don't Buy

People buy emotionally first and logically second. They won't buy in reverse order. You can try to explain why your product makes sense, or why your service is affordable, but until the customer experiences the emotional desire to buy, you're not going to make a sale. Don't put the cart before the horse by trying to sell logic first. Get 'em excited about your product or service, and they'll come up with the logic on their own.

You understand why people buy, but now take a look at the five reasons why they won't buy:

- No need
- No money
- No hurry
- No desire
- No trust

One of the above topics in particular requires a closer look. As we mentioned in Chapter 18, if the prospect doesn't trust you, it doesn't matter how good your product is or how well you represent your business opportunity — the prospect still isn't going to buy from you. Similarly, your price may be terrific, and you may be one of the most enthusiastic network marketers on the planet, but if the customer doesn't trust you, you won't score very well in the initial or the repeat sales category. Following our guidelines is important if you want to build a relationship of trust between yourself and your customers.

The higher the trust, the higher the sales.

Selling is the only part of a company that contributes to profit. All the other parts contribute to cost. Be proud that you sell and reflect that pride to your customers, associates, family, and friends. It's more than just a cliché to say that nothing happens in the world of business until somebody sells something.

Creating a relationship of trust

Sell your prospect on yourself first and build a relationship so that your customer has a reason and the desire to remain loyal to you. How do you do that? Stop broadcasting and start tuning in! In other words, you don't sell yourself by telling the prospect about yourself, your business, and your products. You sell yourself by focusing on the prospect (and later on the customer), asking questions, and learning about the prospect's wants and needs. You also sell yourself by delivering on your promises. If you're not reliable, if you oversell and under-deliver, and if you always have an excuse to explain why this or that didn't happen, you're not creating a relationship of trust between yourself and your customer.

When building a relationship, you're really expressing feelings and attitudes. Both verbal and nonverbal skills, or body language, are required to build a relationship. Seven percent of your feelings and attitudes are expressed through your choice of words. Your tone of voice communicates 38 percent, and your body language expresses the remaining 55 percent. Be aware of these statistics when you're talking to prospects and customers.

Building trust by making a good impression

Your nonverbal skills contribute greatly to the impression that you leave with a prospect or customer. People will watch the way you express yourself non-verbally. They'll listen to what you say, but they'll also look to see whether what you say matches up with the way you look. This isn't a matter of beauty and charm; it's mostly a matter of authenticity. If you're likable, people will respond to you. But if they as much as think they're talking to a fraud, they're not likely to make a purchase, any more than they would agree to join such a person in business. Here are four ways to improve your non-verbal skills:

- **Project a positive appearance.** You don't need to spend money on a new or expensive wardrobe. The point here is to look neat, clean, and crisp. Dress appropriately for the customers you want to attract.

- **Stand confidently.** An erect posture, as opposed to one that's slouched over, projects confidence. People don't expect you to look like a Marine, with shoulders back and stomach in, but if you did, you have to admit you'd look like a confident person.

- **Look your prospect in the eye.** When you talk to someone who doesn't look at you, how does that make you feel? Yep, that's how we feel, too.

Don't expect to build a relationship without giving your prospect or customer a good look through your eyes. However, you need to remember that the con artists of the world are masters at looking their prospects in the eye while lying through their teeth to fleece their victims for temporary gain. For long-term greater success, build your relationships on integrity, and when you look your prospects in the eye, they will get the distinct feeling that they can trust you. Those are the ones who will buy again and again because they're dealing with the "right" kind of person who they know will do the right things.

- **Smile when you're excited.** Make sure that your face and your mouth are in sync. If you say you're excited, look excited! Remember the story of the little boy who asked his dad whether he was okay. His dad answered in the affirmative and asked his son why he asked. The little boy responded, "Well, maybe you should tell your face."

Focusing on the Customer by Asking Questions

Giving someone your undivided attention isn't always easy, but you must do exactly that to build a relationship. Now's the time to ask questions about the prospect, or to make comments that are of interest to the customer. The PIN Profile can help you through this process. PIN is an acronym for Person, Interests, and Needs.

Here's how this process works. (Please understand that the tone and inflection of your voice are critical. You gently probe as an interested friend. Don't attack like a pollster conducting a survey.)

Ask questions about the person. Use open-ended questions, that is, questions that begin with the words who, what, where, when, why, and how. Here are some examples:

- ✔ How long have you been living here?
- ✔ Why did you choose this neighborhood (or city or state)?
- ✔ What line of work brought you here?

Next, ask questions that inquire about the prospect's or customer's interests. Here are some examples:

- ✔ What do you do in your free time?
- ✔ What does your family like to do together?
- ✔ What hobbies do you have?

Finally, ask questions that focus on the person's needs:

- ✔ Why is that important to you?
- ✔ How does that make you feel?
- ✔ What would you like to do differently?

Sales trainer Bryan Flanagan, of Ziglar Training Systems, says that using the PIN Profile generates a lot of information and helps you get a good understanding of the person you're talking to.

Use both verbal and nonverbal skills to build trust. The display of your genuine interest establishes a solid relationship and keeps customers coming back to you for a long time.

Asking Questions Leads to More Sales

Asking questions is important in the sales process for the following reasons:

- ✔ Prospects may not always believe your statements, but they certainly believe *their* answers to your questions.

- ✔ You build rapport by asking questions; rapport leads to trust; and trust establishes a long-term relationship.

- ✔ You put your customers at ease by allowing them to ask those questions — which, not so incidentally, reveal their interest and any possible skepticism, which is vital information for you to have in any successful persuasion effort.

- ✔ Your prospects get to take part in the sales process by responding to your questions.

- ✔ You can uncover needs and concerns that reveal the customer's real emotions.

- ✔ Prospects and customers reveal their buying habits by responding to questions.

Remember that Jesus, the greatest salesman who ever lived, would always answer questions with a question or with a parable. I asked my Jewish brother, Bernie Lofchick, why he always answers questions with a question, and he said, "Why not?" On with the story.

When Jesus answered a question, it was always with a question and/or a parable to go along with it. (If you don't believe me, look at a copy of the New Testament featuring Jesus's words printed in red.) Using that procedure, particularly as you move towards persuading a person to take action, can be very helpful. The method of using parables to sell is, in fact, the most effective way to sell and to teach.

Now look at some specific questions to use in the sales process and some possible answers:

Prospect: Are these products guaranteed?

You (with a smile on your face): Is that important to you?

Prospect: Yes

You: Not only are the products guaranteed, but we have *x* number of years behind the guarantee — and even more important, hundreds of customers who have never used the guarantee.

Prospect: I have some friends who had a bad experience and even lost money in network marketing.

You: So have I, but then I have friends who have lost money in restaurants, service stations, clothing stores, the stock market — big money! But I also have some friends who became wealthy in network marketing, so I decided to follow the model of those who succeeded, not the ones who failed. What is your opinion of that approach?

Prospect: What makes your opportunity different?

You: If it really is different/better and makes sense, would it make sense on your part to look carefully at our opportunity?

Prospect: Yes.

You: Our products are great because . . . (here you briefly describe the products and the benefits and show written testimonials to validate what you're saying). Our plan is different because . . . (explain quickly and identify several failure-to-success examples of ordinary people who became extraordinary successes because of the differences in the opportunity). Our company is different because . . . (give the age, the growth, the size, and the volume, and show company brochures identifying the progress and the principles). Our leadership is different because . . . (discuss the experience and the reputation of the leaders and the mission statement of the company, as well as the philosophy of the principals. For example, at the Zig Ziglar Network our mission is to be the difference-maker in the personal, family, and professional lives of enough people to make a positive difference in the world. Our philosophy is, "You can have everything in life you want if you will just help enough other people get what they want.")

Your prospects won't always answer your questions, but you must always answer theirs; otherwise they will think that you're hiding something because your answer would be unacceptable to them. Be open, frank, and direct in your responses.

You can use both open-ended and closed-ended questions early in the sales process. You can also use direct-agreement questions, which we discuss in a moment.

Asking closed-ended questions

When you're just getting to know a prospect, closed-ended questions are useful for gathering facts. These are questions that can be answered with a yes or no. Here are two examples:

"Have you used these products before?"

"Are you familiar with network marketing?"

Because closed-ended questions don't solicit information, be careful that you don't use too many of them consecutively. If you do, your prospects may feel like they're being interrogated and that what they're saying may be used against them!

Asking open-ended questions

To gather information, as well as to uncover the prospect's needs and emotions, use open-ended questions. We provide examples of these questions earlier in this chapter. Answers to these questions provide valuable information and enable the prospect or customer to engage in a conversation with you. Attitudes, opinions, doubts, fears, and buying habits come through loud and clear in response to open-ended questions.

Open-ended questions always begin with one of the following words: who, what, where, why, when, and how.

Asking direct-agreement questions

At some point in the sales process, you must seek agreement. This point may not occur until after you have demonstrated the benefits of your product or service, or until you've answered an objection. You can also use direct-agreement questions as soon as the prospect shows interest in buying. Here are some examples, complete with a "tie down" phrase, which begs the prospect's agreement with the point you're trying to make. (The tie down phrase is in italic type at the end of the questions).

- ✔ "You agree this is the kind of business that would work for you, *don't you?*"

- ✔ "You'd like to get these kinds of results, *wouldn't you?*"

- ✔ "You can see how your entire family would benefit from these products, *can't you?*"

You can also use direct-agreement questions to close the sale, particularly after the prospect has indicated a readiness to buy.

When you want the facts, and just the facts, use closed-ended questions. When you're after information, use open-ended questions. And to seek agreement or to close the sale, ask direct-agreement questions.

Practice! Practice! Practice! Start using these questions as part of your daily routine. Use them with your family as well as with coworkers. Pay attention to the type of question you're asking and listen carefully to the responses. In no time, you'll be able to use these questions in any selling situation.

Selling Big Requires More than Being a Good Salesperson

Almost anyone can learn the basic sales process, practice it, and be good at it. But good isn't good enough when your business vision includes seeing yourself at the top of your network marketing organization. It takes a special person to sell big, that is, to outsell most of the other people in your company. You must develop two qualities to move ahead of the rest of the pack: loving people and loving your product.

Loving people is quality one

First, you must love people. In network marketing, there is no other prerequisite. Regardless of your background, a network marketing company will accept you and work with you. But if you plan to move to the top of the organization, you had better love people, and you must help them at all levels, regardless of their education, background, or their dreams. If you love helping people excel, you will excel.

When she joined The Pampered Chef, Cathy Barber said she saw herself going to the top of the company within a year. She overlooked the fact that she would have to be in the company for six months before qualifying for her first promotion, which was several levels from the top! But that didn't matter. Her first year in the business, she earned $36,000. Then her annual income jumped to $93,000, and a couple of years later to $130,000. "Try doing that with a job that gives you a 2 percent raise each year!" she says with a chuckle. How did she succeed so rapidly? "By helping other people as they come into the business," she explains. "I help them become directors, and then I show them how to get to the next level, and by doing that, I know I can fulfill my own goals." In mid 2000, Cathy reached the top level of Directorship within The Pampered Chef organization. By year end, she expects to be promoted to independent senior executive director. "If you love people," she says, "and you're willing to put in the energy, you can match my success in a very short period of time."

Loving your product is quality two

Second, you must love your product. Here's what Kathy Smith says about this subject. "Product knowledge is essential, whether you plan to sell a few products or a lot of products. You have to use the product, love the product, and collect stories about how other people love the product and use it to their benefit. This is a skill, but you can learn it. Loving your product is the only way to develop a passion for your product, and once you do that, you can ride to the top on passion."

Growing into an unconsciously competent salesperson

As a salesperson, you will pass through four stages of growth. When you're just getting started, chances are that you're unaware of everything you need to know. You just don't know that you don't know. Therefore, the first stage of growth is called *unconscious incompetency*.

After a short while, you begin to realize that you know that you don't know. For example, you realize you don't know enough about your product, or you need to do more work to overcome certain objections. This second stage of growth is called *consciously incompetent*.

After you've put some time behind you as a salesperson and you've accomplished many of the skills needed to be successful, you understand that you know that you know.

However, your skills aren't yet second nature or automatic. For example, you may have to consciously remember to sell benefits instead of features. This third stage of growth is called *consciously competent*.

Finally, you reach the stage of growth to which all salespeople aspire. You are so good at what you do that you don't know that you know. In other words, you use skills without even thinking about them. You ask questions so easily and listen so intently that you're not even aware that you're using these skills to focus on the prospect or customer. This fourth stage of growth is called *unconsciously competent*. And you want to get there as soon as you can!

As Zig explains, when you communicate the benefits of your product through stories and analogies, your prospects relate those benefits to their needs. They become emotionally involved, and you have a better chance of making your point and your sale! You must get your prospect emotionally involved because most decisions are emotional.

You have to "buy" the value of a product before you can sell it. Until you truly believe that your product delivers more in value than you're asking in price, you're not completely honest.

Overcoming Sales Objections

Just when you thought the sale was about to close itself, your prospect comes up with an objection! Objections are simply the prospect's way of telling you, "I need more information before I can make the decision to buy your product." You can expect to hear some objections before you make the sale, so be prepared for them.

Although you may hate it when prospects come up with objections, you shouldn't. Here's how to deal with them:

✔ **Welcome objections.** You welcome objections because it's only when prospects object that you know for sure that they're interested in your product, service, or opportunity. "I don't have the time" is a frequently stated objection. But it may indicate that your prospect likes everything about the opportunity. All you have to do now is help the prospect overcome the issue of time, and you've made a sale.

✔ **Anticipate objections.** In sales, you're going to hear plenty of objections. Anticipate them so that you're not surprised when they come up. If you expect objections, you can handle them more effectively.

✔ **Understand objections.** An objection isn't a rejection, and it's rarely personal. Many times, prospects and customers use objections to help them make a buying decision. It gives them time to think. They know they want the product, and now they're trying to justify it in their mind.

A customer who says no may be saying "I don't *know* enough" to make a buying decision. Perhaps the prospect needs to hear more about the benefits.

Keep these points in mind when you're dealing with objections:

✔ Children are great salespeople because most of them have hearing problems. You can tell them no a dozen times, and they don't hear it. When your prospect says no, you should hear it, but don't register it in your facial expressions.

✔ When a prospect raises an objection, get excited because that's a sure sign of interest. No objections usually means no interest.

✔ Don't get defensive about objections. You look bad if you let your ego get in the way of objections. Enlighten — don't frighten — the prospect.

✔ Don't tell prospects more than they want or need to know. By holding some critical points in reserve, you may be able to use this information to respond to an objection. Or the information may be useful as a closing tool.

People perpetuate a myth when they say that a professional salesperson can sell anybody. They're confusing the professional salesperson with a con artist. As a sales professional, you can only sell products, services, and opportunities that you fervently believe benefit the buyer more than they benefit you.

Managing Objections

Here's how you can manage objections.

First, question the objection to be sure you understand it. "Your product costs too much," says the prospect. You respond: "The product costs too much?" . . . and then stop talking. Let the prospect continue the conversation by explaining to you why she thinks the product costs too much. After you're certain that cost really is objectionable to the prospect, then you can ask, "How much were you intending to pay?" Once again, stop talking and listen to what the prospect says.

Second, empathize with the customer. Empathy simply means that you care about the prospect, or customer, and you genuinely understand his or her concerns or feelings. Try one of these empathy statements: "Oh, I understand how you feel." "Yes, I hear what you're saying." "I appreciate your point of view." Don't use any of these statements unless you really mean them.

Third, test the objection to make absolutely certain that it's a real concern. Here's how you do it: "So your only objection is the product's credibility. If you can persuade yourself that the price is more than fair and the product benefits exceed the investment, would you be willing to give it a no-risk try?"

The prospect has to answer yes to these questions, or the objection is false. If the objection is false, don't answer it. This sale isn't going to happen, at least not now. Only answer true objections, and always try to answer by talking about benefits and value.

ZIG SAYS

Overcoming the price objection

In sales, the prospect may say, "The price is too high."

And you say, "Let me ask you a question. Do you like the product?"

The prospect says, "Well, yeah, I like it, but the price is too high."

You respond, "Well, don't you really believe it's difficult to pay too much for something you really like?"

The prospect replies, "Well, uh, that's a good point, but yeah, you can pay too much for something, even if you really do like it."

You come back with, "Well, let me ask you a question. Wouldn't you agree that it's better to invest a little more than you had planned instead of a little less than you should? Because if you don't invest as much as you should and the product won't do the job, you lose everything. As it is, we're talking about pennies in difference."

But the prospect still says, "Yeah, but the price is too high."

At this point, you lower your voice — and this takes a little practice — look your prospect right in the eye, and say, "You know, interestingly enough, when (name of the founder) founded this company, (he or she) started it with a basic philosophy. And that was that it's easier to explain price one time than it would be to apologize for poor quality and poor service forever. And I'll bet you're glad (he or she) made that decision, aren't you?"

Now, don't misunderstand. I believe that a skilled salesperson who is thoroughly trained and totally committed and sold on the business can persuade a lot of people to take a lot of actions. But your sales technique really has to come from the heart. Speaking from your heart and speaking with conviction make a big difference in whether you make the sale.

Your customers buy benefits. Features tell and benefits sell. Give your prospects and customers reasons to buy from you by communicating benefits.

Going for the Sale

After you devote the time to studying the sales process and practicing the techniques that we introduce in this chapter and Chapter 18, you can't do much more but go for the sale! Of course, we recommend that you study your company's sales training materials and you frequently attend sales training seminars. Make a personal commitment to sharpen your sales skills by reading books about selling (may we recommend *Secrets of Closing the Sale* by Zig Ziglar?), listening to motivational and instructional audiotapes, and watching videos about selling. Keep yourself on a perpetual sales training and personal growth schedule, and there's no doubt that you will take yourself and your business over the top!

I'm expecting to see you not just *at* the top. No, I'm expecting to see you, and I do mean you, *over* the top — in network marketing!

Chapter 20

Creating Satisfied, Loyal Customers

• •

In This Chapter

▶ Understanding how repeat customers lead to profit and satisfaction

▶ Using systems to keep your customers loyal

▶ Winning customer loyalty with a positive attitude

▶ Doing more than just meeting customer expectations

▶ Enlisting the help of customer advocates

▶ Retaining customers by handling their complaints well

• •

*M*ost network marketers, and business owners in general, are likely to agree that the best way to increase profitability and market share is to maximize customer satisfaction. Makes sense, doesn't it? If customers are satisfied with your business they'll return to buy from you again, they'll spend more money over time, and as these satisfied customers spread the word, a larger percentage of the marketplace will favor your business. Of course! And yet, most of the current research on this subject says that line of thinking is hogwash. Look at this:

✔ In more than 30,000 customer interviews, Dr. Peter ZanDan of Intelliquest has never found customer satisfaction to be a dependable predictor of repeat business.

✔ Approximately 40 percent of customers who said they were satisfied switched suppliers without hesitation, according to a study conducted by Forum Corporation.

✔ Dr. Frederick Reichheld reported in the *Harvard Business Review* that two-thirds or more of customers who chose a new supplier said they were satisfied if not very satisfied with their former supplier.

✔ At the University of Texas, Dr. Robert Peterson's research found that 85 percent of customers who said they were satisfied also said they were willing to try other suppliers.

Knocking yourself out to satisfy your customers won't guarantee that your customers will continue returning to your business. You've got to go one step *better* than satisfaction. You've got to give your customers — both retail buyers and distributors — reasons to be loyal to your business.

When you do, you will build a satisfying and profitable network marketing business. Everywhere you look, from the smallest to the largest communities, customers are aching for the opportunity to find a few businesses that are worthy of their loyalty. This chapter explores a number of ways for you to get your share of loyal customers — and keep them!

Keeping Customers Equals More Profit

It's six to ten times more expensive to win the favor of a new customer than it is to sell something again to an existing customer! Don't miss the impact of that statement. If it costs you $25 to attract a new retail customer, you can save most of that $25 by selling something again to that existing customer. Just look at what that means: It will cost you $25,000 to sell something to 1,000 new customers, while selling something again to 1,000 existing customers may cost you less than $2,500. The $22,500 that you save is money that you keep in your pocket or re-invest in your business.

When you sell to the same people over and over again, it's easier to get to know them. Being attentive to your customers, in a one-to-one relationship, may be the best way to keep customers loyal to your business. When you know your customers personally, it's easier to exceed their expectations, and should you on a rare occasion drop the ball, they will even cut you a little slack.

If you do your job right as a network marketer, most of your customers will get on your autoship program, which means products will be automatically shipped to them every month. However, an autoship program isn't a reason for remaining loyal to your business. It's simply a feature, one that most network marketing companies offer to their customers. A customer on autoship can still have questions or concerns about the products, or how to use them. Even more important, these customers might buy additional products if someone only brought them to their attention!

The danger with autoship is that it's easy to forget about the customers who sign up for it. Big mistake. When the customer doesn't hear from you, the customer begins to think that you don't care. At that point, all it takes is another network marketer to come along with similar products and suddenly your autoship comes to an automatic halt! Interesting fact: According to the Department of Labor, 46 percent of all the people who voluntarily leave their jobs do so because they don't feel respected and/or appreciated. Your customers, even on occasion your mom and little brother or sister, will quit buying from you for the same reasons.

Loyal Customers Require a System

Customers prefer a routine over chaos. They like knowing what to expect. That's why the autoship feature is so popular with most network marketing companies. It's a system that keeps the same customers coming back month after month.

McDonald's isn't a network marketing company, but it's a great example of how systems keep customers coming back. Every network marketer, and every network marketing company, can learn from McDonalds. Customers know almost exactly what to expect when they stop at McDonald's. They know the products, the price, the ordering system, the location of the bathrooms, and the seating arrangements. They're familiar with the taste of McDonald's sandwiches and French fries. And if they have children, the playground may be the calling card that brings them back time after time. In addition, the contests that McDonald's frequently sponsors and the trinkets that they give away are also great attractions for customers.

Most McDonald's restaurants are operated by franchisees, who are also customers of McDonald's. Every franchisee knows, or eventually learns, that McDonald's has a system for everything that needs to be done to operate a successful business. There's a routine for greeting the customer, cooking the French fries, and keeping the playground safe. Violate any part of the system and the retail customer may not come back. Following systems becomes a way of life for the franchisees, a way of life that keeps them loyal to the McDonald's corporation.

Getting customers to follow your systems

Your customers — both retail and distributors — will follow your systems only if you lead them. If you want your customers to sign up for your autoship program, get on autoship yourself. Same advice for your products and services. Use them so that you can speak about them with conviction, authority and enthusiasm. Otherwise, your customers may assume these products are not valuable, or are even inferior — and if they are right, your integrity has been compromised.

If you want your downline distributors to tell two people daily about your business opportunity — because that's the system that works — then make sure *you're* telling at least two people daily about your business opportunity. If you say to your downline that the system calls for attending the company's training sessions, your downline will expect to see you at the sessions, too. If bringing a guest to every opportunity meeting is the system that leads to success in your business, then you should show up at these meetings with at least one guest. As the leader, you must always set the example. Your downline distributors pay more attention to what you *do* than what you *say*.

To become a success in network marketing, you must become a product of your product.

Building Customer Loyalty

It's important to know as much as you possibly can about your products and services. Similarly, it's smart to develop the skills to demonstrate your knowledge. But neither of those conditions is as important as your attitude and your desire to help customers, starting from the very first time you present your product or opportunity to them. Your knowledge may eventually exceed that of every distributor in your company, and your skills may be dazzling, but if your head swells and you become cocky rather than helpful, or egotistical instead of humble, your attitude will eventually chase away your customers.

Your retail *(external)* customers will gladly purchase products from another network marketer — perhaps one who's friendlier. Your downline distributors — who are really your *internal* customers — will demand someone who's genuinely interested in them.

Using the attitude domino effect to everyone's advantage

Be aware of the domino effect your attitude can have: The way you treat your internal customers — your downline — determines the way they treat your external customers. And because your downline should be selling to or servicing many retail/external customers, it's financially critical that you treat those internal customers with courtesy and respect. Otherwise, they might join a different company and take your external customers with them. "Ouch." That's *not* using the attitude domino system to your or anyone else's advantage.

Your attitude offers customers an excellent reason to sign over their loyalty to you and your business. Attitude isn't something you can hide. Oftentimes, your attitude speaks volumes before you ever open your mouth. The way you approach a customer, either in person or on the phone, is the first indication of your attitude. If your attitude is anything less than genuine interest and to be of service, the customer, or the prospect, knows it almost immediately.

A good customer service attitude accepts this fundamental belief: "It's my job to serve the customer." That's not a forced decision. Successful network marketers serve their customers willingly. For one thing, they know if they don't, someone else is likely to! And furthermore, they know that if their attitude turns off their customers, there are plenty of other ways for those customers to get the service they want. Therefore, approach every customer with a good attitude and you will give that customer a good reason to keep buying from you.

It's important to believe that serving customers benefits you. That belief goes a long way in helping you keep a positive attitude. This is especially important on those days when customers get under your skin or on days when you're just not feeling up to par.

For more information about developing a good attitude, read Zig Ziglar's *Success For Dummies* (IDG Books Worldwide, Inc., 1998), especially the section called "Building the Right Attitude" in Chapter 17.

Doing it right the first time

Customers are not fickle people by choice. They have neither the time nor the patience to jump from company to company hoping to find one worthy of their loyalty. All too often, however, that's what they're forced to do. When expectations are not met, or met but never exceeded, customers get antsy. That's when they're easily led to other sources or different opportunities — hoping that *this* time they'll find what they want; hoping that *this* time will be the last time they have to search for a source for a particular product or service; hoping that *this* business opportunity, finally, will be the one that leads to their financial independence.

Keeping customers is easier with a customer retention program

With more than ten years' experience in network marketing, and an income that allows him to travel extensively and not have to go back to a traditional day job, Todd Falcone says he "lives by" his customer retention program. Todd is a networker with ProSTEP (www.prostepinc.com), an Internet-based lead generation system. "Most people in network marketing," he says, "live by the philosophy that once they close the sale, their work is done. That's not the way I operate. Once I sponsor a new member, or bring on a new customer who's using my services, that's when the work begins!"

Todd's customer retention program is designed to pay personal attention to his customers. "My feeling is that once I bring new customers on board, I have to take care of them. I answer their questions, I offer my assistance, and by doing so I've discovered that it's much easier to get more business, more referrals, and — overall — develop a more satisfied customer."

To better serve his customers and win their loyalty to his business, Todd explains that he maintains an e-mail broadcast list for all his customers and he communicates with them regularly. "I provide tips and strategies and I always offer my help. My customers love it. Even those who don't necessarily need my help respond back and thank me for offering help. It's not too difficult to keep customers happy if you maintain this type of relationship with them."

Once they find what they want, and commit their loyalty, it's almost impossible to separate customer advocates from their preferred businesses. For that reason alone, the best decision you can make as a network marketer is to do it right the first time you meet a customer. That's how you'll earn customer loyalty, and that's the only way to build a satisfying and profitable business.

Major point — and a huge bonus: A gung-ho, loyal customer is ripe for being brought into the business. As an example, in the Zig Ziglar Network, an extremely high percentage of our associates join because they have gotten satisfaction and results from our products. Fact: Satisfied customers already have a testimonial. That increases their odds of becoming successful associates.

Gaining Loyalty by Meeting or Exceeding Customer Expectations

Put yourself in the shoes of a customer. You noticed an ad in the newspaper or a neighbor praised a certain business, and based on that information, you've made a decision to visit that business. You won't go to that business without some expectations. You have reason to believe that you can get what you want from that business. You assume your expectations will be fulfilled.

Your customers aren't any different. They give you that first order expecting the best, which is often combined with a degree of trust in you. Your retail customers expect to get the product they need to solve a problem or enhance a particular feature. Your downline distributors expect to get the training and support they need, and leadership to help them excel in their businesses. These expectations motivated these customers to select you!

Ultimately, the customer provides your paycheck in network marketing. From the retail customer who buys your products and services, to the distributor who sells your products and services, you don't earn a penny until one of these customers steps up and favors you!

Recognizing customer expectations

The secret to exceeding your customers' expectations is to first recognize and understand what they are. What do they want? What do they assume they're going to get? What's their image of you and your business? By knowing what's expected, and why, you can incorporate features and benefits to exceed almost every expectation.

Almost all customers share several basic expectations. We use the acronym RATE to remember them (the first three expectations begin with the letter R). This section explains the RATE acronym in more detail:

Reliability/Recovery/Responsiveness

Assurance

Tangibles

Empathy

Reliability

Customers expect you to deliver on your promises. If you tell a retail customer that your product will solve a problem, make sure that it does. If you tell a distributor that you'll call at a certain time, make sure that you do.

Customers don't expect perfection, though it sometimes seems they do. They simply want you to do what you say you'll do. Don't make any promises that you can't keep! Incidentally, women are generally better at keeping promises than men. They are more relationship-oriented while men are more numbers-oriented. Good news, fellas — we can change and improve. It's a choice — and a good one — we can make.

Recovery

Occasionally you're going to make a mistake, particularly if you're serving a large number of customers. When it happens, customers expect you to face up to it and make it right. Fix the problem. But don't stop there. At least apologize. Better yet, give the customer something extra to make up for his/her disappointment.

Mistakes aren't all that bad if you remember to recover. Sometimes mistakes present the best opportunities to create customer advocates.

Responsiveness

A *Wall Street Journal* survey revealed that customers complain most about waiting. Waiting in line. Waiting for an answer. Waiting on hold. Waiting for products to arrive. And of course, waiting for someone to get back to them. Customers want your attention, and they want it when they want it. The rate of your responsiveness can make or break your relationship with a customer. This doesn't mean you must always be there when the customer wants you. However, it does mean that you need to be sure every customer's inquiry, whether by telephone, e-mail, or some other form of communication, gets a response as quickly as possible. At times when you won't be able to respond quickly, you could simply forward your phone calls and e-mails to an associate or an assistant who can respond for you. Always look for opportunities that allow you to get back to your customers, or prospects, faster than they anticipated.

Assurance

The A in RATE means assurance. Customers want the assurance that what you tell them about your products and services is true. That's why it's so important to become a product of your product! Keep in mind that products and services are solutions to problems. Even a product that helps you enjoy life more is a solution to a problem — the problem of not getting enough enjoyment out of life. Whatever the product or service, if you have used it, you'll be able to explain its benefits in greater detail and with the *assurance* that your customers desire. See Chapter 7 for more information about studying your company's products and services.

Tangibles

Everything speaks in your business. In other words, the way you look, the skills you display, the quality of your brochures, your adaptability to technology, the design of your products, and everything else that's part of your business sends a message to your customers. If it's a message they don't like, you're failing to meet their basic expectations. Many network marketers fall into the hype trap and then they wonder why customers don't buy from them, or why they can't attract new distributors into their downline. Most customers believe the adage: *If it's too good to be true it probably is.* Telling people that your product cures diseases, such as cancer, when in fact it doesn't, might attract some people who are desperate, but most people will be turned off by such claims. Telling people they don't have to do any work, just join your downline and the business will build a business for them is utter nonsense, and most people are smart enough to know it today. Yes, there are gullible people who buy into such claims, but not many. People want believability. They want to see it, touch it, feel it and ultimately trust it. Watch what you say and do, because your prospective customers are watching what you say and do, too!

Empathy

Finally, the E in RATE is for empathy. Gone are the days — if they ever *did* exist — when customers put up with businesses that reduced them to numbers. Every customer wants to be treated individually. They expect you to recognize their request or condition as unique. Respond to your customers individually to show them that you care about them. But also respond in a manner that says, "I understand your particular situation, and I can handle it for you."

Of all the businesses in the world, few, if any, are more personal than network marketing. Your relationship with your customers and your downline calls for personalization, tailoring your approach to each individual. Treat all of them as people, not numbers, and you'll retain and build a much larger customer base and a much larger organization.

While the acronym RATE will help you remember the basic expectations of your customers, you'll have to probe to discover expectations that may be specific to your business. How do you do that? Ask! Survey your customers periodically and invite them to give you their feedback.

Creating customer advocates

Here comes a challenge: You can either meet your customers' expectations, or exceed them. If you meet them, your customers will be satisfied, but they won't necessarily feel any loyalty to you. You did only what you were expected to do. However, if you exceed your customers' expectations, you create customer advocates. These customers are not only thrilled about your service, but also eager to tell their family and friends about you, your products and services, and your terrific business opportunity. Customer advocates return to your business repeatedly, and they refer their friends!

"You can create a customer for life, if that's your goal," says network marketing trainer Doug Firebaugh. "But most distributors create 'paycheck' customers. They just want that first commission, so they forget about them [or avoid them] after the sale." This avoidance could also be fueled by lack of conviction that your product is all that good or even that it works, so you avoid your customer to escape criticism and/or rejection. That attitude puts you in a lose/lose situation. If the product doesn't fill the bill, you need to know as quickly as possible and make it right with the customer. If your customer is happy, you need to know about it as soon as possible so you can get a testimonial and references. This approach helps build trust, which is the foundation for all successful, long-term relationships.

Remember, as Doug goes on to say, "If you want to keep your customers for a lifetime, [you must] invest more than you take. Go back to them, ask for their feedback, and always, always, ask for more business."

My Australian friend, Doug Baumber, owns Parts Overnight, a multi-million-dollar company that services Australia, New Zealand, Singapore, Hong Kong and Malaysia. Doug's leading customer recently ordered nearly $400,000 worth of computer parts over a five-month period.

Doug got the account when two of the company's high-tech professionals called to order a thousand dollars' worth of parts. While assisting these potential customers, Doug showed them how to fix their problem without buying the parts. Sensing his interest in doing the right thing, they became steady customers.

You never know what's going to happen when you go out of your way. Take that extra step, go that extra mile, and you will not only build a big retail base, but you will also build a large organization. The old saying is true: People don't really care how much you know until they know how much you care — about them.

"The core of any downline or retail customer base is the relationships you establish with these customers," says Doug Firebaugh. "The attraction to your business is not how people feel about your product as much as how they feel about you. If you truly show up in a caring way for people, and keep their interests ahead of yours, they will keep coming back. Why? Because you have shown them value beyond your product, beyond the sale, and beyond the business opportunity. As the relationship grows, it keeps producing more sales." P.S. It's proof that you can have everything in life you want if you will just help enough other people get what they want.

Keeping Customers Loyal

Beyond exceeding the expectations of your customers, here are several other ways to help you keep customers loyal to your business:

- **Make sure that all communications run two ways.** Don't become a company that speaks but doesn't listen. Give the customer an opportunity to respond. Your retail customers need to know how to reach you, not just how to reach the company. Your downline distributors should be asked for their feedback about how well you're training and supporting them.

- **Make it fun to do business with you.** Want to hear a phone greeting that immediately says it's going to be fun working with this company? Call Ziglar Training Systems at 800-527-0306. A positive, helpful attitude will always make it fun to do business with you.

- **Reward your customers for their loyalty.** People repeat behavior that is recognized and rewarded. Want your customers to keep coming back? Thank them for their loyalty and reward them! Give your retail customers discounts, as well as free introductory products. Congratulate your downline distributors, send them leads to follow up, or recruit a new distributor for them.

"A great way to keep customers buying from you (provided that your product or service is good) is to show them how they can get their products 'free,'" explains Todd Falcone, a leader in the ProSTEP organization. "Even if they aren't distributors, but retail customers, you can invite them to join your sales organization. Then, by helping them recruit a few friends who buy products or become distributors, they'll earn commissions that will more than cover their product costs." That's almost like getting the products free each month. Initially, they'll have to do a little work to sell the product, or to recruit a distributor, but when the commission money pays for their own purchases and provides a surplus, they'll be motivated to find even more customers and distributors.

ZIG SAYS

Projecting a positive image to keep customers loyal

Many of your first-time buyers may not buy again. In some cases it's because they don't feel the product worked, or they decide they really don't need the service. More often than not, however, these customers don't return because of the way they've been treated. First impressions really do count! By always projecting a positive image, you improve your chances of turning the potential one-time buyer into a loyal customer. Here are some positive image techniques we recommend:

✔ Always use customer-friendly words. You'll never impress a customer with how smart you are if you make him or her feel dumb.

✔ Choose a friendly tone of voice. Keep it professional and pleasant.

✔ Watch your body language. The way you stand or sit may say something other than what you mean. Body language can be detected through telephone lines, too!

PEARL OF WISDOM

Todd Falcone says, "The best way that I can reward a distributor is to make sure they become and stay part of the inner circle of leadership on our team. If they are plugged in, participating in the action, involved in conference calls, constantly in contact with others who are productive, it all rubs off on them. Their likelihood of success increases simply by association. We've all heard the saying, 'You become like those you hang around.' It's true in network marketing, too."

TIP

"Leadership, more than anything else, [determines] the . . . turnover rate of distributors in network marketing," reports Doug Firebaugh. "An upline with strong leadership will reduce turnover by at least 30 percent."

Building Your Business from Referrals

The goal of all network marketers should be to build their business from referrals from existing customers. It's the least costly and most satisfying way to build your business.

"When you're building your business from referrals," says former NFL star Jack Maitland, a savvy network marketer in Fort Lauderdale, Florida, "that's when the light in the tunnel looks like financial freedom rather than a train coming at you! Referrals give your business a life of its own, and that's when you know you've arrived, you're a leader, and a champion in your organization." Jack knows all about champions. He's a Diamond leader in the Nikken organization, which he joined in 1996.

Customer advocates are more than willing to give you referrals for building your business. Although sometimes you don't even have to ask them, it's a good idea to get into that practice.

When you get a referral from an existing customer, you save the money it normally would have cost to generate a lead. Beyond keeping your existing customers loyal to your business, the next best step to reducing your customer acquisition costs is to get as many referrals as you can.

Listen to Dan Gaub of Market America when he says, "I don't buy advertising because I don't have to. After 52 months of working my network marketing business, I have 400 loyal customers, and each of them will refer one to six people to me every year. I don't have to sell my products — my customers do that for me."

A new customer costs Dan the grand sum of $5! "When an existing customer brings me a new customer," he explains, "I give my existing customer $5 off a future purchase." And because Dan knows that the average customer generates a $37 commission check each month, he's eager to extend that $5 deduction to every one of his customers every week.

Ask for referrals! At the first hint of a customer's satisfaction, be sure to say, "Who do you know who might want to get the same good results you're getting from my products?" Or, "Who do you know who might be interested in joining my organization?" Even if you don't immediately get a referral, you've planted the seed. Your customer will be looking out for you. Every so often, remember to water and fertilize the seed!

Handling Customer Complaints

Consider these statistics:

- Dissatisfied customers typically tell eight to ten people about their dissatisfaction. One in five will tell twenty. Ouch!

- It takes twelve positive transactions to make up for one negative transaction.

- At any given time, at least 25 percent of your customers are dissatisfied enough to consider looking elsewhere.

- A loyal customer is worth ten times the price of a single purchase.

All of the above is to say that taking care of the disgruntled customer or distributor may be every bit as important, if not more important, than making your next sale.

Differentiating your business

A good way to keep customers loyal to your business is to offer something that the competition doesn't. It could be a product or a service. It could also be a unique aspect of your business opportunity. Mary Kay Cosmetics comes to mind as a good example. Reach a certain level of expertise within Mary Kay's network, and you'll find yourself driving a pink Cadillac courtesy of Mary Kay.

Find something that sets your business apart from the competition, and use it as leverage to keep customers loyal.

There's never been a perfect network marketer, and there never will be. Sooner or later, you're going to disappoint a customer. Some weeks you may disappoint a lot of customers. That's just the way it goes in business. But that doesn't mean you must accept it. When customers contact you to let you know they're unhappy, the best thing you can do is resolve the problem as quickly as possible.

Responding quickly usually saves customers

Seven of ten dissatisfied customers will do business with you again if you resolve their complaints in their favor. Even better, if you will resolve a complaint at the time a customer raises it, 95 percent of the time, that customer will continue doing business with you.

Don't let complaints fester, and do everything you can to make your customers feel that it's okay to complain. Let them know that even if you can't fix every problem, you're at least interested in listening and trying to be helpful. When a customer orders your products, send a postcard and invite feedback, good or bad. If you have a toll-free number, use it to solicit comments from your customers. Be alert for complaints and settle them as quickly as you can.

Keeping your cool helps save customers

The non-emotional, matter-of-fact complaint is a lot easier to deal with than the irate customer who gets rude, angry and nasty. Unfortunately, you may encounter some of these unpleasant folks. If so, here are several steps to help you handle the situation:

- ✔ It takes two people to argue. Think of the irate customer or distributor as someone who's holding one end of a rope and inviting you to play tug of war. Don't play! You'll always lose by arguing with a customer.

- ✔ Let them vent. Sometimes angry customers just need to blow off steam. When you allow them to do so, without talking back or trying to justify the situation, they eventually simmer down. Then you can deal with the problem without being emotional.

- ✔ Use statements that are meant to soften the issue, such as: I understand . . . I agree . . . I realize this was inconvenient for you . . . You have every right to be upset.

- ✔ Once the irate customer runs out of steam and regains composure, use action-oriented words to indicate how you will resolve the situation. Some examples: I will follow-up . . . I'll send the information immediately . . . I'll check on that order and call you back in ten minutes . . . I'll call the corporate office for you right now and get an answer.

Always remember that an irate, abusive customer is not trying to hurt you. Most of the time he or she is hurting, and their disappointment in you might simply be the final straw. Listen carefully and empathetically, promptly solve their problem with you and chances are excellent that later they will apologize — and become a more loyal customer than they were before.

Most disgruntled customers do not complain. They simply go away. Of course, they share their misery with lots of other people who can do nothing for them, such as their friends and neighbors. Why don't they complain to someone who can make the situation right? There are several reasons, including: They don't think it's worth their time because the owner won't listen, or they don't have the time, or the owner doesn't make it easy for customers to provide feedback.

Bottom line: . . . And then some

You build customer loyalty by making certain that you keep all your promises . . . and then some. That your products do all that you say they do . . . and then some. That you give better than good service . . . and then some. In the words of Henry Ford, "If you sell a really good product and continuously give great service, than your profits will be so large they will be obscene." In other words, go the extra mile — a part of the highway to success that is seldom crowded!

Part V
The Part of Tens

The 5th Wave

By Rich Tennant

In this part . . .

*W*ithout a Part of Tens, *Network Marketing For Dummies* just wouldn't be a *For Dummies* book — therefore, this part contains several chapters that are quick, fun to read, and loaded with a lot of useful information for existing and would-be network marketers. You'll find ideas to help you get a fast start in network marketing, along with a resources section that includes information about Web sites, books, magazines, and industry associations. Moreover, Profiles International has agreed to give our readers a free assessment called the Profiles Performance Indicator (PPI — see Chapter 22). This assessment can be completed in less than 15 minutes, and it will give you a thorough analysis of your strengths.

Chapter 21

Ten Plus Two Resources for Network Marketers

In This Chapter

▶ Using the Internet to build your network marketing business

▶ Catching some tips from the products of top network marketers

▶ Discovering resources that can help you become an effective network marketer

*B*uilding a business can be a lonely effort, and when you're working from home, you can easily fall into the trap of "I'm the only one in the world trying to figure out how to do this!" Guess what? You're not! At least not in the world of network marketing. Thousands of people before you have walked the path of success in network marketing, and many of them have created terrific resources, including books, tapes, software, seminars, and Web sites. Latch onto at least a few of these resources because they can help you zip through those bleak days when nothing seems to work and you're left to figure it out.

Many of the products we discuss in this chapter can be purchased in bookstores or online. When we discuss a product that's sold only at the author's Web site, we include the URL for your convenience.

Network Marketing Lifestyles Magazine

`www.nmlifestyles.com`

Network Marketing Lifestyles magazine is a lively bimonthly publication sold by subscription and on newsstands. You can save money when you subscribe from the Web site. Past issues and articles have been archived.

NML publishes articles about the people who move and shake the network marketing profession. Tips, techniques, and tools are featured in every issue. If you're even slightly interested in network marketing, this is a good place to begin.

Direct Selling Association

`www.dsa.org`

Fifty-five percent of Americans have purchased goods or services through direct-sales companies. That's more than the number who have purchased through television shopping and online services combined! How do we know this? Because the Direct Selling Association keeps track of industry-specific data and provides updates on its Web site. The information you find is concise and revealing. The site also provides a directory of DSA member companies. Check it out!

Babener & Associates

`www.mlmlegal.com`

Jeffrey Babener advises network marketing companies on a wide range of legal matters. His law firm, Babener & Associates, serves as an important and informed resource about direct-selling issues. When it comes to knowing the inside story about network marketing, Jeffrey has the scoop, and his Web site reflects his breadth of knowledge and expertise.

Much of the information on this site is directed to executives of network marketing companies and not to distributors. However, distributors can find plenty here, too, especially those who want to be informed about the legal and operational issues that affect network marketing.

You'll find Jeffrey's MLM Article Sampler of particular interest. Click into the Law Library for a variety of articles about how to operate your home-based network marketing business.

mLmSuccess.com

`www.mlmsuccess.com`

This Web site is so informative that you'll want to visit it every day, at least until you're underway in network marketing. Then you'll still want to stop back by every so often.

The site includes the MLM Index — a list of network marketing companies, with contact information. You can search the list by company name or by product or service. The Marketplace invites you to place classified ads for a fee, and of course you can review the ads for free. The Library includes a list of searchable articles — lots of good reading here! — and the Forum allows you to post questions for experts to answer. The Bookstore features a large selection of materials, and a section called Launch Pad includes links to other useful sites. This is a site you don't want to miss!

Direct Sales World

www.directsalesworld.com

Edward Ludbrook, who describes himself as Mr. Network Marketing in Europe, maintains the Direct Sales World Web site without the support of advertising or subscription fees. The site was created in 1997 to provide independent facts, data, and commentary on the world of direct sales.

Ed has been a distributor and a corporate executive and now spends much of his time advising network marketing companies in Europe. Plan to spend some time when you visit Direct Sales World. The Useful Information section includes general resources, which cover topics such as what network marketing is, the history of network marketing, and why network marketing is booming. A Legal Centre, Financial Centre, Bookshop, and Newsletter are also available. We find the site particularly useful for gathering information about network marketing in other countries.

Passion Fire International

www.mlmleadership.com

Passion Fire International is the name of the Web site, and its creator is one of network marketing's most powerful trainers: Doug Firebaugh. This guy will set you on fire with a passion to succeed in this profession. What's better, he'll show you exactly *how* you can succeed.

Here are some of the topics you'll find on Doug's site: Killer Training Secrets, Killer MLM E-Course, Top 25 Training Resource Sites, and Recruiting Fire, Doug's e-mail newsletter. His audiotapes are winning the praises of networkers worldwide, so don't hesitate to buy them. Plus, if you can catch Doug live on the seminar circuit, buy a ticket to hear him!

www.recruitomatic.com

"Old school network marketing is dead," or so says networker Brett Rademacher, who created www.recruitomatic.com. "No meetings. No mailings. All you need to do network marketing is a phone line and an Internet connection," he continues. "Work from the comfort of your home and live anywhere you want." Brett, in fact, lives way up there in Alaska!

As this book explains, technology is revolutionizing the way network marketing is conducted. The old ways are not working anymore, and www.recruitomatic.com shows you how to "effectively use cutting-edge technology to build your network marketing organization *big* and *fast*," in the words of the site's creator.

This Web site includes a special focus on automated lead-generation systems. It also offers a free newsletter for those who wish to subscribe.

www.mlm911.com

A Web site with an attitude! This one belongs to Kim Klaver, who says that people visit her site to "laugh about things they might otherwise cry about." A seasoned networker, Kim provides a variety of helpful, free information including: How to Do Business with or without Your Friends, Family or Neighbors; The 5 Worst Things You Can Say to a Good Prospect; and Target Your Internet Audience.

You can also sign up to receive Kim's free newsletter, and you can join her national teleconferences. Perhaps one of her most insightful offerings is Say 'No' First, in which she instructs you in the subtle "take-away" sales close. When prospects turn negative, doubtful, or rude on you after you've introduced your opportunity, product, or service, Kim shows you how to take back what you offered and tell them why it's not right for them. Have fun at this site!

MLM Insider and Network Marketing Today Magazine

www.mlminsider.com

MLM Insider and *Network Marketing Today Magazine* provide this Web site, which offers many resources: MLM Articles Library, Training & Seminars, Success Stories, Press Releases, and the free MLM Success Tips Newsletter.

Watch out for Internet scams

You'll read that the Internet is a danger zone for network marketing because it's a playground for "carnival barkers" who only want to cheat people out of their money. Lots of fraudulent schemes are popping up on the Internet, and you want to avoid them. Plus, the Internet is chock-full of "crybaby" sites created mostly by ex-network marketers who gave up before they succeeded. They tend to blame everything that's wrong with network marketing — and sometimes the world! — on their former companies. Avoid these sites, too.

Billed as "the definitive source of information on the Network Marketing/MLM Industry," this site provides an Industry News section, which is updated weekly. Here you can find press releases from a variety of companies.

We think that the site's best feature is Compensation Plans Explained. This section includes a guide to understanding the complex phenomenon known as the compensation plan! Check it out.

MLM Nuts $ Bolts

Perhaps you've heard of modeling the success of others? Modeling is a process of finding someone who has already done something you want to do and then doing what that person did — behaving like that person and anticipating your success. Modeling works as long as you remember that you don't want to *become* that other person — you just want to follow the person's success habits.

MLM means multi-level marketing, another word for network marketing.

Jan Ruhe, network marketing superstar, invites you to walk in her footsteps in her book *MLM Nuts $ Bolts: How to Build a Network Marketing Business* (JR Productions, 1997). Jan provides 35 habits that you can model. You can order the book from www.JanRuhe.com, where you can find additional offerings.

Jan's book covers these and many other topics:

- ✔ Writing your personal success story and making it happen
- ✔ Using the phone to become an MLM pro
- ✔ Reaping the rewards of empowering your downline
- ✔ Creating successful strategies for your business

✔ Developing your leadership abilities

✔ Learning to become a master recruiter

Jan Ruhe knows whereof she writes. Early in her networking career, she decided that she would become a millionaire. At the time, she was merely $130,000 in debt! Nonetheless, she made it her business to meet millionaires — not very difficult to do when you live in Dallas, Texas (she now lives in Aspen, Colorado). She interviewed them to learn about their habits, and then she modeled them. Jan will tell you that this approach worked for her, and it can work for you, too.

Performance Tracker

This is one of the most useful tools for network marketers. It helps you plan your daily activities so that you build your business progressively. It's a great idea for anyone who needs to be reminded of what to do and wants to be held accountable for doing it.

The Performance Tracker is a spiral-bound, pocket-sized booklet that includes a month's worth of Daily Performance Worksheets. Each worksheet enables you to track the actions that you performed that day, such as studying your goals, making phone calls, mailing promotions, placing newspaper ads, setting appointments, selling products at retail, spending time in self-development, and so on. Each of these activities is important in the development of your business.

Developed by networker Tim Sales, the Performance Tracker is available at www.brilliantexchange.com, where you can also purchase Tim's video, "Brilliant Compensation."

The Wave 3 and Wave 4 Books by Richard Poe

Richard Poe is not a network marketer by profession. He's a journalist and author, and he's *verrry goood*. Read all of his material about network marketing! Both published by Prima Publishing in 1996 and 1999 respectively, *Wave 3: The New Era in Network Marketing* is a great "getting started" book, while *Wave 4: Network Marketing in the 21st Century* focuses on the way technology is transforming network marketing. Both books include lots of personal success stories, as any good book should!

After you read the *Wave* books, you may decide that you want to give them to family and friends, particularly those who laugh when you tell them you're building a network marketing business. With Poe's credibility behind the books, they won't laugh for long, and they'll soon see that network marketing is an opportunity that may even work for them.

Chapter 22

Ten Characteristics of Top Network Marketers

In This Chapter

▶ Discovering characteristics of the top network marketers

▶ Finding out how your personality and strengths can motivate others and lead you to the top of your business

*T*his chapter takes a look at the characteristics that consistently show up in top network marketers, the people who are leaders and mentors in this profession — and the people who are likely to earn the most money, too! As you'll see at the end of this chapter, we've arranged for you to take a free test that can help you evaluate yourself for some of the characteristics that you need to become a leader in network marketing. The same test can help you evaluate the character qualities of your prospective downline members, too!

They're Dreamers

If you got caught dreaming in school, hopefully you weren't so discouraged that you've stopped dreaming altogether. Contrary to many schoolteachers' admonitions, dreaming is a character quality. Top network marketers are dreamers! They know what they want because they're not afraid to dream.

What is it that *you* want from life? Earl Nightingale said, "In America, anyone can be anything they want . . . the problem is, most people don't know what they want." That's true of people in *all* countries. Life as you'd really like to live it begins with a dream. So get busy . . . dream!

> *All men dream, but not equally. Those men who dream by night in the dusty recesses of their minds wake in the morning to find it was but vanity, but those men who dream by day — these are dangerous men, for they dream with open eyes to make their dreams come true.* — T. E. Lawrence

Jan Ruhe thought she wanted to be a dependent woman. She hoped to marry a man who would take care of her financially and give her the freedom to stay home with their children. Things didn't work out quite that way, however, and when Jan's marriage failed and she won custody of her three children, she was forced to become an independent woman. "Once I learned about Discovery Toys," says Jan, a 20-year veteran of network marketing, "and I considered my own future, I decided that I would become the top producer in my company, and I would become a millionaire. Those were two of my goals, and I needed to reach them because there was so much that I wanted to give to my children and have for myself."

At the time she set these goals, Jan was buried in $130,000 of debt! Some days, surviving was as much as she could manage, but she never gave up on her dreams. "I went to work on myself," she explains, "because I realized I couldn't change anyone else, and I had to change myself if there was any hope of gaining a better life." As you'll recall from earlier chapters in this book, Jan became Discovery Toys' top producer. On Jan's journey to the top, she had another dream: to build a beautiful home in Colorado's Aspen valley. Several years ago, Jan and her husband moved into a 5,000 square-foot dream house in Aspen. "I have everything that's on my master dream list," says Jan, "but I wouldn't have achieved any of it if I hadn't first dreamed."

"There are ten steps to success in network marketing," says Dayle Maloney, the leading money earner with Nutrition for Life International, which sells hundreds of consumer products. "The first step is the dream," he says. "The second step is the dream . . . the third step is the dream . . . in fact, all ten steps are the dream!"

They Don't "Try," They Commit

People who succeed in network marketing make a commitment to become successful. They don't join a company to "try" network marketing. "All millionaires have one thing in common," explains network marketing trainer Doug Firebaugh. "They would not be *denied*." Top network marketers realize there's nothing to gain by trying. Doug says, "The power is in deciding to succeed. There is nothing more powerful in network marketing than engaged activity that has no path to travel except a path to success!"

After you set your goals, you're going to hit some roadblocks. That's not a maybe, that's a positive! You're going to hit the wall. When you do, the only hope of success that you will have is your *commitment* to accomplish your goals. If you've made the commitment, when you hit that roadblock your first thought is "How do I handle this challenge?" Without the commitment, when you hit the roadblock your first thought is, "How do I get out of this deal?"

Berky Palma made a commitment to Nutrition for Life International in the Dominican Republic because she had a dream to create a better life for her family. She's a wife and a mother of three children, all under the age of 8. Her day starts early when she sends her children off to school and her husband leaves for work. Relying on public transportation, she goes into the nearby city and talks to people about her business and the many products she sells, such as household items and nutritional products. She does this all day and well into the evening. In fact, Berky doesn't return home until 11 p.m. Then she irons her children's clothes for the next day, and processes the paperwork from her day's activity before she goes to bed. Did we mention that she was six months pregnant at the time we heard about her?

Berky recently got some good news. She has qualified for Nutrition For Life's car payment program, so she can stop riding public transportation because she can now afford to buy a car. She's also receiving monthly checks in the range of $1,000! Success hasn't come easy for her, but it did come, and it came faster because of her commitment. Without that commitment, chances are good it would not have come at all.

They're Teachable

"The crux of network marketing is teaching and doing a simple, duplicable process," says Dan Hollings, a former teacher and then a distributor of National Safety Associates (NSA), where he earned enough money to walk away and become a consultant to network marketing companies. Top network marketers *do not* reinvent the wheel. They look for companies that have already developed successful systems. Then they learn the systems and replicate them. It's really as simple as that, although many people try to make it complex.

If you don't like to follow directions and you're not comfortable using someone else's system, you should think twice before joining a network marketing company. You'll either feel frustrated trying to reinvent the wheel, or you'll feel uncomfortable trying to follow a system. Either way, you probably won't succeed. Top network marketers are teachable, and they're teachers, too.

In Jerusalem, Shapira Alexander says his obligation as a top network marketer is to develop leaders. How does he do it? By "making my team watch and listen to me, seek me, copy me while I inspire them and keep in touch with them, no matter what level they are on." Shapira is a distributor for Dr. Nona International, which sells health and nutritional products. Shapira continues, "It is extremely important to teach the leaders the most needed skill: passing their knowledge downline and forming other leaders." He adds, "The one who wants to be a real leader has to learn to be a supporting psychologist. Help people dream and teach them to make their dreams come true. Otherwise it's hard to count on serious success."

They Have STEAM

After recruiting more than 500 people for Discovery Toys, Jan Ruhe says that she can spot future top network marketers — those who have STEAM. STEAM is an acronym for Salespeople who are Teachers/Trainers; they are Enthusiastic; they have developed positive, upbeat Attitudes; and they have the desire to earn some extra Money.

So much of our success is controlled by our mental attitude. People with positive mental attitudes are likely to *respond* to life's problems and challenges, while those with negative or poor mental attitudes will simply *react*. Top network marketers respond instead of react!

They're Builders

A satisfying and profitable network marketing business must be built one person at a time, beginning with the person at the top. "Fish stink from the head down," said W. Edwards Deming. Top network marketers realize the importance of building themselves mentally, emotionally, and physically so that by their example they can lead others to success.

How can you build yourself? Read, listen to tapes (especially in your vehicle), watch videos, and attend seminars. Connie Dugan maintains a six-figure income with Oxyfresh (which markets dental products and other nontoxic wellness products for humans and pets), explaining that she spent the first of her dozen years in network marketing as a "sponge." She wasn't a skilled product salesperson when she started with Oxyfresh, and she needed that skill to achieve success. "During that first year," Connie explains, "I became a voracious reader about network marketing. I dialed in to conference calls, I attended leadership seminars, and I listened and learned from the masters who explained how they built their businesses. Eventually, I discovered my own style." She then went on to build a downline that includes more than 5,000 distributors.

Connie says that it's important not to "social work yourself" if you're going to be a top network marketer. "I never want to burn bridges with people," she explains, "but anyone who's not interested in this business beyond getting in up to their ankles, I can't help. If they're not willing to do for themselves, but they expect me to help, then they'd be misusing my energy. I don't want to burn out, so if you want to work with me, you'll have to pass a litmus test so that I can see you've made a commitment to your business. I want to see you at training, hear you on conference calls, and see the list of names that you're working. If you're serious about working your business, I'll give you all the time and more to help you become successful. But I'm not a social worker."

Builders are driven by relationships, not by money, fame, or prestige. Above all else, network marketing is a relationship business. Luis Mogas of Monterrey, Mexico, a distributor for Orbis, which sells home and personal care products, cosmetics, and jewelry, sums up the value of relationship building when he says: "In the search for people who want to succeed, you have to focus on helping them achieve their goals. Your own success will depend on this. If they don't succeed under your guidance, neither will you."

They're Good Finders

There are no perfect companies and no perfect network marketers. Top network marketers understand that perfection doesn't exist in business, and they go out of their way to find the good in their companies and their associates.

Even a company that tries to do everything right will occasionally fall short of expectations. Whether it's their pay plan, product development, marketing programs, or the technology they use, there's always the chance that something will go wrong, won't come together as planned, or may not be good enough. Similarly, network marketers sometimes come up short. They make commitments and don't follow through. Some learn to work the system better than others do. Some are better salespeople, or relationship builders, or trainers. In all of these situations, the top network marketers realize that pointing out what's wrong won't necessarily make things better.

Starting right now, make it a practice to be a good finder. Find the good in your company and your associates. Find the good in every situation. Then be sure to share that information. Tell your company executives what you like about the company, its products and services. Tell your associates what you like about them. And tell yourself what you like about every situation, even one that doesn't work out quite the way you expected. Encouragers are winners and producers.

They're Always Present

Top network marketers maintain presence. Jan Ruhe says, "They're all put together. They look good. They talk well. And they're always upbeat." Doug Firebaugh adds, "Their presence is always noticed. They're present in everything. They're at meetings, they're in conversations, and they're on conference calls. Most of all, they're always present when they are *needed*."

By your presence, you can become the difference maker in the lives of thousands of people. Just the opportunity to share a word of friendship and encouragement with someone could make you a catalyst in his or her life.

"My passion is for the development of others," says "Tremendous" Bill Pike, the highest-paid associate in Youngevity, which markets health and nutritional products. Bill's presence in the lives of his downline distributors has helped many of them become successful, even when others said it couldn't be done. Anita Rawls is a good example. She was a banker in Sherman, Texas, and she joined Bill's downline without seeing any materials, without knowing the compensation plan, and even without experiencing any of the company's products. Why would she take such a risk, including giving up her job? She did it because she knew Bill's presence would make all the difference. A fellow banker told Anita she was crazy to quit her job. But Anita had some big dreams, including becoming a millionaire. Interestingly, a few years after Anita joined Youngevity, the friend who called her crazy lost her job when the bank was sold. Meanwhile, Anita recently purchased a million-dollar home in Sherman!

They're Motivated

"Network marketing is too exciting not to do it!" Those words come from Russ Noland, who for many years avoided network marketing opportunities while he built a thriving — but all-consuming — real estate agency in Houston, Texas. Russ gave up his agency and in a matter of a few years built one of the most successful sales organizations in Excel Communications. He's the epitome of motivation: "Every time I get a new associate started, it's like I got a winning lottery ticket. This person is going to do something big, and I'm going to be a part of it!" Russ goes on to say that much of your success in network marketing depends on your "emotional commitment" to the business.

They're Persistent and Patient

Leaders in this profession realize that not everyone will say yes the first time, or even the tenth time. Success is a matter of persistence and patience.

Dan Gaub of Market America experienced a great example of persistence and patience. "Rick was the first person I showed my business to," he explains. "We had been friends since our teens, 20-plus years. I thought he would join me in an instant, but he said no, and he wished me the best. I was crushed . . . . We would see each other at church, karate with the kids, dinner once a month, and so forth. He was busy with his life and I with mine. From time to time he would ask: 'How's it going,' referring to my business, and I'd say: 'Good.'

Then one day, 42 months after the first time I had approached him, he asked to meet for coffee. He said his life had changed. He had found himself unsettled about his family's future. He became a partner that day, and he has been growing ever since at a fast pace . . . . I never told him he was stupid for not joining me. I kept the integrity of our friendship. It took the right timing of events, and watching me make a six-figure income without rubbing his nose in it, that eventually brought him back. My persistence was in the friendship, not in trying to make him 'do' it. This industry is about the long haul, not the short sprint."

"People everywhere want to be rich," says James Davis, a leader with Horizons Interactive, which sells products and services to consumers and business owners from a variety of Web malls; see www.jdavis.com. "The problem is most people are too busy earning a living to make any serious money. Plus, they're looking for an easy way to make money, but they're so intent on getting rich that they fail to find out what they have to do to get rich. If they *do* find it, it's often too late. There's no quick route to success in network marketing. This is a get-rich-slow opportunity. But if you work it, stay with it, and give it time to develop, you will succeed."

They Have a Heart Condition

"Leaders have their hearts in this business," says Doug Firebaugh. "They operate their business from that capacity and never look back. They have their hearts in their downline's business with a focus of making them more successful than themselves. They have their hearts in their prospects' best interests. And they have their hearts conditioned for success: expecting it, wanting it, attracting it, and obtaining it."

Years ago, an Olympic gold medal winner was asked why he was able to jump so high. He responded, "I simply throw my heart over the bar and the rest of me follows." The reporter persisted and the winner said, "I have never represented anything this big before," and with that he pointed to the U.S. flag.

We frequently hear someone observe about another person that he or she just "didn't have the heart" for what he or she was trying to do. Consequently, he or she even withdrew or had minimal success in the project. It is true that your heart must be in it for you to be at your best. This doesn't mean that you shouldn't be well prepared — because you should — but if your heart is in it, you will prepare properly. The combination of mental preparation and emotional involvement puts you in the position of speaking from your head and heart to the heads and hearts of others.

Audiences, and for that matter, individuals, instinctively know whether your heart is truly in what you are doing. It's more than just a cliché to say that people don't really care how much you know until they know how much you care — about them. If you will just remember that the mind is the gateway to the heart, you will be careful to make certain that you feed your mind good heart material, that which will inspire you to be the right kind of person necessary for you to do the right thing, which is the key to getting what you want.

Several thousand years ago, Solomon, the wisest man who ever lived, said, "Protect your heart, for out of it come the issues of life." Without attempting to add to that, I would simply say that when you get the heart right, based on what you feed it from the mind, your chances of making it big in network marketing dramatically increase.

Take a free test to profile your character qualities

"There are three personality characteristics that I look for in people who will perform at far above average levels in network marketing businesses," explains Jim Sirbasku, CEO of Profiles International based in Waco, Texas. "These characteristics are dominance, influence, and motivational energy."

✔ By *dominance*, Jim says he means aggressiveness, desire to lead, and the power to control situations. "People with this characteristic are — by nature — positive, problem solvers, and 'take charge' types," he explains.

✔ *Influence,* says Jim, is typically characteristic of people who circulate in a large circle of friends and acquaintances, who meet new people easily and frequently, and whose opinions and judgment are respected. "They are persuasive, believable, and able to help others feel confident and optimistic," he continues. "Others often look to people who have influence for leadership and solutions to problems."

✔ The third characteristic, *motivational energy,* shows up in self-starters. Jim explains: "They bring a high degree of intensity and enthusiasm to the things they have

decided to accomplish. These are people who take the initiative, don't need someone to prod them, and find great satisfaction in their work."

Want to know how your dominance, influence, and motivational energy show up? Profiles International has agreed to give our readers a free assessment — with no obligation — called the Profiles Performance Indicator (PPI). You can complete this assessment in less than 15 minutes, and it will give you a thorough analysis of your strengths. This assessment will help you understand the characteristics of successful network marketers and give you several personal benchmarks to consider as well.

To access the assessment, send an e-mail to freeppi@profilesinternational.com. Type **Free PPI** on the subject line or include it in the body of your message. Also include your name, mailing address, and telephone number. In return, Profiles International will send you an e-mail message with directions about how to access PPI on the Internet. Have fun! And remember — you can develop the characteristics you need to succeed in all areas of your life!

Chapter 23

Ten Business-Enhancing Ideas

*T*his chapter gives you ten suggestions that can help you build a more satisfying and profitable network marketing business.

Work "on" Your Business, Not "in" It

At several points in this book, I say, "You've got to be before you can do, and you've got to do before you can have." You can't rearrange the order of those words and expect to get positive results. What we are about to tell you addresses the "do" portion of my philosophy.

Many of the people who start small businesses fall into the "getting ready to get started" trap. Perhaps you've fallen into this trap. You rearrange your desk. You clean up your files. You reposition the phone, the computer, and the printer. You rearrange the furniture in your office. You sharpen all your pencils — three times. And then you go through this routine, with modifications, again, and sometimes again. And if someone asks what you're doing, you say, "I'm getting ready to get started," or words to that effect. Many (maybe most) people go through this stage when they start a business, and it's a challenge that you must resist. If you're still getting ready to get started the second week into your business, you're probably never going to get started.

Even experienced business owners occasionally fall into the getting ready to get started trap. They get bored. Or they lose their confidence, and suddenly they're no longer productive. No matter how long you've been in business, and regardless of the achievements you may have enjoyed in the past, you always have to look out for this trap. It can sneak up on you and ruin a day or a week, and if you don't catch it in time, it can destroy your business.

Here's a test that can help you determine whether you're working *on* your business or *in* your business. Stop whatever you're doing and ask yourself these questions:

- ✔ Is what I'm doing now directly related to achieving one of my goals?
- ✔ Will what I'm doing now help me build my business?
- ✔ Will what I'm doing now result in a sale?
- ✔ Will what I'm doing now improve one of my skills?
- ✔ Could someone else do what I'm doing better or just as well?
- ✔ Am I reinventing the wheel?
- ✔ Could I wait and do this during non-business hours?

Be honest when you answer these questions. You can try to justify rearranging your office by claiming that doing so will improve your productivity. But can you justify rearranging your office during your normal business hours? Not if you answer honestly.

Other "in" as opposed to "on" activities include writing letters and coordinating direct mailings. If you've selected a good network marketing company and/or a good sponsor, all the letters you'll need for your business have already been written. Why are you reinventing the wheel? If you want to tweak the letters or personalize them and store them in your computer, that's fine. But do you have to do it during business hours? As for stuffing envelopes with letters and audiotapes — coordinating your direct-mail pieces — do you *really* need to do that? Are there children in your house? Show them what you're doing, ask for their help, and save yourself time and nonproductive work. If you're the only one in your household, and therefore the only one to do this work, at least do it after business hours.

Whatever you're doing, if you're doing it during business hours and it will not lead to the fulfillment of a goal or result in building your business (such as by making a sale), you're most likely working "in" your business and not "on" it. Don't get caught in that trap.

Organize a Business Mastermind

There's power — and wisdom — in numbers. Consider that challenge you've been grappling with for weeks. Do you think someone else has faced that same challenge and solved it? Absolutely. Just imagine if you had the benefit of that person's counsel. Business would be a whole lot easier and more enjoyable, too.

As soon as you get into business, look for potential members whom you can invite to join your own mastermind group. Arrange to get together with these people every month or so to talk about business issues. These kinds of groups are invaluable in business. You may be able to solve all your business problems by yourself, but chances are, you would benefit from a mastermind group.

Create your mastermind group online and open it up to people worldwide! That's exactly what Jan Ruhe did. After 20 years of developing her Discovery Toys distributorship, Jan is one of the most sought-after speakers and trainers in the world. Ever since she posted her Web site, www.janruhe.com, people from around the world have been writing to her with their questions and concerns about network marketing. "I saved all of their e-mail addresses," Jan explains, "and one day I decided to name this group The Champion Network. Word began to spread, people are joining by leaps and bounds, and now there are thousands on the list! It's free, and it's open to all who want to share ideas about network marketing."

Feed Your Mind Continually

Many people don't have time to become bookworms, but we all have time to be "tapeworms." Please don't underestimate the importance of what I'm saying about listening to audiotapes or instructive CDs as you travel from one place to another. By listening to tapes in your car, you can learn virtually anything, including vocabulary words, sales procedures and techniques, goal-setting processes, leadership skills, attitudinal and personal growth, foreign languages, how to become a better speaker, and memory training.

Stories abound of salespeople who, particularly when they have missed a sale, pop in a motivational tape en route to their next call and their spirits are lifted, their attitudes changed, and their effectiveness increased. The message is that you don't just "sit there to get there." You sit there and learn so that when you get there, you're better prepared to handle any situation.

Don't React to Life; Respond!

Some things you cannot control. You can't, for example, make someone say yes to your business opportunity when he or she is not interested. (And if you did, what kind of distributor would that person become?) You can't make a start-up kit arrive any earlier than it's going to get there. You can't control the number of people who show up for your opportunity meeting minutes before the meeting is going to start. In business, you can be certain that something *will* go wrong on occasion. Be ready for it and, when it happens, try to laugh it off. Throwing a tantrum, getting mad, and yelling at the people in your upline or your downline will only make matters worse.

The choices you make determine your success in life. You're going to make choices that will determine your success as you learn to manage yourself and others. To be effective in making choices, you must understand the difference between *reacting* and *responding*. The following example taken from my book *Top Performance* makes the difference clear.

In January of 1981, I was in Kansas City, Missouri. It had been a particularly difficult week, and that morning I had a lengthy recording session. I finished at exactly 1:00 p.m., and because we had a 3:00 departure time for Dallas and we needed to arrive at least an hour early to get our heavy recording equipment on the plane, my son-in-law, Chad Witmeyer, and I made a mad dash for the airport. We arrived at exactly 2:00, just in time to hear the ticket agent smilingly announce, "Those of you who have a seat on the 3:00 flight to Dallas come over here."

I managed to be first in line. The ticket agent looked at me, smiled, and said, "The 3:00 flight to Dallas has been canceled." I enthusiastically responded, "Fantastic!" With a puzzled expression on her face, the ticket agent asked, "Now, why in the world would you say 'fantastic' when I just told you that the 3:00 flight to Dallas has been canceled?" "Ma'am, I said, there are only three reasons why anybody would cancel a flight to Dallas, Texas. Number one, something must be wrong with that airplane; number two, something must be wrong with the person who is going to fly that airplane; and number three, something must be wrong with the weather they're going to fly that airplane in. Now, ma'am, if any one of those three situations exists, I don't want to be up there. I want to be right down here! Fantastic!"

In a tone that was almost challenging, the agent said, "Yes, but the next flight doesn't leave until 6:05." To that I responded, "Fantastic!"

The lady looked at me in complete shock and said, "Now I'm really puzzled. Why in the world would you say 'fantastic' when I've just told you that you've got a four-hour wait in the airport in Kansas City?" I smilingly said, "Never before have I had a chance to spend four hours in the airport in Kansas City. Do you realize there are people on the face of this earth who are cold and hungry? But here I am in a beautiful facility, and even though it's cold outside, it's comfortable inside. I'm going to go down to the coffee shop, relax for a few minutes, and enjoy a cup of coffee. Then I'm going to finish some important work that I need to do, and here I am in easily the biggest, most comfortable, rent-free office I've ever had at my disposal. Fantastic!"

To this you might well say, "Okay, Ziglar, tell me the truth — did you *really* feel that way?" To this I respond, "Of course not!" At least not initially. Like most travelers I would have preferred to be on my way home, but for the next four hours I did not have that option. However, I did have two other options. I could have chosen to *respond* — which is positive — or I could have chosen to *react* — which is negative. I chose to respond. You can't tailor-make the situations in life, but you can tailor-make the attitudes to fit those situations before they arise.

When the ticket agent told me that my flight had been canceled, I could have reacted sarcastically, *and the next flight would still have left at 6:05!*

Now, my reading friend, there are some things you simply aren't going to change. The *yesterdays* of your life will remain the same, but *tomorrow* is a different matter. In network marketing, people will promise to be at a meeting and not show up. Others will promise to get started next week, and in the meantime, they decide not to get involved at all. Still others will start for a day or two and, after two or three rejections (which really are not rejections but simply refusals to get involved in an outstanding business opportunity), will disappoint you by not doing anything.

At this point, you make a choice. If you choose to react and get upset, your blood pressure will go up, your chances for a stroke will increase, and you won't do one single thing to build your business. What you need to do is simply smile and say, "You know, John and Zig told me this was going to happen, so I understand. But I'm not going to let one or two or even 102 people dictate my future. I know my offer is great and the possibilities are unlimited. I'm simply going to hurry and talk to the next person as quickly as I can." That's the way to build your network marketing business.

Celebrate Your Victories

Getting a prospect to attend an opportunity meeting or listen in on a conference call; getting a sale, even a tiny sale; helping an associate achieve a goal; improving one of your skills — all these events are worthy of celebration. People often get so involved in their business that they gloss over the little victories that need to be celebrated. As a network marketer, you can achieve victories every day in your business. Network marketers thrive on victories and celebrations. Look for the little victories and celebrate them.

One of the truly outstanding things about network marketing is that praise and recognition are given so freely and often. Nothing brings a bigger smile to a face than when someone you've brought into the business, nurtured, and trained walks across an award stage to the applause of his associates and the gleam in the eyes of his mate and/or children. Such recognition really boosts his confidence and makes him feel important because it comes as a direct result of his having done something. It can be just a "little" victory, but for the individual, it can be huge and spur him on to even greater heights.

Ray Velasquez was beaming with pride. He had sponsored Richard Conway of Mt. Vernon, Missouri, into the Zig Ziglar Network (ZZN), and now Richard, who's currently our top producer, was presenting the ZZN business opportunity to a group of prospects in St. Louis, Missouri. As Richard talked about his personal testimony as a network marketer and about the thrill he was experiencing, the income he was enjoying, and the people he was getting to meet, everybody was smiling and laughing. But Ray's smile was the biggest and happiest.

The message is clear: Look for the good, and give lots of praise when you see someone in your downline doing something of significance. Doubly praise your associates when you see them attending training sessions and opportunity meetings to learn more and pick up the feeling of network marketing.

Don't Take Defeat Personally

Tim Sales, one of the most successful Nu Skin distributors, selling nutritional and skincare products, says that he will never forget the lady who cried while she told him how much she wanted to build a house for her mom, and that she was joining his sales organization to fulfill that life's dream. Tim had already helped eight people reach $30,000 a month in income, so he was confident that he could help this woman, who was so moved that tears dripped off her nose while she talked to him.

"We mapped out a plan for her to reach her goal," Tim recalls, "and when she left my house, I thought, 'This lady is real. I can help her get that dream.' But two days later I couldn't get in touch with her! I left messages, and she would not call back. Finally I got her on the phone one morning, and she told me she had quit. I wanted to know why, so I offered to give her money back to her if she would tell me what happened. She took me up on it, and it was an eye-opening experience." The lady explained to Tim that her brother-in-law was first on her warm list, but when she called him to interest him in the business, he told her that she had given up her money for a scam. Furthermore, he told her that it was unethical for her to ask her family and friends for their money just to get into the same scam!

"I was stunned," Tim recalls. "I couldn't respond to her. I found myself sitting in my backyard by the pool thinking, 'That's so true. The dream stealers are everywhere.' As passionate as she was when we set her goals, this lady could not realize that this wasn't a scam. Furthermore, she was unwilling to do her own research to resolve these issues for herself and her brother-in-law. She allowed one person to defeat her and wipe out a dream that she could have accomplished."

At that moment, Tim came up with a plan to help everyone in his downline (and network marketers everywhere). He decided to create a generic tool that shunned hype and told people the truth about network marketing. "We needed a way to give distributors the facts," he said, "and give them a tool so their prospects would get a non-hyped, yet promotional explanation about network marketing. Yes, they were going to meet defeat, people were going to tell them no and laugh behind their backs, but if they knew the truth, they wouldn't have to take defeat personally."

In 1999, shortly after Tim's personal brainstorm, he wrote and produced his video, titled "Brilliant Compensation." You can view the online version at his Web site: www.brilliantcompensation.com. Tim gives the content of the video, and the principles that are taught, much of the credit for helping him build a $25 million business that operates in 24 countries.

Look for Opportunities to Help Others

Anyone who knows anything about me knows about my Golden Rule philosophy. I speak about it in Chapter 11, but here it is once again: You can have everything in life you want if you will just help enough other people get what they want.

For long-term success to be yours in network marketing, you must work with this Golden Rule philosophy. Understand that this is a philosophy and not a tactic. You're dead wrong if you think that you can follow the concept, "I'm going to do something for you because I expect you to eventually do even more for me." That's ugly — and that approach just won't work in the industry or in life.

If you're involved with a network marketing company that believes otherwise, I encourage you to look carefully at your conscience and examine companies that do not deal that way. You can make a few bucks in most cases when you bring somebody into the business; but the real joy, security, and substantial income come as you work with the people you bring in, helping them to become successful. The neat thing is that the more you help others become successful, the more successful you will be. If you bring 1,000 people in and none of them does anything other than join, you've wasted a lot of time and killed a lot of dreams. Your responsibility is to teach, encourage, and develop the people you bring into your organization.

Keep in mind, however, that you're responsible *to* the people you sponsor and not *for* them. Some of them simply join for social reasons and may have little or no interest in really working to build an organization. They're perfectly willing for you to build it for them, but you quickly learn who those people are, and then you wisely invest your time in those who take the business seriously and start to work with their downlines.

Based on 30 years' experience in training in the industry, I can assure you that those who enjoy all the benefits of life (which we've identified as happiness, good health, some degree of prosperity, security, friends, peace of mind, good family relationships, and the hope that the future is going to be better) are the people who follow the Golden Rule philosophy of life. Those who come into network marketing for the wrong reasons may end up with some of the bucks, but they'll miss out on all the things that money can't buy.

Practice Your Affirmations Daily

Remember to use your self-talk affirmations, which we discuss in more detail in Chapter 3. Some people think that repeating affirmations every morning and evening is silly. It may be, but remember this: After you establish in your mind what you're capable of doing and you get a glimpse of your potential, passion is born! And when passion is born, performance takes monumental leaps forward.

You can change who you are and where you are by changing what goes into your mind!

Maintain a Balanced Life

The "hot" topic of today is one that's been "hot" with me for many years — namely, how do you maintain a balanced life? First, consider that to maintain a balanced life, you must deal with your personal, family, business, physical, mental, spiritual, and financial life. A common complaint is, "We're working so hard to get ahead that we don't have time to balance our lives." That simply isn't true. Lack of time is not really the problem; lack of organization and priorities is the problem.

If I were to ask you whether you were honest and at least reasonably intelligent, you would admit that you qualified on both counts. Then if I were to ask you, an honest, intelligent person, whether you got twice as much work done on the day before you go on vacation, you would probably acknowledge that you did.

If planning one day in your business life doubles your productivity, doesn't it make sense that you could bring more balance into your personal life and family life if you planned those areas of your life as well? I'll bet you would agree that you could. And if planning one day of your life has such a huge impact, think what planning your whole life would do for you!

Running your day by the clock and your life with a vision helps you to keep things in perspective. You must deal not only with personal, family, and career issues but also with the physical, mental, and spiritual aspects of life. You also must factor in time for the financial aspect of your life.

Balance does not mean that you spend the same amount of time on each area of life. That would be ridiculous. For example, of the 168 hours in each week, you probably invest 50 percent of that time taking care of your physical needs. You should get eight hours of sleep every night because research says if you don't, you're cheating your body. Remember to factor in your time to prepare for bed and then prepare for work the next morning; that alone uses up several hours of your week.

You probably eat about 20 meals every week, and some people may eat even more than that. If you set aside only 30 minutes for each of those meals and count waiting time, shopping time, cooking time, and so on, there's an additional ten hours. Then if you exercise for 30 minutes four times a week, you add two more hours. So, with half the week already gone (from a time point of view), you must bring the half that includes the spiritual, mental, financial, career, and family into balance. We call this "prioritizing."

What is really important to you? Is the path you're on going to enable you to live well and finish well? (The last part may be more important than the first part!) Do you understand that regardless of how well you plan, some circumstances will throw your life out of balance? For instance, you or a family member may face a debilitating accident or illness or a drug or alcohol problem. Maybe you need a change in direction and decide to go back to school for more education. Getting involved in network marketing can represent a change that requires balance. That's the reason a goals program is of extraordinary importance.

I run my life on a pretty tight schedule, but my schedule works only because I prioritize. My relationship with the Redhead (my wife, Jean) is more important than my work. While at home, my wife and I spend roughly an hour together at breakfast. The same is true at lunch and again at dinner. I do most of my writing in my home office, which makes spending time with the Redhead very convenient. That's one of the reasons, along with a few others, that we're still together after almost 54 years, and happier and more in love than ever. We court each other every day, regardless of what else is going on in our lives.

Is my life balanced all the time? Of course not. I recently finished a six-week professional commitment that no intelligent person would have attempted. Yet during those six weeks I was able to maintain my marriage relationship and my spiritual life as the two top priorities, even though I devoted most of my time to my professional obligations.

In network marketing, you work mostly from your home as you prepare sales presentations, schedule appointments, make telephone calls, send faxes and e-mails, and handle other details of your business. This type of work gives you a huge advantage and a marvelous opportunity to spend time with your family, not just once or twice but several times a day. Because you organize your own schedule, you can include them in it, and if they're willing to help with some of your work tasks, you're sure to get far more done.

Make Success a Habit

In *Success For Dummies,* I devote an entire chapter to the fact that success is a habit. Here are some of the ideas and how you can adapt them to network marketing.

- ✔ In the world of sports, athletes sometimes get in a "zone." A golfer can't miss a ten-foot putt. A pitcher finds the strike zone with every pitch. A quarterback throws the ball on a clothesline to a wide receiver streaking downfield. The same thing happens in network marketing because not only is success a habit, but success begets success. The best time to sponsor somebody into the business is right after you have sponsored someone else because you "get on a roll." The excitement and enthusiasm you generate make a huge difference in your effectiveness. You build what we call an "expectancy" in the mind of the performer.

- ✔ Research proves that parental expectancy has a direct bearing on a child's performance. Teacher expectancy has a direct bearing on a pupil's performance. And employer expectancy has a direct bearing on an employee's performance. This belief is even truer in network marketing. Your own excitement and enthusiasm about the person you've just brought into the business, and that person's willingness to take the training and make the commitment, followed by an honest effort, build an expectancy in your mind. You then communicate that expectancy back to the person you've just trained or sponsored.

For further information that will be very helpful to you in your network marketing career, I strongly encourage you to pick up a copy of *Success For Dummies,* which, incidentally, Wal-Mart made its "motivational book of the year." Wal-Mart also bought thousands of copies for its assistant managers and managers. The book is one of the fastest-selling *For Dummies* books ever. You bet I'm proud of that!

Chapter 24

Ten Questions That You'll Probably Ask about Network Marketing

*W*hat comes to mind when you hear someone mention network marketing or multi-level marketing? If you've never been involved in network marketing before, and if you're even just a little bit curious, several questions are likely to pop up immediately. Most, if not all, of your questions are answered in the pages of this book. However, we chose ten of the most commonly asked questions and answered them in this chapter for your convenience. Once you understand what this profession is all about, it will be easier for you to evaluate whether or not it makes sense for you to get involved. If you do get involved, then you'll be able to confidently explain to others how network marketing works. If you don't get involved, well, that's okay, too, but at least you'll be the wiser when the topic of network marketing is introduced in your presence.

Do I Need a Lot of Capital to Become a Network Marketer?

No. Your upfront investment will range from $20 to $500 in most instances. If you're asked to pay more, find out why! Beware of companies that require you to purchase large amounts of inventory. This is called *front-loading*, and regulators frown on it. There's no need to stockpile products.

After your initial investment, you most likely will be required to purchase a limited amount of products each month to remain active in the network and to qualify for certain commission and bonus money. This investment is usually in the range of $100 a month. (See "Do I Need to Buy Products or Services Every Month?" for more about this purchase.)

You may need money for several reasons after the initial investment:

- **Travel to meetings:** Although your local network may sponsor weekly meetings in your city or area, regional and national meetings may require you to travel and spend a night or two in a hotel. These meetings are not mandatory, but they can help you further develop your skills, as well as motivate and inspire you.

- **Lead generation:** As we explain in Chapters 10 and 11, you probably will be encouraged to develop a list of your friends, family, neighbors, and associates — your *warm list.* Some people choose not to develop this list, however, or they exhaust the list within a few weeks. At that point, you may need to develop leads on your own or as part of a lead co-op.

Going on your own is costly, even when you know what you're doing. You have to place ads in newspapers or on the radio, or perhaps implement a direct-mail program to generate leads. By joining a co-op, you may be able to reduce your advertising expenditures. Rather than purchasing a $1,000 advertisement yourself, you and nine other networkers can contribute $100 each to pay for the advertising. Keep in mind, however, that you will receive only one-tenth of the leads generated, provided that the advertising program works at all!

- **Certification training:** After you join a network marketing company, you should expect to receive basic training at little or no cost. If the training occurs at a public facility, such as a hotel, you may be required to pay $10 to $20 to help cover the costs of the room rental. However, some companies certify their associates to conduct training sessions nationwide. These certification sessions almost always require a fee, ranging from $150 to $1,000 or more. You are not obligated to sign up for any of these sessions, but if you want the certification, you have to pay the fees.

Do I Need to Buy Products or Services Every Month?

Yes. (See "Do I Need a Lot of Capital to Become a Network Marketer?") Keep in mind that you will probably purchase products or services that you would use anyway, such as vitamins, long-distance service, or household goods. "The first thing I tell people when they join Nutrition for Life International (NFLI)," says Dayle Maloney, "is to walk through their house with our catalog and look at what they're already buying that they could buy from NFLI. They'll be surprised — now they can buy (at wholesale prices) a lot of what they need from their own company."

Successful selling involves transference of feeling. Persuading people to join you in the network and use your company's products definitely is selling. If you fervently believe in the company you represent and have a passion for succeeding with that company, the person you're attempting to sponsor will pick up on that feeling. Although he or she may not completely understand the proposal, he or she will buy your passion and belief in the opportunity you're selling. The same is true of the product. You must believe in it to transfer that feeling to others.

A story I tell in my book *Zig Ziglar's Secrets of Closing the Sale* is a perfect example of transference of feeling. A number of years ago when I was in the waterless cookware business, I was having a banner year. A friend of mine in the same position in the company was having a really tough time. One day over a cup of coffee in his home, my friend Bill was really singing the blues. I looked at him and said, "I know what the problem is." He quickly responded that I should tell him what it was because he certainly needed help — he was struggling.

With that I said to Bill, "Your problem is that you don't believe in your product yourself." Bill retorted angrily that he most certainly did and reminded me that he had left his former company as a manager and came aboard this company as a salesman. Then I said, "You can peddle that to others, Bill, but I happen to know you — and I know for a fact that you don't really believe in this product." And with that, I nodded toward the kitchen.

Bill exclaimed, "Oh! You mean that I'm not using our cookware here at home!" I said, "Exactly." Then he went into great detail explaining all his difficulties. His wife had been in the hospital for three weeks and had no insurance. It looked like his boys were going to have to have their tonsils out, and still no insurance. Not only that, but his car had broken down and for a month he had had to depend on buses and taxis for transportation, and that was a lousy way of trying to sell successfully. Then he ended his story by saying, "Zig, I'm going to get a set of the cookware as soon as I can. I do believe in the product!"

To this I responded, "Let me explain something to you, Bill. When you are in front of a prospect and you're in the closing process, the prospect says to you, 'Bill, I'd love to have a set of the cookware, but you see, we're having a tough time. My wife's been in the hospital for three weeks and we don't have insurance. Now it looks like our two boys are going to have to go in for tonsillectomies — and still no insurance. On top of that, for a month I've not had transportation. My car's been in the shop and I've had to use buses and taxis — and you simply can't make it without good transportation.'"

Then I smiled as I said to Bill, "No, Bill, no prospect has ever given you exactly the same excuses that you have given me, but they have excuses of their own. And though you might be saying to yourself, 'Now, think positive,

Bill, think positive,' deep down, as they give their excuses, internally you are saying, 'Yeah, I know exactly what you mean. That's the very reason I don't have a set of the stuff myself!'"

I sold Bill a set of the cookware. Obviously, he wrote his own order, but that week he sold enough additional cookware to pay for his own set — and he was off to the races! If you don't believe in your company and opportunity enough to work at it, and if you don't believe in the products you sell enough to use them yourself, you may as well resign your position now because your future is not going to be very bright.

Yes, selling is transference of feeling. In the Zig Ziglar Network, we repeatedly tell people that you've got to be a product of the product in order to be successful in the business. I'm going to tell you exactly the same thing: You've got to be a product of the product to the degree that you're quite comfortable using the product yourself and selling it to your closest friends and family because you know that it's for their benefit.

Will I Need to Store Products and Then Deliver Them to My Customers?

Yes and no. Many network marketing companies save their representatives the time and hassle involved in warehousing and delivering products by direct-shipping products to customers. In other words, your customer places an order and pays by check or credit card, and the product is shipped to the customer's address. You're not involved in the process.

In other companies, however (particularly those that sell products at home parties), all orders may be shipped to the representative for the representative to deliver to the customers. This process demands storage space as well as additional time and travel on your part, but many representatives see it as an opportunity to sell more products!

Do I Have to Work Full-Time to Make Money?

No. In fact, most network marketers devote only part of their weeks to their network marketing businesses. The majority of network marketers do not expect to earn hundreds of thousands or millions of dollars; they're looking for an additional $300 to $400 a month. Many, in fact, work the business to earn just enough to pay for their own monthly purchases. If you expect to earn more than a couple thousand dollars a month, however, you should expect to work full-time. For more on this issue, please see Chapters 1 and 3.

This Is Just Another Get-Rich-Quick Scheme, Right?

Wrong! Someone may have told you that network marketing is a scheme, but it is a legitimate practice. In 1979, after six years of investigating Amway, the Federal Trade Commission ruled that Amway's multi-level marketing structure is legal and proper. Amway became the benchmark for other legitimate network marketing companies.

Yes, some scoundrels have participated in network marketing. But scoundrels have also been involved in franchising, as well as in the insurance and medical professions, to name just a few. Those who get the facts about network marketing will discover that it is a solid, long-term business opportunity. We discuss this issue in depth in Chapter 2.

Network Marketing Isn't a Real Business, Is It?

Yes, it is! Just because network marketers work from home, and most work part-time, doesn't mean that their businesses aren't real. Network marketing is not a hobby. It's a serious business, and anyone who becomes a network marketer must comply with all local, state, and federal laws that govern the operation of small businesses. That means you may need a license to operate from your home or an office away from home. You may need to register your business name with your state. You may need to incorporate your business. You definitely need to consult with an accountant and a tax advisor.

Ask your sponsor for information about establishing your business. Then read Chapters 9 and 10 for more about getting started in network marketing.

Is Network Marketing the Same as Multi-Level Marketing?

Basically, yes. Many American companies avoid referring to themselves as multi-level marketing, or MLM, companies because of the stigma historically attached to the term (described in the following paragraph).

If any difference exists between network marketing and multi-level marketing, it has to do with the much-frowned-upon practice of front-loading products. In the past, many MLM companies required distributors to purchase large amounts of inventory; store it in a garage, basement, or separate storage facility; and sell it over time. Many distributors either didn't try to sell the inventory or tried and failed. In some instances, the inventory spoiled or was destroyed by extreme temperatures or flooding. These problems weren't swept under the carpet. Quite often, they were publicized, and these tales of woe contributed to MLM's negative reputation.

Beyond North American borders, however, the term *MLM* has not been tarnished. "In Asia and Europe," says magazine publisher Ridgely Goldsborough, "MLM is what it's all about. Any company trying to develop outside the U.S. would be making a mistake not to use the term."

How Often Do I Have to Attend Meetings?

First, you don't *have to* attend meetings. There are no requirements for doing so. However, most network marketing companies sponsor several meetings annually to gather their distributors, reward them for their successes, announce new products, provide additional training, and (perhaps most importantly) recruit new distributors. Not participating in these meetings would be a mistake.

Locally, representatives of your company may meet every week, or at least once a month. Most people enjoy these meetings. They provide you an opportunity to be around positive, eager, and like-minded people.

If My Spouse Isn't Involved in the Business, Is That a Problem?

It could be a problem if your spouse doesn't support your commitment to your network marketing business; it's advisable to have your spouse's support *before* you get involved. Your spouse may object to the time you spend on the telephone or away from home attending meetings, too.

If you can, get your spouse involved. Doing so may require time, but I've heard countless stories of husbands who gave up full-time careers to join their wives in a network marketing business and vice versa. We include a few of these stories in this book. Here's one good example:

"It took me a while to convince my wife that I hadn't lost my mind when I said I wanted to give up our real estate business and join Excel Communications," recalls Russ Noland in Houston, Texas. "I worked on her for several months, and finally she decided to go to an opportunity meeting with me, just to put a stop to the whole thing. But she's smarter than I am. When she saw the opportunity, it made sense to her, and she wrote the check to our sponsor to get started immediately." Now the Nolands are among the top earners at Excel, which markets long-distance phone service.

If Network Marketing Is a Global Phenomenon, How Come I Rarely Hear About It in the Media?

Network marketing exists in at least 125 countries; it's approaching $100 billion in sales globally, driven by 35 million distributors worldwide, according to the Direct Selling Association (see Chapter 1). Then why do you hardly ever read or see any mention of this phenomenon in the media? That would be a good question to ask the business editor of your local newspaper!

Traditional business media respond slowly to anything but traditional business topics. Consider franchising: You hear about it more often today than you did ten years ago, and that's largely because the International Franchise Association, and hundreds of its member companies, have mounted a persistent media campaign designed to educate traditional business writers and editors. Even so, franchising gets less attention than it deserves, and often that attention is negative rather than positive. The situation is similar for network marketing. Many members of the media don't consider network marketing a legitimate profession, and even while they're wrong (as we've demonstrated in this book), if network marketing gets any publicity, it's likely to be negative.

Tim Sales, who produced the video "Brilliant Compensation" at www.brilliant compensation.com, recalls a conversation that he had with a reporter from a major business newspaper who was preparing to write an article about pyramid schemes. "It sounded to me like he was going to write another negative article about network marketing," Tim recalls, "so I said to him, 'Why bother? Ninety-nine percent of the readers are not going to care, and all you're going to do is hammer the network marketers.' I offered him a really good story angle about the big-name brand companies that at the time were just beginning to use network marketing as a distribution channel. He could have written about AT&T, Texas Instruments, and Coca-Cola, who were all partnering with network marketing companies. But he said his editor wasn't interested in that *kind* of story. Apparently they didn't want to tell the positive side of the business." Someday, perhaps, this situation will change, but it probably won't be anytime soon. Meanwhile, you can read about network marketing in these publications: *Money Maker's Monthly* (www.mmmonthly.com), *Business Opportunities Journal* (www.boj.com), *Upline* (www.upline.com), *Network Marketing Lifestyles* (www.nmlifestyles.com), and a host of online newsletters, such as *The Difference Maker* (subscribe by sending a blank e-mail to info@zigziglar.com with "Subscribe DM" on the subject line), published by Ziglar Training Systems.

Chapter 25

Ten Ways to Get a Quick Start in Network Marketing

*T*iming is everything (almost) in network marketing. It's never more critical than in the first week (maybe even days) after you join a network marketing company. You've got to be interested, excited, and "sold" on network marketing before you'll join a company, but then — unless you get started quickly — you may lose your enthusiasm for the business overnight. Protect yourself! Hopefully you'll sign up with a company and an upline that understand the importance of you seeing some results as soon as possible. It's unreasonable, however, to think that you can join a company one day and recruit a distributor the next day. Until you get your start-up kit and review the company's materials and familiarize yourself with its systems, it'll be difficult to sell someone else on the opportunity. Nevertheless, you need to have a game plan because it's human nature to want to get started *now!* Therefore, we are providing ten steps that you can follow to make sure you get a quick start in your business.

By the way, the distributors you'll eventually recruit and sponsor will also need to see results as soon as possible. You can spend weeks contacting prospective distributors, talking to them, sharing information, and selling them on your opportunity. Finally they sign up, and what happens? If you're busy recruiting the next distributor and not paying attention to the distributor who joined yesterday, nothing happens! Well, that's not entirely true. What happens is that your new distributor quits even before getting started! That's discouraging for them and for you. Don't let it happen. Follow our game plan.

Find a Good Company and Join It

Chapters 4 through 8 are loaded with ideas to help you find the network marketing company that suits your personality, interests, and abilities. Take time to read these chapters, study them, and follow our suggestions. By doing the research that we suggest, you can save yourself from joining the wrong company. However, be careful not to become overwhelmed by the process of finding and joining a company. "Don't agonize over this decision," says Russ Noland, one of the top associates at Excel Communications and a much-sought-after trainer. "What's it going to cost you to get involved? Fifty, two hundred, five hundred dollars? If it works, it works. If it doesn't . . . well, you've probably spent more money than that on something else and didn't even have a good time."

There's a company out there for you. Find it and join it!

Get Involved with the Intent to Succeed

Although we don't suggest that you write an elaborate business plan, we do urge you to think about why you're joining a network marketing company. What do you hope to achieve? If you don't think that you have a reasonable chance of realizing your goals in network marketing, or you think that your chances of succeeding with a particular company are marginal at best, why bother? Do something else with your time and money.

One of my favorite phrases is "ya gotta wanna." No, the grammar isn't the best, but the message is crystal clear. It has been said (and I completely agree) that desire is what changes the hot water of mediocrity to the steam of outstanding success. If your conviction is strong that your cause is just and you really do want to make a difference in the lives of others while building your own career and benefiting your family and society in general, your chances of being successful greatly increase.

Many years ago, I encountered a young man who was a victim of polio and was on crutches. He had attended one of our seminars and was persuaded that he could be a speaker. As I talked with him and looked into his eyes, I saw intensity that one seldom sees in a young man. He said, "Zig, the only part of me that doesn't get up and run is these legs. But these crutches get me where I want to go, and my imagination is very active, and I want to go places as a speaker." And then with a serious look on his face he said, "As a matter of fact, Zig, I can *taste* it, I can *feel* it — it's in my bones and I'm going to do whatever it takes to reach this objective."

I lost touch with this young man for about five years, and then one day I got the story. He was not only speaking, but doing so quite successfully, and he was very busy in the process of changing lives and helping other people. You see, helping others was his motive to begin with. That's the network marketing attitude you should have if you expect to succeed in the business.

Be Selective about Your Upline

Say you've found a company that you want to join. You've done your homework and you're ready to get involved. Before you sign the company's agreement and hand over your money, be sure you're comfortable with your intended sponsor. Your sponsor is your lifeline to success in this business. He's the first person you'll look to for a quick start in the business.

Chapter 10 goes into detail about how you can look to your upline for help after you join a network marketing company. It's important to feel comfortable with your upline. Do you like her personality? Is she well organized? Is he dependable — did he call you when he said he would call you or send you information when he said he would? Are you confident that your upline can teach you the ropes of the business?

You don't have to sign up with the first person who offers to sponsor you in network marketing. Unfortunately, many people don't realize that. Take your time, ask questions, feel comfortable, and then commit to a specific sponsor. This is an important step because it's not easy to switch sponsors after you've joined a company. If you want to move out of your sponsor's downline and into a different downline, the company might require your entire upline to approve the transfer. It only takes one person to say "no" and you're stuck! So take your time and choose wisely. It doesn't happen often enough, but some prospective network marketers interview their would-be sponsors in advance of joining a downline.

As Soon as Your Kit Arrives, Contact Your Sponsor

After you complete a distributor application and submit it, it normally takes four to ten days for your start-up kit to arrive. (In some instances, you may be able to pick up your kit at company headquarters or at a company-sponsored meeting.) While you're waiting for the kit, see Chapters 9 and 10 for ideas about how to utilize your time so that when the kit arrives, you'll be ready to get a quick start toward building your business.

When you get your kit, contact your sponsor immediately. A good sponsor knows the contents of the start-up kit, and she will be eager to begin coaching you by phone, in person, via the Internet, or some combination of these communication methods.

Do yourself a favor and follow your sponsor's advice. If you do the homework that we suggest you do throughout this book, you will select a company that has developed a series of systems for its representatives to follow. By following the systems, you can expect to succeed. A good sponsor has mastered the systems and will begin transferring that knowledge to you.

Depending on the contents of your start-up kit, your sponsor may need to meet with you for several hours over a period of a week or two. The kit is likely to include a distributor's manual that lists the rules and regulations of the company, along with product information and the company's compensation plan. It should also include materials to help you build your confidence and your skills for a successful career in network marketing.

Learn One Good Lead-Generating Technique and Use It

Most people who get into network marketing are encouraged to create a warm list of prospects — that is, a list of friends, family, neighbors, and associates who may be interested in purchasing products or services, and possibly even getting involved in the business. Not everyone is ready to use this lead-generating plan when they first start their businesses, however. If you find yourself in that situation, you have to depend on alternative lead-generating methods, such as cold-calling prospects, using direct mail, placing ads in newspapers, or prospecting via the Internet. (No spamming, please!)

Discuss lead generation with your sponsor and find out which techniques work best for your business. Find a technique that you would like to use and start using it! In a short period of time, you will master it. See Chapters 14, 16, and 17 for lots of information about lead-generating techniques.

Learn How to Make Your Presentation

Whether you plan to sell products and services first or your business opportunity first, learn how to make the sales presentation. Again, you should expect your sponsor or company to provide you with a system for mastering this aspect of your new career. The system should give you the words to use and also explain why you use those words, or why you're being taught to make the presentation in a certain manner.

The Zig Ziglar Network start-up kit

One of the prime products in the start-up kit for the Zig Ziglar Network is this very book. John Hayes and I believe that the information in this book will be extraordinarily helpful to the people in our network, just as we are firmly convinced that it will be very helpful in your network. Not only do *we* believe it, but based on what our friends in network marketing tell us, they fully intend to order many of these books for their organizations as well.

In addition, we've created and included in our materials a series of "Ziggets" for network marketers — a taped series consisting of methods for handling objections, among other things. The videos run from 7 to 15 minutes in length and are designed for short, high-impact training/informational/motivational sessions that assist not only new people in the industry but veterans as well. The neat thing is that you can reference them at any time or build a training session around each one. For more information about Ziggets, send a blank e-mail to ziggets@zigziglar.com.

Most people have to practice the presentation repeatedly before they feel comfortable presenting it. That's why you have a sponsor! You can listen to your sponsor make presentations and then practice on your sponsor.

TIP

"I feel utterly ridiculous using the presentation my company gave me." We've heard that said before, and it's usually from a network marketer who's struggling to succeed. If you don't feel comfortable using your company's sales presentation, you have a couple of choices. First, *get comfortable!* It could be that you haven't practiced the presentation often enough. Give it more time. Hook up with your sponsor and practice, practice, practice. Second, develop your own presentation. We hesitate to mention this choice because it's almost always a mistake. If you're going to join a company and then reinvent it, why bother? Good sales presentations are written, tested, rewritten, and retested, and the process continues until the presentation gets results. Do you have the ability to write and perfect a sales presentation?

In order to use the company's presentation, you may have to stretch a bit. You may feel uncomfortable, especially at first. However, our experience is that once the results begin to occur, you don't mind feeling ridiculous. In fact, you no longer will!

REMEMBER

It's important to do your homework in network marketing, as we discuss in Chapters 4 through 8. Before you join a company, listen to the company's sales presentation and consider whether or not you can make the presentation without feeling ridiculous. If you can't, look for another company! On the other hand, don't pass up what could be a great opportunity simply because you're shy, or you don't want to step out of your comfort zone and learn a sales presentation.

Make Your First Real Presentation with Your Sponsor's Support

You have a prospect who's at least mildly interested in joining your business or buying your products or services. This will be your first *real* presentation! Up to now, you've been practicing your presentation on your sponsor, as well as family and friends — some of whom may have responded favorably and even purchased products or joined you in business. Whether you make this first presentation by phone or in person, get your sponsor involved. If you're going to use the telephone, arrange a three-way conference call so that you, your prospect, and your sponsor can be on the line at the same time. If you need help or you're asked a question that you can't answer, your sponsor will be there to back you up.

You may want your sponsor to help you with the first half-dozen (or more) presentations that you make. Even if you've never done anything like this before, you *will* eventually feel confident enough to make presentations on your own.

You may think that you don't need help in making presentations. Perhaps you've been successful as a salesperson in a past profession. Look out! Seasoned salespeople are often the least successful in network marketing, at least initially. Give yourself the advantage of your sponsor's support and guidance.

Commit to Share Your Business with Three or More People Daily

Even if you're working only part-time as a network marketer, you can share your business opportunity, or information about your products and services, with at least three people a day, six days a week. You should commit to a minimum of 18 weekly contacts. If you're a full-time network marketer, you may be able to hit that number every day!

How can you fulfill this commitment? It's easy when you consider all the possibilities. Can you pick up the phone and talk to three people a day? Consult your warm list and start making calls. Or use the mail, e-mail, or fax machine. If you're employed, what do you do at lunchtime? Could you spend lunch with a different co-worker every day and get around to talking about your business? How about attending local meetings, seminars, and workshops that are not related to your business? Spend a Saturday morning at a trade show sponsored by your local Chamber of Commerce, for example, and you may be able to speak with several dozen prospects.

Be careful when you attend events that are not related to your business. Your house of worship isn't the appropriate place to present your network marketing opportunity! Use common sense and tact. Don't offend people before you have a reasonable chance to recruit them as customers or distributors.

One thing is for certain: Products, services, and business opportunities are not capable of presenting themselves. You have to handle that part.

Network marketing is a numbers game. The more people who hear your presentation, the better your chances of building your business. Most people are going to say no, but eventually you'll discover that for every X number of people you contact, Y number of people say yes. Figure out the numbers game for your business and then work it!

Attend All the Meetings You Can

One huge benefit of attending meetings is the opportunity to meet and listen to "unimpressive" people who are making it big in network marketing. Although their education may or may not be limited; they are honest, sincere, hard-working people who have a passion for what they do, and believe with all their hearts that they have a great product and an incredible opportunity. They transfer that belief to the people they meet and, in the process, enjoy enormous success in the business. Even if you've found the world's greatest sponsor, you have much to learn from other professional network marketers in your organization. So get to those meetings! Perhaps the greatest benefit of attending meetings is that you can learn from the leaders in your company. Often you can sit down with them one on one to talk about ideas, challenges, and discomforts.

Don't assume that the leaders aren't interested in helping you. One of the reasons successful network marketers remain network marketers is the opportunity to coach others and watch them fulfill their dreams.

Always Continue Learning So That You Can Improve Your Skills

Someday, you may know everything there is to know about network marketing. But until then, you have a lot to learn. A good network marketing company will sponsor several training events a year to help you build your network marketing skills. Beyond your company, many excellent training programs (several of them are mentioned throughout this book) are targeted to network marketers.

Kathy Smith, who sells for Discovery Toys, credits sales trainer Tom Hopkins for helping her advance in network marketing. "I've been to several Tom Hopkins boot camps," she explains, "and he put it [the profession] all together for me. He doesn't come from network marketing, but from sales, and he tells you the words to say to be effective when you make a presentation." Another Discovery Toys networker, Jan Ruhe, says that training programs by Zig Ziglar and Jim Rohn helped her understand how to succeed in network marketing. Now Jan, who lives in Aspen, Colorado, offers her own training program for networkers: the Annual Aspen MLM Nuts $ Bolts Seminar Weekend (see www.janruhe.com).

As an individual, you should always aim for personal growth. Things are changing rather rapidly, and failure to change can bring disastrous results. I like to tell the story of Larry Carpenter, a wholesome personification of the American dream. He lives a balanced life and is successful in each area of his life. Larry says that much of his success is due to the Born to Win seminar sponsored by Zig Ziglar Corporation. He drove his 200,000-mile Toyota to his first one, maxing out his credit card to make the investment in the program. For 19 consecutive years, Larry has attended Born to Win. What does he learn each year? Always something, but the main thing is that he is constantly reminded of the process leading to balanced success.

Zig Ziglar Corporation is now offering "Born to Win for Network Marketing," which we believe is going to make a difference in the lives of those who attend. It's a how-to seminar in which the attendees are taken through the process of setting goals; building a strong, healthy self-image; developing good relationships; maintaining the right attitude; and making motivation permanent. Getting a quick start in network marketing is far easier when you've already invested time in becoming the best *you* you can be. For free information about "Born to Win for Network Marketing," send an e-mail message to info@zigziglar.com and type **BTWNM** on the subject line.

Appendix

Glossary of Terms

· ·

*E*very profession has its own lingo, and network marketing isn't any different. Spend just a little time with a group of network marketers, and they can have your head spinning with terms such as *upline, downline, generation, leg, matrix, roll-up, breakaway, frontline, front-loading,* and many others. Even more confusing, the definitions of some terms vary from company to company. But don't you worry! This handy glossary will keep you from getting cross-line of your downline. It may even save you from becoming a multi-level junkie!

Accumulated group volume: Also called *group volume, group purchasing volume,* or *GPV.* Refers to the personal sales of a distributor in combination with the sales of that distributor's downline. This definition varies from company to company. For some, the volume may be accumulated for a defined pay period, such as one week or one month. For others, it may be accumulated over an unlimited period of time. In most instances, distributors are required to reach a certain level of accumulated group volume to be eligible for promotion and certain commission and/or bonus money.

Accumulated personal volume: Also called *personal volume or PV.* Refers to the personal production or purchases of a single distributor.

Active versus inactive: Describes the status of a distributor. Active distributors are working their businesses, regardless of title and whether or not they qualify for commission or bonus money; inactive distributors could be taking a little time off, but more than likely they quit working their businesses. Inactive distributors may or may not remain on the company's mailing list. Details vary from company to company.

Associate: In some companies, a distributor is called an *associate,* an *independent representative,* or a *consultant.* (See also *Distributor.*)

Autoship program: Distributors have the option of ordering products that will be automatically shipped to them and billed against a credit card or a debit card or drafted on a checking account. This option saves the distributor the time of ordering monthly, and it also assures the distributor that the monthly qualifications for commissions and/or bonuses are always met.

Binary: A type of compensation plan. Distributors develop two "legs" in their downlines, and compensation is earned and paid on the sales volume of the legs. However, the sales volume must be balanced in the two legs, or the distributor will not be eligible to earn commission. The binary is the most controversial of plans, and many experts say it will not survive the test of time.

Bonus: Remuneration paid to distributors beyond commission money. Bonuses are paid based on distributors meeting certain criteria.

Bonus qualified: Distributors typically are required to fulfill certain requirements to be eligible to receive bonus money. When these requirements are met, the distributor is considered *bonus qualified.*

Bonus volume: Products and services are assigned bonus volume by their respective companies for the purpose of calculating bonus compensation. The value is usually equal to or less than the wholesale price of the item. Bonus earnings are based on the specific compensation plan and qualification requirements of the company.

Breakaway: See *Stairstep Breakaway.*

Commission: Money earned by distributors after they sell products or services. Commission is computed as a percentage of each sale — for example, 25 percent of the retail price. Commission may be paid in the form of a rebate of the appropriate percentage of retail or in the difference earned between the distributor product discount and the actual retail price.

Commissionable volume: The portion of a distributor's sales volume upon which commissions will be paid. Each network marketing company determines how much of each sale will be commissionable. In most companies, this is the same as the *bonus volume.* May also be referred to as *product volume.*

Compensation plan: Also called the *marketing plan, comp plan,* or *pay plan.* It describes the structure, commission, bonus percentages, and performance requirements by which distributors are compensated by the corporate office.

Conference call: See *Three-way call.*

Co-op: Any distributor can form a co-op by inviting other distributors to share equally in the cost of advertising or in implementing a marketing program, such as a direct mail campaign. By pooling their resources, the distributors can increase their buying power.

Corporate office: Refers to the network marketing company itself. Sometimes shortened to *corporate.*

Cross-line: Refers to distributors who belong to the same network marketing company, but who are not in the same downline. A member of one downline is considered cross-line to a distributor in another downline. Trying to recruit or sell to cross-line members is taboo in network marketing.

Distributor: Someone who joins a network marketing company for the purpose of marketing and selling the company's products or services. Also commonly called an *associate, independent representative,* or *consultant.* Distributors are not employees; they are independent contractors.

Downline: A distributor builds a downline by recruiting and/or sponsoring new distributors and by helping them recruit and/or sponsor more distributors. The downline expands exponentially as one distributor recruits two distributors who each recruit two distributors, and on and on. The downline is also called the distributor's *sales organization.* See *Leg* for more information.

Enrolling sponsor: The person who both enrolls and sponsors a new distributor. In some companies, distributors have the option of enrolling new distributors and allowing someone in their downline to be assigned sponsorship of the new distributors.

Forced matrix: A type of compensation plan. A forced matrix plan limits the number of distributors allowed in the downline. The most common forced matrix is a 3 x 7, which means the distributor's downline can include 3 legs and 7 levels. This type of forced matrix cannot grow wider than 3 legs or deeper than 7 levels. This plan has many variables in terms of the number of legs and levels allowed.

Front-end loading: When a network marketing company or a distributor forces a new distributor to purchase large amounts of inventory in order to generate more commissions and overrides. Regulators of network marketing frown upon this practice. See *Seventy percent rule.*

Frontline: This term is used in two ways. When a network marketing company is in its start-up phase, it recruits experienced distributors (especially those who have been active and successful in other network marketing companies). These distributors are called the *frontline* to the company, and they are looked to as leaders within the organization. Similarly, a distributor's frontline refers to the individuals who are on the first level of the distributor's downline. For example, a distributor may recruit and sponsor five frontline leaders with hopes that each of those leaders will build a leg of the distributor's downline.

Genealogy report: A report issued by the corporate office detailing a distributor's downline or sales organization. Sometimes called "organizational report" or "family tree." The genealogy report usually includes names, addresses, telephone numbers, and the level and rank of each distributor within the same downline. The report also provides information about every distributor's purchasing history. Some companies update the genealogy every week or month. More and more companies are posting genealogies on their Web sites where distributors can view them whenever they like.

Generation: Has different meanings within different comp plans. Refers to a group of distributors that belong to one sponsor. At a certain point of qualification in a Stairstep Breakaway compensation plan, the sponsor "breaks away" from his sponsor by taking his downline with him and forming a "generation." The original sponsor will likely earn a generation bonus: a percentage of the sales of the generation's sales volume. In other compensation plans, a sponsor's downline can include generations that do not break away. The sponsor will likely earn a generation bonus. Historically, much of the income of top earners in network marketing is a result of generation bonuses.

Generation override: When a distributor earns money for the sales achievement of a particular generation, the bonus paid is a generation override.

Group: See *Downline.*

Heavy hitter: Refers to a distributor who is extremely successful.

Independent contractor: Distributors in network marketing businesses are independent contractors as opposed to employees. As such, they are self-employed and (in the U.S.) must report any income earned to the Internal Revenue Service for tax purposes. Consult your accountant or tax adviser for details.

Inventory: A supply of company merchandise necessary to provide for your customers and your personal needs. Beware of any company that requires you to purchase large amounts of inventory.

Leg: An organizational line of sequentially sponsored distributors. Usually a downline consists of two or more legs.

Level: Used to describe the position of a distributor in a downline. As an example, if you sponsor a new distributor, that person is on your first level. When that distributor sponsors a new distributor, that new distributor is on your second level, and so on. Depending on the compensation plan, a downline could have an infinite number of levels.

Level bonus override: Distributors are paid a *level bonus* on sales made by members of their downlines. Each level may pay a different percentage. For example, sales by first level distributors may pay 10 percent; second level distributors, 8 percent; and so on. Some companies require a distributor to achieve a certain rank before qualifying to receive a level bonus or to receive increased bonuses.

Marketing plan: See *Compensation plan.*

Multi-level marketing: Refers to a direct selling program that pays distributors for their own sales, as well as for the sales of multiple levels of distributors who are below them in the company's hierarchy. In multi-level marketing, independent distributors represent a network marketing company and sell directly to consumers rather than through conventional outlets, such as retail stores. Also called *network marketing* or *referral marketing.*

Multi-level junkie: A person who works multiple opportunities at the same time or who jumps from one opportunity to another, looking for a better deal. Multi-level junkies are notorious for their lack of loyalty and commitment to a company, and they are rarely successful over a long period of time.

Networking: The act of meeting other people and discussing business ideas and opportunities. For example: "There was a lot of networking going on at the Chamber of Commerce meeting."

Network marketing: See *Multi-level marketing.*

Opportunity meeting: A recruitment/sponsorship meeting. A distributor or group of distributors sponsor an opportunity meeting in hopes of recruiting new distributors. The typical meeting lasts about 30 minutes. During the meeting, one or more experienced distributors provide information about the company and its products and services. Product testimonials are frequently shared at the meetings. Prospective distributors become new distributors at many of these meetings, which is what the meetings are designed for.

Orphan: This term has more than one meaning. Most often it's used to describe a distributor who enrolls in a company without a sponsor. Some companies allow distributors to join directly through the corporate office, which then usually assigns the orphan to a sponsor. At other times, *orphan* is used to describe a distributor whose upline has quit or has become inactive. It's also used to describe a distributor who lives in an area where there are no other distributors and no distributor support.

Personal bonus volume (PBV): The assigned dollar volume for qualification and calculation of bonuses on the products purchased by a distributor.

Product volume: See *Commissionable volume.*

Prospect: A person to whom you offer your network marketing business opportunity; a person to whom you offer to sell a product or service.

Pyramid: Term used by government regulators to describe an illegal sales scheme. Legitimate network marketing companies are not pyramids.

Qualifying volume: The minimum dollar amount (usually based on wholesale sales volume) that a distributor/associate must purchase and/or have moved through his or her downline in order to be eligible to earn commissions.

Rank: By their performance and the performance of their downline members, distributors achieve various levels of rank — for example, Director, Silver Director, Gold Director, Platinum Director, and so on. The higher the rank, the higher the rate of compensation, in most instances.

Recruit: The act of prospecting for new distributors. It's through recruitment that distributors build their downlines.

Referral: If a customer recommends a prospect to a distributor, that's a referral. The distributor contacts the recommended party and hopefully makes a sale.

Residual income: Getting paid repeatedly for the same effort. For example, when a network marketer sponsors a new distributor into her downline, she can earn money every month from the sales of that distributor. She exerts the effort to sponsor the distributor and then reaps the rewards of monthly residual income for as long as she and the distributor remain active in the business. Network marketers also earn residual income from their retail customers. A networker sells a product to a customer one time, but the customer reorders the product every month. Every time the product is reordered by that customer, the network marketer earns a percentage of the sale — that is, residual income.

Retail sale: A sale made to a non-distributor of the company, a sale made at a marked-up price other than the wholesale price, or a sale that is not made solely for qualification or advancement in the compensation plan.

Roll up: When a distributor becomes inactive and is no longer associated with the company, that distributor's downline will *roll up* and become part of his or her sponsor's downline.

Sales kit: Network marketing companies require new distributors to purchase a sales kit (sometimes referred to as a *starter kit, new distributor's kit,* and so on). These kits typically include a distributor's manual that explains the company's regulations, policies, and compensation plan and also include descriptions of products and services, order forms, motivational tapes, and so on. Sales kits should be non-commissionable and reasonably priced, from $19.95 to $99.95.

Seventy percent rule: In accordance with applicable law (of most U.S. states) as well as prudent business practices, a company prohibits its distributors from participating in what is known as *front-end loading* or *inventory loading.* To prevent unjustified inventory buildup for the purpose of qualifying, or attempting to qualify, for advancement, a company requires that each distributor warrants, upon the placement of each new order, that the distributor has either personally sold at retail, resold at wholesale in good faith anticipation of retail distribution, or purchased at wholesale for personal use within a reasonable period of time, at least 70 percent of the inventory. Compliance with this rule is the responsibility of the distributor, subject to periodic and/or random audit by the company. Failure to comply with this rule could result in disciplinary action by the company, including termination of the distributorship.

Spamming: Sending e-mail to people who did not request it or to whom the sender has no previous relationship. Responsible marketers do not spam.

Sponsor/sponsoring: The person who coaches, teaches, and mentors a new distributor, or the act of performing those functions for that distributor. This sponsor is the new distributor's upline.

Stacking: Placing family members or non-producing distributors in his or her downline for the purpose of advancement in the compensation plan. Such a scheme won't be tolerated by legitimate network marketing companies.

Stairstep Breakaway: A type of compensation plan in which a distributor qualifies to *break away* his or her sales organization from its existing upline once the organization reaches a certain level of sales. There are two parts to the Stairstep Breakaway: The front end of the plan is the stairstep, and the back end of the plan is the breakaway. The stairstep usually consists of three or four steps that increase by rank and profitability as the distributor achieves progressively higher sales volumes in a specified period of time. The sales of distributors below you are considered part of your personal group volume, and as the volume increases you "stairstep" your way to higher ranks, and eventually to the back end of the plan where you qualify to break away, taking your downline with you. At that time, your sponsor may qualify to receive generation bonuses on your sales organization.

Termination: Network marketing companies expect distributors to follow their rules and regulations. Violations of the rules and regulations can result in the distributor's termination by the company.

Three-way call: A conversation that includes three people. For example, you're recruiting a prospect, and you want your upline to assist you in closing the sale. While you and your prospect are on the phone, you can connect your upline by phone for a three-way conversation (this is also called *conference calling*). It's a very effective recruiting and training technique.

Unilevel: A type of compensation plan in which distributors are paid for a specified or finite number of levels in their downline. There's no width limit, and varying commission percentages are paid on each level. The more sales volume you and your downline achieve, the more money you can make.

Upline: See *Sponsor.*

Wholesale: The price a distributor pays to the company for products or services. When products purchased at wholesale are sold at retail, the distributor earns a profit.

For the compilation of this glossary, the authors acknowledge the assistance of numerous individuals, including Michael Sheffield and his staff, Jeffrey A. Babener, Ken Rudd, Jane Blackford, Atticus Killough, Jason Gaul, Ronald Wuerch, and Doris Wood.

Index

• **G** •

• *Q* •

• R •

Rademacher, Brett, 32, 314
Raley, Fred, 229, 268
rank, 356
RATE acronym, 301–303
Rawls, Anita, 324
recognition, 19–20
recognizing good management teams, 82–83
recovery, 301
recruit, 357
recruiting, 169–171
    costs of generating leads, 195–196
    enrollment bonuses for distributor, 204
    identifying good candidates, 170
    Internet solutions to, 32–33
    powerhouse associates, 170–171
    questions to ask about, 130
    success linked to, 180
referral
    asking for, 195, 214–216
    customer, 305–306
    defined, 357
    tracking on marketing activity list, 196
    value of customer, 202–203
regulating
    controversial products, 103
    network marketing, 33–34, 61
Rehnborg, Carl, 15
Reichheld, Frederick, 201, 295
rejection by prospects, 221
relationships
    building in network marketing, 275
    creating trust in, 284–285
    cultivating, 228
    importance of, 323
    loving people and your product, 290–291
reliability, 301
repetition
    in advertising, 252
    cultivating relationship, 228
    working leads and, 226–227
repetitive sales, 98
reputation
    of industries, 57–58
    of your business, 41

research and development at company, 86–87
researching
    companies, 60, 67–71
    companies through FTC, 61, 62
    compensation plan, 69
    products and services on Web, 100
residual income
    about, 51–52
    customer base and, 185
    defined, 357
    downline as key to, 169
    reliable products for, 98
    securing financial future with, 52
resources for network marketers, 311–317
    Babener & Associates, 312
    Direct Sales World, 313
    Direct Selling Association, 312
    MLM Nuts $ Bolts (Ruhe), 315–316
    mlminsider Web site, 314–315
    mlmsuccess.com Web site, 312–313
    Network Marketing Lifestyles magazine, 48, 64, 311
    Passion Fire International Web site, 313
    Performance Tracker, 316
    Poe's *Wave 3* and *Wave 4* books, 316–317
    www.mlm911.com, 314
    www.recruitomatic.com Web site, 314
respect from mainstream society, 28–29
responding to life positively, 329–330
responsibility
    of running business, 49–50
    of sponsor, 162, 212
responsiveness, 301
results of products and services, 101, 104–105
Retail Customer Lifetime Value Chart, 198
retail sales. *See also* selling
    defined, 357
    emphasis on, 87
retirement and network marketing, 21–22
rewarding customer loyalty, 304
Right Site, The, 100
Roberti, Jeff, 84, 91, 142, 164
roles in selling, 280–282

• V •

• W •

BUSINESS, CAREERS & PERSONAL FINANCE

Grant Writing
FOR DUMMIES
0-7645-5307-0

Home Buying
FOR DUMMIES
0-7645-5331-3 *†

Also available:
- Accounting For Dummies †
  0-7645-5314-3
- Business Plans Kit For Dummies †
  0-7645-5365-8
- Cover Letters For Dummies
  0-7645-5224-4
- Frugal Living For Dummies
  0-7645-5403-4
- Leadership For Dummies
  0-7645-5176-0
- Managing For Dummies
  0-7645-1771-6

- Marketing For Dummies
  0-7645-5600-2
- Personal Finance For Dummies *
  0-7645-2590-5
- Project Management For Dummies
  0-7645-5283-X
- Resumes For Dummies †
  0-7645-5471-9
- Selling For Dummies
  0-7645-5363-1
- Small Business Kit For Dummies *†
  0-7645-5093-4

HOME & BUSINESS COMPUTER BASICS

Windows XP
FOR DUMMIES
0-7645-4074-2

Excel 2003
ALL-IN-ONE DESK REFERENCE
FOR DUMMIES
0-7645-3758-X

Also available:
- ACT! 6 For Dummies
  0-7645-2645-6
- iLife '04 All-in-One Desk Reference
  For Dummies
  0-7645-7347-0
- iPAQ For Dummies
  0-7645-6769-1
- Mac OS X Panther Timesaving
  Techniques For Dummies
  0-7645-5812-9
- Macs For Dummies
  0-7645-5656-8

- Microsoft Money 2004 For Dummies
  0-7645-4195-1
- Office 2003 All-in-One Desk Reference
  For Dummies
  0-7645-3883-7
- Outlook 2003 For Dummies
  0-7645-3759-8
- PCs For Dummies
  0-7645-4074-2
- TiVo For Dummies
  0-7645-6923-6
- Upgrading and Fixing PCs For Dummies
  0-7645-1665-5
- Windows XP Timesaving Techniques
  For Dummies
  0-7645-3748-2

FOOD, HOME, GARDEN, HOBBIES, MUSIC & PETS

Feng Shui
FOR DUMMIES
0-7645-5295-3

Poker
FOR DUMMIES
0-7645-5232-5

Also available:
- Bass Guitar For Dummies
  0-7645-2487-9
- Diabetes Cookbook For Dummies
  0-7645-5230-9
- Gardening For Dummies *
  0-7645-5130-2
- Guitar For Dummies
  0-7645-5106-X
- Holiday Decorating For Dummies
  0-7645-2570-0
- Home Improvement All-in-One
  For Dummies
  0-7645-5680-0

- Knitting For Dummies
  0-7645-5395-X
- Piano For Dummies
  0-7645-5105-1
- Puppies For Dummies
  0-7645-5255-4
- Scrapbooking For Dummies
  0-7645-7208-3
- Senior Dogs For Dummies
  0-7645-5818-8
- Singing For Dummies
  0-7645-2475-5
- 30-Minute Meals For Dummies
  0-7645-2589-1

INTERNET & DIGITAL MEDIA

Digital Photography
FOR DUMMIES
0-7645-1664-7

Starting an eBay Business
FOR DUMMIES
0-7645-6924-4

Also available:
- 2005 Online Shopping Directory
  For Dummies
  0-7645-7495-7
- CD & DVD Recording For Dummies
  0-7645-5956-7
- eBay For Dummies
  0-7645-5654-1
- Fighting Spam For Dummies
  0-7645-5965-6
- Genealogy Online For Dummies
  0-7645-5964-8
- Google For Dummies
  0-7645-4420-9

- Home Recording For Musicians
  For Dummies
  0-7645-1634-5
- The Internet For Dummies
  0-7645-4173-0
- iPod & iTunes For Dummies
  0-7645-7772-7
- Preventing Identity Theft For Dummies
  0-7645-7336-5
- Pro Tools All-in-One Desk Reference
  For Dummies
  0-7645-5714-9
- Roxio Easy Media Creator For Dummies
  0-7645-7131-1

WILEY

SPORTS, FITNESS, PARENTING, RELIGION & SPIRITUALITY

0-7645-5146-9

0-7645-5418-2

Also available:

Adoption For Dummies
0-7645-5488-3

Basketball For Dummies
0-7645-5248-1

The Bible For Dummies
0-7645-5296-1

Buddhism For Dummies
0-7645-5359-3

Catholicism For Dummies
0-7645-5391-7

Hockey For Dummies
0-7645-5228-7

Judaism For Dummies
0-7645-5299-6

Martial Arts For Dummies
0-7645-5358-5

Pilates For Dummies
0-7645-5397-6

Religion For Dummies
0-7645-5264-3

Teaching Kids to Read For Dummies
0-7645-4043-2

Weight Training For Dummies
0-7645-5168-X

Yoga For Dummies
0-7645-5117-5

TRAVEL

0-7645-5438-7

0-7645-5453-0

Also available:

Alaska For Dummies
0-7645-1761-9

Arizona For Dummies
0-7645-6938-4

Cancún and the Yucatán For Dummies
0-7645-2437-2

Cruise Vacations For Dummies
0-7645-6941-4

Europe For Dummies
0-7645-5456-5

Ireland For Dummies
0-7645-5455-7

Las Vegas For Dummies
0-7645-5448-4

London For Dummies
0-7645-4277-X

New York City For Dummies
0-7645-6945-7

Paris For Dummies
0-7645-5494-8

RV Vacations For Dummies
0-7645-5443-3

Walt Disney World & Orlando For Dummies
0-7645-6943-0

GRAPHICS, DESIGN & WEB DEVELOPMENT

0-7645-4345-8

0-7645-5589-8

Also available:

Adobe Acrobat 6 PDF For Dummies
0-7645-3760-1

Building a Web Site For Dummies
0-7645-7144-3

Dreamweaver MX 2004 For Dummies
0-7645-4342-3

FrontPage 2003 For Dummies
0-7645-3882-9

HTML 4 For Dummies
0-7645-1995-6

Illustrator CS For Dummies
0-7645-4084-X

Macromedia Flash MX 2004 For Dummies
0-7645-4358-X

Photoshop 7 All-in-One Desk Reference For Dummies
0-7645-1667-1

Photoshop CS Timesaving Techniques For Dummies
0-7645-6782-9

PHP 5 For Dummies
0-7645-4166-8

PowerPoint 2003 For Dummies
0-7645-3908-6

QuarkXPress 6 For Dummies
0-7645-2593-X

NETWORKING, SECURITY, PROGRAMMING & DATABASES

0-7645-6852-3

0-7645-5784-X

Also available:

A+ Certification For Dummies
0-7645-4187-0

Access 2003 All-in-One Desk Reference For Dummies
0-7645-3988-4

Beginning Programming For Dummies
0-7645-4997-9

C For Dummies
0-7645-7068-4

Firewalls For Dummies
0-7645-4048-3

Home Networking For Dummies
0-7645-42796

Network Security For Dummies
0-7645-1679-5

Networking For Dummies
0-7645-1677-9

TCP/IP For Dummies
0-7645-1760-0

VBA For Dummies
0-7645-3989-2

Wireless All In-One Desk Reference For Dummies
0-7645-7496-5

Wireless Home Networking For Dummies
0-7645-3910-8

ZigOnline — A Life-Changing Experience: Use It to Get Answers; Use It to Build a Global Business from Your Home!

Have you ever asked yourself any of these questions:

- What qualities do I need most to become successful in sales?
- How should I respond when someone says, "It costs too much"?
- What's the secret to Zig Ziglar's success? And can I get some of it?
- What do I need to do to make sure I accomplish my goals?
- How do I develop and maintain a positive mental attitude?
- When facing life's challenges, how should I respond?
- How do I change my family and professional lives?
- What can I do to look for the good in other people?
- How can I help my kids grow up to be positive in a negative world?

ZigOnline has the answers to those questions and many more. ZigOnline is an indexed multimedia library of Zig Ziglar's material accessible via the Internet. When you use it, you'll discover the meaning of a life-changing experience! Whatever challenges you face in life, personally or professionally, you can rely on ZigOnline for quick but thoughtful solutions. After you search for the topic of your choice, you'll hear Zig address that topic in a three- to seven-minute audio presentation. ZigOnline covers the topics that everyone wants most: money, health, friends, happiness, security, peace of mind, hope in the future, and good family relationships.

By subscribing to ZigOnline, you can improve your own life and help change lives all over the world. ZigOnline is an Internet affiliate program, so you can use it to earn extra income! You can build a global business from your home. If this excites you, point your Web browser to www.zigonline.com/15453 and preview the site for free. You can also subscribe online and immediately start using ZigOnline personally, both to solve life's challenges and to begin building a global business. ZigOnline will show you what to do, step-by-step, so you can get started right away.

ZigOnline
2009 Chenault Drive
Suite 100
Carrollton, TX 75006
Phone: 972.383.3202
Fax: 972.383.3204
www.zigonline.com/15453